FRIENDS AND OTHER STRANGERS

FRIENDS AND OTHER STRANGERS

STUDIES IN RELIGION, ETHICS, AND CULTURE

RICHARD B. MILLER

COLUMBIA UNIVERSITY PRESS

NEW YORK

Columbia University Press
Publishers Since 1893
New York   Chichester, West Sussex
cup.columbia.edu

Library of Congress Cataloging-in-Publication Data
Names: Miller, Richard Brian, 1953- author.
Title: Friends and other strangers : studies in religion, ethics,
and culture / Richard B. Miller.
Description: New York : Columbia University Press, 2016. |
Includes bibliographical references and index.
Identifiers: LCCN 2015043746 (print) | LCCN 2016014143 (ebook) |
ISBN 9780231174886 (cloth : alk. paper) | ISBN 9780231541558 (electronic)
Subjects: LCSH: Religious ethics.
Classification: LCC BJ1188 .M55 2016 (print) | LCC BJ1188 (ebook) |
DDC 205—dc23
LC record available at http://lccn.loc.gov/2015043746

Columbia University Press books are printed on permanent and durable
acid-free paper.

Printed in the United States of America

c 10 9 8 7 6 5 4 3 2 1

Cover design: Lisa Hamm
Cover image: © Richard Renaldi

TO THREE TEACHERS

JAMES F. CHILDRESS

CHARLES E. CURRAN

JAMES M. GUSTAFSON

CONTENTS

ACKNOWLEDGMENTS

THIS BOOK TOOK shape in response to opportunities to develop my ideas about how to chart and expand the terrain of religious ethics. Apropos of its title, it is indebted to input from friends and strangers whose intellectual acuity and goodwill I want to acknowledge here.

I am grateful to Aaron Stalnaker, John P. Reeder Jr., and Richard Rosengarten for critical feedback on an earlier draft of chapter 1. Thanks as well to Maria Antonaccio, Kathryn Bryan, Mark Graham, Charles Hallisey, Gerald McKenny, Todd Whitmore, D. M. Yeager, and Lee Yearley for their commentary and input on chapter 2. Kate Abramson, Colin Allen, Keith Barton, Bennett Bertenthal, John Bodnar, Fritz Breithaupt, Michelle Brown, Kevin Houser, Lisa Sideris, and Aaron Stalnaker helped shape chapters 3 and 4 as members of the two-year project "Virtuous Empathy: Scientific and Humanistic Investigations," funded by the John Templeton Foundation, Indiana University, and the University of Chicago. Arguments for each chapter were sharpened for the Tracy M. Sonneborn Lecture at Indiana University in 2013 and the Maloney Lectures at Davidson College in 2014. I am grateful to Joe Bartzel, Mark Wilson, Andrew Lustig, Trent Foley, Bill Mahoney, Karl Plank, and Kevin Hector for their comments on the material that worked its way into those chapters. Thanks as well to Eric Gregory, Jeffrey Stout, Leora Batnitzky, George Kateb, Ernest Cortés, and others who provided insightful contributions to what became chapter 5 at the conference, "Religion and Power: New Directions in Social Ethics" at Princeton University in 2015.

Jeffrey Reiman, Sarah Irvine Belson, Eva Fetter Kittay, Lucinda Peach, Tibor Machan, and Charlotte Witt provided probing questions the

McDowell Conference at American University in 2006, where I first presented material for chapter 6. Charles Curran, Paul Lauritzen, Charles Pinches, Sharayn Menne, Mark Wilson, and Margaret Mohrmann provided important observations and criticisms as I drafted chapter 7. Maria Antonaccio, William J. Buckley, John Carlson, Charles Curran, Chris Gamwell, Eric Gregory, John Langan, Jean Porter, Melissa Seymour, Lisa Sideris, and Aaron Stalnaker offered constructive insights as I drafted chapter 8. Chapter 9 profited from helpful conversations with John Bodnar, Danny James, Ed Lilenthal, and Glenda Murray.

Chapter 10 was first presented as the Bristol Lecture at Florida State University in 2009 and at the University of Chicago in 2010. Thanks to John Kelsay for the invitation to Florida State and to colleagues and students at both of those institutions for their comments and questions.

Much of the book was presented over the course of the drafting process at meetings of the Ethics, Philosophy, and Politics Workshop in the Department of Religious Studies at Indiana University, on which I frequently relied for critical input during my time as a member of the IU faculty. I owe a special debt of thanks to those who regularly participated at those monthly sessions: Byron Bangert, Joe Bartzel, Kathleen Bonnette, Cheryl Cottine, Constance Furey, Michael Ing, Mark King, Nancy Levene, Dana Logan, Danielle Murry-Knowles, Rick Nance, Bharat Ranganathan, Lisa Sideris, Aaron Stalnaker, Winni Sullivan, Mark Wilson, and Meng Zhang.

As director of the Poynter Center for the Study of Ethics and American Institutions, I was especially helped by the generous organizational and intellectual work of Glenda Murray and Emma Young. I am also indebted to Karen Boeyink, Brian Schrag, Ken Pimple, Stuart Yoak, and Beth Works for their goodwill, spirit of collaboration, and creative work at the Center.

Several friends not already mentioned shared ideas that helped to refine my own: David Brakke, Julia Lamm, Ellen Muehlberger, Gabriel Palmer-Fernandez, and Chester Gillis. I am especially grateful to James Childress, John Kelsay, Paul Lauritzen, John P. Reeder Jr., Nigel Biggar, and Sumner B. Twiss for their insights into all things related to religious ethics. I also wish to thank the staff at Turneffe Island, Belize, where I have retreated periodically over the past fifteen years to write in quiet seclusion.

Since 1988 I have had the benefit of support and insights from participants in the AAR Theology and Ethics Colloquy: Terence J. Martin, Douglas Ottati, William Schweiker, and Charles Wilson. I owe Cheryl Cottine a special debt of gratitude for her work as a research assistant at the Poynter Center and for her editorial eye and input on each chapter.

Dean Margaret M. Mitchell of the University of Chicago Divinity School and Wendy Lochner and Christine Dunbar at Columbia University Press were patient and generous seeing this project through to its completion. I am grateful to them, to Joe Abbott, and to the external readers of the manuscript for valuable insights and suggestions.

As always, I owe a singular debt of love and thanks to Barbara Klinger and Matt Miller for their affection, companionship, and curiosity about the ideas and arguments that found their way into this book.

* * *

Chapter 2 grew out of an initiative supported by the American Academy of Religion that funded seminars at Rice University and the University of Notre Dame on the topic of new genres and rhetoric in religious ethics. It appears here as a revised version of "On Making a Cultural Turn in Religious Ethics," *Journal of Religious Ethics* 33, no. 3 (2005): 409–43.

Chapter 6 grew out of the 2004–5 Interdisciplinary Faculty Seminar, "The Politics and Ethics of Childhood," which I sponsored during my term as director of the Poynter Center for the Study of Ethics and American Institutions at Indiana University. Thanks to Jonathan Plucker, Sandy Shapshay, Aviva Orenstein, Mike Grossberg, Sam Odom, Robert Kunzman, and Melissa Seymour for their participation in the seminar. The chapter appears here, with permission, as an expansion of "On Duties and Debts to Children," *Soundings: An Interdisciplinary Journal* 91, nos. 1–2 (2008): 167–88.

Chapter 7 was first published as "Evil, Friendship, and Iconic Realism in Augustine's *Confessions*," *Harvard Theological Review* 104, no. 4 (2011): 387–409.

Chapter 8 appears here as a revised form of the essay "Just War, Civic Virtue, and Democratic Social Criticism: Augustinian Reflections," *Journal of Religion* 89, no. 1 (2009): 1–30.

Chapter 9 developed out of the 2006–7 Interdisciplinary Faculty Seminar, "Memory: Ethics, Politics, and Aesthetics," which took place while I was director of the Poynter Center. Thanks to seminar members Byron Bangert, Purnima Bose, Maria Bucur, Patrick Dove, Joseph Hoffmann, John Lucaites, Melissa Seymour, Lynn Struve, and Mark Wilson. The chapter was published in an earlier, briefer version as "The Moral and Political Burdens of Memory," *Journal of Religious Ethics* 37, no. 3 (2009): 533–64.

FRIENDS AND OTHER STRANGERS

INTRODUCTION

ALTERITY AND INTIMACY

The principle of *mutual love* admonishes people to constantly *come nearer* to each other; that of *respect* which they owe each other, to keep themselves at a *distance* from one another.

—Immanuel Kant

OSCILLATIONS

One of the dramatic intellectual discoveries in the last several decades is the idea of otherness and, with that, a more expansive grasp of what it means to be human. The other experiences the world in light of particular symbols, lore, ideas, and commitments, thereby revealing distinctive possibilities of identity and agency in pursuit of the good life. Otherness makes a declarative statement: "I am; this way of life can be." The other's existence is thereby a form of address. Alterity exists not as some mute or neutral fact of life; it has the quality of an expressive speech-act. It is both a manifestation and a proclamation. We learn from the other that what it means to be human does not fit into a single, preestablished mold. Indeed, viewing humanity as fitting into a uniform model is one idea that the late twentieth century enabled us to do away with.

Given these developments, we increasingly view ourselves in dialogical terms. One's own way of being is constituted in no small part by one's responses to an other's utterances and, for that matter, to the many expressive speech-acts that address us. The other thereby reveals how one's own outlook is partial and contingent. This is not to say that we approve of or endorse the views of an other. But it does say that one's picture of a good life can be disrupted, broadened, and deepened by possibilities that others bring to one's imaginative repertoire. Alterity can be a promissory note, perhaps a utopian one.

The discovery of otherness along with this fact of being addressed has various implications. One implication is epistemic: the other provides occasions for an increase in knowledge by informing me of a different way of life, a different conception of personhood, a different way of identifying one's self in relation to others—and different ways of conceiving these organizing concepts of "ways of life," "personhood," and "self in relation to others." Presented with alternatives of these kinds, I can grasp my parochialism as a predicament to be overcome. In my encounters with others my knowledge can be deepened, my interests exposed, my ignorance remedied. I can now see things differently, from an other's point of view.

A quite different implication points not so much to opportunities that arise in an epistemological sense as to being-in-relation with others. This implication has to do with normative aspects that inhere in the experience of otherness itself. The idea I have in mind is Stanley Cavell's notion of acknowledgment, or acknowledging others, which is distinct from knowing them.[1] Acknowledgment is a matter of responding to something you are exhibiting—specifically, a matter of revealing a set of feelings or interests in response to your speech-acts. Here the idea is that an other's address speaks in the imperative mood. The statement, "I am; this way of life can be," is an expression that arises from an other's normative commitments, in response to which one's acknowledgment exhibits a moral stance. Acknowledging an other, then, immediately involves one in a dialogue of address and response. But that dialogue presupposes something else—something more fundamental—about acknowledgement, namely, that I expose something about myself in my response, something that is deep and abiding. Acknowledgment, then, is not so much an occasion or an event as it is "a category in terms of which a given response is evaluated."[2] To acknowledge thus presupposes existing in relation to an other, in response to whom I disclose something fundamental about myself.

Seen in these terms, my encounter with an other is less about my predicament-as-parochial than about how my life is normatively conditioned by alterity. The core idea is that the other petitions me to account for myself. My relationship is not a matter of knowing the other but of responding to the other as someone to whom I am responsible.[3] This is not to say that the other is someone *for* whom I am responsible; responsibility is not the same as the morality of justice or care. It rather indicates that the demand to respond to the other requires grasping how our relationships are inescapably ethical. I can respond to an other only in a certain way. How I do so reveals something about my orientation and reactive attitudes, about how I grasp the demands of social existence.

Otherness thereby exposes deficient and donative dimensions to our commerce with the world. We can see this when we think about failures of knowledge and acknowledgment, respectively. Our failure of knowledge denotes an absence, a form of ignorance, an epistemic deficit. Our failure of acknowledgment is, in contrast, "the presence of something, a confusion, an indifference, a callousness, an exhaustion, a coldness."[4] Seen in this way, knowledge is to ignorance as acknowledgment is to apathy.

To acknowledge is not necessarily to endorse another's way of life or vision of the good. It rather makes plain that we do not come to each other on neutral terms. Otherness not only speaks; it requests a hearing. It thereby reveals an ethical asymmetry between me and an other insofar as I am beckoned by another's address.[5] My success or failure to respond to an address reveals something about me in a deep sense. The other challenges in ways that are as epistemic as they are moral. The experience of difference includes the demand for respect, if not recognition, "from the ground up." Alterity requires a reckoning.

Difference, strangeness, and alterity, then, are not only facts that describe others in the world; they are also, obviously, matters of relationality. Difference is relative to the person or persons *to whom* the other is positioned as near or far, commonplace or exotic, familiar or strange, and so forth. That is to say, alterity is itself contingent on specific circumstances and conditions. Those who are strange to me might be familiar to you and vice versa. Equally important, difference cannot be a matter of indifference. As a nonneutral summons *to me*, the other implicates me in her address. She reveals the quality of my reactive attitudes and thus becomes a matter of singular importance.

* * *

The experience of alterity, with its epistemic and normative dimensions, contrasts with another feature of existence according to which, or around which, we carry out our reflections and exercise our concerns. This second feature pertains to matters that are intimate, connected, and familiar. "The shapes of knowledge are always ineluctably local," Clifford Geertz writes, "indivisible from their instruments and their encasements."[6] This statement pertains to more than sources of knowledge alone; it captures the value of intimacy as important to our identity, self-knowledge, and subject formation. Who we are is constituted in no small way by our intimate relationships—by our friendships, loves, and attachments. This matter of our constitution, moreover, extends beyond what we know and acknowledge to ways in which we are intimately known and acknowledged—to our webs of interlocution and intersubjectivity.

The concept of intimacy as it bears on personal identity thus complicates the epistemic and normative dimensions of alterity to which I just referred. How we respond to difference depends on our more explicit and intentional attachments that strongly contribute to our self-understanding. This is not to say that we are sealed into, or closed off by, our intimate relationships. But it is to say that we do not respond to others as if we are blank or empty slates. We come to the world with a stance, an attitude, a set of partial preferences and a sense of location—with what is called, following Donald Evans, an "onlook." An onlook, Evans writes, is a matter of looking "on x as y."[7] Such looking differs from having opinions or abstract conceptualizations toward x, and it is more than having a "perspective" on x. Onlooks involve us by way of feeling, posture, commitment, vision, and intentionality. "In saying 'I look on x as y,'" Evans writes, "I commit myself to a policy of behavior and thought, and I register my decision that x is appropriately described as y; my utterance combines an undertaking with a judgment. . . . One undertakes to do certain things, viewing them or interpreting them in a certain way."[8] Talking about an onlook, in other words, is a way of referring to things

that matter to us, to our basic normative commitments—commitments
that involve us at the very root of our identity and our nonneutral stance
toward others and the world. Moreover, our onlooks are hardly monologi-
cal. Those things that matter to us, that help to constitute our identity,
can be a form of alterity *to* others. I, too, exist as an address that includes
the demand for respect if not recognition.

Seen in this way, our lives ineluctably oscillate between experiences of
intimacy and otherness. Our sense of what is near and dear is a source of
what matters to us. It also conditions how we respond to what is different, strange, and unfamiliar. But the conditioning is hardly one-way. Our
experiences of otherness expose our intimacies as contingent and thus
dependent on social and historical sources. That is to say, our experience
of otherness exposes near and distant sources of the self. This fact of
contingency, moreover, is more than first-personal; it bears on more than
me alone. What is evident about my own contingency is true for others as
well. Accordingly, what is near and dear to others is revealed as contingent
and dependent in their encounters with their others—others that might
include oneself. When generalized in this way, the ethical asymmetries that
shape our relations with others are inescapably reciprocal. Contingent
and mutually conditioning, they oscillate in countless and unpredictable
ways over time.

SELF, SOCIETY, POLITICS

Kant's account of the principles of love and respect provides an appropriate point of departure for this book.[9] Viewing these principles on
analogy with the physical laws of the universe, Kant saw mutual love
and respect as opposing forces of attraction and repulsion that hold
our moral lives together. The principles of mutual love admonish us to
come closer and to be more intimate; those of mutual respect require us
to maintain some distance and respect for difference. His description,
like mine, views attraction and distanciation, intimacy and alterity, in a
paradoxical and dialectical way: they are opposed yet mutually interdependent. Yet, unlike Kant, I do not view these polarities as only describing what he calls our "external relations" with one another. They also

pertain to, and penetrate, the emotional quality of our experience and interpersonal ties.

In the chapters that follow I aim less to explore intimacy and alterity as topics of concentrated analysis than to use them as touchstones for examining normative dimensions of self-other relationships as they are implicated in social life, interpersonal desires, friendships and family, and institutional and political relationships. My overall aim is to explore ethical dimensions of intimacy and alterity in personal and public affairs, focusing in particular on insights made possible by attending to the category of culture as an organizing rubric. Culture is an obvious forum for considering the coeval experiences of intimacy and alterity: cultures bring a range of different individuals together and make possible a distinct, common life. Moreover, cultures often distinguish their customs, traditions, and habits—sometimes dramatically, other times less stridently—from those of other cultures. That is to say, in one stroke cultures instantiate the experience of intimacy and otherness. They make plain the dialectic of attraction and distanciation to which Kant calls our attention. Scholarship in the humanities has pursued these concepts of alterity and intimacy in isolation from each other, typically in the form of theorizing about heterology or theorizing about friendship and special relationships. My premise in this book is different. Rather than quarantine the experiences of intimacy and alterity from each other, I view them in dialectical terms and will thereby seek to illumine features of cultural and moral life that we otherwise leave unnoticed.

Seen not as isolable but as dialectical, the ideas of otherness and intimacy offer a set of ideas that together inform how we should think about a range of questions in philosophy, religious studies, cultural studies, and political theory. Those questions, as I will take them up in this book, concern culture and identity; social criticism; moral authority; empathy and solidarity; family relationships; friendship, death, and self-sacrifice; memory; and political obligation. Critical reflection about these matters, I want to show, draws its sustenance from our engagements and attachments, our experiences of disruption and desire, our outlooks and our onlooks, our openness to utopia and accountability. Along the way we will see how friends and intimates come to us—and remain for us—as strangers in interpersonal and political affairs.

LOOKING AHEAD

The chapters that follow are first and foremost a contribution to religious ethics, a relatively new area of scholarship that examines the variety of ways in which religion and ethics are interrelated. In chapter 1 I describe religious ethics and how this book seeks to widen and dimensionalize that guild's self-understanding. Yet I hasten to add, again echoing Geertz, that this volume is, more broadly, a project "of intellectual deprovincializa-tion."[10] While the ensuing chapters address issues in religious studies and moral philosophy, they also intervene into a wider set of conversations in the humanities, especially in cultural theory, ethnography, and political thought. They offer a vision of knowledge production that resists efforts to support ignorance and apathy about others—efforts that homogenize cultural identity, dichotomize cultural differences into invidious "us-them" contrasts, and generate intractable wedge issues surrounding one or another social controversy.[11] My view, reflected in the arguments herein, is that we do well to trespass established disciplinary territories and break down the intellectual silos along with the cultural barriers that they may covertly or overtly protect. The chapters of this book, individually and taken together, are meant as exercises of scholarly transgression.

Chapter 1, "What Is Religious Ethics?," situates *Friends and Other Strangers* within the wider field of religious ethics, a field that is still trying to define itself. I provide a brief history of the rise of religious ethics and offer an account of how religious ethicists should understand themselves. One of my aims is to provide a clear statement about the emergence and current habits of thought in the guild. Another aim is to clarify how the substantive and methodological arguments in this book are intended to unsettle those habits. Drawing on and revising the overview of religious ethics by James Gustafson, I describe four patterns of inquiry in religious ethics. I then introduce and defend a fifth pattern for religious ethics, arguing for a turn to cultural studies with an eye toward advancing a study of intimacy and alterity in religious ethics and the humanities more generally.

Chapter 2, "On Making a Cultural Turn in Religious Ethics," explores resources and reasons for the study of culture in religious ethics, paying special attention to scholarship that provides what I call an ethics of ordinary life. One of my goals is to show how discourses that seek to explore otherness provide tools for uncovering the intimate details of, and relationships in, everyday life, along with their moral implications. Another goal is to disrupt established patterns of work in religious ethics by calling attention to experiments and arguments in cultural anthropology that have been more or less ignored by scholars in religious ethics. The aim of bringing these discourses into conversation is to open up a wider range of interlocutors and issues for genuinely interdisciplinary work in religion and ethics, work that engages scholars who work in anthropology, psychology, cultural theory, and aesthetics. That hope has a dialogical impetus as well. It aspires to open up pathways along which those who work in cultural studies might find opportunities in and challenges from scholars who work on topics in ethics and religion. I conclude the chapter by discussing exemplary works by Wayne Meeks, Margaret Trawick, and Charles Taylor on the way toward making some prognostications about future directions in religious ethics.

Chapter 3, "Moral Authority and Moral Critique in an Age of Ethnocentric Anxiety," addresses a question that emerges from the previous chapter regarding the ethics of ethnography and social criticism more generally: Can it be *right* for an outsider to morally criticize practices or beliefs that are indigenous to another cultural group or tradition? On what terms, if any, is it possible for social criticism of other cultures and practices to avoid charges of moral chauvinism? I tackle these questions by arguing that they are undertheorized, the frequent effect of which is to tar social criticism in cross-cultural exchanges with charges of ethnocentrism. With that problem in mind I split my question into two parts. The bifurcation turns on distinguishing between *having the right* to offer criticism and *being right* about one's critical judgments. I address each of these parts of my question by showing how it can be answered in the affirmative. My aim is not to discredit concerns about ethnocentrism *tout court*, only to sharpen how and where they properly apply to the practice of social critique. I aim to dispel some anxieties about ethnocentrism and to clarify when criticizing others is a genuine moral problem (and when it is not). Clarifying that idea makes it possible to then identify proper norms for expressing social criticism or, more precisely, nonchauvinistic social criticism in multicultural contexts.

Chapter 4, "The Ethics of Empathy," picks up a thread from the previous chapter by focusing on the idea that social criticism of others should be in some way *empathic*. The general idea—echoing arguments by Dilthey, Collingwood, Polanyi, and Gadamer—is to get beyond putatively value-neutral and detached forms of knowing—knowing on the model of disembodied scientific reasoning. The underlying complaint, stated broadly, is that disembodied forms of knowing fail to grasp how our knowledge is situated and interpretive. A related complaint is that disembodied, scientific reasoning fails to capture the lived, psychological features of the moral life. These two complaints have conspired to generate a demand in the humanities and social sciences for scholarship that is motivated by empathy. I take up reasons that champion empathy and subject them to healthy skepticism. I want to move beyond folk notions of empathy that naively espouse empathic knowing as a necessary remedy to egotistical, chauvinistic, or culturally insensitive forms of knowing and acting. One commonly overlooked problem is that empathy can be mobilized for all kinds of undesirable reasons or in ways that blunt the requirements of true other-regard. I sharpen this line of argument by analogizing the ethics of empathy with Augustine's ethics of love. Perhaps more than any other Western thinker, Augustine was keenly alert to love's potential to advance self-serving motives and ends. In his mind love can be either good or bad, depending on the object loved. Augustine theorized about the virtue of love, and its potential to assist both friends and strangers, in ways that can help us think comparatively about empathy as a desirable moral trait. I thus explore Augustine's effort to redeem love as a step toward constructing norms of empathy that can meet ethical expectations that are often naively assigned to it.

Chapter 5, "Indignation, Empathy, and Solidarity," asks how and on what terms friends may enter into solidarity with strangers who are aggrieved by their experience of injustice. Often we ask ourselves how we might join the cause of others who are victims of wrongdoing and political corruption. I address that challenge first by distinguishing my view of solidarity from the universalist, irenic, inclusivist notions of solidarity as avowed by Pope John Paul II and Richard Rorty. On my account solidarity is not a notion that suggests we overcome differences; on the contrary, it describes an intersubjective social union that is partial and preferential, primed for struggle, and held together by political emotions such as resentment and indignation (among other sentiments). Solidarity draws lines between comrades, on the one hand, and agents of wrongdoing, on the other. We enter into solidarity with others who are victims of injustice, I argue, through feelings of empathic indignation. We can imagine ourselves in others' shoes and thereby grasp what lies behind their feelings of resentment toward regimes of power and inequality. Empathic indignation, moreover, can benefit from religion. Prophetic religions can help cultivate feelings of resentment and indignation—and partisan fellow-feeling—by drawing on the literature of social criticism from their sacred writings and by recalling the history of prophetic voices in their respective traditions. In that way religions can help their members become friends with other strangers to build solidarity and advance the cause of social justice.

Chapter 6, "On Duties and Debts to Children," shifts our attention to a particular case that arose from ethnographic fieldwork I carried out in pediatric health-care settings in the 1990s. I focus on an insight I gained in that research by exploring normative features of our relationships with those who are loved as ineradicably and simultaneously other and intimate—namely, children. That dialectical fact about children cannot but affect the ethos of a family and implicate its cultural traditions in response to the challenges of childrearing. I take as my touchstone the insight that caring for people who are young can be revelatory for the adults who do so. That revelation takes the form of disclosing something to the caretakers about themselves that they otherwise would be unlikely to discover. Children enable us to discover our own hidden alterities. I develop my argument by noting that love and care for children are typically justified as exercises of moral duty toward those who are vulnerable and at-risk. But carrying out such duties is only one dimension of our relationships with young people. Another dimension is an oddity regarding our relationships with them—the idea that children generate debts for us to acknowledge. I examine this oddity by noting that such debts arise as a result of the effects that children can have on adults: challenging us, requiring us to do good owing to their needs and vulnerabilities, and, in the process, enabling us to discover things about ourselves that we would otherwise not know. Children make plain to us that we do not come to one another on neutral terms. That fact invites us to examine basic features of moral responsibility that standard approaches to practical ethics routinely overlook.

Chapter 7, "Evil, Friendship, and Iconic Realism in Augustine's *Confessions*," begins by noting that children often become friends with their parents and other family members, care providers, and fellow children in important and enduring ways. Friendships during and after childhood are attachments that can disclose something about us to ourselves and others. Here I examine how one of Augustine's childhood friendships performs precisely the sort of work I identify in the previous chapter, namely, manifesting something to Augustine that he would otherwise not know—something about his priorities and ends. I show how friendship in Augustine's understanding entails a set of broader metaphysical commitments on which the quality of our intimate relationships depends. Indeed, Augustine views good friendship as a form of intimacy that relies on a fundamental grasp of alterity. We need our friends to be truly other lest they become reflections of our own needs and desires. But our friends and intimates, Augustine avows, are not obviously or readily available to us in their reality and otherness. In his view our intimates too easily become objects for selfish control without an organizing interpretive framework that secures their alterity within a wider, objective order of being and love. Augustine develops his particular organizing framework—what I call a theocentric imaginary—to develop an ethics of desire and heterology, one that helps us see that true friends are those with whom we hold intimacy and alterity together in a dialectical tension.

Chapter 8, "Just War, Civic Virtue, and Democratic Social Criticism: Augustinian Reflections," begins by noting that, for Augustine, the problem of viewing others according to our self-serving desires and projections informs political life no less than more local and intimate relationships. Here I take that insight into a discussion of the ethics and social psychology of war. My aim is to expand the normative framework for thinking about the moral and psychic effects of nationalism and violence. War mobilizes allies, friends, and citizens in opposition to a perceived military and political other. In that mobilization war arouses deep passions and patriotic desires, which often obtrude on moral reasoning and self-criticism during war and in subsequent commemorations. Put differently, war can be the occasion of disordered passions, otherwise known as vices. Frequently those vices find expression when we extol ourselves and our friends and demonize others, especially (but not only) in times of military conflict. The practice of applying ethical criteria—for example, just-war criteria—to assess war must be regularly interrogated given their vulnerability to being hijacked to rationalize wrongdoing and to sanctify disordered public sentiments. I defend these ideas through a close reading of Augustine's writings on killing and war. Augustine reminds us that the morality of actions must consider not only how one's conduct affects the welfare of others but also how one's conduct affects oneself. Equally important, Augustine provides valuable resources for evaluating cultures that encourage violence and killing for whatever cause and that calcify cultural differences in order to valorize one's own. Such behavior often takes the form of demonizing the other and imagining ourselves as morally superior to our enemies, both during war and afterward in our practices of civic memorialization. That fact of public life, he suggests, opens up cultures to normative evaluation and critique.

Chapter 9, "The Moral and Political Burdens of Memory," takes up more general matters regarding memory and justice along with the practices of memorialization and bearing witness to the past. I focus on the question, Do we have an obligation to remember people and past events? I use that question as a starting point to critically examine several recent works that ask whether, and on what terms, we have an obligation to remember, whether memory is linked to neighbors distant and near, how memory is connected to justice and forgiveness, and whether memory sits easily with the kinds of relationships that characterize life in democratic public culture. I pursue these problems on the premise that memory work migrates across fields that we typically sort out in terms of psyche and culture. Memory is doubtless one of the most intimate of our cognitive and affective activities and provides occasions for deep and intense encounters with our intrasubjective alterities. It is expressed in various ways, including deliberate practices of memorialization. Given that memory work can be a deliberate act, the topic of memory opens up a range of normative questions regarding the proper exercise of moral agency in relation to acts of memory work and related practices of self-interpretation, community formation, and public justice. An analysis of memory invites us to consider our duties and debts, our cultural habits, and our relationships with others both near and far. I examine these ideas in dialogue with recent contributions to the ethics and politics of memory by Avishai Margalit, W. James Booth, Paul Ricoeur, Jeffrey Blustein, and various scholars in American religious history.

Chapter 10, "Religion, Public Reason, and the Morality of Democratic Authority," broadens the book's compass by taking up matters regarding religion and public policy in democratic societies. In particular, I discuss the extent to which religious ideas may operate within the canons of "public reason," an idea developed by John Rawls and a version of which I describe to set the stage for determining whether or how religious reasons should inform the creation or revision of democratic public policy. Public reason establishes a normative framework for assessing arguments that may be introduced in democratic deliberations and decision making in the discourse of lawmakers, jurists, and ordinary citizens. Following the work of Corey Brettschneider, I argue that public reason's normative dimensions are properly understood in light of the democratic values of political equality, political freedom, and reciprocity. I argue that those values must be met in democratic reason-giving and policy making for a policy to have democratic authority. The values of equality, autonomy, and reciprocity constrain how we are to debate about other values and, more generally, how we are to comport ourselves in relation to fellow citizens who share a commitment to equality and social cooperation. To theorize about religion and public reason is to theorize about power and authority—specifically, whether and how appeals to religious authority align with the moral demands of democratic authority given democracy's normative understanding of how political power is to be properly shared. To clarify these ideas in concrete terms, I illustrate how constraints on reason-giving enable us to evaluate religiously informed efforts to contribute to public policy deliberations regarding same-sex relations, reproductive cloning, and racial justice.

In the epilogue, "Signposts of the Past and for the Future," I turn to a number of works that traverse the fields of religion, ethics, and culture that were published during the decade in which I drafted the chapters that make up this volume. I examine hybridizing scholarship that interrogates matters of medical ethics, gender relations, the cultural politics of religious revivalism, grassroots political activism, and subject-formation—works that depart from mainstream scholarship in their respective fields by coordinating different research traditions in the study of religion, culture, and ethics. I comment on each monograph with an eye to the promise they hold for future work religious ethics, cultural criticism, and public life.

Taken together, these chapters make an extended case for expanding the field of religious ethics to include critical attention to normative dimensions of culture, interpersonal desires, friendships and family, and institutional and political relationships. It bears repeating that culture is an obvious forum for considering the coeval experiences of intimacy and alterity. Cultures bring different individuals together and make possible a distinct, shared way of life and set of habits. Indeed, as James Clifford observes, "to say that the individual is culturally constituted has become a truism. . . . We assume, almost without question, that a self belongs to a specific cultural world much as it speaks a native language."[12] And cultures typically distinguish their practices, modes of expression, and values from those of other cultures. In that way cultures instantiate the experience of intimacy and otherness in one fell swoop. With that fact in view I will argue for a reconsideration of the field of religious ethics and suggest new directions for future work. One aim will be to identify a cluster of concepts that can catalyze experimental directions of research; another will be to revisit now-familiar ideas and discoveries and theorize about them from new angles. The underlying idea is that cultures generate manifestations and proclamations that reveal something about others' organizing habits, as well as our own onlooks, desires, and attachments. The vision that animates this work is that the field of religious ethics is anything but one that should seek purity in its understanding of morality.[13]

Attending to the themes of intimacy and alterity (with corresponding attention to the concept of culture) will likely seem odd to many scholars of religion and religious ethics insofar as these themes invite us to consider new topics and methodologies for the field. Understanding how such matters might disturb patterns of thought in religious ethics requires us to know something about the subject matter and practice of the guild, along with how religious ethics has come to be a scholarly specialty. With that fact in mind let us turn to an examination of the habits and potential future directions of religious ethics as a way of orienting us for the chapters that will follow.

PART I

RELIGION, ETHICS, AND THE HUMAN SCIENCES

1

WHAT IS RELIGIOUS ETHICS?

A NEW "REGIME OF TRUTH"

Religious ethics is a scholarly area that studies the many ways in which religion and ethics are interrelated. Scholars of religious ethics critically investigate religion's efforts to shape the character and guide the behavior of individuals, groups, and institutions, and they often draw on religious sources to address contemporary or perennial moral problems. The field of religious ethics arose in North American departments of religious studies that took shape or expanded in the 1950s through the late-1960s in response to intellectual demands to study problems connected to religion and ethics by using sources and methods that were often distinct from those employed in church-related colleges and seminary settings. Scholars of religion and ethics thus carved out a place for themselves by identifying a range of issues at the intersections of religion and ethics and by drawing on intellectual developments in the humanities and social sciences to inform their work. Religious ethics thereby emerged as a new discursive formation with a fresh set of rules and practices for identifying what ought to count as important problems for scholars of religion and ethics to examine. Following Michel Foucault, the field created a system of truth understood as a set of "ordered procedures for the production, regulation, distribution, circulation, and operation of statements" according to which "the true and the false are separated and specific effects of power [are] attached to the true." Where ordered procedures for examining religion and ethics were able to enlist systems of power that produce and sustain those procedures, religious ethics became what Foucault called a new "'regime' of truth."[1]

This new regime, however, is not widely or evenly in place within the broader field of religious studies. That is to say, its truths have not secured the special effects of power, leaving it precarious and, at times, uncertain about its proper aims, resources, and methods. In part that is because religious ethics appears "normative" and thus suspicious to scholars who work according to the imperatives of positivist, value-neutral epistemologies or materialist metaphysics. Equally important is the fact that religious ethics is a relatively new field, drawing in ad hoc, unsystematic, and experimental ways from theology, social theory, humanistic cultural criticism, literature, moral psychology, area studies, history, and philosophy. Religious ethics is very much in the process of development. That fact makes it difficult to identify basic or enduring characteristics of the field, and it may frustrate those who want more stability, predictability, and solidity from a research tradition than religious ethics can offer. Compared to more familiar specializations in religious studies—the history of religions, the philosophy of religion, the comparative study of religion, or forms of textual interpretation—religious ethics often requires special justification to other members of the religious studies guild. For reasons that I will explain below, the "regime" of religious ethics is anything but secure. Indeed, course offerings in religious ethics remain either absent from or underdeveloped in more than a few religious studies curricula in the United States, the United Kingdom, and Europe.

With these facts in mind, in this chapter I aim to do three things. First, I will offer conceptual terms for understanding religion, ethics, and their intellectual relationship such that we can understand the locution "religious ethics" and its ground rules for the production, regulation, distribution, circulation, and operation of statements. Without signing on to the relativism and radical historicism of Foucault's work, I wish to draw on his notion of regimes of truth to advance a metadisciplinary understanding of religious ethics. Second, I will provide a brief sketch of the emergence of religious ethics to contextualize its institutional formation and patterns of activity. Finally, I will identify a new frontier for work in religious ethics on the premise that its research directions, rules, and subject matter need considerable expansion and a more ambitious understanding of its range of potential interlocutors and its future mission. One outcome will be to identify sources of truth that can help to empower religious ethics as a bona fide scholarly regime.

RELATING RELIGION AND ETHICS

The subject matter of religious ethics—that on which religious ethicists focus their scholarly attention—would presume, it might seem, working notions of "religion" and "ethics" along with an understanding of the relationship between these two concepts. Yet, strikingly, attention to these matters is generally lacking in religious ethics. Indeed, very little of the intellectual skirmishing that has animated metacritical scholarship in religious studies over the past several decades has had an impact on religious ethics. And with a few notable exceptions religious ethicists have shown little desire to contribute to theoretical and definitional debates in religious studies. Scholars of religious ethics generally view themselves as contributing to an understanding of ethics rather than to an understanding of religion. Clarifying that Islam is not essentially a fundamentalist religion, for example, is relatively uninteresting to religious ethicists unless that altered perception carries with it implications for understanding the moral life in the Muslim tradition. It is also the case that religious ethicists often allow the specific tradition on which they work to stand for religion as a general category, thus enabling a scholar to classify his or her work in Christian ethics or Buddhist ethics as religious ethics.[2] To be sure, the tendency to conflate species with genera is evident, indeed widespread, in the field of religious studies. But religious ethicists' lack of engagement with definitional and, more generally, metadisciplinary matters often leaves them looking marginal to, or uninterested in, debates about theory, method, and purpose in the wider field of which they are a part and oblivious to the history in which they can play a formative role. More than a few scholars in religious ethics appear to be working in an intellectual cocoon.

With those thoughts in mind, and aiming to correct for this relative lack of engagement regarding matters of theory, method, and history, I offer the following proposal. It asks that we deploy a Wittgensteinian

understanding of definitions as a starting point for thinking about definitions of *religion* and *ethics* as a step toward clarifying the locution "religious ethics." That understanding has us seek not a basic essence but a
cluster of traits according to which an item or object can be identified for
the purposes of classifying it in a heuristic way.[3] That is to say, it has us
understand definitions as "provisional attempts to clarify one's thought,
not to capture the innate essence of things."[4] In contrast to the effort to
identify an unchanging essential quality as the basis for assigning a clear,
crisp nominalization, Wittgenstein's approach requires that we view definitions in complex, pluralistic, and less bounded ways.

Wittgenstein would thus have us define *religion* and *ethics* on the
premise that definitions work to classify objects, practices, events, and
the like as "family resemblances." Members in a family can be identified
not because they all possess the same characteristics but because they all
possess crisscrossing and overlapping characteristics that are sufficient for
clustering those members together. We thus aim to identify similarities
rather than uniformities. Some members of a family can be tall, blonde,
and lean. Those who are not may nonetheless share freckles or blue eyes
with some of their taller siblings but not with all of them. Some (but not
all) in each group may be garrulous, competitive talkers. Noting such
features in this way enables us to identify enough similarities to recognize
a set of shared family traits. We can thereby see that all of the people in
question are members of the same family. Wittgenstein illustrates his idea
with the well-known example of how we assign the word *games* to various
playful interactions:

> I mean board-games, card-games, ball-games, Olympic games, and
> so on. What is common to them all?—Don't say: "There *must* be
> something common, or they would not be called 'games'"—but *look
> and see* whether there is anything common to all. . . . Look for exam-
> ple at board-games, with their multifarious relationships. Now pass
> to card-games; here you find many correspondences with the first
> group, but many common features drop out, and others appear. When
> we pass next to ball-games, much that is common is retained, but
> much is lost.—Are they all "amusing"? Compare chess with noughts

and crosses. Or is there always winning and losing, or competition between players? . . . In ball games there is winning and losing, but when a child throws his ball at the wall and catches it again, this feature has disappeared.[5]

Wittgenstein's image of definitions as family resemblances allows us to form ascriptions by finding overlapping characteristics, correspondences, and interrelationships that enable us to mark off one set of data from another. Summarizing his view on the matter, he writes: "We see a complicated network of similarities overlapping and criss-crossing: sometimes overall similarities, sometimes similarities of detail."[6]

With that Wittgensteinian idea in place, consider the following definition of *religion*: a set of beliefs, practices, attitudes, and institutional arrangements that invokes the category of the sacred understood as that which

(a) has extraordinary qualities that entitle it to attitudes and related behaviors of reverence, fidelity, honor, and/or gratitude;

(b) has the capacity to bear importantly on human affairs independently of human volition;

(c) enables or aids persons in resolving or appreciably lessening anxieties about their place, limitations, and experience in the world;

(d) enables persons to experience wonder, joy, hope, awe, or kindred affections;

(e) is deep or far-reaching in effectuality and pertinence to human affairs;

(f) enables persons to communicate or interact by using dramatic ritual performances and other formalized symbolic practices;

(g) provides an institutional basis for social organization and disciplined activity, which may either stabilize or disrupt the status quo; and

(h) requires practices, symbolic forms, and idioms that are assigned noble if not transcendent status.[7]

In offering this account I do not mean to say the sacred designates a discrete ontological entity or transcendental domain that somehow stands apart from human life and social institutions. For scholars of religion the sacred is a *social fact*, amenable to research using the tools of the humanities and social sciences. The sacred can consist of ghosts, animals, ancestors, mountains, deities, forests, hierarchies, authoritative decrees, charismatic leaders, texts, oral traditions, material objects, or legal institutions and traditions, for example. Nor do I mean that religions each have only one sacred object around which to organize their adherents' practices, attitudes, beliefs, or discourses. Religions routinely invoke numerous deities and paradeities, holy figures, institutional arrangements, texts, and physical objects as entitled to the behaviors and attitudes that I mentioned above. Moreover, and equally important, representations of the sacred can be symbolic in ways that defy any simple or unambiguous understanding; the sacred can be ambivalent about its meaning and implications for human life. Nor am I suggesting that religions all avow the same attitudes and behaviors, or even similar attitudes to the same degree, over their long or short histories. By "resolving or appreciably lessening anxieties" I do not mean that religions routinely aim to console their adherents. Religions can "resolve" anxieties by making plain that the resolution of some basic questions, or the satisfaction of some hopes or dreams, is not possible or perhaps even desirable. By noting that religions offer occasions for "persons to experience wonder, joy, hope, awe, or kindred affections," I mean to note that religions often but not always provide ways of encouraging positive outlooks toward experience and motivational bases for human betterment.[8] By "deep or far-reaching in effectuality and pertinence" I do not mean that religious beliefs or practices range across *all* aspects of experience. Religions can have importance or considerable impact on a relatively narrow sphere of human existence; what is important is not the scope of the impact but its palpability. By saying that religion "provides an institutional basis for social organization and disciplined activity, which may either stabilize or disrupt the status quo," I mean to point out that there is, in principle, no one way in which religion relates to established clusters of power.[9] More generally, I do not believe that motives that generate religious activity are untouched by human interest. There is no reason to think that religion is less vulnerable to being instrumentalized than is any other human practice. The sacred is not wholly autonomous; even though it is typically considered of incomparable value, it can be manipulated (and regularly is).

One key feature of my definition is the notion of *entitlement*. Sacred matters are understood to deserve a certain cluster of attitudes, practices, and institutional arrangements. Sacred objects may deserve their entitlements unconditionally or on the basis of some noteworthy quality, communication, or action. The point is that the sacred can be presumed to make certain demands on the basis of possessing a basic value.

Moreover, the entitlements assigned to sacred matters are typically not of the order of other objects of attachment, esteem, and the like. Sacred matters are qualitatively different from other types of value; they enable the establishment of moral hierarchies. Advocates for or representatives of the sacred create a frame of reference according to which particular attachments, concerns, attitudes, and practices are rendered appropriate or inappropriate. One of the key features of the sacred, then, is that it requires a form of acknowledgment in the Cavellian sense I described in my introduction. As I noted there, acknowledgment is a matter of responding to something you are exhibiting. But the kind of response is important. To acknowledge is not premised on having had certain epistemic criteria satisfied; it is not a matter of *knowing*. Indeed, acknowledging according to Cavell occurs prior to and independent of knowing. For Cavell, acknowledgment is not so much an occasion or an event as it is "a category in terms of which a given response is evaluated."[10] To acknowledge is to convey a certain set of attitudes and expectations that paradoxically generate from and create a relationship with an other. Acknowledgment designates not a specific emotive or reactive response but a willingness to account for oneself and, in the process, communicate a set of values and attitudes about oneself toward an other. For that reason Cavell describes the lack of acknowledgment not as an absence but as "the presence of something, a confusion, an indifference, a callousness, an exhaustion, a coldness."[11]

Religious acknowledgment modifies the Cavellian concept of acknowledgment in this way: it is a category in terms of which responses to the sacred's normativity are evaluated—a category that provides the basis for assessing the responses to the entitlements that representatives of the sacred can presume. Persons who are not religious are not only "nonbelievers" or individuals who fail to abide by one of the sacred's instructions or commands. Nonreligious persons include those who are indifferent to the demands of the sacred that they observe others as acknowledging as a matter of social fact.

* * *

Religion as I have characterized it is a complex ascription, not a simple one—an ascription that is premised on needing several—but not all—of the characteristics I have identified to allow us to classify certain beliefs, practices, texts, attitudes, or institutions as "religious" and not something else. Our purposes in invoking this ascription are simultaneously intellectual and practical. We deploy *religion* as a term of classification because thus far we have found this to be a productive way to develop thought, research, and public policy. We can likewise find it useful—again, echoing Wittgenstein—to extend this working definition of religion "as in spinning a thread we twist fibre on fibre" to new domains that can be instructively termed "religion" or "religious." A Wittgensteinian definition is not only complex and plural; it is mobile and thus able to adapt to new phenomena. Matters that are classified as "religion" or "religious" are recognizable not because they all possess the same characteristics but because they all possess enough of the characteristics of sacrality and related symbolism, lore, practice, belief, attitudes, institutional power, anxiety-resolution, wonder, palpability, and ritualization to be usefully marked off, if only provisionally, as distinct from other domains of human activity.

In offering this complex definition, I do not mean to suggest that religion is static or independent of culture, power, or society or that religion is chiefly a matter of personal belief. Religions are historically dynamic, internally varied, socially constructed, situationally located, and culturally diverse. Thus we say that religions are social, temporal, psychological, and practical phenomena that draw their materials from a vast array of human practices and contexts and transmit them intergenerationally in the effort simultaneously to sacralize and naturalize the views they avow. If we wonder whether various human activities can count as "religious," Wittgenstein urges us to "*look and see* whether there is anything common to all."[12]

What, then, of the concept of ethics? Assume—thinking again in terms of family resemblances and for heuristic purposes—that by *ethics*

I mean the critical analysis of ideas that prescribe, permit, or prohibit human behavior. Complexity resides here in the fact that providing prohibition, permission, and prescription can enlist different discourses, as does the work of evaluating individuals, groups, or institutions. Prophetic discourse regarding structural injustices, for example, differs from discourse about practices of moral formation, which differs from efforts to evaluate the impact of new technologies on society, which differ from efforts to demarcate the realm of morality from other realms of human conduct, say, law or etiquette.[13] Yet all of these discourses can inform one another like the fibers that mutually reinforce each other when constituting a thread.

Abstract concepts, along with their analysis, are central to ethical thinking. They enable us to understand the basis and range of moral responsibility and evaluate human behavior as right and wrong, good or bad, desirable or undesirable. Historically, but surely not always in the past, and surely not always today, ethical concepts trace their authority to one or another religious source. When ethical concepts are tied to religious sources, they often prescribe, permit, or prohibit conduct that enables practitioners to link themselves to sacred phenomena in the effort to guide and evaluate their actions or their character.

With these ideas of religion and ethics as heuristic categories in mind, we might better understand what I mean when I say that religious ethics is a scholarly area that studies the many ways in which religion and ethics are interrelated. Religious ethicists examine religious discourses pertaining to the character or conduct of individuals, groups, or institutions. But that summary statement nonetheless requires clarifying the idea that joins religion and ethics in my account, namely, the notion of having a relationship. The relationship between religion and ethics can be conceived along several lines. Ethics might be viewed as *logically dependent* on religious concepts; as *psychologically impelled* by religious attitudes and convictions; as *historically rooted* in religious traditions; as *epistemologically conditioned* by religious ways of knowing; as *linguistically dependent* insofar as they acquire meaning in relation to religious images, exemplars, or ideas; or as *providing terms and tools for clarifying the structure of religious morality or evaluating conduct* authorized by such morality.

I do not intend to explore all of these options here. I rather want to observe that, however many ways we can conceive of the relationship between religion and ethics, the work of religious ethicists generally falls into two patterns of thought. First, religious ethicists examine how religions generate, authorize, interpret, and apply ethical norms and values for evaluating human character and conduct. Here the common orientation is to ask what difference, if any, religious ideas make when it comes to guiding or evaluating human behavior. Do religious ideas provide something that would otherwise be missing from secular or philosophical expressions of morality? That question is often driven by anxiety about whether religion is a marginal factor in personal and public life. It may also be driven by a belief in the uniqueness or autonomy of religion—the idea that religion is immune from broader frameworks by which to understand, compare, and assess it. Second, religious ethicists examine how ethical values (and related claims) place normative constraints on how religious adherents carry out what they perceive as their sacred duties. Here the common orientation is to ask whether religious values or practices heed some basic, nonrelative, normative standards. The focus, in other words, is on the ethics of belief. Scholars operating according to this orientation reject the idea that religion is autonomous and instead subject it to evaluation in light of nonreligious criteria.

Taking these two foci together, we can say that religion and ethics can be interrelated in a dialectical way. Some religious ethicists critically examine how religion authorizes ethical demands and impels human behavior; others focus on how and why religious authorizations of behavior might be subject to approval or critique. These foci, of course, are not mutually exclusive. The intellectual practices in religious ethics can run in crosscutting directions.

These intellectual practices, moreover, can be descriptive, evaluative, or conceptual: religious ethicists describe how religious literature and traditions generate ethical norms and values, evaluate those norms and values, and clarify basic concepts, taxonomic categories, and patterns of practical reasoning according to which those norms and values might be strengthened or better understood. Generally the subject matter to which religious ethicists direct their attention requires them to draw on terms, controversies, questions, and key figures in the history of moral philosophy.

Indeed, an appreciable amount of work by religious ethicists, especially in the 1960s, 1970s, and 1980s, overlaps with the work of Western moral philosophers insofar as both groups seek to clarify the meaning, content, and scope of morality and its relation to various forms of action-guiding sources, including religious traditions. But religious ethics distinguishes itself from moral philosophy by identifying a wider swath of material on which scholars are to focus—material that includes religious stories, political and social imperatives, codes and laws for individual behavior, paradigmatic figures, proverbial or prophetic sayings, and institutional practices, roles, and policies. Religious ethics attracts scholars who wish to examine more of the moral life than is typically the object of study in mainstream moral philosophy.

Religious ethics, thus understood, examines (among other things) morally relevant religious literature, practices, and traditions in the effort to critically ascertain religion's normative dimensions in its efforts to guide human behavior. By the word *critically* I mean to indicate that religious ethicists do not assume that the beliefs or practices of religious adherents may go unquestioned or that they serve as the final arbiter for determining the truth of what a religious ethicist claims. How religious ethicists launch their critical programs of scholarship typically reflects one of the two crosscutting directions I mentioned above. Religious ethicists sometimes begin by thinking about how religious ideas, teachings, or practices organize an account of experience, human nature, and the world as a first step toward critically examining religion's ethical dimensions. Here one underlying premise is that religion is (among other things) a cognitive matter that generates ideas with behavioral import. Other religious ethicists think first not about religious concepts or traditions but about discrete ethical values, scientific data, or general interpretive categories for organizing an understanding of religious claims. Attention to values, data, or interpretive categories, furthermore, might justify placing constraints on religiously authorized claims. Such constraints are introduced on the premise that the values and authority avowed by religious adherents are themselves matters of inquiry and critique, and that criticism of religion can justify itself on terms that are independent of ostensive religious convictions.[14]

As an academic discipline, moreover, religious ethics behaves like other disciplines in that it includes assessing the work of scholars in the guild, precisely as work in the discipline of history includes examining the work of historians and English includes examining the work of literary critics and scholars of literature. This is not to suggest that religious ethicists are, or have been, self-reflexive about how their scholarship might help draw or redraw the contours of their own field. Rarely do religious ethicists critically (or reliably) examine the basic assumptions, terms, and methods according to which general trends are unfolding in the guild.[15]

Yet unlike the disciplines of history or English—and like the disciplines of, say, Latin American studies or African American studies—religious ethics is marked by a modifier, namely, the word *religious*. That term—like *Latin American* or *African American*—identifies the subject matter but not the perspectives or identities of the scholars who work in those areas. One need not be an adherent of a religious tradition or belief system, or a member of a religious community, to work in religious ethics. Insider knowledge obtained from religious adherence, if such knowledge exists, is not a credential for carrying out scholarship in the guild.

INSTITUTIONAL AND INTELLECTUAL FORMATIONS

In the United States religious ethics is a more recent area of academic study than core disciplines such as history or English. As I noted earlier, it arose in North American departments of religious studies in the mid- and late twentieth century in response to demands to study religion with ways that were often distinct from those employed in church-related colleges and seminary settings, philosophy departments, and area studies departments. With the rise of religious studies as a distinct area within the humanities and social sciences, religious ethics emerged alongside the history of religions and religiously relevant area-studies concentrations in course offerings and research projects regarding religion's relationship to ethics and social life. Shifts in topics and institutional settings worked in tandem: moving the study of religion from professional schools such as seminaries to humanities programs in private and public research universities and nondenominational colleges of arts and sciences likewise meant changing the purposes for studying religion and, with that, religious ethics. Departments of religious studies at Brown University, the

University of Virginia, Indiana University, Princeton University, University of Iowa, Stanford University, the University of Tennessee, and Florida State University—some of which were well-established, others newly inaugurated—facilitated the growth of religious ethics in the latter part of the twentieth century by training a new generation of students in the field. Some religiously affiliated colleges, seminaries, and divinity schools, observing these developments, began to reshape their curricula and their priorities for faculty appointments to include a new range of texts, methods, and specializations.

Despite overlooking the vital role that public research universities played in the emergence of religious studies and religious ethics, James M. Gustafson provides a useful short history of the emergence of religious ethics from the late 1940s through the 1990s. He identifies four developments that conspired to generate new institutional settings and patterns of scholarly research in religion and ethics. I would summarize, and partially restate, Gustafson's fourfold account in this way. Religious ethics arose as a result of (1) increased attention to religious traditions such as Islamic, Jewish, Hindu, Buddhist, and Confucian ethics and along with an expansion of the concept of "religion" to designate broad comprehensive or generic frameworks of meaning rather than ostensive traditions; (2) a shift of emphasis from normative ethics to work that is descriptive, comparative, and analytical; (3) a rise of philosophical self-consciousness, driven in no small part by the linguistic turn, such that religious ethics became philosophically more sophisticated and interpretively self-reflexive about its aims and procedures; and (4) the rise of practical ethics in the wake of political turbulence and controversies in scientific research, medicine, war, race, gender, and professional life, generating a need to address public policy and public culture by drawing on the full arsenal of moral reflection, including reflection provided by religious traditions along with precision provided by the tools of moral philosophy.[16]

Gustafson fails to note that the second and fourth items he identifies are in tension given that the descriptive turn reflects a movement away from normative thinking while the practical turn is driven by it. He also understates the authority and impact of moral philosophy in those two developments—a point to which I will return below. With those caveats noted, I believe that his account accurately describes the development of religious ethics at the time his article was published (1997). All four trends contributed to the rise of religious ethics as an area of scholarship that critically examines the interrelationship between religion and ethics. And he is correct when he observes that religious ethics understands its mission not as contributing to the professional formation of religious clergy but as contributing to the public understanding of religion in private and public research universities whose purpose is to address a broader set of needs, questions, and controversies. In this respect, Gustafson observes, "religious ethics was in the same trajectory as the rest of religious studies: For many, the aim for evaluation of publication and teaching was no longer to affect the moral communities of various traditions or ecumenical agencies. Rather, the developing academic guild consciousness (which went well beyond religious studies) set the standards for self-evaluations and for external review."[17]

What Gustafson identifies as emerging from this fourfold development describes well the first critical mass of religious ethicists in the late 1960s and early 1970s, the most distinguished of whom showed expertise in many if not all of the developments that were shaping the field: James F. Childress, Donald Evans, Margaret Farley, Albert R. Jonsen, Karen Lebacqz, Wayne Proudfoot, Ronald M. Green, Beverly Harrison, David Little, Gene Outka, John P. Reeder Jr., Peter Paris, Charles Reynolds, Sumner B. Twiss, LeRoy Walters, and Lee Yearley foremost among them. Imaginative, rigorous, widely read, and intellectually curious, these scholars were trailblazers. They moved into colleges and universities, several with newly formed religious studies departments, and launched an innovative style and range of methodologies for studying religion's normative claims and practical implications. Much of their work was prompted by the recognition that a consensus regarding basic values in American culture had vanished and that institutional authorities, along with their professional experts, could no longer be trusted.[18] They published pathbreaking articles and monographs in leading university press venues, helped create specific fields such as modern bioethics, directed newly established ethics centers, and worked to launch a new academic journal, among other accomplishments. Their early work took the form of careful philosophical, literary, comparative, and historical examinations of religion's contributions to ethical debates about gender, sexual ethics, health care, war and peace, race, religious authority, political authority, and social justice or more abstract discussions pertaining to religious obligation, practical reasoning, moral psychology, and the relation of religion to morality. In the fall of 1973 these and related efforts led to a watershed moment with the first publication of the *Journal of Religious Ethics*, which began as a semiannual publication and now serves as a signature quarterly for scholarly publication in the field. Five years later saw the publication of David Little and Sumner B. Twiss's *Comparative Religious Ethics: A New Method*, the first extended effort to provide conceptual precision to basic terms such as *religion* and *ethics* and to indicate "a method of study that is . . . more rigorous and consistent than some other approaches."[19] Little and Twiss thus attempted to create an analytical scheme that enabled scholars to pay careful attention to *"kinds or types of practical reasoning in different religious settings"* and to eschew either apologetical studies of religions or broad and grossly oversimplified representations of religious traditions as data for comparison.[20] With that framework in place as a way of examining religious, moral, and legal action-guides within Navaho, Christian, and Buddhist sources, Little and Twiss sought to show that the study of religious ethics could be seen as an academic field on par with philosophical ethics. That same year Ronald M. Green, drawing from Kant's theory of moral philosophy and rationality, published *Religious Reason: The Rational and Moral Basis of Religious Belief*, aiming to theorize about a universal structure of practical reasoning in Judaism, Christianity, and the religions of India; and Roderick Hindery, drawing on the ideas of Max Weber, as well as on primary source material, published *Comparative Ethics in Hindu and Buddhist Traditions*.[21] Together these works helped to generate a picture of religious ethics that was rigorous and informed by philosophy and the social sciences. By the end of the 1970s a new style and set of scholarly questions regarding religion and ethics were in place in various parts of the North American academy.

A considerable portion of the early work in religious ethics drew from Western moral philosophy, especially work in analytical, comparative, or descriptive ethics, and practical ethics. In regard to analytical, comparative, or descriptive ethics, philosophical concepts were invoked to clarify basic definitional matters regarding the meaning of moral concepts or to provide a taxonomic framework for examining and comparing religious and moral ideas in a nonconfessional way. As a result religious ethics could be seen not as irrational or as some kind of faith-based parlor conversation but as having a rational structure on par with schools of philosophical ethics. Articles in the first three years of the *Journal of Religious Ethics* were predominantly philosophical in aim and method, examining, for example, the relationship between virtue and duty, the contributions of the philosopher William Frankena to the fields of religious and moral philosophy, the structure of moral theory in religious ethics, the philosophy of John Rawls, the metaethical dimensions of Paul Tillich's thought, Kant's aesthetics, and literature on religious ethics by analytical moral philosophers who work outside the guilds of theology or religious studies.

New monographs reflected this trend as well, one clear example of which is Gene Outka's 1972 book, *Agape: An Ethical Analysis*. Rather than confine his study to any one particular Christian account of the meaning of *agape*, or neighbor-love, for Christian morality, Outka deploys ethical concepts from Anglo-American philosophy to analyze agape as it is conceptualized by a number of Protestant and Roman Catholic theologians. He thus launches a descriptive and analytic study addressing how agape's demands for neighbor-love might square with self-regarding concerns, how to understand agape in terms of rules and virtues, how agape compares and contrasts with other ethical concepts such as justice, and how agape can be justified at a metaethical level.[22] All of these topics are informed by work in contemporary analytical moral philosophy, and they show how agape's requirements can be rendered intelligible by human reason. In effect, Outka draws on moral philosophy to humanize a divine command.

Little and Twiss proceed in a similar manner, noting at the outset of their work that they "found contemporary philosophical work useful in increasing our capacity to understand and compare religious and moral beliefs in different cultures."[23] They craft concepts and definitions to distinguish among morality, religion, and law in the course of developing a general framework for understanding how practical justification operates in religious texts and traditions, a framework that they deploy to analyze the relationship between the religion, morality, and law of the Navajo, in the Gospel of Matthew, and in Theravada Buddhism, respectively. Like Outka's treatment of agape, Little and Twiss's project works to demystify religious commands by showing how they have a rational structure.

In that way their work helps to humanize religious ethics and show how studying it belongs squarely within the academy.

In practical ethics early work done by religious ethicists routinely drew on concepts and distinctions in Western moral philosophy to frame religious ethics in light of deontological or utilitarian methods of moral reasoning and to invoke distinctions such as those concerning intended and foreseen consequences, acts of omission and commission, perfect and imperfect duties, direct and indirect action, categorical and hypothetical imperatives, commands and counsels of perfection, blaming and excusing, and related concepts about human agency, act evaluation, and conditions of moral liability.[24] These categories in moral philosophy were as important for tackling practical moral problems as were the more abstract philosophical concepts for advancing descriptive and comparative work in religious ethics. Indeed, normative work in bioethics, the ethics of war, and economic ethics depended heavily on these concepts and distinctions.[25]

Since the time Gustafson published his overview, religious ethics has become decidedly more historical, descriptive, and comparative.[26] That is to say, greater weight has fallen on the second of the four trends he identifies. The reasons for this development are several. One is that scholars need to generate source material from religious traditions that have heretofore been neglected in order to expand our knowledge of religious traditions' conceptions of moral responsibility and even of "ethics" itself.[27] Thus we see recent contributions that describe various aspects of Jewish, Islamic, Buddhist, Confucian, and Hindu ethics.[28] A second reason is intellectual dissatisfaction with the arid and disembodied nature of many of the philosophical tools first deployed in religious ethics, which rendered religious ethics vulnerable to the criticism—one emerging in antitheoretical quarters of moral philosophy itself—that it was overly abstract and excessively detached from moral experience and the social sources on which it relies.[29] A third reason connects to the enormous influence of Alasdair MacIntyre's 1981 book, *After Virtue*, which seeks to expose the intractability of modern moral philosophical thinking and urges in its place a return to the virtues and an approach to ethical inquiry that is deeply historical, thereby launching a theory of narrative as a way of tracking religion's contributions to moral thought and practice.[30]

A fourth, related reason is tied to the notion that basic concepts in ethics have historical roots and that any adequate understanding and application of them today must grasp how and for what purposes they were originally conceived and used. Fifth is the need for greater clarity at a metadisciplinary level about procedures for description and for carrying out insightful comparison on the premise that disciplined comparative thinking provides ways of putting commonplace ideas in a fresh light and opens up new pathways for thinking about moral responsibility and agency in an increasingly globalized world.[31] A sixth reason may be an aversion to appearing "normative" in academic quarters that are threatened by questions of justification, thereby reinforcing the aspiration to provide putatively value-neutral forms of knowledge.[32] A seventh reason is that political and social controversies in public culture may have receded in urgency in the minds of some of the more recent members of the profession. Perhaps currents of neoconservatism have worked their way into the guild, thereby leading scholars to think there is little need to serve as prophetic voices of social criticism.

One outcome of these reasons for proceeding descriptively, historically, and comparatively is to move religious ethics from relying on *abstract* frameworks (as we see in the work of Outka) to frameworks that insist on reckoning with *particularity* as vital for practical reasoning and moral deliberation.[33] The core idea in that latter framework, reflecting the influence of Aristotle, is that practical reasoning is a special kind of knowledge that requires us to pay attention to circumstances and conditions that intrude on our thoughts, feelings, and contexts. Of special importance is the act of *perceiving* relevant particulars in the formation of moral judgments and visions of how to live well.

That development toward attending to particular facts and circumstances as essential to moral deliberation, in turn, eased the way toward a subsequent development in religious ethics: works that provide detailed scholarly engagements with *specific forms* of particularity. The result of this second development is to *radicalize* particularity, thereby moving religious ethics from a focus on particularity in general terms—what I call attending to *general particularity* as essential for practical reasoning—to an interrogation of particularity in detailed, finely grained terms—what I call *concrete particularity* in ethnographic and similar studies. Of special importance here are the arts of representing specific religious identities, practices, rituals, and modes of seeing. Hence the emergence of several works that focus on ethical aspects of specific religious or political traditions, study specific moral or political controversies, describe various forms of local knowledge and rhetoric, or address ethical concerns directly pertinent to specific identities and groups.[34] All of these factors have contributed, in different ways and with different emphases, to the development of research in religious ethics that places great value on historical contextualization, thick description, and careful analysis and comparison.

EXPANDING THE REGIME

We can read Gustafson's overview of religious ethics, in the spirit of Foucault, as describing patterns of inquiry within a new regime of truth that has developed "ordered procedures for the production, regulation, distribution, circulation, and operation of statements" regarding the interrelationship of religion and ethics. But what is generally missing from this current regime is an attention to culture. By *culture* I mean the total of the inherited ideas, beliefs, values, knowledge, and material products that habituate a people, constitute the shared bases of individual and collective identity and action, and provide the milieu in which persons relate to historical and natural events. Culture on this account includes not only the ideas, customs, habits, and values of a people but also its characteristic artifacts, buildings, visual heritages, and material designs that help to constitute a lifeworld. Culture thus constitutes a symbol system—both material and nonmaterial—that expresses values and helps to give life meaning. On my account culture encompasses (for example) everything from film to political memorializations to rap music to product design to iconic celebrities to televangelism to graphic novels. It ranges from works of elites to alternative or nonmainstream actors who contest and recreate otherwise hegemonic cultural forms. Moreover, cultures provide concepts, symbols, and practices according to which religions express themselves. Given the pervasiveness of culture and how it is saturated with values, including religious values, its neglect by religious ethicists is odd and unfortunate.

With a few exceptions religious ethicists are generally uninterested in the category of culture.[35] Lost in that widespread indifference is information about the routine patterns and practices of everyday experience—customs and codes, socialization processes, ritual practices, kinship systems, criteria of expertise, folk wisdom, visual and aural subcultures, divisions of labor, ascetic disciplines, symbols of meaning, the experience of familiarity and difference, and the complex and often contested ways in which these facts of social life bear on human existence and well-being. Add to this list an inattention to scholarly paradigms, tools, experimental procedures, and pioneering work according to which cultural practices are studied. Religious ethicists' general neglect of culture puts their work at considerable remove from currents in religious studies that draw energies and insights from cultural studies. And it deepens suspicions from antitheoretical currents in moral philosophy that scholars of ethics—whether religious or philosophical—tackle questions that have little meaningful connection to habits and practices in ordinary life.

Looking prospectively rather than retrospectively, then, I will add a fifth trend to those offered by Gustafson: religious ethics will develop in new directions as it is informed by theories of and research about cultural practices, processes, symbols, media, rhetoric, and sources of knowledge, along with the contested ways in which these various cultural matters interact—such contestations, of course, being a crucial part of what cultural theorists regularly study as essential to their work. The basic idea behind this proposal is that making a cultural turn in religious ethics opens up opportunities for critically examining religion, ethics, and their relationships in ways that have gone unnoticed. It is also the case, as I will argue in the next chapter, that making a cultural turn provides insights into the human condition that could inform, as well as challenge, reigning notions of human nature and the self in religious ethics and in the academy more generally.

A turn to culture enables religious ethics to seize a number of specific opportunities for new work in the guild. Experiential data for research, diverse religious and moral values, others' declarative and imperative speech-acts, ideas about self-in-relation-to-others, and self-critical reflection about the representation of difference all invite further, more sustained, analysis. In addition, note that culture is, among other things, a site of dynamic, fluid, intersubjective relationships, and that fact, too, invites fresh thought and exploration. Culture is the constitutive medium of human existence; it is not a secondary layer of causality that redirects or constrains previously established patterns or primitive desires. In this way culture is all-inclusive, working on the plasticity of human desires to organize them in a number of directions.[36] These facts reveal how our lives are contingent and depend on wider patterns of thought, practice, and value. Cultures mediate our commerce with others and the world in ways that get us beyond the antinomies of subjectivity and objectivity, psyche and culture, self and other, character and society, and volition and receptivity. A turn to culture, then, opens up possibilities for exploring dense textures and contexts of religious and ethical ideas and has us think about human agency in potentially new ways.

This is not to say, of course, that religious ethicists should jettison the advances made by increased attention to various religious traditions, descriptive analysis, philosophical reflexivity, or practical inquiry. *Friends and Other Strangers* aims to expand the horizon of religious ethics and shed fresh light on well-established lines of thinking rather than to replace current or previous models of research with a single orthodoxy about how the field should operate. My aims are to liberate, not to constrict.

But if I were merely proposing that religious ethicists draw on cultural theory and cultural studies to broaden the resources on which they work, I would be making a relatively modest proposal, one that speaks only to the guild of religious ethics in an intradisciplinary way and uncritically accepts intellectual currents in cultural studies. My aims are more ambitious. I propose that religious ethics become more wholehearted and more confident, drawing on its own tools and insights to dimensionalize cultural studies, religious studies, and the humanities more broadly. As social critics, religious ethicists must never waver in their work of assessing policy, leadership, and customs as these shape the direction of institutions and aspirations of public culture. All too often work in cultural studies, religious studies, and the humanities, whatever effort it may make to move beyond value-neutral, positivist epistemologies, fails to critically evaluate cultural practices and processes, including those that implicate religious traditions. Worries about ethnocentrism continue to express a tacit if not explicit embrace of moral relativism—itself a moral theory.

Moral commitments are impossible to avoid. Given that fact, religious ethicists would do well to broaden their implied audiences so as to critically address scholars across the academy on matters of normative inquiry. Put in other terms: religious ethicists do well to address others who might become friends of their work upon learning from the insights that the field can provide. In that critical, transgressive, and interdisciplinary spirit the remaining chapters are offered, and it is now time to turn to them.

2

ON MAKING A CULTURAL TURN
IN RELIGIOUS ETHICS

THE PROMISE OF RELIGIOUS ETHICS

Reviewing the first twenty years of the *Journal of Religious Ethics*, Ronald M. Green credits the authors and editors for publishing work of enduring importance in philosophical, comparative, and historical ethics and for creating the preferred venue for scholars who wish to capture the attention of readers familiar with, or interested in, religion and ethics. Despite its success, he goes on to argue, the *JRE* needs to diversify its range of publications and topics of scholarly analysis. In Green's mind "the problem of parochialism and Western bias"—a problem that the inaugural editors hoped the journal would overcome—is considerable.[1] That problem "has expressed itself in the way in which *JRE*'s basic agenda, the problems that are viewed as significant and the issues that merit attention, is still predominantly shaped by the concerns of Christian ethics and theology."[2] A related problem turns on *JRE*'s theoretical and methodological narrowness. Green observes that few articles address issues in humanistic psychology or ethics and aesthetics, and even fewer draw from authors who are trained in cultural anthropology or who deploy methods of original fieldwork.[3] In his judgment the original interdisciplinary goal of the *JRE*—to stimulate discussion between religious ethicists and "normative political theorists, cultural anthropologists, developmental and humanistic psychologists, sociological theorists, and interpreters of the aesthetic"—remains unfulfilled.[4]

In this chapter I want to take up Green's bid for greater interdisciplinarity in religious ethics, focusing on developments in cultural studies, moral psychology, and anthropology.[5] I will defend interdisciplinary work not for the sake of methodological diversity alone but on the conviction that it can open doors for religious ethicists to examine neglected features of experience and craft an ethics of ordinary life. Considerable work in religious ethics neglects the routine culture of everyday experience—customs and codes, socialization processes, ritual practices, kinship systems, criteria of expertise, folk wisdom, divisions of labor, and the contested ways in which these forces interact. Religious ethicists are lamentably uninterested in the workings of culture, and what little reference they do make tends to equate "culture" with "ideas." That fact crowds out an enormous range of meaningful human activity and puts considerable distance between religious ethicists and colleagues in the scholarly study of religion. Scholars of religion and ethics risk losing opportunities for intellectual engagement in their own departments and schools along with an appreciation for ethical genres and rhetorics that might capture the moral imagination of the lay intellectual. Perhaps if religious ethicists would critically examine the local knowledge and vernacular traditions of persons who are affected by the claims that religious communities make, they would widen the orbit of their work.

Developing an ethics of ordinary life invites scholars to consider how religious ethics might proceed "from the bottom up," drawing on cultural ethnography and social theory as resources for social and cultural criticism. This trajectory might develop on the premise, embraced by some moral particularists, that there are goods internal to a practice. On that premise social critics should develop skills of participant observation or cultural analysis so as to familiarize themselves with standards of virtuous activity in particular contexts. Assuming that contextual knowledge is necessary to make sense of others' habits, cooperative activities, and communal relationships, social critics would acquaint themselves with standards of excellence that are indigenous to particular communities and traditions.[6] Or a research trajectory might proceed on the premise, important to the task of connected criticism, that acquiring local knowledge is a condition for holding a culture to its own standards of fairness and that morality is inescapably interpretive of shared meanings.[7] Cognate accounts might hold that relatively abstract, independent moral principles can be developed for social criticism on the assumption that "abstract" ideas are entirely compatible with attention to local goods and traditions and that abstract ideas, as opposed to "idealized" claims, are immune to recent challenges from moral particularists.[8] Yet another trajectory might assess how power assumes its own "microphysics," suffusing and sensualizing our desires, interpersonal relationships, cultural images of the body, and institutional settings.[9]

In any case, whatever research those trajectories might produce, my basic point is this: attention to cultural practices and their relationship to character and conduct can stimulate new work in religious ethics. I do not wish to gainsay the merits of studying specific religious traditions; describing, analyzing, and comparing the ethical dimensions and teachings of religious traditions; clarifying philosophical and methodological assumptions in the guild; or connecting normative principles to cases—the four trends to which James Gustafson calls attention in his overview of religious ethics, as I noted in the previous chapter. I propose that we broaden the agenda of religious ethics beyond these trends by identifying and commenting on cultural forces and institutional settings with which persons identify themselves and find meaning and moral direction.[10] Indeed, I want to show that attending to issues in cultural studies can broaden the agenda of religious ethics and deepen our appreciation of some basic tenets and assumptions in the field. Work at the intersection of religion, ethics, and culture can open up uncharted terrain and stimulate new questions about areas of ongoing interest in the guild. In keeping with a general trend since the 1980s to expand the domain of morality beyond what is characteristically envisioned in Anglo-American moral philosophy that is styled on scientific assumptions, a cultural turn suggests ways of viewing the moral life and human agency to include our dependence on friends and strangers for received sources of wisdom and patterns of self-reflection.[11] To illustrate this point, I will focus on three specific areas of academic inquiry: comparative inquiry, virtue theory, and methodological implications of post-Enlightenment philosophy.

By *culture* I mean, as I noted in my introduction, the total of the inherited beliefs, values, knowledge, and material products that habituate a people, constitute the shared bases of individual and collective identity and action, and provide the milieu in which persons relate to historical and natural events. My definition aims to include not only the ideas, customs, habits, and values of a people but also its characteristic artifacts, buildings, visual heritages, and material designs that help to constitute its lifeworld. Culture thus constitutes a symbol system—both material and nonmaterial—that expresses values and gives life meaning. On this account culture encompasses everything from ballet to civic celebrations to soap operas to architectural design to moral and religious argument to various forms of body art. Culture ranges from works of elites to alternative or nonmainstream actors who contest and recreate dominant cultural forms.[12] Summarizing Plato's capacious view of culture, about which I will say more below, Myles Burnyeat captures part of what I am gesturing toward here:

> Forget about reading T. S. Eliot to yourself in bed. Our subject is the words and music you hear at social gatherings, large and small. Think pubs and cafes, karaoki, football matches, the last night of the proms. Think morning service at the village church, carols from King's College Cambridge, Elton John singing to the nation from Westminster Abbey. Think popular music in general and, when Plato brings in a parallel from the visual arts, forget the Tate Gallery and recall the advertisements that surround us everywhere. Above all, think about the way all this is distributed to us by television, the omnipresent medium at work in every home.[13]

This account of culture does not presuppose that it is static, geographically bounded, or an integrated whole. Cultures are dynamic, not unchanging, and they disperse themselves across barriers of state, religion, and class. Moreover, they exhibit internal diversity, argument, and conflict. "Jewish culture," to take one example, inhabits no single locale or geographical area and is characterized by considerable debate and internal diversity. To properly understand cultures, we must see them as protean, contested, and capable of migrating their materials and traditions across social, political, and economic boundaries. I will be presuming this inclusive, diasporic, and dynamic view of culture as I proceed.

To advance my proposal, I will develop my argument in four parts. In part 1, I will explore a work in cultural anthropology that poses important questions for comparative and cultural work in an age alert to "otherness," asymmetries of power, the end of value-neutrality in the humanities, and the formation of identity. That section charts an experimental moment in cultural anthropology that provides a challenge to and an invitation for parallel work among religious ethicists. Part 1 is thus metadisciplinary, regarding research trends and genres in the humanities that might stimulate cognate work in religious ethics. In part 2, I will deepen my argument by making a foundational case for the importance of culture as a topic of normative analysis. Part 2 will thus take up ontological and moral issues with an eye toward strengthening the case for normative work in religious and cultural studies and will render intelligible some of the questions I raise about anthropological inquiry in part 1. In part 3, I will describe works by Wayne Meeks, Margaret Trawick, and Charles Taylor that carry out a cultural turn in ways that can instruct work by religious ethicists. In part 4, I will conclude by sketching some implications of the first three parts for future work in religious ethics.

EXPERIMENTAL MOMENTS (AND THEIR LIMITS)

CULTURAL ANTHROPOLOGY

One source that might spark a cultural turn and open up new genres in religious ethics is the work of ethnographers George E. Marcus and Michael M. J. Fischer, especially their account of the "experimental moment" that has characterized work of the social and human sciences since the 1980s. According to Marcus and Fischer, anthropologists have become increasingly open to experimental research and writing because they are dissatisfied with grand theories that aspire to provide a comprehensive account of human conduct—"a general science of Man."[14] As an alternative, humanists and social scientists have sought to orient their attention toward describing "difference" and its political implications in local contexts. The acutely felt need for difference and description, Marcus and Fischer add, makes our intellectual situation ripe for "an ethnographic moment in the human sciences."[15] The basic aim is to pursue *heterology*, salvaging voices and practices that resist the homogenizing forces of capitalism in Western culture and across the globe.[16]

Such attention to difference does not necessarily entail traveling to regions that seem culturally distant and exotic from a Western, middle-class perspective. Instead, as James Clifford observes, "ethnography is moving into areas long occupied by sociology, the novel, or avant-garde cultural critique, rediscovering otherness and difference within the cultures of the West."[17] Whether at home or abroad, ethnography identifies distinctive ways in which we fashion identity, develop customs and codes according to which social practices can be evaluated, and resist the leveling forces of consumer culture.

In this period of experimentation no definitive research program has emerged as an alternative to grand theory. As Marcus and Fischer observe, "a period of experimentation is characterized by eclecticism, the play of ideas free of authoritative paradigms, critical and reflexive views of subject matter, openness to diverse influences embracing whatever seems to work in practice, and tolerance of uncertainty about a field's direction and of incompleteness in some of its projects."[18] The result is a situation in which work in the humanities and social sciences can be creatively interdisciplinary. Hybridizing currents in intellectual life invite scholars to draw on a wide range of tools to interpret and represent social reality and to do so without worrying about whether their writing carries the prestige that accompanies work of a more theoretical bent.

In addition to its eclecticism anthropology's "experimental moment" has a critical component, for it points to lay sources of normativity that resist reigning values and institutional power. Hence the title of the book in which Marcus and Fischer survey experiments in ethnography: *Anthropology as Cultural Critique*. Seeking to show how local cultures depart from bourgeois, middle-class Western life, anthropologists have directed their aims toward social and cultural criticism. The experimental goal is not only to affirm the merits of ethnography as a research tool for those who are interested in context and local practices but also to craft a *critical ethnography* that recognizes the evaluative dimension of comparative research in the interpretive social sciences. As described (and endorsed) in *Anthropology as Cultural Critique*, that critical agenda has a twofold component: first, to relativize our "taken-for-granted concepts such as the family, power, and the beliefs that lend certainty to our everyday life," thereby "disorienting the reader and altering perception," and, second, to locate "alternatives by unearthing . . . multiple possibilities as they exist in reality."[19] In other words critical ethnography as conceived by Marcus and Fischer is epistemological and quasi-utopian. Challenging readers' conceptual schemes and offering up alternatives to established practices and norms, it potentially demystifies and liberates.

For ethicists and social critics *Anthropology as Cultural Critique* extends an invitation and a challenge. The invitation is to move across academic boundaries with an eye toward examining a wide range of experiences in familiar and unfamiliar settings and to experiment with genres of writing and representation that depart from established approaches. In general, Marcus and Fischer describe pathbreaking social and humanistic thought as involving intellectual poaching, in which scholars steal tools, terms, categories, and methods from others' research traditions. Moreover, their work provides a rationale for comparative inquiry. Marcus and Fischer argue that comparative study should demystify settled ways of thinking and propose constructive alternatives. Whatever else one makes of their epistemological and quasi-utopian stand, it is an important one for religious ethicists to consider, especially comparative religious ethicists. Comparative religious ethics in some respects echoes the legacy of ecumenism, according to which intellectuals and religious leaders seek to generate better understandings among different faiths in a world that is increasingly interdependent and prone to misunderstanding or violence. However, an ecumenical rationale seems to export the paradigm of interreligious dialogue into an altogether different social and intellectual context, and it focuses on negotiating areas of potential divisiveness rather than on comparing basic concepts or producing finely grained comparative studies of vernacular practices and idioms. Only a few works in comparative religious ethics have developed a clear rationale or normative agenda that moves beyond the metanarratives of religious traditions.[20]

The challenge is to consider whether the epistemological and quasi-utopian aspects of critical ethnography are satisfactory. For reasons that I will develop soon, I believe that, in Marcus and Fischer's hands, they are not. Before we get to that judgment, however, we should turn our attention to recent developments in ethics. Those developments suggest why religious ethicists should accept the invitation to cross boundaries into ethnographic and cultural inquiry as a way of exploring the ethics of difference, moral formation, and everyday life.

PERSONAL AND IMPERSONAL PERSPECTIVES IN ETHICS

Readers familiar with recent developments in religious studies and philosophy know that the trends to which Marcus and Fischer allude have parallels outside anthropology. Many ethicists are dissatisfied with the Enlightenment quest for a comprehensive theory of morality or for a science of ethics—philosophy's equivalent to "grand theory" in the social sciences. One problem is that general, idealized theorizing often requires empirical reality to stretch exceedingly far to accommodate theory's reach. Additional worries claim that impersonal, comprehensive standards are motivationally insufficient insofar as they fail to move or inspire the agents to whom they are addressed. At the same time, there is (or ought to be) a reluctance simply to rehearse the lessons of experience, as if facts were self-interpreting or personal testimony is equivalent to Truth. As an alternative to these tendencies, ethicists and social critics have turned toward normative traditions that either precede Enlightenment philosophy or seek to amend its traditions in light of questions posed by local practices and insights garnered from new developments in the humanities and the social sciences. Hence we are met with increasingly sophisticated work that explores the promise of historicism and narrative ethics, comparative ethics, virtue theory, pragmatism, casuistry and practical reasoning, hermeneutical theory, feminist social criticism, critical social theory, and the like. If the prestige of crafting grand theory has decreased in the social sciences, its luster has diminished no less in religious and moral philosophy.

One contribution to these revisionist efforts is a methodology that supplements an "ethics-near" with an "ethics-distant" orientation, building on a distinction that parallels the difference between "experience-near" and "experience-distant" concepts in the social sciences. "An experience-near concept," Clifford Geertz writes, is "one that someone—a patient, a subject, . . . an informant—might himself naturally and effortlessly use to define what he or his fellows see, feel, think, imagine, and so on, and which he would readily understand when similarly applied by others."

An experience-distant concept, in contrast, "is one that specialists of one sort or another—an analyst, an experimenter, an ethnographer, even a priest or an ideologist—employ to forward their scientific, philosophical, or practical aims."[21] Following Geertz, we can say that an ethics-near approach is one that immerses the researcher in the vernacular moral vocabularies of individuals and institutions. The goal is to attend to local idioms, moral particulars, and the challenges of moral decision making. An ethics-distant approach, in contrast, abstracts from moral particulars to craft impersonal principles as guides for individual or social criticism, policy assessment, and the like. Often the goal is to construct norms that are free of complicity in any specific account of the good life, an impartial set of requirements that privilege no single tradition or point of view. An ethics-near orientation might talk about love as a tireless passion for and attachment to persons or causes, or it might address issues of social justice by providing a fine-grained account of economic hardships felt by minorities in the American inner city.[22] An ethics-distant orientation speaks of love as equal regard for individuals qua human beings, a form of agent-commitment and neighbor-evaluation. Or it speaks of justice as the lexical ordering of basic liberty and the difference principle, the latter of which aims to justify certain inequalities among representative individuals in a society marked by economic disparities.[23]

The respective danger of each orientation is to privilege either vernacular customs, leaving the researcher "awash in immediacies," or detached, impersonal perspectives, leaving the researcher "stranded in abstractions and smothered in jargon." To correct for these problems, Geertz recommends deploying experience-near and experience-distant concepts dialectically, enabling each concept to restrain the other. As Geertz notes, intellectuals must produce "an interpretation of the way a people lives which is neither imprisoned within their mental horizons, an ethnography of witchcraft as written by a witch, nor systematically deaf to the distinctive tonalities of their existence, an ethnography of witchcraft as written by a geometer."[24] The challenge to ethicists is artfully to tack back and forth between personal and impersonal perspectives in the process of crafting arguments and judgments. Coordinated in that way, ethics-near approaches draw on ethics-distant theories to illuminate what is discovered about local knowledge. They do not invoke ethics-distant theories to add prestige to their ethics-near approaches or to cast ethics-near data as mere instances that illustrate comprehensive, ethics-distant orientations. Ethics-distant approaches function, in part, interpretively, to ensure that our perceptions of morally relevant details are clear and perspicuous. In this view ethicists must deploy features of ethics-distant orientations to lift up and refine salient features that emerge from our attention to moral particulars. In the process our understanding of ethics-distant orientations will be illumined and enriched. The relation between ethics-near and ethics-distant orientations is an instance of the hermeneutical circle, in which the tensions between impersonal and personal perspectives remain creatively synergistic. So long as this circle envelops and is informed by local knowledge and practices, it departs from Enlightenment aspirations to construct a general, abstract science of ethics.

IS CULTURAL CRITICISM ETHNOCENTRIC?

What I have said thus far is not meant to romanticize ethnography or cultural anthropology as a research method, only to indicate how those areas might point to analogous developments in religious ethics or stimulate new genres and research trajectories in the field. For social critics interested in coordinating descriptive and normative cultural inquiry, however, difficult questions exist. How, and on what basis, can we incorporate normative ideas within what is otherwise an interpretive, descriptive account? More accurately, what is the proper place of norms or values in hybridized research? May we criticize the culture and practices of those whose world is under review? If we do so, are we insensitive to the challenges of multiculturalism?

Marcus and Fischer reply to these questions in two ways, referring to what they call epistemological and cross-cultural techniques of cultural criticism. Each technique seeks to carve out a place for critical evaluation. The first sets out to describe different cultural practices in order to demystify familiar ways of knowing. Ethnography that informs cultural criticism "is to bring the insights gained on the periphery [of the Eurocentric world] back to the center to raise havoc with our settled ways of thinking and conceptualization." The idea is to reveal how our own practices are as culturally constructed as those of others. "Once this fundamental unity between them and us is recognized," Marcus and Fisher add, "there is a more valid basis for *then* considering substantive differences." The second technique, cross-cultural juxtaposition, attempts to defamiliarize Western readers by using "substantive facts about another culture as a probe into the specific facts about a subject at home." Weak versions of this model use materials from one culture to relativize attitudes or claims within our own; strong versions, which Marcus and Fischer encourage, carry out ethnography at home and abroad and seek to establish strong linkages between the two. In either case—as a form of epistemological demystification or cross-cultural juxtaposition—the goal is to make us conscious of difference by disrupting "common sense, doing the unexpected, placing familiar subjects in unfamiliar, or even shocking, contexts."[25]

I focus on Marcus and Fisher's work because their views enjoy a wide consensus among liberal academics who champion the merits of cross-cultural work and the importance of discovering difference. That consensus stands at considerable remove from—and offers a critique of—political currents in contemporary culture that homogenize cultural identity, encourage anti-intellectualism, and create wedge issues around matters of commitment, tradition, and difference. Yet Marcus and Fischer pull back from advocating cultural criticism to their colleagues in anthropology, exhibiting a resistance if not inarticulacy about ethics that is also widespread in the academy today. When Marcus and Fischer address the place of values in critical ethnography, they erect their own boundaries between descriptive and normative inquiry, endorsing an asymmetric understanding of the relationship between anthropology and other human sciences. "The acutely felt problem of description," they write, "makes this generally an ethnographic moment in the human sciences, for which anthropology has great potential relevance." Humanist scholars interested in alterity are encouraged to poach from anthropological methods. The relationship is, however, not reciprocal; *Anthropology as Cultural Critique* does not encourage anthropologists to borrow from disciplines that are self-consciously reflective and normative. Arguing on behalf of "engaged relativism" in which difference is "redeemed, or recovered as valid and significant, in an age of apparent homogenization," Marcus and Fischer conclude their book by noting that "the statement and assertion of values are not the aim of ethnographic cultural critique." Rather, that aim is "the empirical exploration of the historical and cultural conditions for the articulation and implementation of different values."[26] We are left with the idea that anthropology provides resources for self-criticism but that criticizing others is ethnocentric.

Putting aside the idea that ethics reduces to "a matter of the statement and assertion of values," Marcus and Fischer's desire to bar ethnographers' migration into ethics is a function of two preconceptions, both of which are mistaken. One is their idea that normative domains rely exclusively on experience-distant concepts. Art and philosophy, they write, "thrive on a self-conscious detachment from the world to see their issues clearly. They may draw upon empirical research, but they leave the task of primary and detailed representations of social reality to other kinds of thinkers" (167). Yet as I have indicated, currents in normative discourse have sought to avoid the kind of distance and generality to which Marcus and Fischer refer. A more fulsome understanding of ethics, in other words, would suggest that something other than a unilateral relationship between descriptive and normative discourses is in order.

Their second preconception draws on the connection between relativism and cultural criticism: "In the face of undeniably global structures of political and economic power," they write, "ethnography, as the practical embodiment of relativism and interpretive anthropology, challenges all those views of reality in social thought which permaturely [sic] overlook or reduce cultural diversity for the sake of the capacity to generalize or to affirm universal values, usually from the still-privileged vantage point of global homogenization emanating from the West" (32–33). That is to say, cultural criticism must resist the temptation to use ethnographic descriptions as occasions for applying Western values in ways that end up only confirming Western biases. It is better to use cultural differences to demystify putative "universals" and show where they are relative to a particular time and place.

I agree that comparative work serves an invaluable demystifying function. Yet one problem with this attitude for Marcus and Fischer is that they don't say whether some forms of difference are worth redeeming more than others or whether some forms are worth redeeming at all. It is by no means obvious that all forms of cultural expression will demystify settled habits and customs or that they ought to. Indeed, to suggest that appeals to difference somehow contribute to Western critical self-reflection begs the question: Why should they?

This question is important for cultural critics who wish to avoid a problem that *Anthropology as Cultural Critique* rightly identifies, namely, the danger of romanticizing otherness or providing what might be called "recognition on demand." Recognition on demand produces a reverse ethnocentrism, an uncritical acceptance if not valorization of other cultural practices simply because they are different. As Charles Taylor observes, concerns about recognition grow out of the putative connection between recognition and identity, the idea that "our identity is partly shaped by recognition or its absence, often by the *mis*recognition of others, and so a person or group of people can suffer real damage, real distortion, if the people or society around them mirror back to them a confining or demeaning or contemptible picture of themselves."[27] Yet, as Taylor rightly adds, this concern for recognition is not without its dangers, especially the fact that, in trying to avoid misrecognition, one might abdicate the effort genuinely to understand and assess others on terms different from those they use to understand themselves. Seeking to avoid the problem of demeaning recognitions, we can be naive in accepting "an ethnography of witchcraft as written by a witch."

Marcus and Fischer seek to avoid the problem of naively valorizing otherness in their account of how cross-cultural comparison can serve critical ethnography. In their view we should engage in a kind of reflective equilibrium wherein observers and observed relativize each other's cultural norms in a dialectical interchange. Different norms and practices are assigned equal status as a condition for comparison. Romancing otherness is avoided insofar as the other's cultural practices are scrutinized by "our" standards, which are themselves relativized in light of the other's cultural norms. Putting different cultural norms and practices on an equal footing, cross-cultural juxtaposition can say that it enshrines the virtue of reciprocity.

Readers familiar with Taylor's discussion of "a fusion of horizons" in his treatment of multiculturalism will detect something similar at work in *Anthropology as Cultural Critique*. According to Taylor, in fused horizons "we have been transformed by the study of the other so that we are not simply judging by our original familiar standards." Rather, we "learn to move in a broader horizon, within which what we have formerly taken for granted as the background to valuation can be situated as one possibility alongside of the different background of the formerly unfamiliar culture." We thereby develop "new vocabularies of comparison," leading to judgments that presuppose transformed standards of worth.[28]

Perhaps Marcus and Fischer have something like this fusion in mind in their account of cross-cultural juxtaposition. For Taylor and for Marcus and Fischer one's own canons of evaluation are revised as they are deployed to assess other cultural standards. Neither set of standards enjoys a privileged status because both are presumably syncretized into a new set of criteria. Nonetheless, if by fusing horizons we are to avoid ethnocentrism or its reverse, then it remains unclear whether Marcus and Fischer's first technique, epistemological demystification, actually succeeds, since such demystification makes no reference to reciprocal interchanges or new vocabularies of comparison. More to the point, reference to fused horizons or cross-cultural juxtaposition does not enable us to carry out a full-fledged criticism of others. This is because the main goal of *Anthropology as Cultural Critique* is to fashion a theory for using ethnography as a vehicle for self-criticism. Marcus and Fischer leave little room for finally judging certain cultural practices as unworthy of acceptance. Instead, they suggest that arriving at such judgments violates the canons of tolerance and "engaged relativism."

Equally pressing is the fact that Marcus and Fischer seem unable to avoid a more subtle problem in their account of cultural criticism. Consider again their model of cross-cultural juxtaposition. According to *Anthropology as Cultural Critique*, such juxtaposition attempts to defamiliarize Western readers by using "substantive facts about another culture as a probe into the specific facts about a subject of criticism at home."[29] On that account values and practices from different settings do not retain their original integrity in cross-cultural juxtaposition. In the strong version of cross-cultural juxtaposition, each culture's values are transformed by the other's, thereby producing a *tertium quid*. If that is true, however, the fusion is syncretistic, thereby spoiling the integrity of the "different" culture's customs and standards. While this solution is far less imperialistic than conventional forms of ethnocentrism, it hardly ensures respect for unadulterated versions of "different" beliefs. Marcus and Fischer's technique of cross-cultural juxtaposition should not be viewed as expressing unqualified respect for another's cultural standards, for in strong versions of cross-cultural juxtaposition those standards will not retain their original identity.[30]

The most we should expect in social and cultural criticism is that we avoid denying or assigning esteem in an a priori way. Properly understood, responsible heterology means only that we should not discount a priori the value of other cultures. The idea is to be presumptively open to the merits of other cultural practices without becoming inarticulate or double-minded when wishing to express moral judgment. In that way we can rightly grant others the benefit of the doubt. Antiethnocentrists can be presumptively open to the value of other cultures without also having to transform their standards when evaluating others. Such a presumptive openness, as described by Taylor, "is a starting hypothesis." However, its validity, he rightly observes, "has to be demonstrated concretely in the actual study of the culture."[31]

Normative criticism that poaches from ethnography rightly urges humility when evaluating other cultures. This does not mean, however, abdicating a hermeneutics of suspicion. In the final analysis it leaves open the possibility of judging other practices as worthy or unworthy of approval, recognizing that other cultural practices are no less prone to rationalization than are one's own. When confronted by patriarchy, racial supremacism, religious discrimination or zealotry, ecologically doubtful customs, or other illiberal sentiments, it is not clear why liberals would want to engage in cross-cultural juxtaposition of the sort that Marcus and Fischer describe. Many of these sentiments can be found among ethnic and indigenous cultures whose values challenge the homogenizing effects of Western beliefs and practices. Engaging in cross-cultural juxtaposition may paradoxically require feminists, antiracists, religious liberals, or environmental advocates to narrow the range of values they want to defend.[32]

The issues of cross-cultural criticism, ethnocentrism, engaged relativism, and "respect on demand" are central issues for religious ethics, especially of a comparative sort that seeks to navigate a cultural turn. Religious ethicists would do well to study works such as *Anthropology as Cultural Critique* in order to learn from the invitation it provides and the challenges it raises.

CULTURE, PSYCHE, AND ETHICS

INTERNALIZATION AND EXTERNALIZATION

Lying beyond concerns about interdisciplinarity, cultural criticism, and an ethics of everyday life lurk more fundamental ideas. Here I want to consider topics in cultural theory in light of some familiar issues in religious ethics, focusing not on intellectual poaching but on morality itself. My impulse above was experimental and methodological; my concerns here are more traditional and substantive. One of my aims is to show how the relative inattention to culture ignores something fundamental about our humanity, namely, that we are culture-producing and culture-absorbing creatures. Another aim is to indicate how work in religious ethics too easily assumes that moral norms and virtues are unmediated—the result of individual work, personal experience, or the response to direct divine communication. In contrast to these assumptions, religious ethics that takes a cultural turn rests on the idea that moral thought and experience are mediated and thus dependent on cultural patterns of thought and action. I want to develop these points by focusing on the connection between culture and moral psychology and on the implications of that connection for character and conduct. Typically in religious ethics, attention to moral psychology (such as it exists) pays little attention to the synergism between psyche and culture, between self and society. A cultural turn in religious ethics might alter that inattention and deepen our understanding of some basic issues regarding moral agency, the affections, and the virtues.

In an important argument about Plato's *Republic* Jonathan Lear gives good reasons to pursue this link between psyche and culture. Lear argues that the analogy between the soul and the polis in the *Republic* has less to do with structural parallels between microcosmic and macrocosmic order than with the synergism between self-formation and cultural formation. Early in the *Republic* Plato draws an analogy between the soul and the polis in order to show what the larger picture—the polis—teaches us about the structure of the soul. "We think of justice as a quality that may exist in a whole community as well as in an individual, and the community is the bigger of the two," Plato writes. "Possibly, then, we may find justice there in larger proportions, easier to make out."[33] Justice in the city-state can tell us a lot about justice in the individual—most importantly, about how to order parts in relation to the whole. Lear shows, however, that Plato's putative rationale is deceiving, for it suggests a firewall between the soul and the city-state. According to Lear, Plato's more important aim is to track the movement—the creative and destructive exchanges—between psyche and polis. That is to say, Plato provides "a dynamic account of the psychological transactions between inside and outside a person's psyche, between a person's inner life and his cultural environment, between *intra*psychic and *inter*psychic relations."[34]

Key to these transactions are two processes, what Lear calls internalization and externalization. *Internalization* refers to the process by which young people appropriate the values passed along by parental and other authorities, pedagogical practices, and cultural processes. In Plato's account, Lear observes, "the young human psyche is like a resin, able to receive the impress of cultural influences before it sets into a definite shape."[35] We internalize much from our local worlds before we fully understand what we have received. Hence the crucial importance of education and imitation for the Greeks.

Externalization refers to the process by which a person fashions something in the cultural world according to the drives and interests of his or her psyche. For Plato the key cultural construct is the political community. Such communities have a character that is built up from the predominant characters of their citizens. Remarks Lear: "For Plato, the polis is formed by a process of externalization of structures within the psyches of those who shape it. And, more generally, externalization is a basic psychological activity. For Plato suggests that cultural products in general are externalizations."[36]

Lear notes that in Plato's idea of the polis these two processes operate in relation to different generations. "After we internalize our cultural roles by a process of education, we externalize them in our social roles. . . . Internalization is going on primarily in uninformed youths; externalization is going on primarily in adults who have already formed themselves through prior cultural internalizations."[37] But that generational point should not obscure a more basic one: the traffic between inner states and outer roles blurs the boundary between self and society and, contrary to the idea that the ideal polis is static, shows that psyche and culture are inherently isomorphic.

ETHICS AND THE EMOTIONS

Following Lear, religious ethicists have two reasons for thinking normatively about culture, each of which tracks the implications of internalization and externalization—what might be called the ethics of psyche, culture, and their transactions.

Consider the psyche side of this synergism first. The fact of internalization highlights the dynamics of moral formation and the social construction of the emotions. That is to say, Plato gives us good reasons to believe that our dispositions do not arise sui generis but as a result of psychic struggles with cultural authorities. On this account emotions are cognitive, rule-governed interpretations of moral experience. That idea may seem counterintuitive, given the prevailing notion—often attributed to Plato—that emotions are sensations that resemble itches, throbs, or twitches. In a noncognitive account, emotions are drives that are generated by outside stimuli and, without the coercive control of reason, are at the mercy of external, contingent forces. The emotions are often seen to oppose rationality and expose our deepest vulnerabilities. For that reason they have been deemed inferior wellsprings of agency, the source of incontinence and poor judgment. Viewed in that way, emotions are a kind of raw energy— unprincipled, tyrannical, and teeming with power. Lear reminds us that for Plato this account of the emotions pertains largely to those whose dispositions develop in nonideal contexts—in cities ruled in oligarchical, democratic, or tyrannical ways. In a well-ordered society the appetites can be ruled by reason and integrated into the experience of *eudaimonia*.

Plato's notion of the unruliness of emotions seems to view them negatively, for which Aristotle sought to provide a corrective in his account of human flourishing.[38] But both of these philosophers understood that a noncognitive account of the emotions does little to capture our subjective experience or explain why emotions differ across cultures. If we consider such facts, we can see that viewing emotions as itches and throbs is deceiving. Consider, Taylor argues, the experience of shame.[39] Shame is the feeling that there is something about myself that I should conceal. It derives from a sense of being undignified for having certain qualities. Such emotions cannot occur outside of a horizon of expectations, a moral world in which our conduct is indexed against a hierarchy of values and social norms. Shame flows from a sense of unworthiness, but that sense cannot occur without having standards for distinguishing between honorable and dishonorable qualities. In this way emotions are rule-governed and depend on a wider system of shared meanings. They are expressions of agency shaped by standards of worth, what Taylor calls norms of "strong evaluation."[40] Such norms articulate goods toward which persons order their commitments and from which they derive their bases of self-interpretation.

Viewing emotions as cognitive activities enables us to understand them as intentional. We feel fear *of* danger, grief *over* a loss, hope *for* a happy outcome, umbrage *about* being wrongfully accused. Emotions have an object toward which they are aimed and from which they gain intelligibility. As rule-governed and purposeful, emotions flow from a commitment to a good, and on that basis they express an evaluation of states of affairs. "Experiencing an emotion," Taylor remarks, "involves experiencing our situation as being of a certain kind or having a certain property."[41] That is why emotions should be understood as cognitive. They reflect one's affective awareness of a situation and its bearing on oneself and the world.

If this account of emotions is correct, then we should understand them as moral *and* cultural. They represent how we have come to understand human conduct as measured against a background of standards. We feel in a certain way after having internalized a system of values and ways of seeing. The emotions are "a kind of cultural artifact," as Paul Lauritzen observes.[42] They are structured by codes and expectations that enshrine a culture's account of the good. Grief over a broken friendship is not, on the cognitive account, a crushing flow of indeterminate affection or a release of sadness from an oceanic well of feeling. Rather, such grief derives from esteeming the worth of that friend—from recognizing the value that I placed on her and the profound affection that such esteem evoked. A "sense of loss" could not occur without a prior judgment about the great goods that such friendship brought into one's life.

A cognitive and interpretive account of the emotions suggests a point about their development: they are learned. Consider Plato's view of courage. That virtue, he writes, is "the conviction, inculcated by lawfully established education, about the sort of things that may rightly be feared."[43] One might say, echoing Aquinas's account of the natural virtues, that emotions are "acquired." As culturally mediated, they are transmitted by those who powerfully articulate a society's standards of value. Emotions are learned through interchanges with family members, friends, religious and civic teachers, and cultural authorities. In acquiring a sense of a culture's norms, we gain a sense of how to respond to life's contingencies.

This account of internalization is paradoxically an endorsement of and an embarrassment to much contemporary religious ethics, especially virtue ethics. It is an endorsement in that it focuses our attention on basic commitments and objects of loyalty—what might be called the religious dimension of human affect and identity when such commitments have the sacred as entitled to certain attitudes and behaviors. Such topics are central to religious ethics and provide a research agenda in which philosophers are generally not interested. This account of the emotions is an endorsement of virtue ethics, moreover, in that it points to the moral importance of human dispositions and how we might distinguish between proper and improper ways of feeling.

It is an embarrassment to much contemporary religious ethics because often what goes by virtue theory pays little attention to the wider cultural forces that contribute to the formation of our dispositions.[44] Like the emotions, culture is often seen in noncognitive terms—as neutral if not recalcitrant to reason—a source of contingency, aesthetic arationality, or psychic irrationality that produces goods for privatized consumption. And virtues are thus discussed as if they are self-originating, a property of an individual's "emotional work," voluntary and unmediated. A tacit works-righteousness pervades virtue ethics that ignores the synergism between psyche and culture. The entire thrust of Plato, Lear, Taylor, and Lauritzen is to blur the boundary between self and society, inner states and outer states, psyche and culture, moral and political psychology—viewing both items in each pair as cognitive and intentional.

CULTURE AND MEANING

So much, then, for internalization and some of its implications for an ethics of the emotions in virtue theory. Consider the culture side of this dynamic—what might be called the ethics of externalization. Given what I have already said, this "side" should not be sharply distinguished from the first. The fact that culture is the product of externalization means that cultures—or cultural products—are the result of human creativity. A culture is not morally neutral but a function of human interests and desires.

Yet tracking this side of a cultural turn seems unwieldy if not impossible. Given the ubiquity and amorphousness of culture—the fact that, as an environment, culture surrounds us—it is difficult to identify which of its properties to isolate and evaluate. Culture seems everywhere and thus nowhere in particular. That said, given the affinity between religion and culture, religious ethicists seem uniquely poised to make some headway into cultural interpretation and criticism. Following Geertz, we can say that both religion and culture are symbol systems, expressing and shaping the "world's climate."[45] When cultures develop rites, holy days, codes, images, lore, leaders, icons, scents, music, heroes, and saints, they do so to imbue everyday existence with a sense of importance. Symbols express patterned ways of disposing people toward each other and the world by passing along claims about how experience, especially suffering, is ultimately to be interpreted. Such patterned ways of seeing and feeling contribute to a group's sense of "at-homeness," providing ways for their members to connect with themselves, others, and the natural world. Like religion, cultures provide signs, artifacts, customs, and practices that attempt to give life meaning. And as a system of symbols, cultures seem ripe for analysis by scholars of religion. There are energetic, interpretive, and creative dimensions to existence that explain the proliferation of cultural products. Indeed, given the affinity between culture and religion, it seems odd that few scholars in religious ethics have sought to address the wide gamut of materials that cultures provide for analysis—film and electronic media, drama, civic rituals, art, music, athletic culture, and literature.[46]

Seen as a function of human interests and desires, culture is an embodied rhetoric, a diffuse but ubiquitous web of influences, relationships, and social practices that cultivate a way of being. No less than the emotions, cultures are intentional acts, or the product of intentional acts, that help to form intentional acts among their members. They express the creative and destructive results of intrapsychic struggles in the synergism between psyche and culture. And, as creative and destructive, cultural products cry out for normative analysis, for they provide the repertoire of materials out of which a people habituates itself. Cultures parade appearances of the right and good before us, thereby demanding reflection and evaluation. From Plato's perspective this link between rhetoric and culture requires intellectuals to perform cultural criticism. Without such criticism we would be ill-equipped when trying to distinguish between deceptive and reliable visions of the good life.

Moving religious ethics more directly into cultural criticism means evaluating symbolic forms and what Taylor calls "the social imaginary" to designate how societies attempt to create meaning and memory.[47] This move suggests a broader agenda for religious ethics, one that moves beyond the materials provided by ostensive religious traditions (for example, Christianity or Hinduism) to include the discursive mix of symbols, images, idioms, and values according to which identity and meaning are fashioned in public culture. The idea is to give up the notion that people draw only on traditional religious materials to formulate their account of what is meaningful, right, and good. Viewing religious ethics as a form of cultural criticism thus means tracking individuals' or groups' diverse idioms and practices in their search for meaning and, on that basis, thinking about how traditional religious materials factor into that search. Such a procedure differs considerably from the assumption that religious ethicists should comment on traditional religious texts or elite commentary on the premise that those materials suffice to provide the final vocabularies of religion viewed as a kind of practice. Too much syncretism and inventiveness characterizes the quest for meaning for scholars to assume that only ostensive religious traditions and metanarratives speak to everyday practitioners. At the very least, a "cultural turn" ought to spark reflection about what the concept of *religion* comprises in the work of religious ethics today.

ILLUSTRATIVE WORKS

Intellectual work at the intersections of religious studies, cultural studies, and moral analysis is not entirely absent in religious ethics, although the publications I have in mind operate at the margins of the field. Here I want to discuss three works that reflect hybridizing currents in the humanities, works that examine everyday life, cultural processes, and social institutions and that heed the traffic between internalizing and externalizing forces.

The first, Wayne Meeks's *The Moral World of the First Christians*, probes the moral teachings of first- and second-century Christianity by focusing not on an "ethics of Jesus" or ensemble of New Testament imperatives but on the symbolic and social universe in which early Christian teaching made sense. Meeks explores the intellectual and cultural traditions that early Christians received and reworked as their religion expanded from Palestinian villages to Greco-Roman cities. His analysis proceeds not from the top down, as if morality were chiefly a set of moral rules and arguments, but "from the bottom up," drawing on ideas and methods shared by anthropologists and philosophers. Echoing Plato and Lear, moreover, Meeks attends to "the essential dialectic between community and self." Because the early Christians were converts from one set of cultural and communal values to another, a history of early Christian morality must concentrate on how those converts discovered a new identity and built new "communities of character."[48]

This "bottom up" approach conceives of religion as a framework of meaning, moral formation, and communal edification. Drawing on Geertz's essay "Ethos, World View, and the Analysis of Sacred Symbols," Meeks examines the taken-for-granted patterns of seeing and feeling, the habits by which early Christians disposed themselves to each other and the world. Hence attention to ethos, as defined by Geertz: "the tone, character, and quality of their life, its moral and aesthetic style and mood; it is the underlying attitude toward themselves and their world that life reflects." For Geertz religion is less a set of authoritative propositions than a set of symbols "dramatized in rituals or related in myths, . . . felt somehow to sum up, for those for whom they are resonant, what is known about the way the world is, the quality of the emotional life it supports, and the way one ought to behave while in it."[49]

Viewing early Christianity in light of its symbolic and social universe, Meeks situates his material within a set of concentric circles. The outer perimeter was etched by "the Greek-varnished culture of the eastern Mediterranean, transformed by the power and order of Rome." Within that orbit "the Jewish communities of homeland and Diaspora were a special case. Within the manifold adaptations of Judaism to that larger world, the small circle of Jesus's followers appeared, spread, and became multiform itself."[50] Early Christians thus found themselves positioned within complex strata of influences, customs, and worldviews. From the great traditions of Greece and Rome—the teachings of the Stoics, Epicureans, Platonists, Cynics—early Christians received beliefs about moral formation, wisdom and foolishness, nature's norms, and the moral quality of the emotions. From the great traditions of Israel—Ben Sira, Plutarch, Plotinus, the Essenes—early Christians inherited beliefs about covenantal obedience, sectarian perfection, worldly wisdom, the importance of law, and the authority of scripture. In the preaching, initiation rituals, and institutionalizing of the early Jesus movement, all of these beliefs gained different emphases and direction, depending on the challenges that Christians encountered in specific locations.

At its inception Christianity surfaced as "a deviant movement within a cohesive culture."[51] Early Christians began as a sect within the dominant Jewish culture of Palestine and, like the Essenes at Qumran, were one of a number of eschatological renewal movements that sprang up in Israel under Syrian and Roman rule. The morals that emerged from this apocalyptic sect emphasized separation from the world and concentrated on "the internal cohesion and harmony of the sect itself and with the correlative value of maintaining its boundaries sharply against the rest of the world."[52]

Early Christian morality changed considerably as it migrated from rural to urban settings, and Meeks charts such alterations in social scientific terms. In Palestinian villages early Christians set out to produce a sectarian ethos that emphasized separating from the world and embarking on itinerant, charismatic teaching. In this context ascetic ideals emerged not as marking a path to salvation but as a means of carrying out an evangelical mission. As Christianity moved to cities, Meeks observes, unexpected challenges occurred. New institutional contexts—the synagogue, household, cult, school, church—presumed not the initial encounters between early preachers and a rural culture but the task of maintaining and correcting the faith of early Christian groups in the Greco-Roman polis.

Focusing on ethos, worldview, and morality in this way enables Meeks to spot connections between social context and literary style. He thus highlights diverse rhetorical strategies and genres that early Christians used when addressing different audiences as their religion spread across the eastern Mediterranean.[53] In 1 Thessalonians, for example, we find admonitions from Paul that aim to deepen Christians' view of holiness and their sense of solidarity within a common fellowship; few controversies seem to have vexed the early church in Thessalonica. In 1 Corinthians, in contrast, we see Paul try to resolve moral debates that emerged as the church in Corinth became increasingly institutionalized. The author of the Gospel of Matthew draws on the genre of narrative as opposed to the rhetoric of admonition or quandary resolution to develop what Meeks describes as a sectarian, relational, perfectionist ethic. A quite different genre and set of themes are found in Apocalypse, which seeks to challenge common sense as a guide for life. The *Didache*, a second-century handbook for catechumens, sharpens the distinction between two ways of life to frame rules for church order. The writing of Irenaeus near the end of the second century draws on the Bible to develop a theology of salvation history and symbol system that emphasizes salvific union with God and participation in a great struggle between God and Satan. The effect of Meeks's study is to expand what counts as morally relevant literature in early Christianity, paying special attention to the poetics of Christian moral formation and institutionalization.

In its use of cultural and anthropological tools to show how early Christian morality was mediated through received symbols, patterns of thought, and different social contexts, *The Moral World of the First Christians* is a paradigm of interdisciplinary work. Meeks's turn to culture enables him to capture the aesthetic and affective dimensions of early Christian symbolic systems, the individual and corporate character to which they gave rise, and the rhetorics and genres in which they found expression. Along the way he spotlights the internal diversity and "otherness" of a tradition that, for many religious ethicists, is considered seamless and familiar. Part of that strangeness turns on the fact that early Christians were scarcely interested in careful and elaborate explications of moral values as these might contribute to public philosophy. Instead, their worries were rather pedestrian, focusing on practical questions that arose in the ordinary lives of early converts and communities. Early Christians were trying to resolve questions about whether to eat meat, pay taxes, give alms to itinerant preachers, require circumcision, listen to speakers-in-tongues, and the like. One effect of *The Moral World of the First Christians* is to expose an enormous difference between first- and second-century Christian moral teaching and Christian ethics as it is widely practiced today.

A second work, Margaret Trawick's *Notes on Love in a Tamil Family*, is an ethnographic study of the emotions and family relationships in the Hindu culture of South India. Drawing on fieldwork conducted in 1975, 1976, 1980, and 1984, Trawick examines various meanings and uses of *apnu* (love) in an extended family in a village in Tamil Nadu state near Madras (now called Chennai). She enters the village as a student of S. R. Themozhiyar, from whom she sought to study the epic poem *Tirukkovaiyar*, and eventually moves into his household with her husband and son. Out of that immersion she provides a detailed account of how adults interacted with each other, their children, and their servants in a cramped household of twenty-two people.

For religious ethicists one value of Trawick's work lies in her ability to track love's many expressions in a village economy and elaborate kinship system. *Notes on Love* shows how *apnu* blurs the boundaries of role relations that are especially charged in Tamil culture: husband and wife, brother and sister, mother and daughter, and father and son. Complicating all of these relationships is the practice of cross-cousin marriage,[54] the widespread practice of adoption and exchange of children among family members, reversed gender roles, and the extremely strong bonds that develop between brothers and sisters early in their lives. The overall picture stands in stark contrast to Western ideals of the nuclear family and bourgeois "family values."

Trawick characterizes *apnu* as multilayered and fluid, involving hiddenness, harshness, dirtiness, humility, poverty, servitude, and blinding intoxication. Attending to these personal and interpersonal affections, she avoids sentimentalizing or essentializing love and looks instead at how *apnu* finds expression—often by way of conflict—in kinship relations. Trawick thus shows how desire is both internalized and externalized as it suffuses intergenerational ties. Arguing against the idea that kinship functions in the interests of solidarity, longings for which can be fulfilled, she claims that the institution of cross-cousin marriage is premised on "the fact that it creates longings that can *never* be fulfilled" (152). Kinship is more than a set of patterned relationships, an impersonal structure; it also draws from and imparts a set of yearnings, providing a powerful emotional dynamic in Tamil families.

Notes on Love provides a detailed account of the everyday practices of love—discussing, among other things, the meaning of doing another person's chores, the power that accrues to those who feed others, and the agonizing power-dynamics of offer-and-refusal in overtures between spouses. *Apnu* is intense, fluid, and connected to the most elementary needs and wants. Its ambiguity defines its core because none of *apnu*'s features is straightforwardly felt or practiced as an ideological norm. Instead, Trawick finds, love is routinely complicated by change and paradox. *Apnu* is thus open-ended, generating changing expectations, rivalries, and responses among lovers. In Tamil culture "the closest bonds were concealed by denial of bonds, tenderness was transformed into cruelty, humility could be an expression of pride, servitude a means toward mastery" (112–13). Love was agonistic and fraught with argument in some relationships; it was pacific, supportive, and conciliatory in others.

Ambiguities and paradoxes surrounding *apnu* are mirrored more cosmically in the relations between South Indian gods and goddesses. "South Indian deities . . . are not consistent," Trawick observes: "Each has a dual nature; each is split. In Sri Lankan Buddhism the king of the demons Mara is the mirror image and cross-cousin of Buddha the king of the gods. As cross-cousins, Buddha and Mara are affines. They are welded together as male and female. They need each other. When Mara is conquered he is not expelled from the kingdom of the Buddha (as the devil is expelled from the Christian God's heaven), rather he is enfolded within it" (37–38).

Complementary antinomies likewise characterize Hindu deities: "The Hindu gods, Siva and Vishnu, the light one and the dark one, like Buddha and Mara are rivals and affines: in South Indian myth, Siva is the husband of Vishnu's sister. Siva even begets a child upon Vishnu him/herself. Not long ago the worshippers of Vishnu and Siva fought each other. Each was evil to the other. The more they fought, the more they became alike" (38). These and other religious symbols point to the hiddenness, ambiguity, and paradoxical nature of the sacred. As described in *Notes on Love*, the sacred lies beyond all forms, and any attempt to assign it form involves ambiguity and discrepancy.[55]

In addition to residing in a symbolic universe, love exists in a social one. Trawick enables us to see the patterning of love and how social roles mediate the affections. She notes, for example, that fathers desire continuity through their sons but that sons long for independence. Mothers devalue daughters, but daughters are reluctant to sever ties with their mothers. Brothers and sisters are closely attached and experience their respective marriages to "outsiders" as betrayal; brothers-in-law and sisters-in-law can be extremely close and emotionally intimate, more so than wives and husbands. Trawick notes as well that "mothers do not value daughters as highly as daughters value mothers, or as highly as fathers *and* mothers value sons. However, daughters value mothers very highly. Hence, while men (and some women) worship young, childless male deities and seek refuge in them, women (and some men) are more likely to worship the goddess as mother and seek refuge in her in that form" (169). Viewing love in this way gives depth and texture to the emotions and links personal desire to wider symbolic patterns.

At the same time, *apnu* is not limited to or exhausted by formal structures. According to Trawick, love among Tamils might seem to involve pairing, but soon it extends beyond pairs into a complex skein of relationships: in-laws, servants, children, grandparents, and so on. "Love went beyond pairing," she writes: "Ultimately . . . it negated pair-bonds, especially exclusive ones, and embraced everybody. Then it took the form of the confusion of plurality, when one lost one's identity, and one's loved one's identity, in the crowd. . . . The most strongly maintained value of Anni's household was the value of communal plurality, in which all that stood for self and other, mine and yours, was deliberately, creatively, repeatedly overturned. No single rule was absolute, no single order held eternal sway" (257).

As if to echo Marcus and Fischer, Trawick's account of *apnu* uses anthropological tools to develop cultural criticism, especially cross-cultural juxtaposition. Recall that for Marcus and Fischer cross-cultural juxtaposition attempts to defamiliarize Western readers by using "substantive facts about another culture as a probe into the specific facts about a subject at home."[56] One goal is to make us conscious of cultural differences by disrupting common sense. Such features of cross-cultural juxtaposition appear when Trawick paints different pictures of the self that lie behind ideologies of love and marriage. In Tamil culture marriage is considerably more corporate than in Western, liberal cultures, focusing as the latter do on the needs and desires of individuals. In Tamil Nadu, marriages occur not merely between two people who join together out of shared loyalties and affections and who then learn to handle in-laws and other extended family members. In South India one marries into an extended family and contributes to the reweaving of kinship ties and domestic responsibilities. Marriage is more obviously an "institution," mediating and imposing limits on what can be expected in interpersonal interactions. One marries, in short, not only another person but into a household.[57]

Such facts of life reflect a different picture of the self. Whereas Western individuality is often concerned to define boundaries and autonomy, the Tamil looks for fluidity and intersubjectivity, a self with blurred boundaries. Trawick writes:

As we speak of "intertextuality" among poems or myths in South India, so we may speak of "interpersonality" among human beings there. Considered in himself, a lone man has no meaning. He is suffused with the feelings, the spirits and substances, of those who live near him, and they are suffused with his. We Americans place so much faith in the boundary drawn by our skin, that thin physical membrane, that we build our whole concept of personhood there. Most Indians . . . do not, so they seem strange to us. Because, for them, their living with one another is a concrete, physical fact, we cannot grasp what they are to themselves. . . . The more we fail to face their ambiguity, the ultimate unboundedness of their being, the less we are able to see them. (252)

This picture of "interpersonality," in turn, reflects a wider set of metaphysical beliefs. South Indians are considerably more open than Westerners to indeterminacy, surprise, and lack of control. That fact grounds Tamils' relationships and enhances their ability to handle what might seem to be exceedingly difficult emotional and physical contexts to their Western counterparts. One idea that Trawick asks us to consider is this openness to vulnerability and surprise: "It may help if we can learn to accept the reality and the power of chaos—the unpredictable, the uncontrollable, the contradictory, the illogical, the unexplainable. It may be that chaos works best if our goal is truly *ahimsa*—to let all the living live, to let each one speak and see in its own way. We do not want to consume all others, leaving nothing but our own self. If our own particular vision of truth can take its place among the multitude, then really we have not done so badly" (258).

Though not without limits—Trawick fails to comment on the routine beatings of Tamil children—*Notes on Love* can greatly enhance standard accounts of the ethics of love in two ways. First, Trawick resists dichotomies that typically frame Western (especially Christian) accounts, such as that between preferential and nonpreferential love. To represent the world of Tamil Nadu, that distinction is not terribly instructive. *Apnu* routinely and unpredictably oscillates between those categories in, for example, the widespread practice of adoption and exchange of children. Second, *Notes on Love* invites comparative discussions with Western accounts that have examined the rise of expressive individualism and bourgeois, therapeutic attitudes toward love and marriage today.[58] Trawick shows how love in Tamil culture falls into and energizes patterns and structures. Love is not merely a matter of will and unmediated desire, and it does not seek out "lifestyle enclaves" in which expressive individuals find intense companionship, psychic gratification, and personal authenticity by fencing themselves off from corporate ties and obligations.[59] In Tamil Nadu, love requires a social framework for expression and direction. Moreover, *apnu* does not focus exclusively on the intimate relationship between two persons and their immediate dependents, as is often the case in Western attitudes toward love and marriage. However paradoxical and difficult to track, there is an elaborate "order of *apnu*" in Tamil society that reflects the diversity of love's objects across an extended family of grandparents, in-laws, siblings, cross-cousins, and servants.

A third work, Charles Taylor's *Varieties of Religious Experience Today: William James Revisited*, steps back from particular traditions to track the interaction of cultural attitudes and religious experience in contemporary life. Taking as his point of departure William James's *The Varieties of Religious Experience*, Taylor embarks on a subtle examination of religion's changing place in individual commitment and public culture. According to Taylor, James's thoughts on religion were remarkably prescient, and in many ways (not all of which Taylor approves) his account of religious experience seems remarkably contemporary.

Foremost among James's insights is the idea that religion has become radically individualized and personalized, stripped of theological claims, institutional ties, and shared rituals. The "primordial thing" for James was unmediated religious experience, by which he meant "*the feelings acts, and experiences of individual men in their solitude, so far as they apprehend themselves to stand in relation to whatever they may consider divine.*"[60] Religion is a matter of the affections, the "inner" emotional realm, private and precious to the self. Attending to James in this way, Taylor is able to highlight aspects of Western individualism to which Trawick refers in *Notes on Love in a Tamil Family*. Taylor takes issue with James's account for its disparaging attitude toward social ties and collective experience. Yet as a descriptive matter, Taylor observes, James's work accurately anticipated modernity's emphasis on individuality, authenticity, and inwardness.

James's 1897 essay "The Will to Believe" dimensionalizes his view of religious experience by paying special attention to the psychology of faith and doubt. In a time when the grounds for certitude were increasingly seen to reside in scientific rationality, he argued that certain truths cannot be discovered until one opens oneself to them—prior to attempts to prove or disprove them. He did not set out to defend religious belief, only the idea that those who are religious are not necessarily irrational. For James it is wrong to think that faith is premised on the grounds that truth has already been found, as if truth had chronological priority to faith. Rather, the order is reversed: certain truths are accessible only to someone who is open to their possibility. More akin to hope than to assent for James, faith has chronological priority to truth. Those who accept unbelief close themselves off from experiences that might expand and enrich them. Taylor writes, "The agnostic's closure is self-inflicted, the claim that there is nothing here which ought to interest us a kind of self-fulfilling prophecy."[61] Those who close themselves off to religion risk losing truth out of fear for a certain kind of error. Taylor calls James our "great philosopher of the cusp" because he enables us to hover over belief and unbelief by exposing the trade-offs of each. James was able to sharpen our focus in this way, Taylor adds, because he stripped his subject matter down to the psychology of individual experience, shorn of collective connections and ritual practices.[62]

Taylor sets out to show how we have arrived at this celebration of individualism by developing a typology of "dispensations" that capture religion's changing public status in the history of Western culture: "paleo-Durkheimian," "neo-Durkheimian," and "post-Durkheimian."[63] Stated simply, Western culture has moved from (a) a premodern worldview in which "the presence of God was unavoidable . . . and various invocations of God were inseparable from public life" (64) through (b) a modern regime in which religious beliefs were increasingly separated from the public square but nonetheless evident in various forms of civil religion, to (c) a postmodern culture of expressive individualism in which the spiritual is radically divorced from political and social formations but not absent from individual yearnings for meaning and moral direction. Taylor then develops this account in insightful directions for thinking about the contemporary scene. Especially subtle are his views of the changes in our self-interpretations wrought by the transitions from premodern to modern to postmodern dispensations.

Take, for example, the experience of melancholy. Taylor alleges that we now experience melancholy and the threat of meaninglessness in a radically different way than people did in James's time. Melancholy, Taylor writes, "used to be experienced in a framework in which the meaning of things was beyond doubt. God was there, good and evil were defined."

Contemporary melancholy, in contrast, occurs in a world in which "the guarantee of meaning has gone, where all its traditional sources, theological, metaphysical, historical, can be cast in doubt." This melancholy cuts deeper, Taylor alleges, because it now touches not only me, but everyone and everything. In the present age we experience "the intimation of what may be a definitive emptiness, the final dawning of the end of the last illusion of significance" (39–40).

In part to respond to these developments, Taylor adds, we have created "new ways of being together in society" in our quest for authenticity. After World War II "this ethic of authenticity began to shape the outlook of society in general. Expressions like 'do your own thing' became current; a beer commercial of the early 1970s enjoined us to 'be yourselves in the world of today.' A simplified expressivism infiltrated everywhere. Therapies proliferated that promised to help you find yourself, realize yourself, release your true self, and so on." Observe, he writes, how in urban contexts what once passed as common space has eroded into spaces in which "large numbers of people rub shoulders, unknown to each other, without dealings with each other, and yet affecting each other, forming an inescapable context of each other's lives." In such contexts "a host of urban monads hover on the boundary between solipsism and communication." Taylor's reference to wearing a hat recalls other individualistic modes of communication—the tattoo, the baseball cap, the souvenir T-shirt, the Facebook page, or pierced body—as features of our current attempts to communicate "authentically" in public:

> I wear my own kind of hat, but in doing so I am displaying my style to all of you, and in this I am responding to your self-display, even as you respond to mine. The space of fashion is one in which we sustain a language together of signs and meanings, which is constantly changing, but which at any moment is the background needed to give our gestures the sense they have. If my hat can express my particular kind of cocky understated self-display, this is because of how the common language of style has evolved between us up to this point. . . . The resulting general structure is not that of a common action, but rather of mutual display. (85)

Taylor then uses this account as a framework for commenting on how particular forms of Western self-interpretation have changed from premodern to modern to postmodern dispensations. Common experiences remain possible, he observes, but they are ephemeral and disjointed, as when we rise up to cheer our favorite sports team or join the raucous crowd at a rock concert: "There is a heightened excitement at these moments of fusion, reminiscent of Carnival or of some of the other great collective rituals of earlier days. . . . These moments seem to respond to some important felt need of today's 'lonely crowd'" (88).

Varieties of Religious Experience Today is an apt illustration of work that takes a cultural turn, but it differs from the preceding two examples. It is apt because Taylor coordinates resources from several disciplines to interpret contemporary religion, culture, modern psychology, and their expressions in everyday life. It is different because Meeks and Trawick explore an ostensive religious tradition. Taylor's account has less to do with a religious tradition than with how broad historical and cultural transformations have affected, and have been affected by, religious experience and piety. Using James's thought as a springboard, Taylor looks at developments in Western society, tracking what he calls "the social imaginary." His main questions are, How do Westerners see themselves now? How is that self-image different from prior images? And how does that self-image find expression and reinforcement in cultural forms? As he attempts to answer these questions, he examines how the externalization of a religious psychology, presciently foreseen by James, has altered our individual and collective self-interpretations.

* * *

Meeks, Trawick, and Taylor draw on the ideas of "normative political theorists, cultural anthropologists, developmental and humanistic psychologists, sociological theorists, and interpreters of the aesthetic" in ways that suggest new avenues for religious ethics. Their works build on developments in cultural studies, postmodern discussions about the poetics and politics of representing "other" cultures and practices, and cultural and psychological theory—intellectual movements that have affected virtually all of the humanities (including religious studies) during the past several decades. If nothing else, their works show how connections between religious ethics and currents in the academic study of religion can be strengthened. What do these works, and the idea of taking a cultural turn, suggest more generally for the field of religious ethics?

Put briefly, a cultural turn in religious ethics as I have described it here is likely to become more Greek and Hegelian than is currently the case. I say "Greek" because it will be more attentive to moral psychology and the conditions of human flourishing than we generally witness in religious ethics today. That is to say, religious ethics that makes a cultural turn of the sort I have described is likely to identify and compare local vocabularies of *eudaimonia*, their articulations, and their formations.[64] What energizes the transactions between psyche and culture are visions of the good life, a life of human flourishing. For that reason religious ethics that makes a cultural turn is likely to be more naturalistic than nonnaturalistic, focusing on goods to which persons attach themselves as providing constituents for human well-being.[65] I say "Hegelian" because religious ethics will have to view culture not as inert or irrational but as externalizations of the human spirit, with all of its creative and destructive capacities. Culture is nonneutral and should be subject to moral evaluation because its institutions enshrine, perhaps successfully, aspirations to the good. If nothing else, a turn to culture will open up attention to patterns of creativity and consumption as proper subjects of social criticism.

Taking together these various ideas, we can say that a cultural turn in religious ethics focuses our attention on how our lives are mediated—on how transactions between self and other, individual and society, and persons and institutions are mutually formative. Advancing work that reflects a cultural turn will mean developing undergraduate and graduate education in a more interdisciplinary way than is currently the case in religious ethics. Moreover, a cultural turn suggests something about the work of ethics itself. That is to say, we cannot assume that questions in ethics disclose themselves ahistorically, as if they arrived untouched by cultural forces, social processes, and institutional contexts. In religious ethics, no less than elsewhere, reason has a material, embodied life. Our questions and privileged research agendas themselves arise from the transaction between psyche and culture. Religious ethics thus occupies a paradoxical and reflexive space, for it both emerges from and attempts to monitor efforts to create meaning and direction in personal and public life.

Religious ethics that makes a cultural turn will thus be characterized by three distinctive features. First, it will endeavor more vigorously to provide an ethics of ordinary life, drawing from and assessing vernacular traditions, folk heritages, popular culture, and lay perspectives in the lifeworld of a people. Second, it will recognize that such traditions materialize from the intrapsychic struggles between soul and polis and thus disclose properties of culture more generally. Finally, it will draw on an eclectic array of tools in the human and social sciences to assess idioms of the right and the good. In that capacity religious ethics might provide its own experimental moment while deepening our understanding of cultural differences, the emotions, and the moral quality of everyday life.

3

MORAL AUTHORITY AND
MORAL CRITIQUE IN AN AGE
OF ETHNOCENTRIC ANXIETY

TWO FORMS OF DISAPPROVAL

In the first chapter I said that religious ethicists should never waver in their work as social critics and that one aim of this book is to provide confidence in and reasons for evaluating social practices in a world of cultural differences. In the previous chapter I complicated that proposal by asking whether criticizing other cultural groups or traditions is ethnocentric. I addressed that question only cursorily, however, focusing on Marcus and Fischer's notion of "engaged relativism" in *Anthropology as Cultural Critique*. My comments there addressed how outsiders might practice nonethnocentric moral criticism in a way that avoids moral relativism while heeding the interpretive turn in the humanities and social sciences. That answer raises a more basic question, namely, whether outsiders ought to engage in moral criticism of others' cultural beliefs and practices at all. In this chapter I want to take up the question of ethnocentrism directly. My core question is this: can it be *right* for an outsider to morally criticize practices or beliefs that are indigenous to a particular cultural group or tradition?

My question goes to the very heart of expressing moral criticism. On the one hand, we all make moral judgments on a regular basis, and we presume some level of authority in the process. But we rarely step back and ask if we are right or wrong in making that presumption. On the other hand, we live in a culture that often questions authority. We are frequently skeptical of persons in positions of power whose moral judgments target the lives of others, often with real consequences.

With these facts in mind, in this chapter I want to focus our thinking on the ethics of moral authority and the practice of moral critique. I will be exploring relational aspects of moral authority in the course of determining when and on what terms offering moral judgments about others is justified. Developing an ethics of moral authority and the practice of critique means that I will be thinking about virtues and norms that should guide the conduct of moral critics in public life. I want to organize my thoughts around instances when moral critique might go awry—indeed when it often seems to go awry—namely, in cross-cultural contexts. That is to say, I want to think about especially difficult instances of moral criticism as a way of sharpening our understanding of the ethics of moral authority and the practice of critique. Thinking about hard cases can strengthen how we think about the practice of moral critique across cultures, as well as within our own culture.

To focus my discussion, consider this example: in response to a spate of self-immolations, in which more than forty Tibetan monks have taken their lives since March 2011, Stephen Prothero writes about the Dalai Lama's studied moral neutrality about the issue: "I know it is impolitic to criticize the Dalai Lama, a Nobel Peace Prize winner who is revered as a bodhisattva by many Buddhists. But he deserves criticism in this case. Why not create [what the Dalai Lama describes as] 'some kind of impression' that killing is wrong? Why not use his vast storehouse of moral and spiritual capital to denounce this ritual of human sacrifice? If the Dalai Lama were to speak out unequivocally against these deaths, they would surely stop. So in a very real sense, their blood is on his hands."[1]

We are often uncomfortable with these kinds of statements, even if we agree with the values they express. Sometimes our discomfort resides in doubts not about the merits of the criticism but about the credentials of those who utter them. We wonder what makes them believe they have the authority to say what they say, given how different they are from the contexts, institutions, and cultures they criticize. It is not that we disagree with their statements or that we don't share their indignation. We question their authority because we worry that such critics' indignation may be culturally insensitive or ethnocentric.

The general question I take up in this chapter is whether public intellectuals, academics, and spokespersons for political or religious organizations are moral authorities and on what terms we ought to credit them as such. By *authority* I mean having a certain standing within a relationship, a standing that vests an individual or group with responsibilities, entitlements, or power to affect the lives of others. That standing presumes the ability to produce what Bruce Lincoln calls "consequential speech." Authority, Lincoln writes, is a term used "in connection with the capacity to perform a speech-act on its hearers," producing consequential speech that is "greater than that of simple influence, but less than that of a command." *Authority*, as I will be using the term (following Lincoln), is the "effect of a posited, perceived, or institutionally ascribed asymmetry between speaker and audience that permits certain speakers to command not just the attention, but the confidence, respect, and trust of their audience."[2]

I want to examine the idea of moral authority on the assumption that there are credentials necessary to possess it and thus ways to forfeit it or to deny it to others. I have in mind examples, not unlike Prothero's, in which we are skeptical about its exercise, namely, when critics judge the practices or beliefs of foreign traditions or cultures. I believe that the idea of moral authority and anxieties about ethnocentrism are particularly difficult matters today, given the ubiquity of cross-cultural encounters in an increasingly globalized world along with the commonplace experience of moral disagreement and disapproval. I want to reduce our skepticism about exercising moral authority when judging others in foreign cultures, and if I succeed in that case, then I may well strengthen our ways of evaluating the practices of moral critics in a range of contexts—near and far—more generally.

Anxieties about ethnocentrism often fuel our skepticism about the pronouncements of moral critics. I understand ethnocentrism to be the reactive attitude of parochial bias when encountering or judging others. It is more than mere stereotyping, and it is more than simple provincialism. As a reactive *attitude*, ethnocentrism includes a disposition or frame of mind about others who are different. An ethnocentric response to otherness combines narrow-mindedness with moral hubris. The result of that alchemy is bias in the process of forming or justifying one's judgments. Ethnocentrists operate on the dogmatic assumption that their ethnic, cultural, national, or religious standards are superior to anyone else's.

The attitude is not only a matter of personal aesthetics or taste; ethnocentrism often has a public life, connected to practical decisions about who is deserving of one or another form of treatment. Ethnocentrism, then, can cause suffering. It underwrites the chauvinist tendency to denigrate other people because they are different, often citing cultural or ethnic difference as a reason to exercise power and control.

I have said that I aim to examine the practice of moral criticism, and I want to be clear about the kind of moral criticism to which I am referring. I am referring, in part, to the idea of expressing a negative moral judgment in a general, impersonal way. This form of disapproval would say, "*That* cultural practice fails to pass muster by *these* standards." The practice in question may be one that is alive and well, such as religiously sanctioned suicide in political protest, or a feature of the past, such as African slavery or foot binding in China. *These* moral standards, moreover, aspire to be objective and universal; they are not authorized on local or indigenous terms alone.

But in addition to examining impersonal moral criticism, I want to examine moral criticism that is direct and interpersonal. This latter form of criticism would say, "*Your* cultural practice fails to pass muster by *these* moral standards." As before, *these* moral standards aspire to be objective and universal rather than relative and local. The effect of this latter form of criticism is to say that there is something about *you* that should be a matter of guilt or shame. That is to say, there is a difference in the illocutionary force of the utterance.[3] This form of criticism is highly personal insofar as it touches on matters of identity, the social sources of recognition, and matters of moral psychology.

Call, then, these forms of moral criticism, the "impersonal" and the "interpersonal," two forms of expressing disapproval. Each is often charged with being ethnocentric when uttered cross-culturally. The fact that they have a different illocutionary force makes no relevant difference to those who question their universalist aspirations. That said, and as I will soon make clear, there is an important difference between these two types of criticism when it comes to asking whether, and on what terms, one has the authority to express them. There is a heavier burden of proof, I want to argue, when it comes to justifying interpersonal moral critique. In those cases the stakes are higher given the direct and felt nature of the indignation. We typically grasp this difference when we say to a critic, "Where do *you* get off criticizing *me* for *that*?" There is something about the intimate nature of the criticism that puts additional constraints on those who deliver it.

With these preliminary thoughts in mind, let us return to my core question about moral authority and moral criticism: can it be *right* for an outsider to morally criticize practices or beliefs that are indigenous to a particular cultural group or tradition? I ask this question, as I noted above, with concerns about ethnocentrism in mind. I want to sort out my question into two parts and answer each part in the affirmative. My aim is not to discredit concerns about ethnocentrism *tout court*; ethnocentrism is a serious moral problem, as my earlier comments make plain. I only wish to clarify how and where concerns about ethnocentrism properly arise. Along the way I want to indicate how ethnocentrism is, or has become, a much more expansive problem than my initial description— ethnocentrism as the reactive attitude of narrow-mindedness and moral hubris that biases our processes of forming or justifying judgments— suggests. Current concerns about ethnocentrism have us worry that it is an inescapable feature of the human condition as finite, historical, and contingent. For example, the declared goal of the Association of Third World Anthropologists is to make "anthropology less prejudiced against Third World peoples by making it less ethnocentric in its use of language and paradigms."[4] Echoing this line of thinking, Benson Saler argues that ethnocentrism is unavoidable in anthropology but that anthropologists should seek to "transcend it to some productive extent" by making anthropology "less parochial and rigid, and more pluralistic and supple, in its use of language and paradigms." But viewing ethnocentrism as Saler does—as "probably unavoidable as a cognitive starting point in the search for transcultural understandings"—has left us confused when it comes to feeling indignation and expressing moral criticism.[5] I wish to diminish anxieties about ethnocentrism and clarify when criticizing others is a genuine moral problem and when it is not. That is to say, I want to shrink the tumor of ethnocentrism without suggesting that I will make it go away entirely. Performing that therapy will open up a horizon for identifying proper ways to express moral disapproval and, in turn, understand how and on what terms we may accept the authority that critics presume when they express moral critique across cultural boundaries. One counterintuitive conclusion to which I will bring us is that being an outsider, far from discrediting a critic, may well be to a critic's moral advantage in cross-cultural exchanges.[6]

ON HAVING A RIGHT AND BEING RIGHT

The question about whether it can be right for an outsider to morally criticize practices or beliefs that are indigenous to a particular cultural group or tradition has two parts. The first part is whether one *has* the right to carry out moral criticism. In addressing this question, as we will see, the difference between impersonal and interpersonal expressions of disapproval is of considerable importance. The second part is whether one *is* right in one's moral assessment. In addressing this question we focus on the actual substance of the judgment itself. We investigate the merits of the judgment to determine whether it is correct. These two invocations of the term *right* are independent of each other. One can have the right to perform an act that, as it turns out, is morally questionable if not wrong; and one may be right (or justified) in committing an act while presuming an authority that one lacks. We might say, for example, that Jack generally has the right to express himself freely and thus the liberty to speak about religious believers or their prophets and heroes in a prejudicial way, however much he is wrong to do so given the insulting nature of his comments. And we might say that Carrie lacks the right to unilaterally change the grading policy of her faculty adviser, however much her policy is better than his.

In these ways we distinguish between having a right to do A and being right in doing A. With this distinction in mind I want to sort out the question of moral criticism along two lines, what I will call questions of *moral authority* and *moral critique*. Questions of moral authority turn on whether one has proper standing to express moral disapproval. When we pose questions about moral authority to a critic, we are not questioning the substantive merits of the critique. Indeed, we might be ceding its substantive merits. What we question is whether the critic has the proper credentials for uttering it.[7] Soon I will turn to reasons that we typically invoke to deny critics moral authority to criticize others, even critics who are correct in their judgments.

Questions about moral critique, in contrast, pertain to the substance of a criticism. They do not have us focus on the credentials of the critic. We engage in matters of substance when we debate the moral acceptability of one or another practice. Here, too, anxieties about ethnocentrism arise. But in this context they focus on whether members of the cultural group in question can be rightly expected to accept the relevant values espoused by the moral critic, reevaluate their practices, and revise them accordingly. Issues of that sort need to be kept distinct from controversies surrounding moral authority.

Regardless of whether concerns about ethnocentrism are attached to matters of moral authority or moral critique, such concerns often impede the practice of moral criticism. Thoughtful moral critics typically worry about sounding culturally imperialistic, provincial, or patronizing. But sometimes those concerns overreach. And, as my previous comments suggest, they overreach in different ways given the distinction between moral authority and moral critique. Grasping when and how moral criticism is justified can provide therapy for some of the anxieties that surround expressions of disapproval. I will turn directly to these two distinct matters, moral authority and moral critique, below. If nothing else, these matters help us understand different foundations for complaints about "being ethnocentric."

Before I do so, however, I need to identify the foil of my argument, a theory that often empowers allegations of ethnocentrism, namely, moral relativism. In the next section of this chapter I want to clarify moral relativism and note specific challenges it poses to expressing moral disapproval. While I believe that moral relativism is an incoherent moral theory, we do well to grasp its seductions and how it attaches to the intellectual ascendancy of cultural anthropology along with an appreciation of cultural and religious differences. That appeal has been diminished, to be sure, by the recognition that some other cultures hardly discourage their members from judging and, at times, ostracizing, imprisoning, or demeaning *their* outsiders (and their ostracized insiders). Worries about moral chauvinism or cultural imperialism are scarcely embraced in a cosmopolitan way.

What will emerge from my critical overview is a general, diffuse account of moral relativism, something in the spirit of what has been called, following Theodor Adorno, "bourgeois relativism."[8] As Lee Year-ley notes, bourgeois relativism "is not the product of a sophisticated intellectual position. It is only the raw notion that people have no clear cut way to adjudicate conflicts among ways of life or ethical judgments, and therefore they ought to (or perhaps only can) embrace fully the ways of life and judgments they presently have."[9] This form of relativism believes that there is something wrong about judging others' practices. On this account, ethnocentrism is inescapable—even if unintended—in moral criticism, and it automatically undermines the authority that critics assume when judging others' practices.

ON MORAL RELATIVISM

In the previous chapter I proposed that moral critics should avoid denying or assigning esteem to other cultures in a peremptory way. My main idea is that, having encountered alterity and a wide range of beliefs and practices, we should not naively affirm or chauvinistically discount the value of other cultural beliefs and practices—that we should be presumptively open to and curious about the merits of other cultures without having to transform our own standards when evaluating others. In my view we do well to express a form of respect that assigns others a presumptive benefit of the doubt, proceeding on the principle of interpretive charity.[10] After considered reflection we then determine whether one or another cultural practice or belief should be affirmed or at least permitted.

This position might be confused with moral relativism in that it does not depend on a moral theory that eschews reference to place and context to provide moral justification. But it should not be. Moral relativism is the thesis that no single, transcultural standard exists to evaluate human conduct; rather, there are many cultural and moral standards and no way to adjudicate among them when they conflict. I will return to this thesis soon. The position I have just espoused—that we do well to express a presumptive benefit of the doubt when evaluating others in the process of determining whether one or another practice or belief merits affirmation—accepts other practices and beliefs on the condition that they offer resources for human well-being and human flourishing in a way that respects the rights of others. It thus expresses an acceptance of alterity that is constrained by certain nonrelative standards and expectations. That is to say, it proffers a theory of critical pluralism, which I will describe more fully below.[11] Before I do that, however, clarifying some basic categories is necessary.

Moral relativism often takes its bearings from *descriptive cultural pluralism*.[12] Descriptive cultural pluralism is the claim that various cultural, religious, and other systems of morality exist. It is an empirical observation about the diversity of morals: moral beliefs and practices rely on reasons that are shaped by cultural values, symbols, and worldviews, which vary across time and location. Descriptive cultural pluralism reports that there is no one moral theory or set of beliefs according to which human beings justify their conduct. Frequently, however, descriptive cultural pluralism provides the empirical foundation for claiming that disagreements between and among cultural systems are intractable. That claim involves an additional layer of argument, namely, the idea that differences between cultural beliefs and moral systems cannot be resolved because no transcultural standard exists to adjudicate them or to judge any one of them as better or worse than another.

The additional layer of argument to support the idea of incommensurability is espoused by *metaethical relativism*. Metaethical relativism is the technical name for moral relativism as it is typically used, and I will stick to that latter terminology. Moral relativism is the philosophical thesis that differences among moral systems are, in principle, irresolvable because no universal standard exists for assessing their claims. On its account, all moral beliefs and practices are equally valid. And they are equally valid not because they have all met the same ideal or ideals but because none can be invalidated. None can be invalidated, moreover, because no ultimate standard exists that would enable us to assign (or withhold) validation. Moral relativism, then, is a thesis of equal moral validity—the idea that all moral systems are equally valid for people to follow. As a practical matter, moreover, moral relativism produces a doctrine of abstinence. We are to abstain from morally judging other cultures because we have no universal basis for doing so. Indeed, any such judgment would be inescapably parochial, imposing on one culture the norms or ideals that are indigenous, and relative, to another.[13]

Moral relativism is not only a negative thesis, however; it includes an account of moral justification, namely, that moral judgments have normative force relative to a particular group of persons or epistemic circumstances. For the moral relativist, moral justifications are local matters, the products of contingency, time, and circumstance. The point is not simply that there are different ways of morally achieving the same end—say, honoring the dead—or morally diverse values that organize the same set of relationships or institutions in different cultures—say, marriages and families.[14] Moral relativism makes the stronger claim that one moral code may prohibit what another moral code allows. This means, for example, that a moral judgment such as "stoning adulterers is morally wrong" may be true relative to one culture and false to another. According to moral relativism, the claim that stoning adulterers is morally wrong can be true and false at the same time.

Moral relativism thus seems incoherent and psychologically unsatisfying, leaving us ambivalent if not paralyzed about making moral judgments and expressing moral disapproval. One way to undermine its claims is to attack the empirical foundations on which it often rests, foundations provided by descriptive cultural pluralism. That is to say, if the assumptions on which descriptive cultural pluralism rests are untenable, then so are the more robust moral philosophical claims that depend on them.

On examining the writings of several prominent cultural anthropologists who avow moral relativism—E. E. Evans-Pritchard, Ruth Benedict, and Melville Herskovits, among others—Michelle M. Moody-Adams identifies four problems with descriptive cultural pluralism on which Evans-Pritchard et al.'s claims rely. First, Moody-Adams notes, descriptive cultural pluralism presupposes that cultures are self-contained, discrete, and isolable, with fixed boundaries that enable us to mark off one culture from another. But that picture of culture, she rightly observes, is simply wrong. Cultures change and interact with other cultures; their boundaries are porous, and they undergo ongoing development and revision. Second, descriptive cultural pluralism views cultures as integrated and homogeneous, inviting us to identify values and practices that enjoy widespread consensus. Once again, however, facts defy the presupposition. Cultures contain divergent, contradictory, and dissenting tendencies; they are internally variegated. Third, descriptive cultural pluralism views cultures or their practices as frozen essences, immune to change and subject to description in an "ethnographic present" that fails to capture a practice's potential for evolution or amendment. But cultures have histories; they change over time owing to the previously mentioned facts about them: they interact and cross-pollinate with other cultures and have internal diversity. Finally, descriptive cultural pluralism views human action deterministically, suggesting that members of a culture have no basis for agency, choice, or critical evaluation of their practices. To be sure, Moody-Adams notes, cultures exert a strong influence on human behavior. But the fact that they are subject to internal criticism makes it plain that their influences are not monocausal or deterministic. For these reasons we can hardly say that descriptive cultural pluralism is a neutral or uncontroversial position. It makes claims that overgeneralize about cultural values and practices, and it fails to grasp the historicity, fluidity, and internal diversity that characterize the real life of cultures themselves. For these reasons, Moody-Adams argues, descriptive cultural pluralism is empirically underdetermined, and any moral theory that relies on it is wrongheaded.[15]

But for moral relativists these empirical challenges can be sidestepped. While it may be true that some moral relativists presuppose a view of culture as essentialized, homogeneous, and dehistoricized, they need not make such empirical assumptions. Moral relativists can avoid Moody-Adams's fourfold criticism by trading in the notion of "culture" for the notion of "historical diversity." They can say not that their values reside within different cultures that are frozen and then sealed off from each other but that their values arise from ongoing historical narratives that have appreciable differences from other narrative histories and corresponding values.

For that matter moral relativism is not undermined if we take the opposite view and identify facts in support of moral consensus instead of moral diversity. Consider the converse of descriptive cultural pluralism, namely, the idea that moral relativism can be refuted by identifying the existence of common moral systems, norms, or principles—what are called "cultural universals" or facts about a "common morality" or evidences about "overlapping" norms, values, or traditions. The core idea is that there is evidence of increasing agreement across cultural and national boundaries about universal moral principles such as human rights. That fact suggests reasons for being confident about the existence, or prospect of, a common morality, not moral incommensurability.[16]

But in response to the putative existence of such universals the moral relativist needs simply to observe that the cultural norm in question enjoys consensus in current circumstances—by members of present cultures. There is always the possibility of new or future moral systems, which might reject existing cultural universals, thereby exposing the relativity and contingency of erstwhile universalist claims. As Steven Lukes observes, "even if much or all of human morality turned out to be shared in common, there would still be the potentiality of diversity emerging, and that shared morality would, in the moral relativist view, be relative to all currently existing societies."[17] The consequence of this challenge is to unsettle the place of facts within efforts to support *or* refute moral relativism. Universalism does not depend on the empirical existence of universals, and relativism does not depend on the empirical absence of universals. Moral relativism, Lukes notes, is a philosophical claim. It means "the denial of universal applicability."[18]

So we must be cautious about how facts play into claims for or against moral relativism. But that insight fails to save moral relativism from a more fundamental problem, one that is logical, not empirical. Recall again that moral relativism is the thesis that no single, transcultural standard exists to evaluate human conduct; rather, there are many cultural and moral standards and no way to adjudicate among them when they conflict. Moral relativists reason from the facts of moral diversity to the conclusion of moral relativity, equal moral validity, and often a doctrine of abstinence. The problem is not that such diversity is premised on empirically untenable assumptions but that the conclusion is a non sequitur. One could reason instead from the concept of moral diversity to the conclusion that all moral systems except one's own are wrong. Indeed, that was often the conclusion of Christian morality in response to its encounter with other moral systems and beliefs, including reforming and nonmainstream movements within its own history. The discovery of the Americas provided only more opportunity for the experience of diversity to produce judgments about error and consequent acts of intolerance. And Christianity is hardly an exception to a more general pattern of responding to moral diversity by avowing moral error. One can respond to moral diversity as an objectivist or a moral realist, claiming that what passes as acceptable behavior in other systems is not merely different but morally wrong.[19] The main point here is this: one can reason from the facts of moral diversity to the conclusion that other moral systems are in error, not that they are all equally valid.

Thus understood, moral relativism rests on a logical mistake. Yet regardless of its philosophical problems, it retains popular appeal. One explanation for this is that moral relativism has an existential "justification." The idea is that we are often struck by the fact that members of diverse cultures find meaning and well-being in their respective systems of belief and practice, and we have difficulty viewing such systems as morally erroneous because we can see humanizing features in them. In his discussion of multiculturalism Charles Taylor has captured something like this existential point well: "Merely on the human level, one could argue that it is reasonable to suppose that cultures that have provided a horizon of meaning for large numbers of human beings, of diverse characters and temperaments, over [a] long period of time—that have, in other words, articulated their sense of the good, the holy, the admirable—are almost certain to have something that deserves our admiration and respect, even if it is accompanied by much that we have to abhor and reject."[20] Lukes makes a similar observation. Moral relativism retains its appeal, he observes, "from its *recognition* of the variety of human ways of living and the sheer improbability that we just happen to have found the best way, the one true morality." To state the idea in another way: "There are many such best ways, where what is best is internal to a range of alternative conceptions of the good."[21]

This existential account is what I have in mind when I refer to "bourgeois relativism." (I do not mean to impute this position to Taylor or Lukes.) This form of relativism expresses the idea that there is something wrong in applying one's standards when judging others' practices—whatever philosophers might say about the incoherence of relativism as a moral theory. Bourgeois relativism would have us believe that, given the variety of human ways of living now and over the vast expanse of human history, one cannot be *right* when judging others. Such judgments would seem to be, at a minimum, presumptuous given our limited range of experience, and they often lead to acts that are not only intolerant but brutally inhumane. Not infrequently, as Yearley notes, bourgeois relativism becomes a way of embracing the comfortable way of life to which one had been previously drawn.[22] Ironically, it becomes a way of affirming the status quo, leaving standards of taste and their underlying modes of production untouched after reviewing other ways of life in different cultures.[23]

Whether moral relativism is viewed as a formal moral theory or as a bourgeois courtesy, it has implications that are extensive. By that I mean that it can fuel worries about ethnocentrism that can go overboard and weaken our confidence when uttering moral criticism. Moral relativism has us think that ethnocentrism is wrong not because it is the reactive attitude of chauvinism that fuels biased ways of judging but because, given the facts of cultural or historical difference, ethnocentrism cannot be avoided in moral criticism. That is to say, moral relativism has us focus not on ethnocentrism's morally problematical features but on the fact that it is an inevitable feature of judging others. I want to reject the idea that we are doomed to be ethnocentric without denying the problem of narrow-mindedness and moral hubris. Stated differently, one can be ethnocentric even if moral relativism is incoherent. With that thought in mind I want to return us to my core question: can it be *right* for an outsider to criticize the beliefs or practices that are indigenous to a particular cultural group or tradition?

ON MORAL AUTHORITY: VIRTUES AND NORMS

The question of moral authority, as I have noted, has us focus on whether one has the right to carry out moral criticism. It brings us squarely into the ethics of ethnography, among other matters. Observe that for a moral relativist my question poses a dangerous challenge. It is something of a trick question. That is because either answer—yes or no—is nonrelative. If the answer were only relative to the one asking the question, it would have little force. Put another way: for a consistent moral relativist neither answer would guide the behavior of others—at least those others who exist outside the relativist's frame of reference. But my question—Can it be *right* for an outsider to criticize the beliefs and practices of other cultures?—aims to produce an answer that addresses anyone who is worried about chauvinism. The plain sense of the question asks if it can be right for *any* outsider to morally criticize the practices or beliefs that are indigenous to another cultural group or tradition. If expressing moral criticism is wrong for any outsider, then its wrongness is nonrelative. For that reason, in addition to those I identified earlier, I find moral relativism to be incoherent. It cannot explain how its standards supervene on the conduct of others across the board. Aaron Stalnaker puts the point precisely: moral relativism "claims a universally binding status that it denies to other norms, and is thus self-referentially incoherent."[24] The moral relativist who says that it is universally wrong to utter a criticism across cultural boundaries commits a self-refuting error.[25]

Suppose, however, that the critic hails from a culture that routinely discourages its members from passing judgment on other cultural practices. She comes, say, from a society that is generally pluralistic and permissive, a society of bourgeois relativists. The relativist can say to her that he is not making a case against *any* outsider critic but against a special kind of outsider critic—a critic whose background should free her from worrying about other people's business.[26] In other words, suppose the relativist says that he is identifying an incongruity between a critic's practices and her own social background. He's pointing out to the critic that, given her context and upbringing, she shouldn't be passing judgments about other people in other cultures. He's working to ensure that she adheres to the norms of her own culture, which require her to abstain from judging others.

This reply relies on some contingent features of the critic's background along with some speculation about how deeply she has internalized it. But the more pressing problem is that it changes the subject from the source of moral norms to the scope of moral sympathy. By saying that the cross-cultural critic should mind her own business, the relativist is telling the critic how far her moral concern should extend. The relativist is saying that the critic should limit her causes of indignation to cases closer to home. The cross-cultural critic errs in the relativist's eyes by having extensive sympathies that connect her to victims who are distant and strange rather than near and dear.

But on this point the critic can rightly ask the relativist why her sympathies must be so limited. There is nothing about having norms that are justified relatively, she might say, that should restrict her grasp of human suffering. In effect the critic responds to the relativist by identifying a category mistake. She says that he confuses matters of moral *justification* with those of moral *scope*. The critic is a defender of extensive moral scope, and that fact requires her to pay attention to other people's suffering. Once again we encounter problems with bourgeois relativism that are rarely sorted out.

Let us return to the question of the moral authority of critics who express disapproval about beliefs or practices that are indigenous to a particular cultural group or tradition. That issue requires us to think about authority more generally. As I have noted, by *authority* I mean the capacity to utter "consequential speech" and to "effect . . . [an] asymmetry between speaker and audience that permits certain speakers to command not just the attention but the confidence, respect, and trust of their audience."[27]

Moral authority goes beyond this general account of authority in one important way. Matters of moral authority have us ask whether the asymmetry between a moral critic and her audience is premised on having the proper epistemic and moral credentials to express "consequential speech" in the form of normative judgments, judgments about right and wrong behavior. We ask that question in part because moral criticism generates an asymmetry between the critic and the target(s) of her criticism. We capture this asymmetry when we describe the critic as assuming the moral "high ground." The geographical image captures a relationship of social power. In cultures that generally avow some egalitarian claims, the asymmetry that arises in moral criticism requires justification. We typically resent persons who blithely position themselves in relation to us in that way. Thus we have moral expectations that attach to those who have authority assigned to them or who arrogate authority to themselves. College students grasp this problem when they say that they have a view on one or another controversial ethical matter, but they are not in a position to judge how others should address it. Some of those students might be tapping into an ethos of liberal tolerance and exposing their bourgeois relativist credentials.[28] Others, however, might instead be expressing a lack of confidence in their moral authority, wondering whether or on what terms they can separate themselves from their peers.[29] They are thinking about the ethics of moral authority, and that is a different matter from bourgeois relativism entirely.

In my view a critic is a legitimate—and justifiably confident—moral authority if she or he meets five conditions. The critic must

(1) give reasons to explain and justify her or his disapproval,

(2) have (general) moral and epistemic probity,

(3) exercise due diligence,

(4) aspire to render a judgment that is informed by judicious perspective-taking, and

(5) express her- or himself with a style and a grasp of social location that is context-sensitive.[30]

These five conditions provide the terms for justifiably assigning moral authority to critics. By "giving reasons" I mean providing arguments that include intelligible and relevant concepts, values, and distinctions that aim to justify criticism to others, including those who are criticized. By "(general) moral and epistemic probity" I mean making a good-faith effort to seek the truth in particular arguments and in the practice of moral criticism more generally.[31] By "due diligence" I mean painstakingly investigating circumstances and causes of a cultural practice in order to understand its context and history. By "informed by judicious perspective-taking" I mean examining a cultural practice in a way that does not pre-judge it, perhaps by viewing it from another's point of view. By expecting a critic to express her- or himself "with a style and a grasp of social location that is context-sensitive," I mean being mindful of structures of power on which the critic depends and that may themselves play into the conditions that make necessary the practice under scrutiny. We dismiss moral critics when they fail to meet one or more of these conditions because we judge them as speaking glibly, understood to mean "speaking in a morally arbitrary way." Such critics lack proper respect for the task of exchanging ideas and making a case to those who are judged. Seen in this way, these five conditions identify the virtues of moral criticism. I consider them necessary attributes of character among moral critics, enabling us to accept the asymmetry that obtains between moral critics and their audiences.[32]

A phony moral critic might nonetheless be correct in her judgment. When we deny moral authority to a "correct" moral critic, we sometimes explain her correctness as aberrant. The critic might be right in this or that case, but she is generally untrustworthy and thus ineligible to claim moral authority. She might have arrived at the right judgment only accidentally. A critic might be correct in hindsight as a matter of luck. We deny moral standing to critics who are liars, cranks, or bullshitters.[33] They either willfully deceive or do not care about whether they are correct. Or the "correct" moral critic has forfeited her moral authority owing to incongruities between her utterances and aspects of her conduct. I will say more about this idea of incongruity soon.

Worries about ethnocentrism, as I have noted, often lead us to question the moral authority of a critic. Often, the antiethnocentrist will say that the moral critic is wrong to criticize because she lacks epistemic and moral probity, one of my five conditions for having moral authority. Her frameworks of value are implicated in, for example, a colonial past or in other Eurocentric interests, or they are limited by a perspective that cannot but be saturated by a false sense of cultural superiority. When a critic is denied authority for those reasons, she is asked: "Where do you get off criticizing others?" Or she hears, "Judge not, lest ye be judged." In such instances moral authority is denied because the critic is judged as less than perfect.

This way of discrediting moral critics, however, is problematic for what I hope are obvious reasons. Few of us can meet unflinching standards of moral and epistemic probity. All of us are imperfect, and we must make decisions and exercise agency within morally tarnished circumstances. If sainthood or historical innocence is a condition for having the right to criticize, the practice of moral criticism is precarious. Thus we need stronger reasons to deny critics moral authority. Realistic assessments of human nature and history require that we set the appropriate bar for assigning moral authority.[34] This is not to say that one may lack moral and epistemic probity and pass as a moral critic, only that evidence of some imperfection is not sufficient to deny one standing as a moral critic. This is why I say that to have moral authority a critic must show *general* moral and epistemic probity along with giving reasons in an argument that is disciplined by due diligence, perspective-taking, and context-sensitivity. My wording bears repeating: by "(general) moral and epistemic probity"

I mean making a good-faith effort to seek the truth in particular arguments and in the practice of moral criticism more generally. I do not mean that the critic must have an unblemished moral record or operate in pristine historical circumstances to presume moral authority.

But things are different, as I suggested earlier, when criticizing others in interpersonal terms. Here the disapproval is direct and personal; the psychological stakes are more acute. And thus our standards for assigning moral authority are higher.

In a discussion of whether Israeli public officials have the right to condemn Palestinian terrorists, G. A. Cohen addresses matters of moral criticism and moral authority in ways that are instructive for this discussion. Cohen does not deny that Palestinian terrorists, like all terrorists, commit acts that we should find morally unacceptable. That is to say, Cohen utters an impersonal judgment that terrorism is morally wrong. His question is whether Israeli public officials—in particular Dr. Zvi Shtauber, Israel's ambassador to Britain—had the right to express a moral condemnation of Palestinian terrorism in a radio broadcast in 2003. Cohen's view is that Shtauber did not have such a right, however correct his judgment might have been. In his discussion of Shtauber's utterances Cohen identifies three reasons we should deny moral authority to critics who utter moral condemnation. These reasons amend the five virtues that I attached to moral authority earlier and point to an underlying principle that we do well to note.

The first reason for denying moral authority has to do with whether moral condemnation is a matter of the pot calling the kettle black—what is known as *tu quoque*. We deny moral authority to critics who are *hypocritical*. Such critics lose their legitimacy when their moral conduct is subject to the same judgments they avow. They might have committed worse versions of the same wrongs that they condemn. Or they might have committed— or be committing—the same acts that they are judging as wrong. Consider, for example, denouncements of homosexuality by closeted homosexual politicians and Christian ministers. Such critics forfeit the moral high ground when their character or their conduct exposes a clear inconsistency between their standards and their behavior. We discredit such critics, in other words, by saying, "Look who's talking." We say that the moral condemnation they utter applies to (and against) them as well.[35]

This first reason refines my criterion of general moral and epistemic probity that I attached to being a moral authority uttering impersonal moral criticism. We deny hypocrites moral authority because they lack moral and epistemic probity in a specific way. We may have no moral difficulty with the practice that *they* denounce. Instead, we see that *they* purport to have moral difficulty with the very same practices that they commit. So we deny them moral authority because they accuse others of wrongdoing on terms that apply equally, or similarly, to them. Denying moral authority to hypocrites thus has its own interpersonal illocutionary force. When we identify hypocritical moral critics, we say, "Where do *you* get off condemning *them* for *that*?"

A second way that we deny moral authority is when we show that a critic is *complicit* in the wrongdoing she condemns. Here we charge the critic with being causally related to the action under scrutiny, an action that *we* judge as unacceptable.[36] The critic might have cooperated by providing incentives, goods, or services that aimed to make a wrongdoing possible. She is an accomplice. In this instance we express disapproval that includes the critic within the scope of the overall moral judgment. She is part of the wrongdoing under review because she is intentionally instrumental to its performance. She thus bears some responsibility for the act in question, yet she fails to assume responsibility for the very thing she is criticizing. Indeed, her failure to see her complicity exposes a form of denial that is itself morally troubling. But that fact is secondary to this reason for denying moral authority. This reason, again, is that the critic helped to create that which she says should not exist. That form of inconsistency denies her the moral high ground.

A third way that we deny moral authority is when we say that the critic *prompts* the wrongdoing. Here we say, "You made me do it." And this "making me do it" can be of two sorts. One way is to limit my choices so that I have no recourse but to do the wrong you condemn. You might have directly coerced me to do the act such that I do it under duress. Or you might have blocked or removed access to morally acceptable pathways of action. This is not to say that the critic caused the wrongdoing. It is rather to say that the critic is involved in the wrongful act by imposing her will on the circumstances of my action, restricting my opportunities to respond in morally acceptable ways. That involvement denies her moral authority to criticize me. Here again the point is that the critic's agency is sufficiently implicated in the wrongdoing to deny her standing to criticize the persons who carry it out.

Another way the claim, "You made me do it," discredits a moral critic is exemplified in Cohen's principal focus, namely, incidents in which the critic creates a grievance to which another responds by carrying out wrongful acts. Here, Cohen suggests, is where we should concentrate when asking whether Israeli public officials have the right to condemn Palestinian terrorists. "You made me do it" here means, "You created a moral grievance in response to which I lack—and you prevented me from acquiring—acceptable measures."[37]

This version of "You made me do it" does not simply take the form of showing how the critic limited morally acceptable pathways of action. In this instance the critic creates an injustice to which the wrongdoing is addressed. The wrongdoing would not have occurred absent the grievance for which the critic is responsible. Say that Jackson publicly and repeatedly insults me, and I verbally lash out in response when speaking privately to him later. Jackson can criticize me for overreacting, but he cannot criticize me for reacting with indignation. Jackson's options for expressing disapproval are thus limited by the fact that he created a grievance and is implicated in the morally compromised conditions in which I reacted. Jackson loses the moral high ground in relation to me by virtue of generating reasons for my grievance against him.

My argument thus far has aimed to show that critics must meet some standards in order to possess moral authority. I would tie all of them together by saying that the ethics of moral authority is a matter of integrity. By *integrity* I mean being true to one's professed commitments and values as those are constrained by the virtues and norms I have enumerated above.[38] The virtues of moral criticism and the special norms for uttering moral condemnation refine the idea that there should be palpable consonance between the standards and character of a moral critic. The absence of moral probity, or the failure to exercise due diligence, or the fact of moral hypocrisy, for example, points to a discrepancy between the moral critic's behavior and her utterances. In those instances we are justified in asking, "Where do *you* get off criticizing *them*, or *me*, for *that*?" The virtues and norms I have identified aim to specify how we track inconsistencies in the pronouncements of moral critics.

The idea that criteria exist for possessing moral authority enables us to shrink the tumor of ethnocentrism and expand our ways of thinking about moral authority. Recall my core question: can it be *right* for an outsider to morally criticize practices or beliefs that are indigenous to a particular cultural group or tradition? In many respects the virtues and norms I espouse considerably erode the distinction on which my core question rests, namely, the distinction between insiders and outsiders. A critic who offers reasons, has general epistemic and moral probity, exercises due diligence, examines matters from different perspectives, and speaks in a way that is context-sensitive goes a long way toward so familiarizing herself with her target culture as to render the notion of "outsider" status meaningless. Put differently: a critic who abides by the virtues and norms that I have identified expresses her criticism empathically. She includes, among the things she considers, how the world looks according to the other's point of view. She thereby engages in perspective-taking. That is not to say that the critic agrees with the other; that fact would obviously undercut the charge of wrongdoing. The critic who abides by the standards for authority I am defending crosses the boundary between self and other, rendering the other familiar on terms set not by the critic but by the other. Nonchauvinistic moral indignation, in other words, can and should be empathic.[39] At the very least the virtues and norms of moral criticism should give us pause about lionizing insider status as bestowing special epistemic and moral credentials.

Suppose, nonetheless and for the sake of argument, that we adhere to the distinction between insider and outsider critics and that we are skeptical about the moral authority of the latter. Suppose that we view the notion of empathic moral indignation as nonsensical. The virtues and norms of moral criticism that I am recommending should nevertheless lead to this conclusion: it is not obvious that outsiders who express moral disapproval are open to the charge of lacking moral authority simply by virtue of being outsiders. There is nothing about being an outsider that connects to the idea of moral incongruity or the absence of moral integrity. Viewing outsider status in that way overlooks important facts and distinctions.

Let us approach this point another way. Anxieties about ethnocentrism sometimes energize suspicions about whether a critic may arrogate to herself the moral high ground. The idea is that she lacks moral authority by virtue of being an outsider. But those anxieties can be considerably lessened if we look at reasons we have for questioning moral authority. Tarring outsiders with the charge of incongruity—on par with hypocrisy, complicity, or causing a grievance—simply because they are outsiders is wrongheaded. Outsiders may well be innocent of these problems and deserve the moral high ground. Our reasons for denying moral authority are more finely grained than when we focus on outsider status alone. Critics who satisfy my criteria can be confident that their utterances should be recognized as expressed in good faith—*as nonchauvinistic*. We should remember that often the best criticism (moral or otherwise) comes from "outsiders."[40] Works such as Alexis de Tocqueville's *Democracy in America* are a clear case in point.

One challenge to my account is to pick up and amplify one of Cohen's reasons for denying moral authority to outsider critics, namely, the fact of causing a moral grievance. We might say that it cannot be right for outsiders to morally criticize practices or beliefs that are indigenous to another cultural group because those outsiders are part of a regime that caused the group's grievances. Being associated with such a regime, in this view, discredits a critic's moral authority. Cultural groups thus say, "Where do *you* get off criticizing *us* for *that*?" by associating the critic with historic wrongs. But this form of discrediting overgeneralizes. It relies more on matters of association than of complicity or prompting. There is no reason to think that a moral critic endorses the unjust legacies with which she is associated. Discrediting a critic on the basis of association frees cultural groups from criticism that comes from postcolonial quarters. It takes advantage of the morally compromised circumstances in which criticism is uttered in order to discredit outsiders. If a critic is to be properly discredited, however, something specific about *her* has to be identified as incongruous. Otherwise she can be stereotyped as a basis for denying her moral authority. That kind of discrediting would be ironic indeed.

ON MORAL CRITICISM: THIN AND THICK MORALITY

Suppose that a critic exhibits the virtues and abides by the norms for articulating moral truths and moral condemnation. She has moral authority.
We thus return to my core question and tackle it in light of the concept of
moral critique: can it be *right* for an outsider to morally criticize practices
or beliefs that are indigenous to another cultural group or tradition? Here
we are focusing on determining whether one's moral critique *is* right. I ask
this question, moreover, with the existential allure of moral relativism in
mind. How can we carry out moral criticism if we hold the view "that
it is reasonable to suppose that cultures that have provided a horizon of
meaning for large numbers of human beings, of diverse characters and
temperaments, over [a] long period of time—that have, in other words,
articulated their sense of the good, the holy, the admirable—are almost
certain to have something that deserves our admiration and respect, even
if it is accompanied by much that we have to abhor and reject"?[41]

One way to address this question is to begin by noting the fact of
value pluralism, which is distinct from descriptive cultural relativism and
moral relativism. Value pluralism begins by making an empirical claim. It
holds that different values exist according to which people organize their
lives—values that vary in time and location. It points to the diversity of
morals. But value pluralism typically combines that observation with a
normative claim, namely, that such values should be respected or valued
by others insofar as they provide people with a vision of the good life.
Value pluralism thereby avows certain attitudes toward others, namely,
that they are owed acknowledgment.[42] By avowing a nonneutral stance
toward the beliefs and practices of others, value pluralism thus grants
the factual claims of descriptive cultural pluralism but denies the claims
of moral relativism. Like descriptive cultural relativism, value pluralism
reports facts about the diversity of morals and alterity. Not unlike moral
relativism, value pluralism introduces some normative ideas about such
facts, avowing attitudes that we should take toward others' practices and
beliefs. More important—and unlike moral relativism—value pluralism
admits of some restrictions regarding what may be respected or esteemed
across diverse cultures, religions, and moral systems. These restrictions

identify nonrelative norms according to which we can assess the values and corresponding practices and beliefs that others hold. In this way value pluralism is a mixed theory that allows for an appreciation of diversity without undermining the capacity for making moral judgments based on universal principles.

What might such restrictions be? Consider a line of argument that is premised on the idea that human beings are free and responsible. More specifically, it draws on the idea of moral subjectivity, the notion that we are free to deliberate about, question, and revise our respective visions of the good. We live life, as Will Kymlicka puts it, "from the inside, in accordance with our beliefs about what gives value to life."[43] As moral subjects, we freely develop and revise our desires against a background of meaningful options. Value is assigned to our autonomy as the capacity to self-critically adopt and evaluate our immediate, first-order desires in order to determine whether they are indeed desirable and worthy of our commitment. Accordingly, we deserve others' respect in order to make such decisions under our own authority. Correlatively, others deserve our respect in order to make decisions about the good under their own authority. Respecting the nonrelative value of moral subjectivity is a necessary condition for allowing persons to act freely and responsibly.

To see the force of this idea, let us embark on a thought experiment. Imagine a religion or philosophical doctrine that assigns to its adherents the notion that they are the sorts of beings who do not, cannot, or should not deliberate about and revise their understandings of the good. In other words suppose the existence of a religion or philosophical doctrine that rejects the idea that we are moral subjects. Adherents to this doctrine are required to believe that they are, and have been, conditioned by the claims of the religion or philosophical outlook in question, and they are instructed to follow its codes in unquestioning terms. They understand "responsibility" to mean operating as instruments to carry out policies or directives as if they were agents of some other will, either real or metaphorical, and never in ways that allow those adherents to reflect on the meaning of what they are doing or to change their attitudes toward it. The force of the thought experiment is to pose this question: would we assign to that religion or philosophical doctrine the name *morality*? In what sense are its adherents anything other than automatons? The force of the experiment is to expose an invariant feature in the concept of morality, namely, its presupposition of moral subjectivity. That is to say, it requires us to ask about the conditions of the possibility of having a morality at all. Invoking the concept of "the moral" requires us to accept a basic assumption, namely, the fact of moral subjectivity, the idea that whatever beliefs or values we hold, we adhere to them "from the inside," as subjects with the capacity to consider, evaluate, and, when necessary, revise our respective understandings of the good. (Putative) moralities that deny their practitioners moral subjectivity—the freedom to adopt and revise their commitments against a background of cultural and other beliefs and ideals—trade on counterfeit currency. They deny the foundational terms according to which we can have expectations of moral responsibility.

This is not to deny that religious, cultural, and philosophical traditions have their esteemed sources of authority and are entitled to the attitudes and actions of the sort I described in chapter 1. It is not to suggest that exhibiting moral subjectivity requires an individual to doubt any and every cultural or religious authority on the model of radical skepticism. It means, more modestly, that we understand individuals to have the freedom to deliberate about the meaning of the good in order to determine whether, and on what terms, their account of the good merits acceptance as desirable. That is to say, when we use the term *morality*, we are presupposing some underlying invariants—especially the idea that moral responsibility assumes the existence of persons as subjects rather than as instruments of another's will. No notion of "the moral" is coherent that rejects the notion that human beings are moral subjects.

This notion of moral subjectivity is a component of what is called "thin" as opposed to "thick" morality. Thick morality consists of our denser moral understandings and names those goods that we endorse or that we believe make a claim for endorsement. It identifies the deep, inner reasons and self-defining commitments according to which we find purpose and direction in life. It is particularist and local, often steeped in tradition and history. Thick morality is what value pluralism identifies when it calls attention to the diversity of morals. Thin morality, in contrast, places limits on how we carry out those thicker commitments and purposes. It consists of norms and ideas that, compared to our denser moral understandings, are general and abstract.

What is important in this duality is that the thin morality of moral subjectivity constitutes the precondition for the existence of any thicker account. We should grasp thin obligations as deriving from recognizing what it means to be a subject with convictions. We ought to grasp this obligation, moreover, as bearing on all of our relationships. Thin obligations arise in response to the fact that others are moral subjects, each of whom lives life "from the inside" and possesses the authority to envision and (within limits) pursue his or her vision of the good. Thin morality has as its basis the idea of mutual respect for persons, the norm of equal respect.

Thin morality, as the name implies, seeks not to express the whole of morality, only some elementary and central components. It identifies what is minimally acceptable for a moral system. In this way thin morality places invariant restraints on the pursuit of values that range across cultures and traditions. And it does so by virtue of a value that attaches to the very idea of being a moral subject. That value, and the entitlement that it confers, must be heeded as a constraint on our pursuits of other values or goods. Whatever else we may seek according to our denser moral understandings, our efforts should be bounded by respect for persons as having inherent dignity. Any morality that fails to heed that value denies others their entitlement to exercise their moral responsibilities as free and equal persons.[44]

Earlier I indicated that I would invoke the label "critical pluralism" to describe my position. Critical pluralism brings thin and thick morality together in this way: it disavows the idea that any single moral theory or set of beliefs provides a universal account of the human good. But it also denies the idea that the concept of pluralism produces the conclusion of moral relativism, namely, the idea of equal moral validity. Critical pluralism is a species of value pluralism insofar as it acknowledges various moral systems as worthy of acknowledgment. But as a critical theory, it places limits on what can be proffered as an acceptable candidate for morality. As described by Moody-Adams, critical pluralism is "a conception of the plurality of moral values that leaves room for the critical analysis and rejection of some ways of life and some practices as outside the range of moral acceptability."[45]

A critical pluralist, then, can provide an affirmative answer to my question, Can it be *right* for an outsider to morally criticize practices or beliefs that are indigenous to a particular cultural group or tradition? A critical pluralist would add that she is not necessarily in a position to judge the whole of another, thick morality in a sweeping or comprehensive way. So her affirmative answer is qualified. But she is equipped to ask fundamental questions about matters of equal respect. As opposed to a moral relativist, she can inquire into whether certain invariant norms are avowed and sanctioned by a moral code or cultural practice under review. She can inquire into whether individuals or groups are assigned proper respect as moral subjects. And she need feel no reservation about declaring violations of those norms as immoral and a proper source of guilt or shame for those who commit them. Thin morality might appear rudimentary when compared to the more elaborate and complicated moral codes of particular cultural or religious traditions. But that morality enables her to possess moral sympathies that have universal scope. On those universalist terms she may utter moral indignation on behalf of victims of moral wrong. Her status as an outsider may be of cultural or sociological interest, but it is irrelevant to the moral facts at hand.

ETHNOCENTRISM AND RESPECT

Earlier I said that I would be offering different grounds for thinking about ethnocentrism and how those differences enable us to think more precisely about it. I want to dispel what I think are some wrongheaded ideas that pervade cultural studies and strengthen the basis for confident expressions of cross-cultural moral criticism. We are now in a position to see what I mean. Ethnocentrism can circle around worries about moral authority or moral critique. When we understand each of these concepts correctly, we can understand how and where we ought to flag ethnocentric practices and conceits.

Put another way: I began this chapter by describing ethnocentrism as a matter of parochial bias when encountering or judging others, a reactive attitude that combines narrow-mindedness with moral hubris. But as we've seen, ethnocentrism can metastasize when it is nourished by moral relativism. In that context ethnocentrism is typically seen not as a reactive attitude but as an inevitable feature of judging others in contexts of cultural diversity. But if I am correct about how and why we deny critics moral authority, and if I am correct about critical pluralism as providing terms for moral criticism, then the problem of "ethnocentric inevitability" should disappear.

This is not to deny the problem of chauvinism in cross-cultural encounters. But that problem should be understood for what it is, namely, a moral problem. We are chauvinistic not simply when we judge others, or when we disagree with others, or when we disapprove of others, but when we judge or disagree or disapprove arbitrarily. Moral chauvinism is a garden-variety moral problem that needs little stage-setting to grasp. This is why we should reject the claim of ethnocentrism's inevitability without denying the problem of narrow-mindedness and hubris. As I noted earlier, one can be ethnocentric even if moral relativism is an incoherent moral theory; the problem of being ethnocentric does not hinge on the idea of incommensurable moral perspectives. At one level, then, I am shrinking the tumor of ethnocentrism; at another level, however, I am showing that it can be practiced quite broadly, independent of any claims about moral relativity. Moral chauvinism arises when we judge other persons arbitrarily—in ways that fail to respect them as persons, as equal sources of moral claims and deserving of good-faith reasons and arguments. The virtues and norms of moral authority that I have identified aim to keep the exercise of criticism from being biased and chauvinistic.

Viewing moral chauvinism as a matter of speaking arbitrarily brings together the two main threads of this chapter. I have been arguing on the premise that we distinguish matters of moral authority from matters of moral critique, noting the distinction between the right to do *A* and being right in doing *A*. But distinguishing between these two matters is not to separate them. We can tie my claims together with the principle of respect for persons. We deny moral authority—we spot instances of moral chauvinism—for substantive reasons. We criticize another's arrogation of moral authority by saying that her criticism fails to respect the persons she addresses or about whom she speaks. More precisely: critics who lack moral congruity, a first-personal (or agent-referring) moral deficit, carry out acts that have second- and third-personal implications. That they speak arbitrarily—failing, for example, to exercise due diligence, impartiality, or context-sensitivity—reveals an attitude toward their interlocutors that violates a cardinal norm of critical pluralism as I have described it, namely, the norm of equal respect. To be justified, moral authority must itself heed basic principles on which its utterances morally rely. Critics who lack respect express their disapproval chauvinistically. Thus understood, chauvinism is not just one more way of expressing disapproval. It is an objective moral wrong.

BEYOND CROSS-CULTURALISM

Everything I have said in this chapter focuses on questions of moral authority and moral critique with an eye toward endorsing the possibility of expressing moral disapproval while avoiding chauvinistic bias in cross-cultural contexts. But what I have said about expressing moral critique, especially when discussing moral authority, has wider implications for thinking about the ubiquitous circulation of moral ideas in public culture. I want to conclude by making a few observations along these more general lines.

Consider these examples of moral concern and moral disapproval. Since 1985, the lead singer of U2, Bono, has devoted considerable time, celebrity status, and money to spark international relief action on behalf of victims of famine and war in Africa. After the 2013 government shutdown in the United States, former vice presidential candidate Sarah Palin described Washington lawmakers as a "corrupt bastards club on steroids." Environmentalist Bill McKibben has proclaimed the "end of nature" given consumerist habits and practices. The former Pope Benedict XVI frequently condemned Western secularism, materialism, and sexual permissiveness in his public statements. Throughout 2012 and 2013, television host and syndicated columnist Bill O'Reilly expressed righteous indignation regarding President Obama's health-care plan. During his tenure on *The Colbert Report* comedian Stephen Colbert routinely mocked the beliefs and practices of Mormons. Media celebrity, actress, and philanthropist Oprah Winfrey has amassed a worldwide following by offering confessional self-help advice and sponsoring a televised book club. Author, professor, and journalist Michael Pollan regularly exposes the unhealthy practices of American agribusiness and the politics of food.

Pastor Tim Warren has spoken out against gay marriage and abortion rights. Political commentator, blogger, and philanthropist Tavis Smiley predicted that the 2012 U.S. presidential election would be the most racist election ever. Talk-show host Bill Maher regularly chides political liberals for not speaking out against Muslim extremism and violence.

Popular culture assigns authority to these spokespersons. They all have a certain kind of standing—call it cultural authority—by virtue of gaining access to the airwaves, the lecture circuit, or the pulpit. They use various privileges or opportunities to utter "consequential speech." They are perceived, correctly or otherwise, as having considered views about the moral life, cultural attitudes, and the proper design of public policy and social institutions. My question is whether they are moral authorities, properly understood. That question would have us ask whether they meet ethical criteria for uttering a moral criticism, however much we agree or disagree with their particular normative judgments. We should thus ask whether they provide good reasons, exercise due diligence, explore alternative perspectives in their moral utterances, exhibit context-sensitivity in their pronouncements, possess general moral and epistemic probity, and demonstrate palpable congruity between their pronouncements and their behavior. That is to say, we should ask whether they exhibit respect for persons. Whenever we listen to cultural authorities who speak on moral issues, we should be asking not only whether we are persuaded but also whether those who might persuade us have the credentials needed to express moral criticism authoritatively. Our responses to their pronouncements may be those of approval or of disapproval. In either case we need to draw on the right concepts and distinctions that enable us to understand why.

PART II

SELVES

AND

OTHERS

4

THE ETHICS OF EMPATHY

Atticus stood up and walked to the end of the porch. . . . "First of all," he said, "if you can learn a simple trick, Scout, you'll get along a lot better with all kinds of folks. You never really understand a person until you consider things from his point of view—"

"Sir?"

"—until you climb into his skin and walk around in it."

—*To Kill a Mockingbird*

EMPATHY'S APPEAL AND MORAL HAZARDS

About the ethnographic understanding of others, especially non-Western others and their conceptions of the human person, Clifford Geertz writes:

The Western conception of the person as a bounded, unique, more or less integrated motivational and cognitive universe, the dynamic center of awareness, emotion, judgment, and action organized into a distinctive whole and set contrastively both against other such wholes and against its social and natural background is, however incorrigible it may seem to us, a rather peculiar idea within the context of the world's cultures. Rather than attempting to place the experience of others within the framework of such a conception, which is what the extolled "empathy" in fact usually comes down to, understanding them demands setting that conception aside and seeing their experiences within the framework of their own idea of what selfhood is.[1]

Controversy surrounding "extolled 'empathy'"—and Geertz's desire to put it aside as a basis for ethnographic understanding—arose during a dustup among anthropologists following the publication of Bronislaw Malinowski's *A Diary in the Strict Sense of the Term*. In that work Malinowski revealed his not-too-generous attitudes toward the cultures he was studying and, in the process, demolished "the myth of the chameleon fieldworker, perfectly self-tuned to his exotic surroundings, a walking miracle of empathy, tact, patience, and cosmopolitanism."[2] But the issues surrounding Malinowski's *Diary*, Geertz observes, go beyond those of demystifying the project of ethnographic fieldwork or the moral probity of the fieldworker. Malinowski's alienation from his ethnographic subjects was epistemological, striking at the heart of understanding itself. That fact opened up a more general point about understanding, namely, that it must attend to the fact of alterity, regardless of one's cosmopolitan dispositions (or lack thereof). For Geertz the following epistemological challenge thus presented itself: if anthropologists are to cling "to the injunction to see things from the native's point of view," then how can they proceed given that they "can no longer claim some form of psychological closeness, a sort of transcultural identification, with [their] subjects?" "What happens to *verstehen*," Geertz wondered, "when *einfühlen* disappears?"[3]

Geertz's questions, written in the early 1980s, augur an interest in empathy that now pervades the humanities, social sciences, and public culture. Contrary to Geertz's declaration that we "can no longer claim some form of psychological closeness," many avow that empathy is a genuine desideratum in social life, psychological development, and human understanding. Owing to empathy, it is alleged, we can participate in the cognitive and emotive states of others. Indeed, empathy appears to explain how we can overcome the gap between self and other and communicate with others in meaningful and effective ways.

Consider these examples. As a presidential hopeful and throughout his executive terms, President Obama frequently claimed that empathy, or being able to "place yourself in someone else's shoes," is a desirable moral trait. When faced with the task of replacing Supreme Court Justice

David Souter in 2009, Obama focused not on matters of ideological orientation but on personal character, saying he wanted someone with "empathy"
for "people's hopes and struggles."[4] After the shooting of Congresswoman
Gabrielle Giffords in Tucson in 2011, he advised the nation to use the
occasion to "expand our moral imaginations, to listen to each other more
carefully, to sharpen our instincts for empathy."[5] Before he was president,
when speaking to the graduating class at Northwestern University, Obama
remarked that "there's a lot of talk in this country about the federal deficit.
But I think we should talk more about our empathy deficit—the ability to
put ourselves in someone else's shoes; to see the world through those who
are different from us—the child who's hungry, the laid-off steelworker, the
immigrant woman cleaning your dorm room."[6]

Obama is not alone; a wide range of scholars and cultural commenta-
tors promote empathy as a cure for many social and interpersonal ills.
Cognitive scientist Kent Kiehl's research on the psychology of hardened
criminals is premised on the claim that the ability to empathize is necessary for healthy human relationships, without which we suffer cognitive
and emotional handicaps that can lead to enormously callous and cruel
behavior.[7] In a similar vein Simon Baron-Cohen explains evil and human
cruelty as a function of a lack of empathy and has constructed a ques-
tionnaire to determine an "empathy quotient" for children and adults.[8]
Philosopher Stephen Darwall identifies empathy as central to morality
conceived in "second-personal" terms—morality understood as an ability to see another as a "you" and as having the same reciprocal relation
with "me."[9] Ethologist Marc Bekoff believes that empathy is innate not
only in humans but in other animals, including nonprimates; primatolo-
gist Frans de Waal speaks of empathy as providing "nature's lessons for
a kinder society."[10] Psychologist Martin Hoffman argues that empathy is
so important to our psychic and social lives that it must have evolutionary
roots.[11] Literary scholar Robert Katz writes that being able to imaginatively empathize is essential to creative activity ranging from theatrical
performance to biographical writing—creative activities in which we
adopt or imagine another's persona.[12] Jeremy Rifkin provides a sweeping
interpretation of human civilization in terms of the evolution of empathy
and argues that today the Age of Reason is being eclipsed by an emerging
"Age of Empathy" that provides an entirely new picture of human nature

and destiny.[13] In the realm of education the website *Center for Building a Culture of Empathy* is devoted to expanding the inculcation of empathy in children's schools.[14] That same idea drives an initiative by the Ashoka Organization, a group of social entrepreneurs founded by MacArthur Fellow Bill Drayton that has embarked on what it calls an "Empathy Movement." Business-growth strategist Dev Patnaik writes that the cultivation of empathy is the key to success in economic competition.[15] The actress Meryl Streep has been quoted as saying, "The great gift of human beings is that we have the power of empathy, we can all sense a mysterious connection to each other," and that empathy is "at the heart of the actor's art."[16] A theory of "narrative medicine" has emerged that emphasizes storytelling as an "empathy-inducing methodology recommended to physicians who wish to practice medicine more efficaciously."[17] Indeed, so alluring is empathy that Microsoft CEO Eric Horvitz has designed a computerized voice-based system to ask patients about their symptoms and to respond to them empathically.[18]

This appeal to empathy—the idea that we should "place yourself in someone else's shoes"—invokes a term of recent vintage that touches a deep cultural nerve. In the early twentieth century the experimental psychologist Edward Titchener coined the term *empathy* to translate psychologist Walter Lipps's notion of *Einfühlung* ("to feel one's way into another"). In *Beginner's Psychology* Titchener writes:

> We have a natural tendency to feel ourselves into what we perceive or imagine. As we read about the forest, we may, as it were, *become* the explorer; we feel for ourselves the gloom, the silence, the humidity, the oppression, the sense of lurking danger; everything is strange, but it is to us that strange experience has come. . . . This tendency to feel oneself *into* a situation is called EMPATHY;—on the analogy of sympathy, which is feeling *together with* another; and empathic ideas are psychologically interesting because they are the converse of perceptions; their core is imaginal, and their context is made up of sensations, the kinaesthetic and organic sensations that carry the empathic meaning. Like the feeling of strangeness, they are characteristic of imagination. In memory, their place is taken by the *imitative* experiences, which repeat over again certain phases of the original situation.[19]

Titchener thus conceived of empathy as a kind of kinesthetic and affective imagination, an experience that joins the emotions, physical sensations, and creative perspective-taking.

Recommending that we affectively and cognitively take another's point of view is more than a pie-in-the-sky hope; it has a strong scientific basis. Empirical studies of empathy suggest that it has deep roots in human psychology—that "intuitive aspects of empathy are available to infants"[20] and that a child's neural circuits discharge during her observation as well as during her execution of the same actions she sees others carry out. These neural mechanisms enable us to mimic others in infancy and, over time, acquire the ability to imagine ourselves in others' situations. Some theorists avow that rudimentary forms of mimicry provide the basis for empathy and reciprocal interactions.[21] Studies in child development also show that infants as early as a few days old work hard to track the eye and mouth movements of their care providers. Infants depend on caretakers as reference points in order to learn how to feel and connect with the world. The capacity to attend to and learn from others in a mimicking way, many psychologists argue, provides the psychological foundation for interpersonal knowledge, human development, and shared experience.[22]

This picture of empathy as a rudimentary feature of our infant lives, childhood development, and interpersonal experience suggests that Geertz's understanding of "the Western conception of the person as a bounded, unique, more or less integrated motivational and cognitive universe, the dynamic center of awareness, emotion, judgment, and action organized into a distinctive whole and set contrastively both against other such wholes and against its social and natural background" is a fantastic overgeneralization. Moreover, at a moral level it suggests that expecting to adopt another's perspective does not demand too much and that empathizing may very well be a universal inclination. That is to say, expectations surrounding the *desirability* of empathy seem psychologically well-grounded and realistic.[23] Equally important for contemporary culture, evidence of empathic tendencies among humans enjoys the support of empirical study and scientific authority.

But what, more precisely, is empathy? Answering that question is more difficult than it might appear. Indeed, the scholarly and popular literature about empathy is enormously vague about the concept. As I want to discuss it here, empathy refers to the ability to "place yourself in someone else's shoes" cognitively, emotively, and self-reflexively. Seen in this way, empathy must meet epistemic, affective, and metacognitive conditions. It describes a psychological state in which our thoughts and emotions are conditioned by our imagined or real perceptions of another's feelings and frame of mind.[24] When we empathize, we think and feel as we take the other to think and feel, given our perception of how *that person* perceives her or his circumstances. Empathy designates, among other things, participation in another's thoughts and feelings—the experience of attunement. And in clear instances of empathy we are aware that our feelings and point of view have become attuned to what we take another's feelings and point of view to be. That is to say, in prototypical instances of empathy, one is aware that "*I*" am empathizing and am mindful of that fact. Such mindfulness, moreover, renders empathy subject to moral responsibility and virtue. I will return to this idea below.

Understood in this way, empathy seems appealing because it highlights our ability to get beyond ourselves, to connect with others, and perhaps to act in a prosocial way—beyond indifference and egocentrism. It is an attractive idea because it suggests that we can imaginatively engage others on their own terms. Recall the deficits of knowledge and acknowledgment that I noted in my introduction, namely, ignorance and apathy. Empathy denotes an ability to overcome both of those deficits in one stroke. It suggests that we are not happy in isolation, that we are naturally social animals eager to attune to others' feelings and thereby share in them. Moreover, knowing that others can or should be empathic allows us to assume that they can be so disposed toward us; the human potential for empathy opens up expectations that we can rightly have of our neighbors toward us. Empathy's potential for other-regarding and self-regarding dispositions is therefore vast.

Empathy, then, is a kind of fellow-feeling and imaginative understanding of the other. But it is a special kind, often confused with sympathy and compassion. All of these emotions enable us to connect to others' contexts and emotive states. But distinctions among these feelings are important. Sympathy consists in "feeling for" an individual, typically when she or he is suffering, and often with care or concern. It need not adopt feelings from another's point of view. Parents may feel sympathy for their child's emotional difficulties without participating in those emotions themselves. We sympathize *for* but empathize *with*. Compassion is arguably closer to empathy in that it consists in vicariously "suffering with" another individual—emotively sharing in a misfortune and hoping for the better. But empathy can include feelings other than those associated with suffering with another, and it need not include well-wishes. An empathic person can share the emotion of anxiety in connection with a friend's recent job interview or joy over a colleague's personal accomplishment; we don't associate those forms of fellow-feeling with compassion. Empathy includes a potentially wider range of emotions, beyond those we associate with distress, and it need not include hoping for the better.

Moreover, empathy is not itself a single, discrete emotion, like anger or joy or fear. It should rather be seen as a participatory experience. Thus we might speak of empathic experiences or "empathic emotions."[25] Accordingly, empathy comes with no specific emotional content; it is promiscuous, relying on (or responding to) various emotional and cognitive states of others. When we empathize, we have an experience of others in which we undergo a change that attunes us to another person's perceived frame of mind and emotional state. We imagine what it's like to be in another's shoes—not in their shoes as if *we* were wearing them but as we imagine *them* to be wearing them. We've imaginatively taken up their perspective on a situation.

Perhaps the best image for empathy is the tuning fork. One prong of the fork picks up and replicates the note that the other prong is sounding. There is attunement between the two prongs, a transformational communication from one to the other. They not only share the same note, moreover; they share the shame vibration as they resonate back and forth. And the shared note can be one of a wide range of possibilities.

Understood in this way, empathy has implications for what we seek to identify and cultivate in social relations. When we show empathy, we can not only show others how they think and feel; we can show them that we agree with them about how to think and feel.[26] We show that we grasp their thoughts and feelings, and we communicate our willingness to participate with them in a common emotional life. This makes empathy central to the formation of like-minded groups who can agree on norms of feeling. Far from being only a one-to-one dynamic, empathy can provide a basis for the formation of communities, solidarity, and the experience of social concord.

* * *

So much, then, for a definition and general description of empathy. But having clarified these conceptual matters, we should note that empathy is not obviously desirable. And it is on this matter of desirability that I want to focus the remainder of this chapter, namely, on the *ethics* of empathy, or the issue of good empathy. Focusing on epistemological controversies surrounding empathy as a potential basis for human understanding (as Geertz does) misses a key point, namely, that esteem for empathy might be morally naive and superficial. Whether we have the ability to empathize is a first-order, scientific question that is open to empirical study. Indeed, a considerable amount of research in childhood studies, animal studies, and brain science is devoted to determining whether and to what extent we can know and feel as others do.[27] Empathy appeals to scholars who have what might be called "naturalist commitments"[28]—the idea that certain features of the moral life are or should be rooted in an understanding of human nature. So we study aspects of human behavior and social life empirically to determine, among other things, what is possible for us, what our inclinations are, what our tendencies happen to be. We typically turn to the findings of psychologists who research such matters. Empathy is one topic that has become rich territory for such study, and for that reason there is a robust "science of empathy."

Within this science the standard account begins by establishing empirical facts about empathy on the premise that such facts might tell us something good about human nature. In the background of that mainstream attitude is the priority of science to philosophy. But the question of empathy's *desirability* is an altogether different question from a scientific one. It is a second-order question, one that is philosophical, not empirical. It has us ask, What makes for good empathy? Is the capacity to empathize desirable? Too often we assume that discovering facts about the ability to empathize answers the philosophical question about empathy's desirability. This reductive naturalism can be a considerable source of confusion.

It fails to grasp that placing "yourself in someone else's shoes" can be hazardous and quite contrary to morality. Without too much work we can see that empathy can be amoral and, indeed, can have a dark side, for seven reasons.

First, one might empathize in ways that only partly meet my three conditions. A young child might seek to imitate the behavior or emotive dispositions of his or her parents, for example, but whether such responses are genuinely empathic—whether they satisfy my knowledge, emotive, and self-awareness conditions—is doubtful. Empathy may activate involuntary response mechanisms, but such reactions hardly count as morally praiseworthy given that morally good deeds and character implicate our choices and deliberative capacities.[29] At most we can say that imitative behavior of young children is protoempathic, or a precursor to empathy, but nothing more.

Second, empathizing with one person might mean neglecting one's duties toward others. Empathy is vulnerable to "familiarity bias," the tendency to attune our thoughts and feelings to those of someone near and dear or to those of someone whose concerns seem urgent and immediate.[30] But such bias may draw the empathizer away from other, more deserving claimants for empathy or prosocial action. What may pass for empathy on one description may be a form of tunnel vision on another. Empathy can lead to a neglect of moral responsibility and a failure to address the needs of others.

Third, empathy can suffer from first-person bias, in which the empathizer presumes that her or his own experience or range of feelings provides the entire imaginary template for perceiving how another is thinking and feeling. The experience of connecting with another may thus suffer from experiential narrowness and, with that, presumptuousness.

Fourth, one might empathize too much with another and, in the process, recoil and detach. Overarousal in response to another's distress can lead the empathizer to identify too closely with his or her target and then turn away. Empathy is subject to "egoistic drift" and, with that, a return to self-concern and neglect of another's circumstances. Thus we change the television channel when we see victims of earthquakes, hurricanes, or famine.[31] It's not that we are apathetic toward such people or about such circumstances but that we empathize too much.

Fifth, studies of hostages show that empathy might lead to a severe loss of self. For example, a hostage might identify with the more powerful hostage-taker to such a degree that no return to a sense of self is possible.[32] Empathy, then, can lead to an erosion of one's own identity and personal agency.

Sixth, empathy can be prompted by, or connected to, unworthy motives. Those who take pleasure in another's pain, for example, empathize for reasons that are self-aggrandizing and debasing of another. For example, a sadist can resonate with and thereby enjoy the pain that he or she inflicts. And, the knowledge gained from empathy may enable one to manipulate another for one's own ends. Torturers and glib ad executives exploit their capacities to empathize in order to harm others or to gain advantage.

Seventh, empathy may be short-lived and thus negligible as a psychological trait. We hardly credit people for having fleeting feelings or responses; we see those as unreliable and superficial. We hardly count as virtuous a feeling or emotive state that passes quickly. Virtues identify things that matter to us, and things matter because they engage us in enduring ways.[33]

These hazards were well-known to eighteenth- and nineteenth-century philosophers of the moral sentiments—most notably, David Hume and Adam Smith—and they have received renewed attention among critics skeptical of empathy's potential contribution to morality.[34] *New York Times* columnist David Brooks observes that being empathic does not guarantee good behavior. According to Brooks, "the problem comes when we try to turn feeling into action. Empathy makes you more aware of other people's suffering, but it's not clear it actually motivates you to take moral action or prevents you from taking immoral action." This is true even when costs to ourselves are low. Brooks adds: "You may feel a pang for the homeless guy on the other side of the street, but the odds are that you are not going to cross the street to give him a dollar."[35]

Philosopher Jesse Prinz puts the challenge more pointedly. Empathy is intrinsically local and biased, he argues, blinding us to problems of institutional inertia, the rights of distant neighbors, and inequalities in the distribution of goods and opportunities. It blocks us from adopting an impartial and general point of view: "Environmental destruction and widespread diseases cannot be combated by addressing the plight of a few individuals. With empathy, we ignore the forest fire, while watering a smoldering tree."[36] Being empathic "is good when directed at our friends, but the norms of friendship are all about preferential treatment." Empathy is thus subject to familiar critiques of partiality and prejudice. But these problems do not lead Prinz to disavow a theory of the moral sentiments. We do well, he argues, to rely on emotions other than empathy as a basis for moral approval and motivation—guilt, reward, anger, concern, disgust, contempt, and the positive feelings associated with charity.[37] When empathy infects these other emotions, it only turns them inward, restricting our moral feelings to those who are near and dear.

All of this is to say that the ability to see and feel the world from another's perspective, however appealing, has normative challenges. Any account of the ethics of empathy must thus be chastened by a healthy dose of philosophical realism. To count as morally good, empathy must include the ability to recognize the moral demands that a situation imposes on one's behavior.[38] Accordingly, empathy's epistemic condition requires a wider repertoire of understanding than one gains from generalizing on the basis of one's personal experience or perspective. Empathy's affective condition requires that motives for empathy be genuinely other-oriented and durable. Empathy's metacognitive condition requires that the empathic person be reflective about the boundary that distinguishes between self and other. Determining the ensemble of supporting virtues that meets these requirements is a philosophical question, not an empirical one, and it defines the ethical challenge that faces any full-bodied understanding of empathy.

Before I set out to develop such an understanding, however, I want to make clear that these various perils reveal how empathy *simpliciter* is neither necessary nor sufficient for morality. To see that it is not sufficient, consider the problem of overarousal. As I noted above, empathizing with victims of disaster might lead one to turn away from their situation in agony or despair. In that instance empathy can be detrimental to morality. To see that it is not necessary, consider the fact that prosocial behavior need not require adopting another's feelings and frame of mind. Indeed, morality often requires us to respond to persons whose emotive and cognitive states are unknown, inaccessible, or foreign to us. Moreover, some persons—high functioning autistic persons, for example—abide by moral rules and expectations in ways that lack affect or attunement.[39] Their morality need not rely on empathizing as a necessary condition.

But empathy's lack of sufficiency or necessity for morality should not lead us to conclude that it is altogether unimportant to the moral life. The ability to empathize may enable us to detect occasions for exercising our moral responsibilities; it may increase our moral sensitivities to the plights of others and may lead us to remedy them.[40] Given that fact, empathy might serve as a virtue that conduces to other virtues. The ability to empathize, even if not obviously good, may facilitate the exercise of other morally desirable dispositions and traits. Perhaps for that reason it has champions today. Moreover, the capacity to empathize can open our hearts to sharing positive experiences of others that are justified and understandable. But if empathy is to count as a virtue in these ways, then its moral grounding must be established.

Taking a first step in this direction requires us to resist the temptation to view empathy in isolation from a wider cluster of moral norms and feelings. Empathy is an easy target of criticism when it is seen as standing alone as a candidate for virtue. With that thought in mind, I want to explore empathy's potential as a virtue by taking a detour through the work of Augustine. My main aim is to indicate how and on what terms we might view empathy as a virtue, understanding "virtue" to designate a habit of good judgment, feeling, and action, an excellence of character that disposes one to achieve a desired purpose and feel right about pursuing and achieving that purpose. Virtue designates a reliable and characteristic trait of a person, one that is connected to an objective value. Typical virtues include generosity, justice, courage, temperance, compassion, practical wisdom, discernment, discretion, and the like. Philosopher Linda Trinkaus Zagzebski provides a good start at defining the concept of virtue: "A virtue . . . can be defined as a deep and enduring acquired excellence of a person, involving a characteristic motivation to produce a certain desired end and reliable success in bringing about that end."[41] To Zagzebski's definition I would add, drawing from Aristotle, that virtue includes feeling in the right way about success in achieving one's end. When we talk about morality in these ways, we are thinking neither in terms of adhering to our duties nor in terms of producing a balance of good over bad outcomes. That is to say, we are not thinking in deontological or utilitarian terms. The language of virtue has us talk instead about persistent, reliable traits of character, features of a person that we find morally admirable if not exemplary. Often moral theorists, especially those working out of the Aristotelian tradition, see virtue as constitutive of a rich and rewarding life.[42] The disposition to empathize, I want to argue, is a potential virtue—a potentially good personal trait to have. But in order to be a virtue it needs to be understood in thicker terms than its proponents or opponents grasp. Augustine, I will propose, provides one way of conceiving a thicker account.

Before proceeding in this vein, however, a few other caveats are in order. Augustine never wrote directly about empathy; the term and its pedigree in moral sentimentalism are of recent vintage. Perhaps Augustine thought that we are too antagonistic with each other to overcome the distance between us or—relatedly—that we are too self-absorbed and narcissistic to do so. Augustine would likely agree with empathy's skeptics who doubt our ability to get beyond apathy or egocentrism. He could easily endorse worries about empathy and proximity bias, first-person bias, egotistical drift, projection, or base motives. All of these problems, he would say, are but other names for human sinfulness. He would likely have added that since we are all sinful and corrupt, it makes no sense to participate in another sinner's affections and point of view. The other must give us *good reasons* to empathize, as I will make plain below. Augustine would be skeptical about whether any such reasons exist.

But as a teacher of rhetoric, Augustine also knew about emotions, as well as the communication of feeling more generally. Whether or not Augustine held something like a concept of empathy, he was fluent with ideas of harmony and concord, the lust for cruelty experienced contagiously at gladiatorial games, and feelings that drive a conspiracy to perform evil deeds. Indeed, he carefully examined the moral quality of his feelings of pity and the problem of enjoying "pangs of sorrow" in his responses to tragic theater.[43] All of these states seem akin to empathy insofar as they include the transformational communication of feelings and, in some instances, imaginative perspective taking.

Equally important, Augustine had a clear idea about what constitutes a virtue, and he deployed that idea in his discussions of Christian love in ways that can instruct discussions of empathy. By this I do not mean to suggest that Augustine is the only source to which we might turn for insights for conceiving of virtuous empathy. We could draw ideas from Greek philosophy or early modern philosophy—in different ways to be sure—by engaging Aristotle or Hume, for example. But Augustine posed the same challenges to the idea of love that I have identified with empathy—challenges concerning egocentrism, base motives, bias, and the like. Exploring those challenges along with Augustine's effort to address them can directly inform a conception of virtuous empathy for moral theory.

THE ORDERING OF LOVE IN AUGUSTINE

For Augustine love can be either good or evil, depending on the object loved. That is to say, love is not necessarily or obviously a good thing; everything turns on the object to which love attaches itself.[44] Indeed, Augustine viewed human nature as having loves that were inclined toward egoism and self-absorption—loves whose object was, in the final analysis, oneself. Like empathy, love can be misdirected or, as Augustine would say, disordered. We can be drawn to the wrong objects or be motivated to love for the wrong reasons. Given love's importance and its tendency to err, Augustine considered the ordering of love to be *the* organizing question of the moral life. Determining how he conceives of love's proper ordering—good love—can provide lessons for rescuing the idea of empathy from the perils to which I have referred.

Love for Augustine is a form of striving, a creative movement of the soul. To love something means first to desire it. Seen in that light, Augustine's account of love appears to be conative—based on the satisfaction of one's subjective desire—rather than evaluative—based on an appreciation of another's objective value and goodness.[45] In his mind our conduct is explainable in terms of our loves: what we love inclines us to act in one or another way. Love provides the internal wellspring, the inner dynamism, of human behavior.[46] We are motivated to act by our underlying loves—by what we might call, today, things that *matter* to us. Moreover, echoing Plato, love for Augustine is unitive: it inclines us to attach ourselves to an object, thereby enabling the will to focus its energies and interests. Love joins the lover to her beloved object and reveals to others what is important to her. Moreover, and equally important, our efforts to attach to a beloved object are a function of a more basic feature of human nature, our ontology. We attach ourselves to objects that seem to matter because we experience our mortal condition as incomplete and vulnerable to decay. Our loves are driven by our finitude, our contingency, our impermanence. Attachments offer the promise of stability and completeness to creatures who are dependent and deficient.

For Augustine, then, love directs us toward ends to which we attach ourselves in our quest for happiness and well-being. Love is teleological, directing us to goods that (we hope) enable us to realize our true natures. But love can be deceived about true happiness; unaided by grace, love is impatient and unreliable. Not unlike empathy, love, for Augustine, can be wrong about why and how it connects us with another.

The idea that love can be wrong is a point that Augustine develops by way of a set of distinctions. The first has us distinguish, as I have indicated, between the objects of our loves. We can love objects that are impermanent or permanent—creaturely objects that are subject to decay and death, or the Creator God who is unchanging and eternal. In Augustine's language *cupiditas* is a form of love in which we attach ourselves to impermanent goods as if they were everlasting. Such loves are motivated by the anxious desire to complete our natures in relation to the temporal goods to which we are attached. *Caritas*, in contrast, is a love of the Supreme Good as true and unchanging. Such love seeks the unchanging good as an object of beauty and truth for its own sake. Augustine writes: "I call 'charity' the motion of the soul toward the enjoyment of God for His own sake, and the enjoyment of one's self and one's neighbor for the sake of God; but 'cupidity' is a motion of the soul toward the enjoyment of one's self, one's neighbor, or any corporeal thing for the sake of something other than God."[47]

The distinction between *cupiditas* and *caritas* aims to clarify how the objects of love render it good or bad. One crucial Augustinian question, then, is whether we love impermanent objects as if they were permanent. For Augustine evil arises when we seek to overcome our fundamental lack as mortal creatures by attaching ourselves to changeable goods in excess of their quality and being. We confuse transient for unchanging goods and thus attach ourselves to objects that are finite and contingent in our anxious quest for enduring happiness. We overvalue earthly goods and subject ourselves to them. Augustine understands such desires as sinful because they are disordered; they are literally unruly in that they disrupt the proper organization of our attachments. According to Augustine, the pursuit of happiness is doomed to fail when we attach our hopes to goods that are fated to decay.[48] Rightly ordered love, in contrast, directs human action to its true final end, which is union with and enjoyment of God, the Supreme and unchanging Good. Humanity finds happiness not in attaching confidently or proudly to earthly realities that are exclusively its own but by embracing in *caritas* the unchanging good of the Creator.

One Augustinian distinction, then, has us look at love's objects and adds the concept of right rule or right order. But Augustine did not hold to the idea that loving earthly, transient goods was necessarily a bad thing. His polemics against the Manichees prevented him from defending an entirely otherworldly ethic, an ethic of radical detachment from this-worldly matters. Neither Augustine's metaphysics nor his theological ethics is dualistic. His anti-Manicheism thus required him to coordinate his ideas about *what* we should love with his ideas about *how* we should love changing and unchanging goods.

Augustine refines this latter topic by distinguishing between *amor uti* and *amor frui*, or use-love as distinct from love that is the source of permanent happiness.[49] *Amor frui* is love of God as the source of unchanging goodness and fulfillment. According to Augustine, God is to be loved ceaselessly. *Amor uti*, in contrast, is love that is useful and proper when ordered to the love of God. That is to say, creaturely objects may be loved when they are placed within a wider framework that enables us to grasp their contingency and fragility. They should be seen as mediations of a wider goodness in relation to which they possess their being and beauty. *Amor uti*, when rightly ordered, arises from seeing earthly goods as iconically pointing beyond themselves to a more basic principle of beauty and truth. Love for such objects is thereby not a matter of *subjection*. According to Augustine, when our desires are properly ordered, we can love finite objects without being ruled by them; rather, we may love them in a way that is ruled by norms that draw from divine wisdom in nature and revelation.

Augustine's account of useful goods opens him to the charge that Christians are to use earthly realities for the selfish purpose of loving and enjoying God.[50] But it is more accurate to see Augustine as encouraging his readers to love earthly goods as objects that have their own goodness by virtue of having been created by God. The key Augustinian idea is to understand earthly goods within a larger framework according to which their value and purpose can be properly understood. When Christians reconceive creaturely objects in that way, they can attach themselves to them without unrealistic expectations about what they provide by way of happiness.

Grasping how Augustine viewed love as rightly ordered thus requires us to see how he connects ideas about *what* to love with *how* to love. Love of the unchanging Good does not mean that we detach ourselves entirely from other, finite goods; the concept of attachment for Augustine is not a zero-sum matter. Rather, embracing God as the common good of all releases humanity from expecting finite, contingent goods to provide unchanging happiness and satisfaction. Those who love God are not denied the opportunity to love lesser objects; quite the contrary. Individuals who love God can attach themselves to finite goods proportionately, on terms that finite objects can sustain.

Augustine thereby generates the idea that virtuous love enables one to love earthly objects without being ruled by them. Often Augustine describes disordered love as *libido dominandi*—love that seeks to dominate, love that is imperious and unfairly demanding in personal and political affairs. But in the account I have just described, the dominating lover is actually being dominated by his object of love; he is being ruled by his frustrating desire to possess and control that which is contingent and impermanent. Augustine saw the psychology of such love, the love of *cupiditas*, as double-sided: the lover imposes his will on his object of attachment while being possessed by his sought-after object of possession. The object is loved conditionally—loved for what it offers on terms defined by the self. *Cupiditas* thereby fails to reckon with the true otherness of the loved object. In the love of *cupiditas* the lover assimilates or homologizes reality to himself. Viewing the world as created in the image of himself, he paradoxically seeks to become sovereign over that to which he is subjected.[51]

Virtuous love, in contrast, can respect the alterity, the otherness, of the object of its attachment. *Caritas* emphasizes the importance of seeing reality as it is rather than as one wishes.[52] That is because *caritas* is itself a kind of freedom from anxiety and insecurity. It enables the self to love confidently and wholeheartedly,[53] unafraid of what another brings to a relationship. Love that is inspired by *caritas* can thereby bring together a desire for intimacy with the recognition of another's uniqueness and alterity as an independent source of value.

For the self who converts from *cupiditas* to *caritas*, then, a series of transformations occurs. The first obvious shift is in the objects of one's love. Here it is important to note that Augustine marks not only a difference between objects of attachment but proposes two different modes of valuation. That is to say, in distinguishing between objects of love, he proceeds on the premise that love is an expression of value. Whatever we love we deem as good. The second shift is in the ordering of one's loves toward earthly things proportionately, as is their due. We are to attach ourselves to goods in relation to their goodness, neither too much nor too little. We are not to overvalue or undervalue objects of affection.

The third shift is more subtle, and it combines points from the first two. This change has us move from thinking about love in quantitative to qualitative terms. Disordered love is excessive love, love that attaches itself with expectations that go beyond what its object can provide.[54] Rightly ordered love not only recalibrates our attachments; it qualitatively transforms how we do so. That is because love now attaches us to objects whose value we can rightly ascertain. In this way *caritas* changes the criteria according to which earthly love should be assessed. As John M. Rist writes of Augustine's account of love, a person who loves rightly "knows that it is the love of God for his creation that has made it loveable. . . . All value judgments are underpinned by God's action as the sole non-conventional source of value."[55] In the love of *caritas*, beloved objects are grasped as having objective value, thereby assuring their alterity.

Augustine makes this point about how love properly directs us toward the goods of this world when discussing the relationship between Christian love and the pagan virtues that are the legacy of Greek and Roman philosophy. His explicit aim is to redescribe the Greek and Roman virtues of temperance, courage, justice, and prudence as different forms of love. According to Augustine, each of these pagan virtues refines how we are to attach ourselves to the Supreme Good, as well as to earthly goods. Temperance is "love giving itself entirely to that which is loved"; courage is "love readily bearing all things for the loved object"; justice is "love serving only the loved object, and ruling rightly"; and prudence is "love distinguishing with sagacity what hinders and what helps it."[56] In our commerce with the world and its earthly goods we should order our desires in ways that are proper to the objective value of things, independent of our particular interests and anxious cravings.

One of Augustine's aims in his discussion of Christian love and the pagan virtues is to argue on behalf of the interconnection of the virtues—the idea that having one virtue means having them all. His Platonic way of thinking led him to conceive of virtue's unity and internal variations. Augustine's core point is that actions that appear virtuous—actions that seem temperate, courageous, just, or prudent—are counterfeit excellences unless they are motivated by rightly ordered love. True justice or true courage depends on the quality of the agent's motivation. What might pass as an exercise of justice when viewed externally might be done out of mixed or impure motives. Rightly ordered love assures that one's just actions will be carried out for the sake of the recipient, not for some ulterior purpose.[57]

These points are well known. What is less well known is that Augustine conceives of the interconnection of the virtues in a way that shows their mutual interdependence. By that I am referring to how the core virtue, love, is properly channeled by the pagan virtues of temperance, courage, justice, and prudence. Love for Augustine works to order the pagan virtues; equally important, the pagan virtues channel specific ways in which we are to express our love. Augustine had no problem thinking about love by drawing on collateral philosophical terms or in light of what he would call pagan ideals. For Augustine, virtuous love should be disciplined in ways that cohere with the dictates of reason and reality. And it is here that we can start to draw lessons from Augustine for thinking about empathy as a potential virtue.

Augustinian charity brings in its train a cluster of feelings and dispositions. Like emotions in general, feelings of love include emotional processes that are difficult to distinguish from each other without knowing what belief states they imply. As Nancy Snow writes, emotions are "composites of belief and affect" and, as such, are "qualitatively indistinguishable from each other unless reference is made to the beliefs that partially constitute each type of emotion."[58] That notion echoes Augustine's view of charity in relation to the pagan virtues. *Caritas* has God, and only God, as its object. The virtue of temperance would be keeping "itself entire and uncorrupt for God" on the belief that sources of corruption exist that can weaken one's convictions. The virtue of courage is "love bearing everything readily for the sake of God" on the belief that experience can force us to make difficult choices between earthly and higher goods. The virtue of justice is "love serving God only, and therefore ruling well all else, as subject to humanity," on the belief that others make claims on one's commitments that require us to determine their proper due. The virtue of prudence equips us to make "a right distinction between what helps it towards God and what might hinder it" on the belief that what appears to be good may be deceptive; thus we must "watch with most anxious vigilance, lest any evil influence should stealthily creep upon us."[59] Regarding each of these virtues, Augustine is saying that we presuppose a set of reasonable, realistic beliefs about the world that require us to love in virtuous ways that are distinguishable from each other. Love depends on the guidance of practical reason, drawing as it should from beliefs about the demands imposed on our character by everyday experience. Those beliefs enable us to differentiate between our psychological states in our responses to the difficulties we encounter in ordinary life—difficulties that we should respond to temperately or justly or courageously or prudently.

VIRTUOUS EMPATHY

The implications for these ideas about love and the emotions for thinking about Augustinian virtue, and empathy as a potential virtue, are twofold. One implication is that virtuous empathy, like *caritas*, requires right ordering. By that I mean that empathy, like Augustinian love, is conditioned by its object, which, in turn, conditions its manner of expression. That is to say, the *what* of empathy is important to assessing its moral quality, which likewise affects *how* empathy ought to be felt and expressed. For that ordering to happen, neither empathy nor love can do the entire work of virtue on its own. Virtuous empathy must be a disposition toward experiencing others that has a certain kind of strength and discipline.[60] In broad terms we might say, echoing Aristotle, that empathy must resonate with the other according to the right motives, in the right way, in relation with the right feelings, and toward the right ends. This is one way of saying that virtuous empathy is interconnected with other virtues. Being virtuously empathic means possessing a cluster of other morally desirable traits that enable us to empathize in ways that reveal and express a strong and noble character. Guided by the virtues, empathy would allow for a kind of intimacy that is able to grasp the alterity, the difference, of another, to empathize with feelings or perspectives that are themselves justified, and to respond to the other in a way that is mindful of the demands that she and others place on us. Virtuous empathy, so construed, would thereby be connected to three virtues that would discipline its formation and guide its expression.

The first of these virtues is respect for others as ends in themselves. Call this virtue the disposition of respect for persons. Like Augustinian neighbor-love, good empathy must heed the objective value of an other and grasp that others place demands on oneself that may not (and likely do not) accord with one's own wishes and projections. Virtuous empathy must thereby heed the potential strangeness of others, their foreignness and separateness. That demand may well put strains on the imagination of the empath, but at a minimum it means that one does not encounter the other on terms that incline toward projection or wish-fulfillment. Indeed, it means that one does not encounter the other on neutral terms. Rather, one encounters the other as someone who imposes reasons to which one should respond. Virtuous empathy, thus understood, is conditioned by the demand to acknowledge another as a bearer of reasons and feelings.

This idea of acknowledgment is philosophically loaded. It is not a form of respect of persons that is value-neutral. It rather denotes the expectation of responding to particular others as having claims on one's own feelings and thoughts. Empathy means being drawn out of ourselves into the reasons, feelings, and perspectives of another.[61] That experience can never be a neutral, abstract, or value-free matter.

If that is true—if experiencing empathy means entering a space that is saturated with claims and reasons—then virtuous empathy requires having to make judgments about the moral merits of the reasons to which the empathic individual is responding. That is to say, virtuous empathy must be, of necessity, judgmental. Herein lies the second virtue on which virtuous empathy relies: the virtue of good judgment. When coordinated with the idea of virtuous empathy, this means our empathic responses are to be guided by reasons in response to others' reasons. We are required to ascertain whether the other is giving us good reasons to empathize. The other is making a potential claim on one for attunement that we might do well to decline; the other might be envious, self-pitying, sarcastic, or spiteful, for example. Virtuous empathy, then, must be guided by certain beliefs about what an other is properly due. Not unlike Augustinian *caritas*, empathy is evaluative. The object is itself a source of value, and what we value conditions our empathic interactions. Empathy thus entails judging the character of, and the emotive and cognitive state of, the other with whom one can empathize.[62]

The question of whether another deserves our empathy points to a third virtue on which it relies, namely, the virtue of justice. And this virtue has implications that are both interpersonal and general. Justice, as I have said, requires us to ask (among other things) if the other to whom we are responding deserves our attunement. We hardly wish to resonate with the putative courage of a terrorist, for example or, in a therapeutic setting, with the dispositions of child predators or pathological liars. At a more general level empathy must be disciplined by justice such that we are not drawn by bias toward those who are near and dear at the expense of others whose claims on our resources may be more pressing. Contrary to the idea that empathy enables us to be more just—the intuition lying behind Obama's statement about character traits to look for when selecting a Supreme Court justice—it is rather the case that justice constrains how we ought to be empathic.

So much, then, for one conclusion drawn from Augustine regarding the mutual interdependence of the virtues, namely, empathy's dependence on moral excellences for its proper expression. The virtues of respect for persons and prudence help to ensure that empathy is felt according to the right motives in response to the right emotions and in the right way.

These virtues remind us that emotions are rule-governed activities. And justice works to ensure that our empathy does not provide cover for partiality and prejudice.

A different problem has to do with the problem of empathy's scope—the challenge of being disposed toward the feeling states of a wide range of others. This challenge goes beyond that of acknowledging the concrete alterity of particular others to that of being open to an expansive range of others—what I will call the challenge of being *extensively empathic*. Here, Prinz's criticisms of empathy as preferential and parochial are most telling. The question is, To what extent, if at all, can we cultivate empathy in ways that get us beyond special relations, beyond local ties and familiarity? Think, for example, of persons who carry out humanitarian relief efforts in remote parts of the globe and who describe their aid to needy strangers as arising from empathy. How do we conceptualize empathy that extends beyond the near and dear to those who are distant or strange, in a cosmopolitan way?[63]

On these matters Augustine provides only a few thoughts. His main idea is that Christians are to build on local or particular loves in ways that enable them to then develop extensive neighbor-love.[64] For Augustine Christians are to understand that rightly ordered love begins with a form of proper self-love that is premised on the idea that one must love God as better than oneself: "He alone has a proper love for himself who aims diligently at the attainment of the chief and true good; and if this is nothing else but God . . . what is to prevent one who loves God from loving himself?" To this Augustine adds: "What, then, you aim at in yourself you must aim at in your neighbor, namely, that he may love God with a perfect affection. For you do not love him as yourself, unless you try to draw him to that good which you are yourself pursuing."[65] On this Augustinian description, desires and affections that are structured by the love of self and God provide the basis for desires and affections toward others. One might restate Augustine as saying that one can only love others if one is first, and fundamentally, wholehearted about love, a wholeheartedness that grounds one's ability to feel for and relate to others. On that description self-love is a kind of confidence that underlies one's repertoire of emotions. Individuals then can build from that repertoire as they gain knowledge about others and the world. Love can thus proceed from special relationships (self-love) to relations with new or distant neighbors. Put in more contemporary terms: for Augustine it seems natural to think that we can proceed from a moral psychology of wholeheartedness to an extensive ethics of care.[66]

Virtuous empathy is not to be confused with Augustinian *caritas* because virtuous empathy ranges across a cluster of an other's cognitive and feeling states, whereas Augustinian *caritas* is foundational for all the other virtues. That said, Augustine's ideas about *caritas* and its cultivation for extensive neighbor-love provide a model for thinking about the psychological development of extensive empathy in a way that meets Prinz's objections. We would first resist the idea that particular or special relationships are preferential ones in a pejorative sense, as if attention to the specifics of a close relationship excludes the potential for making unbiased or impartial judgments.[67] We would say, then, following John P. Reeder Jr., that new emotions can use materials from previous emotive states to respond to new or different experiences. We learn from capacities that we have acquired from previous experiences as we respond to new situations. With regard to acquiring the ability to empathize extensively, the idea is that we work from empathic capacities developed in intimate or familiar contexts. We draw from that palette of emotions as we deepen our disposition to empathize with those who are new or different. Drawing from our previous experience of special relations is no impediment to the cultivation of extensive empathy; quite the contrary. Those special relationships, and the cultivation of our capacities for attunement, provide the emotional bedrock and rudimentary memory for empathizing in extensive ways. We "put ourselves in others' shoes" by learning about new and different contexts, and roles within them, as we grow from more familiar settings to less familiar ones. Our disposition to empathize with the stranger need not suppose that our experiences simply repeat the intimacies of previous experiences or that our encounter with the stranger must closely resemble our more intimate relationships.[68] Indeed, as Nancy Sherman and Martha Nussbaum observe, we often enter lives that are different from our own through fiction, cinema, drama, and journalistic narratives.[69] When we do so, we need not feel the same kind of attunements that we have had toward a family member or friend. But those connections can provide a repertoire of imagination and affect on which we draw when perceiving the states of others who are unfamiliar.

* * *

These two conclusions drawn from Augustine enable us to conceive of empathy as a potentially desirable trait that should be cultivated in childhood development and beyond. This means that empathy must be conditioned by other excellences of character that likewise require nurturing and support.

Empathy is desirable, in other words, not because it denotes the good of "feeling-sharing" or acquiring the "native's point of view." Whether such "feeling-sharing" or perspective taking is morally desirable begs ethical questions. The virtuous nature of virtuous empathy depends on *reasons* that discipline empathic responses. Moreover, empathic responses to distant others need not repress empathy's roots in special relations and family experiences. They can build up from them, resourcing from empathic memories and the associations that those memories provide.

Thus understood, good empathy is a disposition that has us oscillate between intimacy and alterity. In response to the affective and cognitive states of those who are familiar, virtuous empathy requires us to grasp an other's difference. In response to those who are distant and strange, virtuous empathy requires us to draw from our emotive and cognitive capacities rooted in our intimate experiences and then to extend our scope of concern to include acknowledging and responding to an other. Virtuous empathy's contingency is one of its defining features, given that empathy is not a single state or a single emotion but the capacity to respond to a range of others' states, both cognitively and affectively. But empathy as a species of virtue is not promiscuous. It requires respecting others, evaluating their feeling and cognitive states, and determining what they and others are due. Good empathy thus disciplines and orders our reactions. It does so to determine how, and whether, we should participate in the cognitive and affective states of friends and other strangers as we try to determine how best to exercise our responsibilities and deepen our sensitivities toward them.

Moreover, if I am correct about how to conceive of good empathy, then we do well to reconsider the relationship between philosophy and science, between ethics and human nature, in empathy research. The standard account, as I have indicated above, has us look at the science of empathy as if it can tell us something about empathy's desirability. That account presumes the priority of science to philosophy. My view is to reverse the relationship of science and philosophy and reject the mainstream account. Philosophy's priority to science would require us first to understand what makes for good empathy and then to study human beings in that light. That is to say, we should require scientists to explore how human beings can get beyond empathy's perils and limits. They should study, for example, whether building from proximate relationships to extensive ones is something that humans have sufficient capacities to develop if they suffer from unstable family relationships at a very young age. Or they could study whether certain forms of role-playing are better than others for cultivating extensive empathy. Or they might seek to ascertain whether children are more prone to self-loss in self-other relationships in early youth than in adolescence. For that matter, scientists might examine whether the capacity to empathize with the less fortunate is conditioned by class or socioeconomic background. In any event, understanding good empathy enables us to set the questions according to which empirical research can profitably proceed. As Augustine would surely remind us, it is important to have our priorities in the right order.

5

INDIGNATION, EMPATHY, AND SOLIDARITY

REASON AND PASSION

Consider the following headline from the *Chicago Tribune*: "Union Official: 'Solidarity' Is Key for Striking BP Refinery Workers."[1] The headline draws from comments by Steve Garey, a member of the National Oil Bargaining Policy Committee, who was speaking before hundreds of striking workers and their spouses at Lloyd McBride Union Hall in Gary, Indiana, in February of 2015. The strikers were receiving money from the union's strike fund, which pays less than a normal take-home salary, during the strike. Concerns had arisen that some strikers would end up crossing the picket line at the Whiting (Indiana) BP refinery, like union workers elsewhere in a national strike that targeted fifteen oil refineries, affecting 6,550 workers. In Garey's mind it was important for strikers to make sacrifices now for their long-term benefit, as well as for the benefit of future generations of oil workers. For that reason "solidarity" was key.

Garey's effort to keep the union's ranks in line provides an apt illustration of Michael Walzer's insights about political activism and struggle. In his book *Politics and Passion* Walzer argues that we do well to remember that politics is an arena of contest and conflict, of political and moral differences, of passion and reason.[2] Strikes, bargaining, demonstrations, lobbying, campaigning, fund-raising, grunt work, caucusing, strategizing, sacrifice, charisma, compromises—these activities are the embodied stuff of political life.[3] Political action is messy, frustrating, uncertain, unstable, and often incorrigible to shared, rational principles. Such plain facts of politics are often obscured by the more rationalist and deliberative approaches to liberal political theory of the sort generated by John Rawls and by Dennis Thompson and Amy Gutmann. Political life includes what Walzer calls "nondeliberative activities."[4] But this is not to say that politics is the agonistic realm of power of the sort championed by poststructural theorists under the sway of Michel Foucault.[5] Equally important for Walzer, the "nondeliberative" facts of politics should not suggest that political life is simply a matter of *realpolitik* driven by rational interest or enlightened self-interest. Matters are not quite so simple. Despite its rationalist resonances in political philosophy informed by rational choice theory, the idea of "interest" is also a form of passion; *our* use of the term *interest* domesticates, instrumentalizes, and rationalizes what was once a thicker, more controversial source of moral and political motivation, namely, self-love, pride, or vanity—putting oneself before or above others.[6] The fact that "interest" or "self-interest" is both a kind of rational principle and a passion should teach us something more general about politics: it is an arena in which the distinction between reason and passion is blurred. We do not reduce our political reasons to "mere" passion, and we deceive ourselves if we look at our adversaries as motivated solely by their passions. Calvin, Locke, Rousseau, Smith, Thoreau, Marx, Gandhi, Fanon, and Friedman are cited all too frequently by defenders and opponents of the "status quo"; it is unlikely that we can look across a political divide and fail to see passions that aren't informed by reasons or reasons that are uninformed by passions.

That being the case, Walzer observes, how we conceptualize matters of political agency, identity, and commitment needs to be reframed. It is also the case that how we conceptualize political difference needs to be reframed. The organizing question is not, How are we to cope with another's passionate unreason? It is rather, Which side are you on?[7] That is to say, the fundamental question when thinking about political activism is not only about the reasons that shape one's view of justice but also the emotions, stories, and relationships that ground one's purposes. Discussing the place of passion in politics, Walzer writes:

> No political party that sets itself against the established hierarchies of power and wealth, no movement for equality or national liberation, for emancipation or empowerment, will ever succeed unless it arouses

the affiliative and combative passions of the people at the lower end of the hierarchies. The passions that it arouses are certain to include envy, resentment, and hatred, since these are the common consequences of hierarchical domination. They are also the emotional demons of political life, . . . bound to call up anxieties . . . that I assume we all share and have good reason to share. But anger at injustice and a sense of solidarity are also among the passions aroused by anti-hierarchical politics, which means that we also have good reason not to surrender too quickly to anxiety.[8]

By blurring the reason-passion distinction and taking due note of the erotic, combative, and imaginary features of political activism, Walzer enables us to think about political action as arousing the feelings of Steve Garey's key term: *solidarity*. Considerations of solidarity bring into sharp relief the focal question that I just mentioned: Which side are you on?

Walzer's way of putting these points leads me to ask what, more precisely, *is* solidarity, and what passions enable us to build ties that are proper to it? Walzer lists several emotions—envy, resentment, hatred, anger at injustice, and solidarity itself—as commonplace in our experiences of inequality. But this list is more of a suggestive menu than a full account of political emotions, and it assimilates solidarity into that menu as if it were a passion like the others. That assimilation overlooks the self-conscious aspects of solidarity that we do well not to overlook. And it pits one set of passions (such as envy) against another set (such as anger at injustice) without suggesting ways to evaluate their differences. Walzer leaves us with an inviting set of ethical and social-psychological questions regarding reason, passion, and partisanship that we do well to consider further.

It is toward clarifying political emotions that explain answers to the question, Which side are you on? that this chapter is aimed. My central point, made evident by its title, is that indignation and empathy, when understood as virtues, properly belong to the menu of political emotions that contribute to the "affiliative and combative passions" of people at the lower end of the hierarchies of power, wealth, and cramped opportunities in private and public affairs. Indignation and empathy can explain how feelings of solidarity are aroused and how they can bring morally committed citizens together into an imagined community. But here, too, matters are not so simple; political emotions as sources of solidarity are not merely players in the story that "misery loves company." It may rather be the case, as Shakespeare writes, that "misery acquaints a man with strange bedfellows."[9] To understand this point, and to grasp the difference between misery's "company" and its "strange bedfellows," some conceptual and terminological brush-clearing is in order.

POLITICAL SOLIDARITY

Solidarity is a shared, socialized emotion, not one that can be held by individuals alone, like fear or envy. To exist, it must be intersubjective. And such intersubjectivity must be consciously preferential and primed for struggle. Solidarity is an "in-group" idea, and it suggests a social psychology of collective resolve that draws its energy from members' real or vicarious shared experiences. But solidarity has been generally undertheorized, romanticized, and dulled of its partisan edge in recent literature. What should we mean, more precisely, by *solidarity*?

By *solidarity* I do not have in mind the notion given emphasis in contemporary Roman Catholic social teaching informed by the ideas of Pope John Paul II. Taking as his inspiration the name of the free trade union that quickly expanded into a powerful, nonviolent social movement in Poland in the 1980s,[10] and drawing on a larger body of his previous work in phenomenology, John Paul II introduced solidarity into the lexicon of Roman Catholic social teaching in his encyclical *Laborem exercens* (*On Human Work*, 1981) and invoked it often in subsequent encyclicals. In *Laborem exercens* John Paul II used *solidarity* to describe ways of prompting social change that did not rely on Marxist ideas of class struggle. The pope drew on the idea to speak in support of worker solidarity "against the degradation of man as the subject of work."[11] In his subsequent writings, however, John Paul II used the idea more frequently and in a different register—not to denote partnership in the struggle against degradation in the workplace but to describe universal responsibility and especially care for the weak and poor. In *Sollicitudo rei socialis* (On Social Concern, 1987) the pope states that solidarity "is not a feeling of vague compassion or shallow distress at the misfortunes of so many people, both near and far. On the contrary, it is a firm and persevering determination to commit oneself to the common good; that is to say, to the good of all and of each individual, because we are all really responsible for all." For John Paul II solidarity is a virtue tied to a cosmopolitan, humanistic vision to describe obligations to all members of the human family, and it is understood as a distinctively Christian virtue when it is informed by "total gratuity, forgiveness, and reconciliation."[12] It presupposes an understanding of human beings as creatures of God and as sharing a common nature. John Paul II first invoked *solidarity* as a term to describe ways of prompting social change that did not rely on Marxist ideas of class struggle and subsequently developed it as a virtue in response to globalization. Although he understood solidarity as a way of standing tall against the "structures of sin"—what others call institutionalized forms of social injustice—his aversion to conflict, division, and partisanship take the edge off of the term. For the pope, solidarity "helps us to see the 'other'—whether a person, people or nation—not just as some kind of instrument . . . but as our 'neighbor,' a 'helper' (Gen. 2:18–20), to be made a sharer on a par with ourselves, in the banquet of life to which all are equally invited by God."[13] John Paul II's views of shared responsibility might help Steve Garey's efforts to widen the perspective of his strikers to include the welfare of future generations of union workers, but the pope's inclusivism doesn't help Garey explain why they shouldn't cross the line to the other side. Solidarity is not only about "collaboration" and "dialogue"; it is also combative, self-consciously drawing lines between "us and them."

Nor do I have in mind the notion of solidarity that informs Richard Rorty's account of a postmodern bourgeois liberal utopia as he develops that idea in several of his essays and in *Contingency, Irony, and Solidarity*.[14] Rorty's idea of solidarity involves a number of claims. One idea is that solidarity is a way that people place themselves into a larger context in order to give meaning to their lives. For Rorty *solidarity* contrasts with *objectivity*, which describes how people seek meaning by describing themselves as standing in immediate relation to an objective nonhuman reality.[15] That is to say, "solidarity" indicates a way of making sense of our lives; it is a concept that draws from antirepresentational, pragmatist ideas about how to handle matters of truth. Solidarity on this view is an antimetaphysical category, not a political one, and

Rorty deploys it as part of his defense of postmodern bourgeois liberalism. Here solidarity is not about taking sides about matters of social injustice; it is a category that aims to help us relax about the absence of transcendent, objective truth.

The second of Rorty's ideas, closer to my topic, is that solidarity, seen in liberal terms, is a form of community shaped by two criteria: (1) a negative norm, to wit: that cruelty, especially humiliation, is "the worst thing we do";[16] and (2) the positive norm to expand our definition of "we" to include more of the human population until no one can be considered less-than-human, thereby "creating an even larger and more variegated *ethnos*."[17] Here we see how Rorty and John Paul II are fellow travelers: both describe solidarity as a nonpartisan, cosmopolitan ideal, conceived either on the basis of an objectivist vision of common human nature or on the basis of rejecting precisely that way of thinking. Depoliticized and depolemicized in this way, solidarity prevents us from either asking or answering Walzer's question, Which side are you on?

In contrast to this universalist and utopian picture of solidarity, I propose that we view it as a social relation that is partisan, primed for struggle, mindful of itself as organized (or close to it), and energized by feelings of resentment and indignation (among other emotions). Solidarity on my view is preferential, and it draws lines. It is a concept about power. For the purposes of shorthand, call this view of solidarity, one that brings together strange bedfellows, political solidarity. The modifier seems obvious, but it is meant to conceive of the idea as something other than an inclusivist disposition and to make plain that it is a form of moral agency collectively expressed in terms of organized political affiliation, a culture of shared expectations, mutual understanding, and resolve.

Solidarity consists of more than concord, unity, or common agreement, but it certainly has those features. The political solidarity that I propose is a kind of moral sovereignty, an imagined community that is energized—I am tempted to say ruled—by the commitment for a better life and a better society, a commitment shaped by shared norms and ideals. Such a society has an ethos that is shaped more by an egalitarian ethic of self-respect and mutual respect than by an ethic that focuses on avoiding cruelty or promoting universalist humanistic visions; it targets privilege, has a polemical edge, and agitates against the power that money can buy.

Solidarity, of course, is a double-edged sword. White supremacists are typically described as cultivating partisan and polemical solidarity, and their ties extend across an extensive territory, both real and imagined. For that matter, groups that essentialize aspects of cultural identity and dichotomize cultural differences into invidious "us-them" antagonisms also have an answer to the question, Which side are you on? It is thus crucial to underline the seemingly obvious point I just mentioned, namely, that political solidarity that aims at establishing a kind of moral sovereignty should be ruled by substantive egalitarian principles. It would be on that basis that we can distinguish between good and bad solidarity—solidarity among white supremacists or cultural warriors and solidarity among those working for a society of political and social equality.[18] In my ensuing comments I will be presuming a notion of political solidarity of a morally desirable sort.

RESENTMENT AND INDIGNATION

The fact that political solidarity has an inner resolve with a polemical edge can be explained with reference to feelings of resentment and indignation. These sentiments—what Peter Strawson calls "moral reactive attitudes"—make for political solidarity among strange bedfellows in the rough-and-tumble of political life. In his essay "Freedom and Resentment" Strawson asks us to remember "what it is actually like to be involved in ordinary interpersonal relationships, ranging from the most intimate to the most casual." He notes how much it matters to us "whether the actions of other people . . . reflect attitudes towards us of goodwill, affection, or esteem on the one hand or contempt, indifference, or malevolence on the other." He thereby calls attention to our attitudes and emotional responses that express how we react to others' attitudes and responses expressed toward us. Gratitude, resentment, forgiveness, and love are among the "personal" (as distinct from the "objective" and impersonal) reactive feelings that we have in response to how others regard us.[19]

With these thoughts about interpersonal attitudes and feelings in mind Strawson asks us to consider the "moral reactive attitudes" that arise in our responses to experiencing or seeing another's conduct or attitude of indifference, contempt, or malice. The reactions that flow from witnessing indifference, contempt, or malice are directed at the perpetrator's intentions or attitudes. Strawson identifies three moral reactive attitudes in response to malice, contempt, or indifference: resentment, indignation, and guilt. A person who is wronged typically has the moral reactive attitude of *resentment*, understood as a first-personal category of feeling aggrieved. A third party who witnesses wrongdoing typically has the moral reactive attitude of *indignation*, which Strawson calls a "vicarious analogue" of resentment. Resentment and indignation, then, are feelings of having been offended; they are emotions that can fuel the expression of a grievance. And the agent of wrongdoing, upon reflecting on the wrong she or he has committed, has the moral reactive attitude of *guilt*.[20]

Strawson does not devote much time to what can count as the moral wrong to which the attitudes of resentment, indignation, and guilt are proper responses. His essay addresses the free will/determinism debate, not matters of moral and political psychology. Strawson's general view is that these moral reactive feelings are responses to departures from expectations of goodwill that we naturally have in social life. One of his core points is that we care how others regard us and that our feelings are often in dialogical response to an other's expressed attitudes and actions of goodwill or ill-will in everyday life. He sidesteps whether there exist *wrong* feelings of resentment—for example, delusional, moody, or narcissistic bases for feeling a grievance. But for resentment and indignation to be justified responses to another's malice, they must be tied to claims of justice. They must be feelings we have that are desirable, and their desirability must be established on terms other than the depth or sincerity according to which they are felt. Morally reactive feelings, no less than solidarity, can be a double-edged sword.

In the third section of *A Theory of Justice* John Rawls draws an important distinction between *moral* sentiments, feelings, and attitudes, on the one hand, and *natural* sentiments, feelings, and attitudes, on the other, that speaks to this lacuna in Strawson's essay.[21] For the sake of simplicity, I will call this the distinction between *moral* and *natural* feelings. What distinguishes them? A moral feeling, Rawls states, "invokes a moral concept and its associated principles." An account of one's moral feelings thus "makes reference to an acknowledged right or wrong."[22] A natural feeling, by definition, does not include a connection to a moral concept or standard. Natural feelings are learned, according to Rawls, across the arc of childhood development as we proceed from relying on parental authority to activities and roles that we experience as we move out of the family and into relationships in school, recreation, and the like. These natural feelings can serve as precursors to moral feelings, but they remain ethically indeterminate until they can be explained in relation to concepts of the right or the good. We might feel anger, with all of its visceral and related dimensions, but that feeling is not a feeling of resentment or indignation unless it is, in Walzer's language, "anger at injustice."

Anger, then, is a reactive attitude but not a moral one until it is tied to ethical concepts. Then we can label it the morally reactive attitude of resentment or indignation and thus overcome the lacuna in Strawson's argument. This is not to say that indignation or resentment are emotions that must be felt solely in relation to an *abstract moral principle*, however. "Anger at injustice" typically includes more than a feeling that we experience after reading the headlines. Or more precisely: resentment or indignation typically includes more than a response to witnessing the violation of an egalitarian principle. Our passions run deep precisely because we see peoples' lives at stake. As a moral reactive attitude, "anger at injustice" is socialized: it typically means "anger at injustice suffered by *us* or by *them*." Although Rawls would like us to have moral feelings that are "free from contingency," he notes, rightly in my mind, connections between moral feelings and natural ties such as love and trust that ought to be cultivated in the family.[23] Indeed, Rawls sees the connection between moral feelings and their natural, social undercurrents as important for explaining not only their depth but also their *moral salience*:

A reference to the relevant principle [of right or good] is made in explaining one's [moral] emotions. When the natural ties of friendship and mutual trust are present, however, these moral feelings are more intense than if they are absent. Existing attachments heighten the feeling of guilt and indignation . . . even at the stage of the morality of principles. Now granting that this heightening is appropriate, it follows that violations of these natural ties are wrongs. For if we suppose that, say, a rational feeling of guilt . . . implies a fault on our part, and that a greater feeling of guilt implies a greater fault, then indeed breach of trust and the betrayal of friendships, and the like, are especially forbidden. The violation of these ties to particular individuals and groups arouses more intense moral feelings, and this entails that these offenses are worse.[24]

On this point—the synergism between moral reactive feelings and the ties that deepen them—we can observe an internal connection between solidarity and a moral grievance, where solidarity is viewed not merely as another passion but as a self-reflexive relationship of people who are bound together in a partisan way. Resentment or indignation is anger at injustice that has been experienced by *us* or by *them*. Those feelings can unite people, and the conflict that injustice creates brings to mind shared commitments to basic fairness. That is to say, conflicts wrought by injustice enable us to move from solidarity that is *aroused and felt* to solidarity that is *mindful and self-aware*. Solidarities arise in contexts of cultural pressure and political crisis. Indignation and resentment awaken us to remember which side we are on.[25] But resentment makes for more familiar bedfellows; the grievance is immediate and first-personal (*we* have been wronged). Indignation, in contrast, is felt somewhat from a distance. How to lessen that distance is a challenge for thinking about reason, passion, and political solidarity. With that challenge in mind I turn to my third concept, empathy.

EMPATHY

Earlier in this chapter I proposed that we view solidarity as a social relation that is partisan, primed for struggle, mindful of itself as organized (or close to it), and energized by the moral reactive feelings of resentment and indignation (among other feelings). Now we see that such feelings must be tied to concepts such as justice. Thus far I have been talking about resentment and indignation in the same breath, as if they are both equal to the task of arousing feelings and awareness of political solidarity. Here again, however, matters are not so simple. Resentment is a first-personal feeling in response to *being a victim of* injustice; indignation is mainly a third-personal feeling in response to *witnessing* injustice. How might those of us who witness but do not undergo a particular set of injustices join cause with, and enter into solidarity with, victims of such injustice? What can explain how political solidarity might generate moral sovereignty among strange bedfellows?

To these questions I propose empathy as a way of mediating between those who witness injustice and those who are bound in political solidarity by moral reactive feelings of resentment. Empathy is a complex and controversial concept, as we saw in the previous chapter, but a concise definition and set of contrasts with other emotions can clarify what I mean and why I consider it relevant to this problem of mediating between third-personal and first-personal feelings of a grievance. It is also important, I want to suggest, to the formation of a robust imaginary community bound together in political solidarity.

As I noted in chapter 4, empathy refers to the ability to "place yourself in someone else's shoes" cognitively, emotively, and self-reflexively. It describes a psychological state in which our thoughts and emotions are conditioned by our perceptions of another's feelings and frame of mind. When we empathize, we think and feel as we take the other to feel, given our perception of how she perceives her circumstances. Empathy designates, among other things, participation in another's feelings—the experience of attunement. And in clear instances of empathy we are aware that our feelings and point of view have become attuned to another's feelings and point of view. As I noted earlier, in prototypical instances of empathy, one is aware that "I" am empathizing and am mindful of that fact. For that reason empathy has an important ethical dimension insofar as it is something about which I am aware and can regulate for good or ill.

Recall that empathy is not itself a single, discrete emotion, like anger or joy or fear. It is rather the experience of resonating with what we imagine others' feelings and frames of mind to be. For this reason we can speak of "empathic emotions."[26] Empathy has no specific emotional or cognitive content; one's empathy relies on or responds to the perceived emotional and cognitive states of another. We imagine what it's like to be in another's shoes, which can be of all different sorts. Empathy thus helps to provide the glue that holds social relationships together. When we empathize, we show others how they feel and we communicate that we can agree with them about their feelings.[27] We show that we grasp their feelings and express our willingness to stand in solidarity with them in light of their situation and grievances.

Here we do well to return to the difference between empathy and compassion. Although these feelings can shade into each other, their differences reveal something important about empathy's potential for widening the base of political solidarities. We might feel compassion for those who feel resentment upon experiencing injustice, but that is different from empathizing with their grievance. Compassion asks us to "feel for" others in their distress and frequently includes efforts to ameliorate their condition. It is often seen as a motivation for assisting others and helping to alleviate their suffering. Empathy, in contrast, is not a matter of "feeling for" but "feeling with" someone else. It asks us to see the world from another's presumed perspective and it can energize feelings that seek not to alleviate distress but to rectify an injustice. Compassion does not rectify; indeed, it usually contrasts with justice-as-rectification. Empathy is different insofar as it can engage energies and desires that seek to right a wrong and for that reason it can provide a valuable psychological basis for joining others' political causes.

To be sure, empathy is another double-edged sword. As I noted in the previous chapter, some people empathize as a way to gain advantages over others, enjoy the pain they inflict on others, or feel undesirable emotions with others, such as spite or ill-will.[28] Empathy that mediates in the service of political solidarity, then, must be conditioned by other excellences, such as the commitment to a just society. Like resentment and indignation, good empathy depends on other virtues. But the capacity to empathize helps to explain how political solidarities can come about among those who are either resentful or indignant about injustice. Indeed, given that empathy includes reciprocity—imaginatively placing oneself in another's shoes—it seems well suited to carry the weight of both reason and feeling in the life of morally committed citizens. As a concept of both principle and passion, empathy boasts the capacity to strengthen the inner resolve that political solidarity requires. Bringing indignation and empathy together, we can continue to blur reason and passion in ways that explain solidarity and maintain its partisan, self-reflexive, and polemical edge.

RELIGION

I have described political solidarity as a kind of imagined moral community bound together by a commitment to justice that can include passions of indignation and resentment. The question arises: what (if anything) might religious communities contribute to this account? What kind of ethics of belief arises from a view of political action defined in these social-psychological and moral ways?

Here I will be brief and only suggestive. My principal thought is that religions with prophetic traditions have resources for developing *empathic indignation*. This category, empathic indignation, is the linchpin of my argument about sources of political solidarity. Religions have bases for cultivating feelings of political solidarity with those who are justifiably aggrieved, and they serve the wider public by drawing on those resources to cultivate dispositions and fellow-feeling among their adherents to build ties with strange bedfellows. The imagination can be aided by the prophetic voices, poetry, imagery, and inspiring denouncements of injustice found in religious texts, teachings, and traditions of interpretation. On this view the ethics of belief—focusing on religion's moral responsibilities in public life—would be to turn down the volume of feel-good religious stories and scholarship and focus instead on how those at the bottom of hierarchies of wealth, opportunity, power, and sources of esteem can be joined in their efforts to create a better, more egalitarian society for themselves and others. It would also mean resisting the allure of in-group religious solidarities evident in the new traditionalism (among other places) and have religious adherents instead think about building affiliations with those who suffer injustice.[29] Religions can also help political solidarities from backsliding from egalitarian relationships to oligarchical patterns of organizing and decision making.[30] They can also build solidarities within their own ranks and invite friends and strangers to stand united with them against religious and other forms of prejudice and injustice.[31] That is to say, religions with prophetic resources have strong bases to fuel social criticism within and among groups bound together in political solidarity. Religions can help ensure that the reasons that bring partisan groups together are principled and self-critical. Thus understood, religions can empower their adherents by calling on the literature of their social critics to draw together friends and strangers in justifiably partisan and polemical ways.

6

ON DUTIES AND DEBTS TO CHILDREN

BEYOND POSTETHNOGRAPHIC AUTHORITY

In chapter 2 I proposed making a cultural turn in religious ethics to expand the methodological practices and intellectual agendas in the field. My proposal was to encourage scholars to examine cultural circumstances and institutional settings with which persons identify themselves and find meaning, direction, and sources of moral formation. A turn to culture would enable religious ethicists to examine neglected features of moral experience and craft an ethics of ordinary life, looking closely at routine aspects of everyday experience—customs and codes, socialization processes, ritual practices, kinship systems, criteria of expertise, visual culture, folk wisdom, divisions of labor, the experiences of familiarity and difference, symbols of meaning, and the contested way in which these facts and forces are mobilized by congeries of power and resistance in culture and society.

In offering this proposal I issued two caveats. First, I do not wish to romanticize ethnography or cultural anthropology as a research method or to weaken the confidence of religious ethicists about the value of critically examining religion, ethics, and their interrelationships. I mainly want to indicate how work in ethnography and cultural anthropology can stimulate new research programs in religious ethics and contribute to new genres in the field. Second, I do not mean to suggest that religious ethicists or others need to visit regions or settings that are culturally distant and exotic in order to explore otherness or to carry out good ethnographic work. Recall again the observation made by James Clifford:

"Ethnography is moving into areas long occupied by sociology, the novel, or avant-garde cultural critique, rediscovering otherness and difference within the cultures of the West."[1] There is no reason to presume that otherness is not embedded in what is familiar and intimately present.

Recent work in religious ethics and moral philosophy has taken up one or another facet of these ideas. G. Scott Davis criticizes the exaggerated claims in the humanities and the natural sciences about the work that "theory" can perform, recalling several of the concerns I rehearsed in chapter 2 about the limits of "grand theory" in the social sciences. Davis urges comparative religious ethicists to turn to history and anthropology to carry out their work with more modest and edifying purposes than theorists typically avow.[2] Jeffrey Stout, a philosopher of religious ethics and pragmatism, visited religious communities and activist organizations in New Orleans, Houston, the borderlands of south Texas, Los Angeles, and the Bay Area to examine their practices of grassroots political organizing for his book *Blessed Are the Organized: Grassroots Democracy in America*.[3] Todd Whitmore, a scholar working in the Catholic social justice tradition, has carried out seventeen months of ethnographic fieldwork to write about matters of justice, race, ethnicity, colonialism, and religion in the violent struggles in Uganda and the South Sudan, spending much of his time in Internally Displaced Persons camps and asking how people in extreme poverty and armed conflict sustain hope.[4] Elizabeth M. Bucar, drawing on feminist thought and rhetorical theory, carried out extensive interviews over four months in Iran for research that resulted in a work in comparative religious ethics, *Creative Conformity: The Feminist Politics of U.S. Catholic and Iranian Shi'i Women*.[5] A generation ago, bioethicist William F. May immersed himself in various health-care settings that help patients and families cope with how illness assaults both body and identity, a study that led to the book *The Patient's Ordeal*.[6] Articles and books by Stout, Whitmore, Bucar, and May all exhibit the hybridization of discourses in ethics, the humanities, and social sciences to which I earlier referred.[7]

My own effort in this direction ranged from 1993 to 1998, a period in which I took on the role of participant-observer in several pediatric medical contexts in Bloomington, Indiana; Indianapolis; and Boston as part of a project in religion, the culture of biomedicine, and professional ethics.

During that time I was formally mentored by anthropologists and social scientists who study culture and the professions in a yearlong seminar funded by the Lilly Endowment before I immersed myself in the office of a local family-care provider, an urban burn unit, and two intensive care units—one in a high-tech tertiary care and research hospital. Much of that mentoring aimed to ensure that I produced not merely a study of local interest but a work of moral theory that spoke to more general questions and paradigms of thought in pediatric medical ethics.

The bulk of my ethnographic work occurred in 1997 and 1998, when I was a participant-observer in a children's hospital that I call Baylin Pediatric Medical Center.[8] I set out on that project to examine the finely grained features of professional and patient experience in order to see how children and families cope with chronic or acute illnesses. In many respects the study was prompted by my long-standing interests in theodicy, broadly construed—the problem of explaining innocent suffering to those who believe in a just universe. I wanted to know, among other things, what cultural, religious, and other resources professionals and families rely on to address the challenges of caring for those who are young and ill, often gravely ill. More precisely, I wanted to explore what sense of order or meaning professionals and parents retained when confronting the raw and merciless face of childhood suffering. With knowledge gained from ethnographic participant-observation, moreover, I hoped to chart the intimate geography of pediatric medical ethics, commenting on concrete experiences in law and medicine along with their cultural and moral dimensions. Methodologically, I sought to develop a reflexive ethnography for medical ethics by coordinating information gained from clinical immersion with ideas garnered from recent developments in theories of practical reasoning and the interpretive turn in the human sciences.

What I gained from that immersion is an insight of the sort that rarely works its way into ethnographic or postethnographic reflections—works in which the fieldworker looks back on the circumstances and interactions that informed his or her work. Postethnographic writing tends to be more memoirist and autobiographical than anything else. It is more about securing ethnographic authority than about providing a new round of discoveries.[9] The postethnographic insight that I experienced, in contrast, was that broad philosophical ideas can continually arise from particular experiences and cultural encounters if we work to remember and reflect on them after the fact.

This chapter is less about securing ethnographic authority than about exploring a set of ideas that were prompted by my previous ethnographic work. I will get at matters, and some of the parameters of my ensuing argument, in this way. What I learned from my clinical immersion, among other things, is that the modern research hospital deploys the latest results of scientific research to ameliorate a patient's pain while it often stumbles, clumsily and inarticulately, to alleviate human suffering. This is not because hospital professionals are insensitive to human suffering or uninterested in responding to it but because they sometimes lack the tools for understanding the idioms and traditions that constitute how patients and families undergo their setbacks and hardships. Suffering is shaped in no small part by cultural, religious, and ethnic identity. It is not a one-size-fits-all phenomenon, as if reducible to general diagnostic formulas.

One of the cases that clarified this matter of suffering's different articulations involved the parents of a four-year-old boy, Billy Richardson, who suffered from Hurler's syndrome and the effects of treating it. Hurler's syndrome is a rare, inherited metabolic disorder caused by an enzyme defect that produces an abnormal accumulation of mucopolysaccharides in the body's tissues. Billy was admitted to Baylin for a second bone marrow transplant to provide a continuing source of an enzyme that he lacked.[10] Patients like Billy develop cardiac abnormalities; umbilical hernias; skeletal deformities; and enlarged tongues, livers, and spleens. Their somatic and mental growth is impaired, and they acquire physical features that give the syndrome its former name of gargoylism. Billy had all of these conditions and several other serious medical problems as well. Although his transplant was successful, he soon experienced multisystem organ failure and was admitted to the hospital's intensive care unit (ICU) for aggressive treatment.

Billy's parents, Michelle and Kyle Richardson, met with Baylin's ICU and oncology staff many times to discuss whether to continue life-support for their son. I conversed with Michelle Richardson throughout Billy's admission at Baylin and attended almost all of her meetings with house staff. Those meetings were understandably fraught with anxiety and uncertainty about whether and on what terms Billy could be described as improving. But Billy's case was not only or chiefly a matter about whether to continue one or another form of medical technology—an all-too-familiar question in end-of-life controversies in biomedical ethics and practice. The controversy was rather about the proper framework for understanding Billy's situation. The dispute, in other words, was more metaphysical than it was about the details of ethical decision making or scientific diagnosis. The ICU and oncology team interpreted his condition against a series of medical data based on his fluid retention, heart rate and blood pressure, caloric intake, the size of his lung fields, the strength of his immune system, and probability of survival based on information about patients with similar conditions. Michelle and Kyle understood all of these data and placed them within a religious framework that was shaped by Calvinistic beliefs about how God is in final control of human destiny. They invoked Christian theological convictions to strengthen their resistance to what they experienced as a collusion of professional power and expertise in the hospital. Both parents relied on those beliefs to question what appeared to them to be a hasty time table on the part of the doctors and to forestall removing Billy's life-support. In Michelle's mind Billy's fate should be determined according to "God's time table," not the doctors'. In her opinion the doctors' reading of Billy's data was shaped by a set of human and professional interests that failed to acknowledge the workings of divine providence.

I recall this incident not to rehearse a drama of medical and moral disagreement but to consider a comment that Michelle made in one of our many conversations about Billy. Michelle claimed, among other things, that her son's condition was part of a larger divine plan in which God invites others to grow in neighbor-love. Specifically, his condition confronted society with this question: can others respond charitably to him given his strange appearance, his developmental delay, and the requirements of caring for his many needs? Billy was a figure of radical alterity. In Michelle's mind modern secular society and its many ableist prejudices make it difficult for the average person to accept a child such as hers. Billy posed a moral challenge to our capacities and virtues and our alleged commitment to equality. Keeping Billy alive was, in part, an occasion for increasing the possibility of selfless love in the world and for contesting society's standards and cultural conceits about what counts as "normal" or "ideal." Michelle supplemented her argument with several examples about physicians, children at her church, and members of COTA (Children's Organ Transplant Association) who were deeply affected by Billy's story and who went out of their way to express their support for the Richardsons. Michelle summarized these ideas to me: "[Billy] touched so many people. He changed us. Oh, my God. I've done things I'd never thought I'd do. There's nothing I can't do. He enriched life; day-to-day stuff."[11] Indeed, so important was Billy's condition that Michelle often spoke of him as an agent in his own right, a "fighter" whose unpredictable ups and downs in the ICU were a source of strength to her own religious faith.

Michelle's ideas never persuaded me that Billy's costly and increasingly futile treatment should be continued. But her comments did capture something more general about caring for children: children can challenge adults in ways that are morally significant. And that fact can put adults in children's debt. Children challenge their caretakers with questions about how to exhibit unconditional love and how to express that love according to the finite and uncontrollable demands of their special needs.

Here I want to reflect on a claim that Michelle and Kyle made—and that others at Baylin grasped as reasonable, often repeating it to me in their role as pediatric care-providers—regarding how children, given their challenges and demands, can transform the ends and identities of those on whom they rely. To be sure, children can produce ill effects in their relationships with adults. But there are doubtless many young persons in our experience of educational, family, recreational, medical, or other settings who have left us deeply affected and all the better for it. With Billy and other such young persons in mind we do well to consider how adults are, in part at least, dependent subjects in their interactions with children.[12]

As a way of framing this discussion, let me begin with this fact: the idea that adults have duties to care for children is generally obvious and uncontroversial today. Typically we say that adults have such duties given that (a) young people, as dependent, vulnerable, and undergoing the process of development, have "claims against the world" for care, nurture, and education; and (b) adults have the capacities to address such claims.[13] Less obvious—perhaps counterintuitive—is the idea that I proposed above, namely, that adults can have debts to children. Such debts arise owing to the effects that children can have on adults: challenging adults, requiring them to do good, and, in the process, having adults discover aspects of themselves that they would otherwise not know. Although adults do not depend on children in the same way that children depend on adults, adults can nonetheless be indebted to children for morally significant reasons, among which is their ability to reform adults' picture of themselves and their ends.[14] We might say that adults are paradoxically sovereign and subject, free and bound, in their relationships with children.

In this chapter I will scrutinize this paradoxical fact about the relationship between adults and young people in light of recent work in moral philosophy and religious ethics. I will step back from the case of Billy Richardson and my clinical immersion to focus on a broader range of intimate relationships with children that involve the provision of care: parenting, of course, but also teaching, advising, coaching, and providing for a child's physical, emotional, or psychological needs in relatively stable relationships over time. I will call adults who occupy such roles "caretakers," "caregivers," or, to emphasize the fact that we are dealing with relations between older and younger persons, "caring adults."

I want to make sense of the idea of a caregiver's debt to a child and to identify how it poses a challenge to moral thinking about adult-child relationships. I also want to show how we can resolve or at least appreciably lessen the tension between the experiences of being sovereign and subject in light of an understanding of *responsibility* that gestures toward phenomenological understandings of the concept often ignored in contemporary moral philosophy and, to a lesser extent, religious ethics. If nothing else, I hope to show that caregivers' relationships with children are fraught with rich moral dimensions that are easily overlooked in practical ethics—an oversight to which we are especially prone if we concentrate exclusively, as contemporary moral philosophy has tended to do, on duties owed by adults to young people.

TWO ONTOLOGIES

One way to view the experiences of being sovereign and subject is to sort out who owes what to whom by viewing the adult-child relationship bilaterally or, to adopt another image, as moving along two different streams.

One stream flows from caregivers to children on the premise that adults owe children care and protection of some sort. The other stream flows in the opposite direction: children act on caring adults in ways that are morally significant insofar as they are transformative. Caregivers can be indebted to children for many things, among which is the power to change adults' self-interpretations along with some of the ends they seek. As a result, a distinct set of obligations reveals itself: adults can owe children a debt of gratitude for teaching them something about themselves. Adults who attend to a young person's needs can find that caring opens up and transforms horizons of expectation, meaning, and the ends of the caregiver.

Soon I will sharpen the difference between these two streams by classifying the first as moving us to a *principled* understanding of caregiving as opposed to the second, which directs us to a *constitutive* understanding of caregiving. Corresponding to this distinction is the idea that children can be either a *predicament* for adults to address or a *gift* for adults to appreciate. To make sense of these distinctions, I want first to show that the tension between duties and debts to children points to a deeper ontological divide. That divide points to two different accounts of the self that underlie each of the streams to which I just alluded.

The first stream, the stream of duty, suggests a top-down or at least one-way connection between caring adults and children. The idea is that such adults have a duty to care for young persons owing to their needs and vulnerabilities, their relative lack of self-sufficiency. Putting the point this way suggests an asymmetry or hierarchy between adults and children, between benefactors and beneficiaries. Caregivers are providers to those who are unable to provide for themselves. The ontology that such an account suggests is one in which persons with rather fixed identities and capabilities provide for those who stand in need of assistance. Obligations fall to those who, in the words of Michael J. Sandel, are "individuated in advance"—more or less bounded selves who act on behalf of others.[15]

Certain views of duty suggest that kind of ontology of caretakers. We typically assume that children have negative and positive rights that establish duties on others to abstain from or to carry out certain actions. On this view adults are obligated to ensure that a child's rights are honored, even if the child does not or is not able to identify a rights-claim or rights violation. The ontology underlying this account assumes that adults are rational agents with capacities of practical reason and that it falls to them as free and responsible persons to act on behalf of others who have less or diminished autonomy. Our picture of justified paternalism in the care of children is framed in precisely this way.[16] The relationship is one, in short, of an agent with a relatively settled and fixed identity acting to care for others with less-developed powers of self-determination and practical reason.

Sandel's objections to liberal doctrine, or to what he calls "deontological liberalism," have done much to shape our interpretation of liberal thinking along these ontological lines.[17] In his critique of John Rawls's *A Theory of Justice* Sandel argues that Rawlsian liberalism rests not on uncontroversial premises but on an account of the self that is fraught with arguable assumptions. Chief among those is the idea that we begin in liberal doctrine by assuming the plurality of persons—distinct and different persons who are subjects of possession and self-possession prior to experience. For Rawls, Sandel writes, "the self is prior to the ends which are affirmed by it."[18] This assumption of selves "individuated in advance" is key to an account of deontological morality more generally. Sandel writes: "To be a deontological self, I must be a subject whose identity is given independently of the things I have, independently that is, of my interests and ends and my relations with others."[19] Sandel thus highlights liberal doctrine's dependence on a view of the self that is "fixed prior to its ends"—a self that finds its nature not in the ends that it discovers but in the very exercise of choice and obedience to principles that are conceived independently of contingency and experience.

In the concluding section of *A Theory of Justice*, devoted to securing the stability of the doctrine of justice-as-fairness, Rawls speaks to these various points. Seeking to establish the good of justice—justice as something that we would desire to act upon—as part of his larger aim to establish the stability of his theory, he writes: "The desire to act justly and the desire to express our nature as free moral persons turn out to specify what is practically speaking the same desire." He elaborates: "The desire to express our nature as a free and equal rational being can be fulfilled only by acting on the principles of right and justice as having first priority. This is a consequence of the condition of finality [imposed on the terms of the original position]: since these principles are regulative, the desire to act upon them is satisfied only to the extent that it is likewise regulative with respect to other desires. It is acting from this precedence that expresses our freedom from contingency and happenstance."[20]

Following this line of argument, we are moved to abide by principles of justice *as principles* owing to the fact that they function to regulate our desires on terms that are free from implication in those desires. That is to say, the good to which we are drawn in abiding by justice is the "revelation" of our natures as free from inclination, a revelation made plain by our very power to regulate inclination according to terms that are independent of it. In this way our sense of justice, our motivation to strive for it, "contains within itself its own priority."[21] Our desire to act justly reveals our natures as free moral persons. And, equally important, in recognizing the priority of principle to desire, we presume ourselves as having appropriate distance from our ends.

Rawls's subsequent efforts to secure the stability of his theory eschew these metaphysical claims altogether, arguing for the stability of liberalism as a political (as opposed to metaphysical) theory on the basis of an overlapping consensus of reasonable comprehensive doctrines.[22] The details of how Rawls develops his position are less important to my argument than how Sandel's discussion of philosophical anthropology can highlight some basic tendencies in our understanding of relationships more generally, including caregivers' relationships with children.[23]

With these thoughts in mind consider Tamara Schapiro's Kantian discussion of childhood, adults' responsibilities, and justified paternalism within an egalitarian ethic. In response to the question, "What is a child, such that it could be appropriate to treat a person like one?" Schapiro develops a picture of children on analogy with Kant's understanding of a prepolitical society as a way of considering how egalitarians might coherently distinguish between adults and children as two classes of people. What characterizes children and societies in the state of nature is their incapacity for self-rule or, more precisely, a constitution according to which they can govern themselves. Instead, they reside in a nonideal state of underdevelopment, lacking the resources necessary for independence from others. For that reason, Schapiro notes, childhood (like existence in the state of nature) is a "normative predicament" from a Kantian point of view.[24] What is important for both adults and societies is that they have a basis according to which to judge and adjudicate conflicting claims. An adult *qua* adult is a person who can "adjudicate her conflicting motivational claims on the basis of something like [a] principle; because she is reflective, being wanton is not an option." A child is a predicament, in contrast, because she "cannot adjudicate those conflicts in a truly authoritative way for lack of an established constitution, that is, a principled perspective which could count as a law of her will."[25] What is necessary for immature individuals is a perspective according to which they can step back from their motivational claims and determine as a matter of principle which ones to act on. Accordingly, children are "provisional" selves whereas adults, as developed persons, possess hegemony over their impulses and feelings.

From this perspective adults have paternalistic responsibilities to children in the same way that Kant's "active" citizens have duties toward "passive" citizens in political arrangements: the latter are a temporary deviation from the norm of active citizenship, not to be treated as a permanent underclass.[26] Analogously, adults should think of children as a temporary deviation from adulthood and contribute to the formation of their identities as self-governing agents. On this account we might say adults are to relate to children as potential equals. Schapiro writes: "If childhood really is a nonideal status, then we ought to regard the undeveloped nature of children's agency as an obstacle to morality, a condition which in principle ought to be eliminated. The idea here is not that children are an obstacle to morality, but that their predicament is an obstacle to morality. Being a practical agent is hard enough; being an undeveloped one is even harder." Adults should thus make it their end to do what is in their power to help children work their way into adulthood. To see what this requires, we need to keep in mind what children have to do: "Their task is to carve out a space between themselves and the forces within them. They are to do this by trying on principles in the hope of developing a perspective they can endorse as their own."[27] On these grounds, Schapiro argues, our intuitions permitting the paternalistic treatment of some persons—children—can make sense within an egalitarian framework.

For my purposes the key terms in this account are twofold: children exist in an *undeveloped* state (in contrast to adults) and must find a way to "carve out a *space* between themselves and the forces within them." The implication is that an adult, in contrast, is relatively fixed in relation to her or his ends and has sufficient distance from them to judge their merits as maxims of action.

Consider, second, Onora O'Neill's account of obligations that adults owe to children. O'Neill argues that there are duties to others that do not entail a specific set of rights or obvious rights-claimants. O'Neill wishes to produce an understanding of obligation that gets beyond an account of justice as rights-centered, one that implicates the virtues. In Kant's terms such virtues are "imperfect duties." Developing her own line of Kantian argumentation, O'Neill argues that there is a responsibility to care for others that derives from the Kantian rejection of indifference and that such an account generates obligations—imperfect duties—that do not correlate with others' rights.

To see this, O'Neill has us consider the opposite of care, namely, apathy toward others. Individuals who commit themselves not to care for others assign to themselves the value of indifference as a policy of action. In so doing, they deny themselves the care and beneficence of others, for it would be inconsistent to expect others to reject indifference while not rejecting it oneself. Herein lies the force of Kant's principle of universalizability: a principle of action is unacceptable if I cannot will that it be a principle for all. Assuming that I will need assistance and care from others, I deny myself such resources by committing myself to indifference and neglect as a program of action. A key premise here is that we are all incomplete in one way or another. Put differently, only agents who are entirely self-sufficient can coherently embrace a life plan that neglects the needs of others; we who are finite and vulnerable agents have no such freedom. O'Neill writes:

> No vulnerable agent can coherently accept that indifference and neglect should be universalized, for if they were nobody could rely on others' help; joint projects would tend to fail; vulnerable characters would be undermined; capacities and capabilities that need assistance and nurturing would not emerge; personal relationships would wither; education and cultural life would decline. . . . Those with limited and variable capacities and capabilities *must* plan to rely in various ways on one

another's capacities and capabilities for action, so *must* (if committed to universalizable inclusive principles) be committed to doing at least something to sustain one another's capacities and capabilities, hence committed to rejecting inclusive principles of indifference and neglect.[28]

People who are indifferent deny goods to others that they (have or will) expect for themselves given the conditions of finitude in which all of our action occurs. Assuming that I rely on the caring actions of others, it would be unfair not to act toward others in caring ways, leaving them vulnerable to danger or harm while relying on deeds or institutions that enable me to avoid danger or harm. The duty to care, in short, is a function of justice, broadly conceived. If I fail to do unto others as others have done unto me, then I selfishly absent myself from (broad) patterns of reciprocity on which social life relies. Persons with benevolent dispositions, in contrast, understand something that is basic to the human condition: we rely on the kindness of each other—friends and strangers—in our various quests for growth and self-discovery. Love and care are not always acts of supererogation but flow from the character of persons who know that our lives are marked by conditions of finitude.[29]

O'Neill's account shifts attention away from rights-claimants to matters of moral agency, obligation, and the shape of our character and dispositions. This fact puts it within close proximity to the second moral stream I mentioned at the outset of this chapter and to which I will return shortly. First it should be noted, however, that an account of obligation—construed either with an eye toward permissible paternalism or in light of the more capacious framework of imperfect duties—resonates with Sandel's general account of the self presupposed by "deontological liberalism." The shared premise in each account is the idea of the plurality of persons. That is a Rawlsian way of marking our differences, as well as presuming that our identities are relatively set and stable as a condition for noting our differences. I act on principles on the assumption that I stand at a distance from my ends and am guided by principles that mediate my desires and interactions with my ends. The "I" who exercises moral responsibility is an ego that is bounded in advance from his or her ends and attachments. You might say in this account that relationships are marked by an *external* connection to another person's alterity.

I want to provide an alternative to that account, however, one that presumes not only a different picture of agency but also a wider account of moral responsibility. It is one that avoids Sandel's complaints to Rawls and to deontological liberalism more generally. Before I do that, however, I want to sketch the ontology implied by indebtedness in relationships between caretakers and children. That ontology presumes something quite different from a self that is individuated in advance or "fixed prior to its ends." It presumes a self that is affected by its relationships, a self that is vulnerable to change in the face of the other. This view understands agency, in the words of Margaret Urban Walker, as "impure." "Impure agents," Walker writes, "are saddled with weighty responsibilities and the open-ended possibility of acquiring more due to circumstances beyond our control." Responsibilities are likely to outrun the commitments of impure agents given the tendency of relationships to absorb unanticipated vicissitudes of luck. Such agents are thus required to adopt a series of virtues of practical reasoning and character, including a "reliable capacity to see things clearly, to take the proper moral measure of situations, so that a fitting response may be fashioned."[30]

Walker's ideas shed considerable light on the ontology of indebtedness. In adult-child relationships children are, or can be, quite "other," challenging adults to determine what is right or fitting and imposing responsibilities beyond an adult's settled commitments. Young persons can test the limits of adults' patience, humble adults with their candor, and demand that adults visit worlds they have either never imagined or from which they departed after their youth. Children can have adults talk and behave in ways both endearing and foolish, have adults relearn and revisit parts of their own lives that they might wish to forget, and have them attend to the grit and messiness of life that they would otherwise be able to control or avoid altogether. In short, children bring caring adults into new worlds of discovery and self-discovery and, in the process, test the virtues of impure agency.

Seen in these terms, the experience of caring for children is "agent-referring." Caregivers encounter their own capabilities and limits when interacting with children, capabilities and limits about which otherwise they would likely be oblivious. Lacking such interactions, adults' worlds would be more sanitary and controlled, less complicated, and riddled with fewer contingencies. Caregivers typically feel deeply implicated in the formation of children's lives, their development, and their trials and tribulations. The experience of caregiving in these and related ways involves what William F. May calls being "open to the unbidden."[31] Such openness, Sandel observes, "invites us to abide the unexpected, to live with dissonance, to reign in the impulse to control."[32] On this view children are less problems or predicaments to be solved than they are what Gabriel Marcel calls a "mystery," by which he means a problem in which the identity of the questioner is at issue.[33]

This agent-referring point is closely tied to an adult's experience of vulnerability when interacting with a young person—the experience of being incomplete and transformed by a close relationship with a child. This transformation, I propose, puts a caregiver in a child's debt, one that can be appropriately paid through expressions of gratitude. In this account the character of caregivers is marked by an *internal* connection to a young person's alterity. Caregivers are required to respond to children in ways that draw out new and different (adult) capabilities and, in the process, acquire unaccustomed skills in response to a child's needs. For this reason the debt has a moral dimension. Virtue is found or enhanced in the encounter with childhood difference, strangeness, and unpredictability. Caretakers must adapt themselves to children's needs, and in that process they become indebted to what a child offers (or demands of) adults. In this way caregivers' moral lives are conditioned by circumstances of luck. And for this reason we can plausibly describe a child as a gift for which one can be grateful.

To be sure, an adult's debt to such a gift is of a peculiar sort.[34] Typically we see debt as a condition that arises after we have been intentionally given or promised something for our benefit. We see a child's debt to caregiving adults precisely in those (donative) terms, as beneficiary to benefactor. As Kierkegaard reminds us, one comes into debt by receiving love.[35] Yet we can come into a debt for reasons that go beyond whether a putative benefactor's motives are an expression of goodwill. Consider, for example, a needy patient's debt of gratitude for receiving an anonymous organ donation. Typically, the recipient knows nothing of the donor's motives. At a minimum the recipient cannot impute benevolence on the part of the anonymous donor *to the recipient* as a basis for determining indebtedness. An anonymous donor's goodwill is diffuse and nonparticularized. Nonetheless, we typically assume that the needy patient stands in the donor's debt.

A caregiver's debt to a child is close to debts of this philanthropic sort insofar as it is not a function of a targeted act of beneficence. That said, a caring adult's debt has aspects that are not captured by the analogy of anonymous organ donation. In caregiving relationships a debt can arise not from a child's specific or diffuse benevolent motive but from a child's need to be benefited. Children tax adults with other-regarding, nonreciprocal demands. These demands are often nonnegotiable, moreover, given their urgency and necessity. A debt accrues here not from receiving but from having one's character marked by the requirement to care in unconditional ways.[36] Assuming that being "open to the unbidden" and having dispositions to give unconditionally are indeed good traits, we can say that children put caregiving adults in their debt.

Such a debt is unusual insofar as it arises in relation to someone who is not self-consciously giving. In that respect the debt is like and unlike one that accrues in cases of anonymous organ donation. Like the needy patient's debt to an anonymous donor, a caretaker's debt to a child arises not in response to a targeted act of beneficence. Unlike the patient's debt to an organ donor, however, an adult's debt to a child emerges from a demand instead of something akin to a contribution or sacrifice. In this respect a child's need for unconditional care might be seen as a contingent aspect of a caregiver's life akin to an act of grace. As an invitation for adults to acquire or develop virtue, it is something that they cannot control or initiate. In adults' caring relationships with children, a complex ethics of heterology unfolds: gift and demand can overlap.[37]

VOLITIONAL AND COGNITIVE AGENCY

So we have two moral streams with two different ontologies. The first uses the language of entitlement and duty. Whether we are thinking only of perfect duties or of imperfect ones as well, the first stream has deontological resonances. And, fitting as it seems to that tradition of thinking, it suggests a view of the self whose identity is fixed and bounded. It is the identity of an agent whose character is formed in such a way as to give unconditionally—without regard to his or her own interests. The truly moral agent, in this description, gives without expectations of return. Hence, my suggestion that we view this account as one of "principled caregiving."

The second stream speaks not in the language of entitlement and duty but in the language of teleology and virtue.[38] It refers not to the self as benevolent or beneficent but to the self as affected by the very challenge of being benevolent in unconditional ways. Here we are reminded that raising a child involves a kind of spiritual exercise—self-discipline in the cultivation of a kind of character. The focus here falls on how some of a caretakers' ends change, or must change, when they interact with children and on the ways such adults are put in a child's debt for contributing to the formation or reformation of their character.

Accompanying each of these ontologies is a corresponding account of agency that differs from the other in important respects. Sandel provides useful guidance here with his distinction between *volitional* and *cognitive* agency. In his mind these accounts differentiate between the philosophical anthropologies presumed by liberal and communitarian theories of justice, the ontologies of "unencumbered" and "encumbered" selves. My proposal is that these concepts function heuristically to help us sharpen the difference between the two streams of duty and debt with their corresponding ontologies of independence and interdependence.

Volitional agency refers to the experience of relating to our attachments as a matter of will. The basic question is, "How do I overcome the distance between what is me and what is mine, between self and other, given the premise that self and other are plural persons, individuated and distinct?" Moral principles mediate our decisions and actions as we overcome that distance. The key point is that the process is premised on a picture of each self as bounded off in advance. The question "What ends shall I choose, and how shall I choose them?" is obviously addressed to our powers of choice. The language of duty ensures that our volition is morally constrained and thus properly directed.

Cognitive agency refers to the experience of relating to our attachments as a matter of reflection. Here the task is not to overcome the divide between self and other, assuming selves as bounded in advance, but to *establish* boundaries between myself and my attachments given my intimate connection to them. Reflection, like principles, mediates in this process, but it does so by enabling us to detach and withdraw from our ends, not to draw closer. Here the picture is of the self as "at least partly unformed."[39] The question is not, What ends shall I choose? but rather, What kind of self am I? And this question is addressed not to the will but to the understanding. About the challenges of cognitive agency, Sandel writes: "The problem here [is] not the distance of the self from its ends, but rather the fact that the self, being unbounded in advance, [is] awash with possible purposes and ends, all impinging indiscriminately on its identity, threatening always to engulf it. The challenge to the agent [is] to sort out the limits or the boundaries of the self, to distinguish the subject from its situation, and so to forge its identity" (152). Relating to others on this account relies on powers of self-examination. Here our freedom turns not on choice but on internal analysis. "In reflexivity," Sandel notes, "the self turns its lights inward upon itself, making the self its own object of inquiry and reflection" (58).

Caregivers' debts to children are a function in part of children's capacity to prompt such self-examination. A child's otherness, invites—indeed requires—a caretaker to reflect on who he or she is and what he or she represents to a child. In that process the caring adult doesn't draw near so much as apart. Caregivers must ascertain what distinguishes "me from mine" and discover the boundaries that mark off what they value in the flux of contingency and inner feeling. Such adults thereby involve themselves in a reciprocal process of self-differentiation, moving from less-formed to more well-defined and bounded identities.

These accounts of agency enable us to see different ways in which caring adults relate to children. That is to say, volitional and cognitive agencies involve two kinds of deliberation. The first sort, Sandel notes, "attends to the desires of the agent alone," while the second "extends to the subject of desires and explores its identity." When we focus on our moral obligations, perfect and imperfect duties mediate our relationships with objects of desire and attachment, our children. Our attention is on what we owe them as recipients of benevolence and beneficence. But debts penetrate deeper. They point to how adults can be affected by children and thus move "further to reach the subject of desire" (161). Debts point not merely to the exercise of agency but to its reconstitution. The relationship becomes partly definitive of who one is. Hence my locution to capture this aspect of care: "constitutive caregiving."

Some philosophers, O'Neill foremost among them, argue that the experience of vulnerability deserves a greater role in moral theorizing. For O'Neill, however, vulnerability is a fact from which, or about which, we reason to arrive at principles of obligation as necessary moral laws: "Those with limited and variable capacities and capabilities *must* plan to rely in various ways on one another's capacities and capabilities for action, so *must* (if committed to universalizable inclusive principles) be committed to doing at least something to sustain one another's capacities and capabilities, hence committed to rejecting inclusive principles of indifference and neglect."[40]

On the second ontology that I have sketched, in contrast, vulnerability is less a premise from which to construct principles of morality that meet the test of consistency than a fact according to which we must understand the very essence of identity and personal relationships. It reveals something about the adult-child relationship that challenges deontic theorizing about the ethics of care.

I believe that these principled and constitutive notions of caregiving each describe palpable aspects of caring adults' interactions with children. There are some things that adults choose to do or not to do when caring for children, and that fact reminds us of volitional dimensions of caregiving and how desires are constrained by principles to care in unconditional ways. But caregivers' behavior is directed not only by principles but by changing conceptions of the self that being available to children requires of a care provider.[41] Those changes, and the adjustments they require, are catalyzed in no small way by the passage of a young person from infancy to childhood to adolescence and early adulthood.

ON RESPONSIBILITY

What began as a basic tension has now unfolded into an ontological divide that has corresponding agential, epistemological, and relational dimensions. As sovereigns and subjects, caring adults have relationships with children that seem fraught with layers of schizophrenia. I suspect that most caregivers live or have lived in these two universes of duty and debt, liberty and contingency, and independence and interdependence. For caring adults children pose a problem to be solved and a gift to our self-interpretations.

Yet we should ask whether these dual universes and the demands of residing in them are indeed so self-divisive. I believe that there is a way out of this kind of moral and ontological dualism, one in which we can affirm features of the divide to which I have brought us without sacrificing the integrity of agents who care for children. Finding that way requires us not to rethink obligation, as O'Neill asks us to do, but to revisit a more basic question, namely, how do we understand *responsibility*? That is to say, we can get beyond this tension between duty and debt, or at least ease it to tolerable levels, by situating it within a wider framework of responsibility—what I will call a prejuridical account of responsibility.

The key to this move is to identify two aspects of responsibility that typically are ignored in discussions of the concept. But before we move to that step in the argument, we should consider an obvious objection. There is a clear difference, one might claim, between my doing something and having something done to me, between *doing* and *happening*. More to the point, my argument has failed to mark how the difference between doing and happening relies on different accounts of the proper domain of moral accountability.[42] *Doing* focuses on actions within my power and assigns responsibility to conduct that I carry out under my knowledge and control. Things that *happen* to me, in contrast, put me in the position of patient instead of agent. Assigning responsibility to someone for events in which she is only passively "involved" may wrongly expand the domain of moral accountability. In such an expanded account, her responsibility would include actions that are done *to* her, as well as to actions done *by* her. One undesirable outcome of such a view is that it could lead to judgments that hold sufferers accountable for things done wrongly to them—to "blaming the victim."

A prejuridical view of responsibility enables us to get beyond this difficulty and yet consider moral aspects of agency, as well as of suffering. The point about prejuridical responsibility is to say that there is a morally relevant domain of experience that exists as a prior condition for considering matters for which we are directly accountable. That is to say, we can identify a realm of moral experience that avoids the temptation to attach blame or praise while nonetheless requiring us critically to reflect on our moral stance regarding factors that condition our agency. The key to understanding such an account of responsibility in these terms is to underscore its prejuridical quality. It is not constructed to establish criteria for passing favorable or unfavorable judgments about actions that we (or others) have performed. The concept provides a background set of assumptions for marking the horizon within which we blame, acquit, or praise someone.

As I noted above, understanding responsibility in this prejuridical way requires us to identify two aspects of responsibility that are typically ignored in discussions of the concept. Each of these ideas harks back to discussions of morality and agency by thinkers such as George Herbert Mead, Gabriel Marcel, and H. Richard Niebuhr.[43] First is the idea of *responsiveness*. My responsibility is an expression of a more fundamental background feature of moral experience, namely, that I am both an agent and a patient, an actor and a sufferer. My moral resources are tapped not only by the question, What ought I to do or be? but, more fundamentally, by the question, What is going on? In what circumstances do I find myself? How do these circumstances offer enabling and limiting conditions for my exercise of freedom? Our being is a matter, as Heidegger famously observed, of *Mitsein*, of being "in between" a variety of actors; social, cultural, and historical conditions; feelings; and discourse.[44]

Niebuhr is perhaps best known for his attempt to probe moral aspects of this picture of the self, one that moves beyond Heidegger's melodramatic notion that we are radically finite, contingent, and moving inexorably toward death. In Niebuhr's mind our contingency and finitude mean that the moral life is characterized less by independent initiative than by our interpretive responsiveness to agencies that circumscribe our conduct, enable our action, and act upon us. We are patients as much as agents, acted on as much as acting, and this complex dynamic of activity and receptivity is typically missed in teleological and deontological moral theories. Our first task in this account is not to determine what to do but how to make sense of situations in which we find ourselves invited or required to so act. Responsibility thus involves interpretation and anticipation, a dialogical sensibility of our interactive lives. "The idea . . . of responsibility," Niebuhr writes, "may summarily and abstractly be defined as the idea of an agent's action as a response to an action upon him in accordance with his interpretation of the latter action and with his expectation of response to his response; and all of this in a continuing community of agents." In this way Niebuhr proposed an alternative image for ethics, the image of us as "responders."[45]

This image has the advantage, in Niebuhr's mind, of making suffering a more pronounced aspect of ethical reflection. A central theme in a responsibility-oriented ethics, suffering is a feature of everyday life that is too easily overlooked in moral theory. The key point for Niebuhr and others of his ilk is to arrive at a paradigm for describing features of experience that capture our sense of vulnerability or of being acted upon: suffering in the sense of receiving or having to yield. Niebuhr writes: "It is in response to suffering that many and perhaps most people define themselves, take on character, develop their ethos."[46]

The second idea, in many ways corollary to the notion of responsiveness, is that responsibility entails not only accountability for our actions but, more fundamentally, *responsibility to* others.[47] This idea signals the more active side of a prejuridical account of responsibility. The change in the preposition, from *for* to *to*, is decisive. It draws attention away from morality conceived in juridical terms, where we sort out matters in terms of praise or blame. Responsibility *to* reminds us that our "thrownness" entails an intersubjective morality, one in which we come to make sense of experience in light of the exchange of meanings and messages that help to form our character.[48] For Niebuhr the idea of responsibility "holds in the center of attention the fundamentally social character of selfhood. To be a self in the presence of other selves is not a derivative experience but primordial."[49] To exercise responsibility for, we must first exercise responsiveness to a wider environment of discourse, agencies, and interests.

Adults who begin families provide an apt illustration of this point. The transition from being a nonparent to a parent demands a fundamental change in one's self-picture. Crossing the threshold from nonparental to parental status is a matter of acting as much as having to adapt one's character to demands that are placed before one. Put differently, the role of parenting involves not only making principled choices but also acquiring new patterns of self-interpretation. With this picture, then, we begin with a more capacious view of responsibility than is typically assumed. It is a concept according to which I understand myself as responsive and in dialogue, thrust into a matrix of forces and circumstances as a condition for acting on principles or pursuing certain ends. Such an account provides stage-setting or background conditions for specific instantiations of moral judgment.

* * *

In proposing that we think about agential, epistemological, and relational distinctions against the backdrop of an inchoate understanding of prejuridical responsibility, I am not proposing that we adopt the idea of responsibility as an overarching framework for moral theory or a principle from which to launch a particular decision-procedure to resolve moral quandaries.[50] My suggestion is more modest: that a prejuridical view of responsibility enables us to get over the ontological and moral divide to which I have devoted most of my remarks in this chapter. Understanding our lives as responsive to and in dialogue with others renders intelligible how we can care in both principled and constitutive ways that cohere with a more basic account of agential integrity. The unencumbered and encumbered self reposes against the backdrop of the responsible self. The image of us as "responders" enables us to grasp that caregivers' adherence to perfect and imperfect duties and their vulnerability to being transformed by relationships with children are pieces of a larger dynamic. That dynamic is not initially framed by the question "What are my appropriate duties or goals?" but instead by the question "What is the situation in which I am located and in which I am to be responsive to an other whose needs address me now?"

On these terms caring adults have duties and debts to children. The language of duty speaks to how children depend on adults; the language of debt speaks to how caring adults can depend on children. My central point is that we should not view these experiences of liberty and contingency as producing a moral and ontological dualism. Rather, we should see them as expressions of concerns and care that flow from the integrity of a dialogical self. However schizophrenic these universes of duty and debt might seem at first glance, they are joined by an understanding of caring adults as having inner connections to others in ways that require a sustained dialogue with them. That dialogue draws caregivers near to and apart from children, in an ongoing dialectic of availability and interpersonal individuation.

7

EVIL, FRIENDSHIP, AND ICONIC REALISM IN AUGUSTINE'S *CONFESSIONS*

The icon and the idol determine two manners of being . . . not two classes of beings.

—Jean-Luc Marion

EVIL'S CONUNDRUM

Children often become friends with their parents and family members, care providers, and fellow children in memorable and enduring ways. Friendships, during and after childhood, are special attachments that reveal something to us about ourselves and say something about us to others. In that respect a friendship is a speech-act, manifesting or proclaiming aspects of our desires and playing out various struggles between psyche and culture. In this chapter I want to examine friendship in some detail, returning to the ideas of Augustine to help clarify matters of human desire, attachment, and self-understanding. I want to explore how one of Augustine's childhood friendships performs precisely the sort of work that I identified in the previous chapter, namely, revealing something to him that he would not have otherwise known about himself—something about his desires, priorities, and ends. And, as chapter 4 makes plain, Augustine's account of love includes a set of broader metaphysical commitments on which the alterity of our attachments depends. The point holds for friendships as a subset of our loves. In Augustine's mind we need our friends to be truly other lest they become reflections of our own needs and desires. But our friends and intimates, he avows, are not obviously or readily available to us in their reality and otherness. Augustine claims that our friendships too easily become occasions for narcissism and imperialistic control without an organizing framework that secures their place within a wider order of being and desire.

I will take up these ideas by tying together Augustine's conceptions of friendship, alterity, and attachment in his classic work *Confessions*. I must do so from oblique angles, however, because the issue that Augustine takes up immediately in *Confessions* concerns not friendship but the nature of evil within the context of his psychological development and social relations. Early in *Confessions* Augustine offers two conceptual frameworks for understanding evil to organize the reader's understanding of his various tribulations.[1] One account provides a psychological explanation, focusing on the will's excessive attachment to earthly goods in its anxious desire to secure a permanent mooring in the sea of time and circumstance. According to Augustine, evil arises when we seek to overcome our fundamental lack as mortal creatures by attaching ourselves to changeable goods in excess of their quality and being. We confuse mutable for immutable goods, drawn as we are to objects of beauty that are finite and contingent in our restless quest for enduring happiness. In the process we elevate the value of temporal goods to a status they neither deserve nor can sustain. Augustine understands such desires as sinful because they are disordered. They fail to draw the correct measure in our commerce with the world and leave us unhappy and unsatisfied. Indeed, such pursuits of happiness are doomed to fail given that we have tethered our hopes to goods that are fated to decay.[2] Our desires will remain unquenched and our sense of internal order will remain off-kilter insofar as we fail to draw delight and direction from God as the Supreme Good. Confused about the qualitative difference between eternity and time, between unchanging and changing goods, we attach our loves to gifts of death (4.10.15). In these terms Augustine concludes the first book of *Confessions* after recounting his years of infancy and early youth: "In this lay my sin, that not in [God] was I seeking pleasures, distinctions and truth, but in myself and the rest of [God's] creatures, and so I fell headlong into pains, confusions and errors" (1.20.31).

This picture of desire provides Augustine a psychological explanation for why humans commit wrongdoing, an explanation that seeks to defend divine justice against Manichaean criticisms of Christian beliefs. According to Augustine, humanity, not God, is responsible for evil's existence in the world. Evil arises not from God's creation but from a will that turns away from God "and lapses into fornication"—an image that Augustine uses in *Confessions* to describe our defection from the Supreme Good in the quest to find happiness in more immediate and tangible realities (2.6.14). Desirous for security, anxious about mortality, we attach ourselves to temporal goods as if they were everlasting. We thereby turn the world into a theater of idols.

Augustine famously complicates this psychological account with his story of stealing pears in book 2 of *Confessions*. As an adolescent he conspired with friends to steal a neighbor's pears, a seemingly trivial act of vandalism to which Augustine attaches great significance.[3] He wonders what could have motivated him given that he had plenty of better pears immediately available to him. His answer only darkens the picture of evil that he has offered to that point in *Confessions*: he stole them for the sake of stealing itself. "There was no motive for my malice except malice,"[4] Augustine admits, adding, "I feasted on the sin, nothing else" (2.6.12). Other vices make motivational sense insofar as we seek out beauty in those acts, however counterfeit that beauty might be. But there was no beauty in stealing the pears—no good, the desire for which can explain the boys' theft. He asks, "To do what was wrong simply because it was wrong—could I have found pleasure in that?" (2.6.14). His answer connects the act to a metaphysical nullity: "From that theft . . . I found nothing to love" (2.8.16). Not even the "shadowy beauty with which even vice allures us" can explain his theft (2.6.12). To the idea that he loved not the theft but the camaraderie of those with whom he conspired, he sticks to this same point: the "gang-mentality too was a nothing" (2.8.16). In that "unfriendly form of friendship," he confesses, "I was greedy for another's loss without any desire on my part to gain anything or to settle a score" (2.9.17). It was deprivation—the privation of a good—and nothing more that drove Augustine and his friends to thievery. Explanations for such an action are wanting, as there was no substantive end to which the act could be aimed as a basis for moving the will.[5] Augustine rather aspired to divine-like sovereignty and freedom, uncreated and noncontingent—independent of any rational end to which his conduct might give account. He sought arbitrary liberty, liberty whose exercise was his alone to authorize. A narrative about what seems like a minor sin thus provides a conceptual window into evil's deeper mystery. For Augustine the ground of arbitrary, unmotivated evil in the will is a surd, dark and inaccessible, mute and irrational.[6] It is approachable by way of querying and approximation, but it finally defies human categories of psychological understanding.[7]

It is tempting to conclude that Augustine is either confused or equivocal about the relation between evil and human agency because he seems not to care about resolving the tensions between his explanatory and nonreductive accounts. The tension consists in an account of evil as motivated, prompted, and (improperly) ordered toward a finite good, on the one hand, and an account of evil as spontaneous, radically and arbitrarily free, and sui generis, on the other. Understood within the sweep of *Confessions*, however, the pear scene works less to overturn Augustine's psychological explanation than to segue into his second main account of evil, his ontological account, which he introduces in book 3. Understood ontologically, evil is a deficiency, a diminishment of good. Here we detect resonances between the ontology of evil and Augustine's nonreductive claim that the theft of pears and the gang mentality of his friends were each "a nothing." When we philosophize about evil in relation to "that which is" rather than in relation to human agency or "reasons for action," Augustine avows, we are to conceive of it in terms of the diminishment of being.

Here, too, Manichaean ideas provide a foil. When recalling his discussions with the Manichees about the origin of evil, Augustine notes that his efforts were frustrated by a picture of a deity that was "confined to a material form with hair and nails" (3.7.12). Tellingly, Augustine adds that a worldview "restricted to seeing material shapes with my eyes and imaginary forms in my mind" left him with "no inkling of what there could be in us which would give grounds for saying that we are made in the image of God" (3.7.12). More to the point, the idea of an anthropomorphic god offered no room for notions of immateriality and infinity, "present everywhere, as a spirit is, and as God is," as found in Platonic and Christian philosophy. A metaphysic understood as including immateriality and infinity enabled Augustine to conceive of evil not as some part of creation or as some substance that a material deity once fashioned. Rather, Augustine came to define evil as an absence, a *privatio boni*. He writes, "Evil is nothing but the diminishment of good to the point where nothing at all is left" (3.7.12).

How to harmonize these two accounts of evil, the psychological and the ontological, is not obvious. Augustine's psychological view seems not to track his ontological view; excess and deficiency describe altogether different manifestations of evil in the world. In general his psychological experience of desire seems disconnected from his philosophical theory of being—no small problem for a memoir that seeks to make sense of history and experience in light of the reasons behind them.[8] Regarding the topic of evil, this detachment borders on alienation. We are presented with metaphors that identify evil affections according to opposite extremes: inordinate love that is, at the same time, a kind of vacancy. In the *City of God* Augustine speaks to this point when he describes Adam's defection from God as "like trying to see darkness or to hear silence." Hence evil's conundrum: can we coherently say that we indeed love darkness and silence in our excessive attachment to light and sound, to color and melody? Augustine himself articulates this question when he asks, "Who can observe things that are lacking?" (*City of God* 12.7).

I want to explore this conundrum not in the abstract but as it helps to launch inquiry into Augustine's understanding of desire, friendship, and alterity in *Confessions*.[9] I do so not out of an idiosyncratic interest but because Augustine himself invites us down this path by turning from his discussions of evil in *Confessions* 1–3 to the story of the death of an unnamed childhood friend in book 4. Augustine narrates his feelings in response to this death as if he wants us not to untangle the inner tensions of the conundrum of evil but to grasp its potential to speak in religious and philosophical terms about friendship, moral psychology, and the epistemic aspects of virtue. During this phase of his life, Augustine's world was populated by idols, created by an anthropocentric imaginary, and driven by self-love known as *cupiditas*.[10] Reflections on death and friendship resume after his conversion in response to a second significant death, that of his mother, Monica, narrated in book 9. Here Augustine revisits love and the affections within a theocentric imaginary, one that leads him to repoetize friendship and to grieve in ways that express an altogether different emotional repertoire. At this later point in his life he mourns in ways that are iconic rather than idolatrous, motivated by a love of neighbor informed by *caritas*. An iconic, theocentric imaginary enables him to perceive mutable goods neither as temptations to excess nor as vessels of nullity but as disclosively real and truly other.

In what follows I will show how Augustine's conundrum of evil exposes the intertwining of psychological and ontological aspects of the materialist relation to the world and the narcissistic orientation to his friends that characterized his late adolescence and early adult life. For Augustine narcissism and idolatry are two sides of the same coin, forged together by the self as the reference point for conceiving of both God and neighbor. What is basic about such loves is that, as forms of projection, they cannot point beyond themselves to something more, only to something less.

But Augustine will leave us with more than a judgment about how not to love in *Confessions*. He will contrast the worldview he possessed as a Manichean with his ability, informed by a Platonized Christianity, to perceive mutable goods iconically. When viewed in this way, sensible phenomena point beyond themselves to enduring principles that secure temporal reality's objectivity and alterity, making that reality available to us independently of our desire to grasp it for confidence and control. Anticipating a theme of Iris Murdoch, Augustinian ethics emphasizes the importance of seeing reality as it is rather than as one wishes.[11] As I will show, in *Confessions* Augustine represents *caritas*, iconicity, and heterology as mutually supportive facets of mind and will. In a universe viewed iconically rather than idolatrously, mutable goods point beyond their surface beauty to objective values according to which they find meaning and provide order and direction to human affections. Desires can thereby become indexed against an order of things that is independent of human wishes and constructions. This order of things can serve to determine whether our desires, inexorably arising from the soul, are indeed desirable.

Noting that Augustine acquires what Donald Evans calls a different "onlook" can help us understand Augustine's conversion from *cupiditas* to *caritas*. As I indicated in my introduction, Evans describes an onlook as a matter of looking "on x as y."[12] According to Evans, having an onlook differs from having an opinion or abstract conceptualization of x; an onlook entails more than having a "perspective" on x. Onlooks rather involve us by way of feeling, posture, commitment, vision, and intentionality. Evans proposes five features of an onlook: (1) it is "commissive," reflecting a policy or an expression of intention; (2) it is autobiographical, involving the self both behaviorally and attitudinally; (3) it is expressive of feelings, which are logically connected to the words and ideas that shape an onlook; (4) it involves a posture toward the world—it is not neutral or detached; and (5) it has a "verdictive" component, such that looking "on x as y" means "placing x within a structure, organization, or scheme."[13] For Evans the commissive and verdictive aspects of an onlook are especially important. "In saying 'I look on x as y,'" he writes, "I commit myself to a policy of behavior and thought, and I register my decision that x is appropriately described as y; my utterance combines an undertaking with a judgment. . . . One undertakes to do certain things, viewing them or interpreting them in a certain way."[14]

Augustine's conversion meant acquiring an onlook that enabled him to see the world emancipated from his narcissistic tendency to assimilate it to himself—as if the world could be conceived (like a material deity) in his own image. In Augustine's early years his relation to the world is self-referring in a pejorative sense. *Caritas* brings in its wake an onlook toward the world in its alterity and, with that, its independent goodness. That gift of otherness, along with its ethical implications, is made plain in Augustine's recollection of Monica's death in book 9 of *Confessions*, for which the death of his childhood friend serves as a clear contrast.

Developing these claims and the connections among *cupiditas*, idolatry, and narcissism will require several steps. That discussion will prepare us to see how Augustine triangulates *caritas*, iconicity, and heterology as graced dispositions of the mind and will—as describing what it means to love the neighbor "in God." These ideas will also generate insights about vision, friendship, and virtue to which I will direct our attention. Augustine's grievous responses to the deaths of his friends provide a window into his more general understanding of what counts as real and how the virtuous mind and will recondition his onlook toward the world and his understanding of the self-other relationship. That is to say, his moments of grief point to different modes of feeling and friendship as well as to an epistemology of the real, the latter of which is often construed reductively in Augustinian ethics. I will seek to nuance that account before concluding. To explore these points, let us turn to Augustine's account of love, loss, and grief as he first describes them in *Confessions*.

CUPIDITAS, IDOLATRY, AND NARCISSISM

Augustine initially describes his unnamed friend in book 4 not in terms of particularities or peculiarities that mark him off as a distinct individual but in terms of the two friends' similarities. Indeed, the fact that Augustine fails to mention his friend's name—a signifier of individuation—is telling. Departicularized, the young man's *res* lacks a *signum*. The two men mirror each other in body, age, and outlook; what was important for Augustine was his friend's likeness, not his difference. The two shared the fact that they were "intellectually astray," agreeing about matters of superstition and myth on the basis of Augustine's persuasive rendering of Manichean ideas. But their friendship, while including a measure of unity and affection, fell short of "true friendship," in which people are bound fast in charity (4.4.7). Here we see echoes of Augustine's earlier concerns about an "unfriendly form of friendship" of the sort that he mentioned in book 2. What appears to make such bonding possible in Augustine's mind during this stage of his life is mimesis—the apparent identity of difference, the mutuality of self-imaging.

Indeed, the two young men's similarity is intense; their friendship is less a bonding of two distinct persons than an absorption of two souls into one, a reduction of identity—both personal and numerical. Augustine writes: "I felt that my soul and his had been but one soul in two bodies" (4.6.11).[15] Their relationship mimics in reverse the idea of Christ as two natures in one person; theirs is an inverted Christology, a parody of loss and exaltation. Equally important, the two friends are starkly codependent. "My soul could not bear to be without him," Augustine writes; at his friend's bedside "I did not leave him, so closely we were dependent on each other" (4.4.8). Augustine "shrank from life with loathing" because the idea of his friend's death left him with the unendurable consequence of being "only half alive" (4.6.11). For these reasons the idea of difference—and, with that, objectivity and individuation—left Augustine deeply addled. When confronted by his friend's apparent embrace of Christianity after having been baptized in a state of unconsciousness, Augustine felt "aghast and troubled" by his friend's "new found independence." Yet Augustine deferred telling his friend his true thoughts about his baptism on the premise that "once he was in normal health again I would be able to do what I liked with him" (4.4.8).

Augustine's grief at the passing of his friend was considerable: "I was beset by misery and bereft of my joy," he writes. "I was miserable, and miserable too is everyone whose mind is chained by friendship with mortal things, and is torn apart by their loss, and then becomes aware of the misery that it was even before it lost them" (4.6.11). His grief's lack of order smacks of the inordinate value he attached to earthbound goods. But exactly what Augustine grieved and how his grief arose from a wider repertoire of emotions are not obvious. Plainly, it was not the loss of the friend that distressed him. His grief was diffuse and self-indulgent. He confesses that it was not out of hope that his friend would "come back" that he mourned. It was rather the tide of emotion itself on which Augustine centered his being. "Weeping alone brought me solace," he writes; sorrow substituted for his friend "as the only comfort of my soul" (4.4.9). He experienced a loss of self in his sadness, a profound sense of despair. "I wept very bitterly and found repose in the bitterness," he admits (4.6.11). A species of *cupiditas*, Augustine's grief had himself as its object.

Augustine's mourning became melancholia, driven not (as Freud would have it) by internalized self-reproach but by obsessive narcissism and myopia. According to Freud, mourning is a feeling of sadness and distress upon the experience of loss. But Freudian melancholia is more: it is a pathological expression of mourning—the internalization of dejection such that the grieving person experiences a radical, punishing loss of self-esteem. "The distinguishing mental features of melancholia," Freud writes, "are a profoundly painful dejection, abrogation of interest in the outside world, loss of the capacity to love, inhibition of all activity, and a lowering of the self-regarding feelings to a degree that finds utterance in self-reproaches and self-revilings, and culminates in a delusional expectation of punishment."[16] Freudian melancholics believe that they deserve the grievous state they are in. They blame the victim—themselves. But Augustine did not blame himself for his friend's death. Rather, he experienced his friend's death passively, as if death had visited him. That feature of Augustine's response mirrored the Manichean god in whom he believed—a deity whose goodness was, in the words of Peter Brown, "singularly passive and ineffective."[17]

Augustine's melancholia prompted a new level of self-examination, crucial to his narrative's forward movement. In the wake of his friend's death, he writes, "I had become a great enigma to myself, and I questioned my soul, demanding why it was so sorrowful and why it so disquieted me" (4.4.9). He found one answer in his psychological account of evil, focusing as it does on excessive attachments to earthbound loves. It was his friend, "whom I loved as though he would never die, and still more amazed that I could go on living myself when he was dead—I who had been like another self to him" (4.6.11). So he exclaims, "Woe to the madness which thinks to cherish human beings as though more than human!" (4.7.12).

From this confession Augustine turns in book 4 to a discussion of beauty, about which he also wrote a nonextant treatise. "What is it that entices and attracts us in the things we love?" he asks. He answers that we are drawn to objects of beauty, understood as having beauty in themselves and in their relations to other things: "In material objects there was both a quality inherent in the whole—beauty—and a different quality that was seemly in something that was harmoniously adapted to something else, as a part of the body to the whole, or a sandal to the foot" (4.13.20). Yet despite his ability to conceptualize a formal reality—the fact of harmony in relationships—Augustine could not grasp incorporeal reality as such; he "looked instead toward shapes and colors and distended mass" (4.15.24). Given his experience of peace as concord and vice as discord, he came to the conclusion that unity was the supreme good and "in disintegration some indefinable substance of irrational life was to be found, which was the essence of supreme evil" (4.15.24).[18] His conception of the deity, in turn, remained within an anthropocentric imaginary, unable to reckon with ideas in terms other than human. He thus addresses God: "I was prepared even to think you changeable rather than admit that I was not what you are. . . . I persisted in walking after things that had no existence either in you or in me or in any creature, ideas not created for me by your truth but invented in material shape by my own vanity" (4.15.26).

Augustine's onlook toward sensible reality as described in book 4 was idolatrous, understanding that term in more than the familiar sense of elevating temporal realities to the status of eternal goods. The notion of an idol also bespeaks an epistemology, a way of seeing. As Jean-Luc Marion writes, "The gaze makes the idol, not the idol the gaze."[19] More specifically, as Margaret R. Miles observes, throughout his work Augustine presents us with two epistemologies regarding sensible reality, one that accepts sensible things as they present themselves to him, another that refuses to take their reality as given and looks beyond their surface appearance to probe their "structure, their essence, and the source of their existence."[20] That is to say, with Augustine, as with Plato, everything depends on the terms according to which we receive and interrogate sensible reality. For Augustine, Miles notes, "a sensible object can be either a distraction or an indispensable starting point. Nothing about the object determines whether it will act as one or the other."[21] At the heart of the distinction between an idolatrous epistemology and an iconic one is whether one accepts surface beauty as sufficient or whether one questions it to discern more enduring principles underlying it. "The idol absorbs the gaze, dazzling it and saturating it with the visible, ravishing it," Miles writes.[22] It thereby contracts rather than expands the idolater's range and depth of vision. An idol is a *res* without an objective *signum*. The icon, in contrast, "summons the gaze to surpass itself by never freezing on the visible, since the visible only presents itself here in view of the invisible."[23] In this way the icon makes sensible reality available on terms that are not established by the observer's own desires or interests. In book 10 of *Confessions* Augustine illustrates how the iconic imagination works:

> And what is this? I put my question to the earth, and it replied, "I am not he"; I questioned everything it held, and they confessed the same. I questioned the sea and the great deep, and the teeming live creatures that crawl, and they replied, "We are not God; seek higher." . . . To the sky I put my question, to sun, moon, and stars, but they denied me:

"We are not the God you seek." And to all things which stood around the portals of my flesh I said, "Tell me of my God. You are not he, but tell me something of him." (*Confessions* 10.6.9)

Augustine asks these questions on certain epistemological assumptions. He presumes to determine the significance of sensible reality not by jettisoning that reality but by interrogating it and thereby discerning more fundamental facts about it. In this case sensible reality discloses a difference between creation and Creator, a fundamental distinction according to which the former points to how the latter creates and sustains that which is.[24] Such are the illuminations of the iconic epistemology whereby the mind is summoned by sense perception to surpass itself.

Augustine's discourse on beauty, desire, and the imagination in book 4 reminds us that his theological ethics includes an aesthetic. That discourse, moreover, is connected to his preceding recollections regarding the death of his unnamed friend. Overwrought with despair, he admits to finding no repose in God "because when I thought about you [God], you did not seem to be anything solid or firm. For what I thought of was not you at all; an empty fantasy and my own error were my god" (4.7.12). Augustine was thus unable to see the world as manifesting anything, as having any beauty. The world was empty of potential for hierophany. Full of his own desires, Augustine saw not presence but absence, a privation of that for which he looked. "My eyes sought [my beloved] everywhere," he writes, "but he was missing; I hated all things because they held him not, and could no more say to me, 'Look, here he comes!' as they had been wont to do in this lifetime when he had been away" (4.4.9). Within a universe populated only by decaying goods, sensible reality becomes dark and incommunicative. Augustine thus confesses his first reaction to his friend's passing: "Black grief closed over my heart and wherever I looked I saw only death" (4.4.9).

Taken as a whole, Augustine's memory of friendship and death draws on both sides of evil's conundrum to illustrate the motivations lying behind his friendship along with the visual and emotional poverty to which it led. That is to say, his affection was marked by both excess and deficiency. Augustine is saying that these two concepts of evil, far from being opposite extremes, reinforce each other. Loving too much, according to Augustine, is not to love at all. On that basis he can say that evil's dual manifestation indeed illumines rather than obscures his experience.

It is nonetheless tempting to think that Augustine's narrative of death and grief hews to only one side of evil's conundrum regarding this "unfriendly form of friendship." James Wetzel offers one such reading in his commentary on book 4 of *Confessions*. Wetzel rightly observes that in book 4 Augustine describes "having done his level best to love a mortal human being as if he were immortal and presumably divine." But Wetzel adds to this point: "The result is not that Augustine loved something of lesser value in place of something greater, but that he lost touch with the man he was loving and so had no way to take in the magnitude of his loss."[25] Eric Gregory repeats this idea when he writes that Augustine confesses "not that he loved too much, but that he did not really love (either the world or God) at all."[26] But these remarks fly in the face of Augustine's frank admission that he had loved his friend "as though he would never die"—cherishing "human beings as though more than human!" The contrast that Wetzel and Gregory present between loving a lesser value in place of something greater and losing touch with one's beloved is a false one.

Augustine makes plain that his excessive attachment was driven by a desire to see his own image, to address his own needs on the premise that he and his friend were alike. That tendency drew from his habit of homologizing reality to himself, of projecting an anthropomorphic account of power and sovereignty onto the cosmos. As a consequence he loved his friend as a private possession rather than as someone whose goodness could be shared. Here, echoes of the narrative of theft in book 2 resonate: Augustine first understood his friendship as something to be stolen and privately kept, depriving others of a basic goodness. In his desires, as in his metaphysics, Augustine used himself as his reference point. As he strives to make plain throughout *Confessions*, how we love is a matter of the wider frameworks that shape the imagination.

Augustine's youthful friendship had its own inner poverty, the inability to embrace another who was independent and beyond his control. Indeed, it is not clear that Augustine lost touch with his friend because it is not clear that his friend was ever available to him as something other than created in his own likeness. Here, Wetzel is correct to say that Augustine's failure to love his friend in God "left his friend to be the creature of Augustine's fears and desires."[27] Augustine's point is that loving too much and loving not at all are paradoxically one and the same. He underscores that idea by confessing in book 4 that he was left thinking not about how his beloved's passing meant the loss of someone who had an independent set of interests and promise. Augustine's focus was rather on what his friend's death meant for his own self-absorbed concerns about his mortality. He admits to being "amazed that I could go on living myself when he was dead—I who had been like another self to him." Equally important, Augustine experiences his friend's death as the taking of a possession that he had previously stolen for himself. Echoing the pear scene, he reports that he was as much the object as the subject of theft: "I believe that the more that I loved him, the more I hated death, which had taken him from me; I hated it as a hideous enemy, and feared it, and pictured it as ready to devour all human beings, since it had been able to make away with him" (4.6.11).

LOVING THE NEIGHBOR "IN GOD"

Earlier I stated that book 4 of *Confessions* stands in clear contrast with book 9, in which Augustine recounts his feelings in response to the death of Monica. Book 9 tells us of the deaths of several friends: Monica, Verecundus, Nebridius, and his son, Adeodatus. Notably, Monica is named only once in *Confessions*, a signification that Augustine reserves for his prayers at the conclusion of that book.[28] We can only speculate about why Augustine refrains from reflecting at length on his friendships—a crucial feature of his life[29]—until they cease. Starkly, strangely, Augustine frequently associates friendship with death. Perhaps friendship represents the most intimate kind of temporal good whose passing reveals the power of time over earthbound things—the subject of Augustine's probing philosophical analysis in book 11 of *Confessions*. Perhaps friendship is too easily underwritten by *eros*, a love that becomes extinguished in its satisfaction.[30] Perhaps, in a Heideggerian fashion, friendship is part of Augustine's being-in-the-world, only to be reflected on when it is disrupted or taken away. Whatever might explain the association, it is impossible to ignore how death shadows intimate friendships throughout Augustine's memoir.

In book 9 Augustine, his mother, his brother, his friend Alypius, and others retire to a villa in Cassiciacum to live together. Their ideal was to form a community of Christian celibates. At this point in his life Augustine slowly removes himself from his work as a rhetorician, after which time he is baptized, thereby redeeming his mother's prayers and patience. He tells of how his mother was a subservient wife, dutiful and capable of correction about matters of continence. Indeed, he goes to great lengths to describe her ordinariness and her sinfulness, a point to which I will soon return.

In Ostia, before their planned departure for Africa, they experience a shared epiphany, the third and climactic vision in the book. The hierophany they experienced is prompted by their shared reflection about the communion of saints. They then launch their sojourn by discussing the great pleasures of eternal life as opposed to earthly existence. Augustine writes:

> Our colloquy led us to the point where the pleasures of the body's senses, however intense and in however brilliant a material light enjoyed, seemed unworthy not merely of comparison but even of remembrance beside the joy of that life, and we lifted ourselves in longing yet more ardent toward *That Which Is*, and step by step traversed all bodily creatures and heaven itself, whence sun and moon and stars shed their light upon the earth. Higher still we mounted by inward thought and wondering discourse on your works, and we arrived at the summit of our own minds; and this too we transcended, to touch that land of never-failing plenty where you pasture Israel forever with the food of truth. Life there is the Wisdom through whom all these things are made, and all others that have been or ever will be; but Wisdom herself is not made: she is as she always has been and will be forever. Rather should we say that in her there is no "has been" or "will be," but only being, for she is eternal, but past and future do not belong to eternity. And as we talked and panted for it, we just touched the edge of it by the utmost leap of our hearts; then, sighing and unsatisfied, we left the first-fruits of our spirit captive there, and returned to the noise of articulate speech, where a word has beginning and end. (9.10.24)

Theirs is not a vision of the sort that Augustine describes in book 7 of *Confessions*. There, Augustine ascends in Plotinian fashion from the experience of sensible objects to experiencing the condition of reflection itself, attaining "*That Which Is*, in the flash of one tremulous glance" (7.17.23). That epiphany was solitary and intellectual, and it brought no informational content. Equally important, Augustine was unable to hold fast to what he had attained, drawn back as he was to sensible experience by time and habit. Nor is the Ostian vision like Augustine's conversion epiphany in book 8, which was mediated by the verbal communication of the word of God and included theological content but was mediated to him alone, in solitude. With Monica Augustine's experience has less to do with light or hearing than with relative silence. And, of course, in this instance Augustine is not alone: he embarks on a journey with a fellow traveler. Together they imagine the tumult of human flesh, earthly life, human dreams, and the soul all falling silent, along with "every tongue, and every sign, and whatever is subject to transience." In that silence, he writes, "if anyone listens, all these things will tell him, 'We did not make ourselves, he made us who abides forever'" (9.10.25). Augustine and Monica are informed that they are dependent, not self-originating; they are finite beings, not Being itself. There is a qualitative distinction between Creator and creation, between time and eternity.

Here, as in the passage from book 10 noted above, Augustine expresses an iconic epistemology. Sensible reality points beyond itself to its permanent structure and its source of origination. Equally important, it communicates content. Their vision is Christological and sacramental, wherein they encounter the Logos through whom they believe creation is made and structured. Within such a framework earthly goods have relative value and death itself is not to be feared. Soon we are told that Monica herself neither despaired over her imminent death nor worried about the whereabouts of her burial. Addressing God, Augustine writes of Monica: "[She] desired only to be remembered at your altar, where she had served you with never a day's absence. From that altar, as she knew, the holy Victim is made available to us, he through whom the record of debt that stood against us was annulled. . . . To the sacrament of that ransom-price your handmaid made fast her soul with the bonds of faith" (9.13.36).

After Monica's death Augustine reports that he does not weep at her funeral, but he does weep later, and he brings the narrative portion of *Confessions* to an end by expressing anxiety about whether his grief is excessive or inappropriate. "I found comfort in weeping before you about her and for her, about myself and for myself," he writes (9.12.33). At that critical juncture he asks publicly to confess and begs his readers not to judge him harshly for his grief surrounding Monica's passing. But whether excessive or not, Augustine's grief is clearly not the feeling of despair of the sort he experienced with the passing of his unnamed friend. His grief draws on an altogether different emotional repertoire, focusing on Monica's future life rather than on his own fated mortality. "Let no one wrench her away from your protection," Augustine implores in his prayers after her passing.[31]

Equally important, in describing her life, Augustine sees Monica not only as a devout and obedient Christian but also as a sinner like himself in need of mercy and forgiveness—in her ordinariness as well as in her saintliness. Once again we find him homologizing reality to himself, but this time the likeness is mediated by theological concepts of sin and reconciliation rather than the terms of this-worldly agreements such as he enjoyed with his unnamed friend. Like his boyhood friendship, Augustine's relationship with his mother was one of intense bonding, a cleaving of two into one. But his attachment to Monica is not cast in terms of having "one soul in two bodies." He rather describes the bonding as between two distinct persons. "For there had been but one life," he writes of his relationship with Monica, "woven out of mine and hers" (9.12.30).

Augustine's grief and subsequent prayer are presented to the reader as public matters. His account presumes an iconic epistemology that allows for a gaze that moves beyond mere appearances—private appearances—to a more expansive and potentially inclusive vision. Moreover, such an epistemology has moral and interpersonal implications. Monica was not a victim to the theft wrought by death, someone kept from him and others as fate's private possession. Indeed, Augustine openly pleads with his readers to pray for her salvation. In his grief Augustine mourns not for himself, nor about himself, but on her behalf. That the epiphany in Ostia is prompted by a reflection about the communion of saints seems hardly accidental. He prays for God to forgive her and accept her into the eternal community. In other words Augustine mourns for her hopefully and charitably, with an eye to her independent interests. His grief has been reordered, structured in ways that reflect a turn from vice to virtue—from *cupiditas* to *caritas*—enabling him to mourn and love his mother for her own sake. He is able to see Monica as other, independent of his own projections and points of self-reference.

Augustine's response to his mother's death enables us to grasp how *caritas*, iconicity, and heterology are triangulated into an altogether new onlook in *Confessions*. As Kim Paffenroth observes, all of Augustine's friendships in book 9 of *Confessions* demonstrate that he "has learned how to have earthly loves that lead to and include God, rather than distract from knowledge or love of him."[32] Paffenroth's remark recalls a comment Augustine makes while reflecting on the death of his boyhood friend: "Blessed is he who loves you, and loves his friend in you" (4.9.14)— loving in a way that he admits he could not do as a youth. But exactly what it means to love a neighbor "in God" is seldom clear in Augustine's work. I propose that thinking in terms of an onlook that triangulates *caritas*, iconicity, and heterology provides an important clue. Together these ideas structure Augustine's graced dispositions of mind and will.

Metaphysically, Augustine views sensible reality within a Platonized Christianity as pointing beyond itself and as structured by a timeless principle that has been rendered available to humanity through reason and revelation. Epistemologically, that fact provides a framework that enables him to grasp reality in its own right, independently of his anxious wishes or projections. Normatively, knowledge of these facts, empowered by grace, turns the mind and will away from themselves to others' needs and interests, however ordinary or extraordinary. Monica's death, the apex of the narrative portion of *Confessions*, thereby provides a clear contrast to the "unfriendly form of friendship" interpreted by way of evil's conundrum in book 4.

FRIENDSHIP: FROM HAVING TO BEING

Augustine's ethics of alterity—love of the other for her own sake—is part of a broader project of seeing the world in a way that is freed from an anthropocentric imaginary. He stands with Iris Murdoch, who writes, "It is a *task* to come to see the world as it is."[33] But for Augustine, "to see the world as it is" requires an onlook that is both a gift and a task. It is a task insofar as it requires a reorientation of human tendencies and dispositions; it is a gift insofar as it arises from the mind and will transformed by grace.

One outcome of Augustine's conversion from *cupiditas* to *caritas* is the ability to experience friendship in a radically altered way: the conversion from having a friend to being a friend. In book 4 Augustine anguishes over the friend he lost, an experience conditioned by the idea of friendship as a possession. In that context death is a thief, stealing what it can in a seemingly heedless and arbitrary way. In book 9 Augustine's grief over his mother's passing is conditioned not by the thought of possession but by what it means to be a friend to her in her final days and in her death. He changes from experiencing friendship passively to experiencing it actively. Put another way, Augustine's friendship with Monica was a matter of *being* rather than *having*, to recall a distinction from Gabriel Marcel's phenomenology.[34] For Marcel, being and having point to two different ways in which we relate to other things and persons. *Having* pertains to things or persons that are external to me—possessions that I can lose, dispose of, or use instrumentally.[35] *Being* corresponds to relationships that exist on different terms. In relationships of being the encounter with another is not one of externality but of mutuality, a matter of participation. With being, as opposed to having, one makes another's ends one's own. Relationships of being are embodied, constitutive of who one is. They thus differ from relationships in which we proceed "on a level where . . . the contrast between within and without retains a meaning."[36] Strikingly, Augustine describes his relationship with Monica, as I noted earlier, in precisely such embodied terms: "For there had been but one life, woven out of mine and hers."

The fact of embodiment suggests that Augustine's onlook undergoes a dramatic transformation from one in which God and world are seen in anthropomorphic and bodily terms to one in which to be embodied rather means to be related-in-difference. Augustine is thereby enabled to love temporal goods that exist across a range of differentiated possibilities.[37] To love is to share something fundamental to one's being in a way that respects difference. Augustine can thus distinguish himself from his mother not by keeping part of his life secret or by running from her as he had rebelliously done in his youth. With his relationship reframed and thus reconstituted, he achieves distance from her in terms of ontology, not volition.[38] He poeticizes Monica by situating her within a new set of relationships, describing her as a member of the "brethren" under God rather than as his mother and as a "fellow-citizen" in the "eternal Jerusalem" (9.13.37). In that context Augustine asks God not to allow death to steal Monica but to preserve her for those willing to pray for her and remember her.[39] All of this reflects how his focus has shifted from what he putatively gained from friendship to what he can offer it.

Augustine's reflections on the death of Monica suggest that he understands friendship's flow of giving and receiving in a new way. However much Augustine's intersubjectivity emphasizes mutuality and reciprocity, it remains the case that he represents true friendship—embodied friendship—as more a matter of giving than yearning to receive. To be a friend according to Augustine's description requires unconditional self-giving and availability. In this way he reveals features of love that serve as the antitype to evil's conundrum: desire can be appropriately attached to the goods of another when it is freed to see those goods on their own life-giving terms.

Moving across the sweep of *Confessions*, we should now see that Augustine leaves us with stark alternatives when it comes to friendship and the emotions. We are presented with the idea of self-centered and idolatrous love which is not true love at all—both too much and not enough. The alternative to that love is Christian love of the neighbor "in God," in which an encounter with the beloved triangulates *caritas*, iconicity, and heterology. The corrective to narcissism for Augustine resides in an onlook toward the world shaped by Platonized Christianity and empowered by graced excellences.

That fact seems to provide little by way of hope or direction for non-Christians or non-Platonic Christians when it comes to an ethics of friendship and love. For non-Augustinians, to see the world as it is may be more of a task than a gift of any sort. But Augustine may leave his readers with more general, workable ideas about friendship and love if we step back from the particulars of *Confessions*. His key insight is that the apparent love of another can be fraught with immediacy and, with that, a lack of differentiation and respect for the beloved as an individual with claims of her own. True friendship requires a framework for interpreting the meaning of one's love on terms that are meaningful to the lover as well as the beloved. Augustine finds in Platonic Christianity an instance of what, he suggests, we all need in order to have true love: a horizon within which we contextualize our loves and acquire the ability to value our friends on terms that they can esteem. That is to say, Augustine believes that in order to befriend another, we must understand what friendship *is* as a prior condition. We cannot grasp friendship inductively or intuitively, building up a general account of friendship based on serial relationships that we acquire over time; we need a wider onlook according to which we are able to perceive what a particular friendship signifies.[40] Such an onlook performs work that is similar to that of a moral rule: as action-guiding, it helps the agent set the future.[41] If one's onlook is to enable us to grasp the otherness of our friends, moreover, it cannot be conceived in our own image. That is to say, our experience of any particular friend requires the mediation of an interpretive framework according to which that relationship makes sense on terms other than those we concoct for our own advantage.

GRIEF AND VIRTUE

Augustine's two accounts of grief in *Confessions* should remind us of the great importance of grief as a concept in moral psychology among classical writers in the West. It should also instruct us (more importantly, at least from Augustine's point of view) that there are ways of mourning that can be either morally undesirable or commendable. Mourning need not devolve into Freudian melancholia. Rather, grief can be marked by either virtue or vice. This presupposes the idea that, for Augustine, emotions are not merely raw feelings, akin to itches or throbs. Emotions are instead moral responses, registering what we value through the passions. Our feelings thus presuppose objects that, when properly perceived, prevent us from being self-indulgent or from attaching ourselves inordinately to them. Augustine writes: "In general, as a man's will is attracted to or repelled in accordance with the varied character of different objects which are pursued or shunned, so it changes and turns into feelings of various kinds" (*City of God* 14.6). Emotions express an interpretation of an event, the embrace or loss of an objective good. Ideally, dejection is the expression of a properly ordered appreciation, for we would not feel a loss were we not previously attached to something genuinely valuable that has now ceased to be.

Viewing grief as potentially virtuous seems odd, of course, given our tendency to understand virtue in positive terms, as ennobling or self-enhancing. Certainly the classical tradition on which Augustine relied associated the virtues with a good and genuinely happy life. But that fact should not prevent us from seeing how responses to loss and disconnection can also be expressions of moral excellence. Virtue, Aristotle reminds us, means feeling pleasure and pain in the right manner. Schooled in the virtues, we should feel "at the right times, with reference to the right objects, towards the right people, with the right motive, and in the right way," as he says of strong and noble character.[42] Casting similar ideas in Christian terms, Augustine writes: "Citizens of the Holy City of God, as they live by God's standards in the pilgrimage of this present life, feel fear and desire, pain and gladness in conformity with the holy Scriptures and sound doctrine; and because their love is right, all these feelings are right in them" (*City of God* 14.9).

All of this is to say that grief, like other emotions, is conditioned by the order of love that underlies it. Augustine's sadness as recalled in books 4 and 9 of *Confessions* tells him something about how he orders his loves. He understands desires and affections as depending on how an agent is ordered—either toward oneself or God. As he writes in the *City of God*: "And so a rightly directed will is love in a good sense and a perverted will is love in a bad sense. Therefore a love which strains after the possession of a loved object is desire; and the love which possesses and enjoys that object is joy. The love that shuns what opposes it is fear, while the love that feels that opposition when it happens is grief." In this account the desirability of our desires is a function of our deeper loves. Augustine thus concludes: "Consequently, these feelings are bad, if the love is bad, and good if the love is good" (*City of God* 14.7).

Moreover, and equally important, Augustine's account of virtue tells us something about the complexity of desire and freedom in the moral

life. Here evil's conundrum in *Confessions* provides an instructive coun-
terpoint. Books 1 through 3 teach us that vice combines inordinate desire
with arbitrary freedom—freedom that aspires to be Godlike, uncreated
and noncontingent. Vice is thus both excessive and empty, as I noted
earlier. Virtue contrasts in a parallel, twofold sense: desirable desires are
ordered by charity, which, in turn, enables the self to choose in ways that
are free from an image of the self as uncreated. All of this is made possible by the infusion of charity spread across the heart—a Pauline notion
that courses throughout much of Augustine's work. In *The Spirit and
the Letter* Augustine writes about the proper and improper motives of
moral action with this compound idea regarding desire and freedom in
mind: "And if the commandment be done through fear of penalty and
not through love of righteousness, it is done in the temper of servitude
not freedom—and therefore it is not done at all. For there is no good fruit
which does not rise from the root of charity. The man in whom is the faith
that works through love, begins to delight in the law of God after the
inward man, and that delight is a gift not of the letter but of the spirit."[43]
For Augustine proper action is carried out in a way that is free from the
self's worries about its own welfare, liberated from fear of failing or falling short. As well, it is done with affections that are themselves shaped by
charity, enabling one to delight in the Good for its own sake.

With that more general account in mind we can say that, for Augustine, charitable grief—*dolor* informed by *caritas*—is grief that is free
from anxiety about the self's own mortality and contingency, grief that
is capable of imagining in loving terms what is fitting to another who has
died. Virtuous grief thus repoeticizes death, viewing it not as a *finis* but
as having a *telos*, beyond the appearances of mutability and mortality.

AUGUSTINIAN REALISM REVISITED

If I am correct about how *caritas*, iconicity, and heterology triangulate in
Augustine's ethics of love and friendship, then we need to rethink what is
commonly meant by the notion of "Augustinian realism." As influentially
defined by Reinhold Niebuhr, realism in the Augustinian tradition typically positions itself between various forms of idealism, on the one hand,

and cynicism, on the other. Realism for Niebuhr aspires toward aims that reckon soberly with facts about human will-to-power, sloth, and fallibility while refusing to accept such facts as the final word about what can and should be imaginatively explored in the exercise of human responsibility. As Niebuhr puts it in "Augustine's Political Realism":

> The terms "idealism" and "realism" are not analogous in political and metaphysical theory; and they are certainly not as precise in political as in metaphysical theory. In political and moral theory "realism" denotes the disposition to take all factors in a social and political situation, which offer resistance to established norms, into account, particularly the factors of self-interest and power. . . . "Idealism" is in the esteem of its proponents, characterized by loyalty to moral norms and ideals, rather than to self-interest, whether individual or collective. It is, in the opinion of its critics, characterized by a disposition to ignore or be indifferent to the forces in human life which offer resistance to universally valid ideals and norms.[44]

Realism, as it has come to be known in theological ethics, requires normative reasoning to reckon with certain indisputable facts about social life that reveal the limits of our will and understanding along with our dependence on and vulnerability to powers that lie beyond our control. Augustine's account of human nature, Niebuhr avowed, underwrites that line of thinking.

The core feature of Augustinian realism understood in this way is its commitment to accounting, especially accounting with the conditions of finitude within which human action occurs. Describing Niebuhr's brand of realism, Robin W. Lovin writes, "Realism implies *recognition of the limits* of purely moral solutions to political problems and calls for *attention* to the realities that shape social, political, and economic conflicts."[45] On that account the realist must be responsive to certain incorrigible facts about history and human proclivities along the way toward developing social criticism. Such facts embarrass those who aspire, optimistically, to utopian ideals of love, social harmony, and equality. Failures in social criticism to account for what Niebuhr understood as moral recalcitrance disqualify such criticism from passing as plausibly realistic.

Realism according to this description counsels against this-worldly moral perfectionism.

Augustinian realism of the iconic variety I have described differs from the political realism made famous by Niebuhr. Iconic realism need not deny that human action occurs within conditions of finitude for which social critics and activists must account. It puts limits on the human desire to conceive of reality by way of a narcissistic and anthropocentric imaginary. But iconic realism identifies the practical limits of human thought and action not as a condition for being realistic *but as a consequence*. Iconic realism insists that knowledge of the conditions of finitude is mediated by onlooks that presuppose and express epistemic and volitional dispositions that situate human desire and action within a broader, theocentric framework. Augustinian moral and social criticism thus requires habits of interpretation as much as it does accounting.[46] For Augustine the task of interpretation was assisted by Platonic philosophy and its understanding of the relationship between sensible reality and its underlying, permanent structure.

For the iconic realist, what presents itself as real must indeed include a proper reckoning with human limitations but not only those that frustrate moral perfectionism. The real is first and foremost a matter of what becomes available, donatively, through proper disclosure. As I have noted, for the iconic realist, gaining knowledge of reality is a gift as well as a task. Regarding matters of this chapter—friendship and intimate relationships—the real thus frees the iconic realist from forming relationships driven by anxious needs and imperious attachments. That is to say, iconic realism makes possible the disclosure of the other on terms over which we have neither sovereignty nor control.[47] Understood in this way, iconic realism is as much about freeing us to grasp what is possible as it is attentive to binding us to the constraints within which our imaginations should do their work. Augustine's iconic realism thus enables a manner of being-in-the-world according to which we may love on terms that are attuned to the neighbor in her or his alterity. It enables us to be available to others, experienced as gifts that we are thereby open to receive.

PART III

COMMUNITIES

AND

INSTITUTIONS

8

JUST WAR, CIVIC VIRTUE, AND DEMOCRATIC SOCIAL CRITICISM

AUGUSTINIAN REFLECTIONS

Europe since the outbreak of war has been comparatively quiet, and in consequence indiscriminate hatred has been far less noticeable than it was during the last war. But as the conflict grows more serious, we cannot expect this state of things to last; already there is less moderation in public speeches and private conversation than at the outset. Worse, there is already suppression and distortion of truth "in the interests of the state"; and news has become propaganda and advocacy of a case. One man's lies are not justified because they contradict another's.

—G. E. M. Anscombe, "The Justice of the Present War Examined"

SOCIAL CRITICISM, POLITICAL MORALITY, AND ORDINARY LIFE

Augustine's idea that we tend to view others according to our own self-serving desires informs his political thinking no less than his understanding of interpersonal morality. In fact, Augustine would likely query the boundary that we often erect between personal and public morality, focusing as he does on how virtues and vices mediate between self and society. Those mediations blur the boundaries of psyche and culture and guide the reciprocal dynamics that shape them.

In this chapter I examine how Augustine's concerns about an anthropocentric and narcissistic imaginary inform his contributions to political morality and to the ethics of war. His idea that we must be responsive to the neighbor in his or her alterity, as we will see, aims to restrain collective passions during times of cultural and national conflict. In personal as in political affairs Augustine offers a religiously informed heterological ethics to guide human attachments during times of political strife.

To develop these ideas I must proceed, once again, by way of oblique angles. I want to begin by attending to one of Augustine's signature contributions to morality, namely, the idea that war can, in principle, be just. This notion, developed over the centuries into what is known as just-war doctrine, presupposes that war is not a morally neutral institution but is rather one that is subject to norms and values.[1] Enshrined in just-war doctrine, those norms and values enable citizens to ask about war's cause, authority, aims, timing, and risks, along with war's proper and improper methods. Certainly one of our beliefs about political morality today is that ordinary citizens have a stake in this doctrine during times of war or rumors of war. That is because just-war doctrine provides a moral framework not only for political leaders and military officials but also for socially responsible citizens in public life. The underlying assumption is that the ethics of war can inform everyday judgments about political and military decisions and that being a responsible citizen means holding oneself and public officials accountable to just-war criteria. For citizens who concern themselves with the morality and prudence of military action, just-war tenets provide a basis for analysis, criticism, and approval or dissent.

Of course I am talking about moral and political discourse in democratic societies, where political sovereignty and authority lie in the will of the people. Democracies both presuppose and, ideally, habituate the practice of social criticism, by which I mean the practice of assessing policy, leadership, and customs as these shape the direction of institutions and aspirations of public culture. Democratic societies view such criticism as part of the franchise assigned to the office of citizenship. Just-war doctrine is significant, in other words, for moral as well as for political reasons. Citizens have a stake in just-war doctrine insofar as they have a share in popular sovereignty and want to make a difference in the moral quality of the *res publica*.

I suspect that this connection between just-war doctrine and democratic social criticism is self-evident in political contexts where the ethics of war is a matter of public deliberation and debate. One of my aims in this chapter is to indicate why that connection is less obvious than it seems and how it might be strengthened. G. E. M. Anscombe, writing at the outbreak of England's entry into the Second World War, captures some of the issues to which I want to call attention, namely, the cultural effects of war on the dispositions and affections of a nation's populace. War both relies on and inspires expressions of political allegiance, but it can also tempt citizens toward xenophobic self-deception and disrespect of others—modern versions of the psychological and moral problems to which Augustine regularly called attention in his work.[2] Echoing these ideas, Anscombe described England in this way in 1939: "There is a widespread tendency to make what our country chooses to do, the criterion of what must be done, and to call this patriotism."[3] That tendency can impoverish practical reasoning and conscientious self-analysis, leading Anscombe to instruct her readers that "it is our duty to resist passion and to consider carefully whether all conditions of a just war are satisfied in this present war."[4] Further, emotions surrounding war are typically highly charged and, as such, can produce distorted or reified memories that are transmitted to future generations in the ongoing formation of political identity. Given that "already men are talking of Germany as a pariah nation" and that Germany must "henceforth be kept down and never allowed to become powerful again," it seemed inconceivable to Anscombe that anything like a lasting peace would be possible.[5] Seen in these terms, war can be an occasion for vice insofar as it can generate passions that weaken a commitment to personal and public justice. Not infrequently we unfairly valorize ourselves and our friends, and derogate others, during international conflict. Anscombe's concerns about the relationship of character, war, and civil society are regrettably rare in the ethics of international affairs, a fact evidenced in the gap between just-war doctrine and matters of civic virtue, political membership, and democratic social criticism.

Readers familiar with the just-war tradition know that the explanation for this gap is genealogical: just-war doctrine arose in illiberal, undemocratic contexts, in which the idea of popular sovereignty was either inconceivable or anathema to those who conceived it. Yet even if we set aside this problem of political pedigree, a more pressing problem lurks: we (generally) deploy just-war doctrine chiefly as a morality of statecraft,[6] a set of norms according to which political elites and military soldiers should manage the destruction of war, not as a morality for assessing the sentiments and passions of citizens more broadly. As currently understood, just-war doctrine's connections to the virtues of democratic social criticism remain undertheorized. The tradition's intellectual and cultural origins are premodern, and its potential role as guide for the individual conscience stands removed from the network of cultural and psychological forces that bear directly on political identity and the civic imagination. While it is true that just-war criteria can instruct the private citizen's moral deliberations,[7] little work has been done to indicate how and on what terms the ethics of war might inform and guide the powerful longings of patriotism and the existential features of membership in an ongoing political community—cultural forces and desires that press upon the workings of conscience. This connection—or lack thereof—between the ethics of war and the desires that animate a common life is of no small importance given the just-war tradition's idea that the good of political community is desirable enough to defend with lethal violence if necessary.

Another way to put this point is to say that the ethics of war presumes a psychology and sociology.[8] Given the powerful emotions that animate a common life, it would seem necessary for just-war doctrine to function self-reflexively vis-à-vis the shared desires and values to which it is attached. In the moral life generally, and during war in particular, it is vital to determine whether our desires are indeed desirable. War excites passion, and passion sometimes undermines practical reason. This means that moral judgment guided by the just-war tradition is precarious. Moral discourse about war can slip from functioning as a critical, reflective idiom to an idiom of rationalization regarding political decisions and military practices in war. The ethics of war thus requires a kind of moral steadiness in relation to the feelings that enliven the political community and the institutions that serve human needs and aspirations. It must affirm the good of community while resisting the temptation to assign that good absolute value lest it fall prey to political expedience or self-righteousness, along with their penchant for cost-benefit analysis and instrumental reasoning "in the interests of the state."[9]

The need to articulate self-reflexive features of just-war doctrine suggests two ideas, the desirability of which I will stipulate here. One stipulation says that the ethics of war ought to inform and build on the habits of civic virtue—that it should provide a framework not only for forming policy and practice but also for forming (or reforming) citizens' political character over time. With that in mind I want to develop a connection between just-war tenets and a corporate, popular "sense of justice," as John Rawls designates it.[10] I will thus present an argument about virtues that dispose us toward prophetic social criticism—virtues that draw from and augment the virtue of justice and strengthen moral resolve in the face of political power.

This concern about character opens up a second idea: the connection between dispositions and the wider culture that shapes them. What is lacking in just-war discourse is attention to the cultural forces that inform, and often corrode, expressions of courage and a commitment to fairness in times of national duress. On that score we must attend to how social location affects our perceptions of ourselves and others. Because our affections are shaped by ethos and culture, it behooves us to consider how cultural images and political rhetoric bear on the imagination, feelings, and "habits of the heart."[11] That is to say, given the dynamic relationship between character and culture, moral assessment of the former cannot overlook the quality of the latter.[12] We must therefore interrogate how cultures ask their members to imagine themselves and their opponents when they consider putative claims to justice in the recourse to war.

With these points in mind I will make the following argument: as a moral framework for democratic social critics, just-war doctrine cannot ignore the workings of the imagination, along with its cultural influences, as those bear on the formation of character, the exercise of practical reason, and civic virtue in the polis. The killing, sacrifice, and death involved in war pose deep questions about meaning and loyalty. And for that reason questions about the stakes of war involve psychological and sociological dimensions that can be easily overlooked when war's morality is viewed as a matter of political statecraft alone.

In this chapter I want to address connections between just-war doctrine and civic virtue, the dynamics of culture and character, and the habits of democratic social criticism in light of my previously expressed interest in thinking about ethics and ordinary life. My argument in this chapter will unfold in four parts. My organizing idea will take up concerns about the effects of war on public culture with an eye toward expanding just-war doctrine's potential as a practical morality in civil society. To do that, I will first revisit Augustine's account of the morality of killing in order to reconnect just-war tradition to a theory of the virtues. Along the way I will correct a widespread misunderstanding about Augustine, namely, that he justifies war as an expression of Christian beneficence to protect innocent persons at risk. Second, I will consider virtue and the emotions to indicate why we cannot omit attention to the dynamic relationship between character and culture, between the private and public formation of the virtues. In passing I will note why that relationship helps us understand that considerations of war's morality must subsume not only matters of political statecraft but also the moral character of culture and the responsibility to assess it. Third, I propose three specific civic virtues that should be indexed to just-war doctrine in the context of modern, liberal democracies: the dispositions of self-restraint, critical self-analysis, and openness to deliberate publicly about moral matters in a context of cultural pluralism. I will indicate briefly how these virtues have concrete implications for popular consent, dissent, and decisions about whether to participate in war. I will conclude by noting that just-war doctrine involves a spiritual exercise—an ascesis—demanding that political elites and ordinary citizens discipline their attitudes, practices, and representations of the other according to the demands of respect and fairness— including respect for outsiders whose interests may not be one's own. That point will take us to an odd and controversial idea that harks back to Augustine, namely, that virtue—including political virtue—is grounded in the practice of confession and the habituation of what Paul Ricoeur suggestively calls a "just memory."[13] I will elaborate on that idea as I conclude the chapter.

The outcome of this discussion will be to conceive of just-war doctrine as a component in a larger theoretical apparatus, namely, *just-war morality*. Just-war doctrine is often deontic and criteria-driven, providing norms for assessing political policy and military action. The tendency to view the doctrine in these terms is understandable given its account of war as a "rule-governed activity."[14] Seen in this way, just-war tenets function as a supplement (and potential corrective) to legality and, more important, as an apology for morality against the doctrine's chief rival in social ethics, namely, political realism. Developed with an eye to rules and principles, just-war doctrine naturally inclines us to consider the dignity of individuals and the rights of states in conflict situations.

Viewed only in deontic terms, however, just-war doctrine too easily produces a "checklist" approach to the ethics of war, in which practical reasoning becomes a matter of assessing discrete acts against a set of disembodied criteria. Just-war morality implies a wider framework according to which we view the application of just-war criteria as an exercise of civic virtue and properly habituated social criticism. On these terms we can say that the ethics of war implicates matters of embodied practical reason, desire, and political identity. And for that reason it sharpens our moral attention on the political obligations of ordinary citizens before, during, and after war. Or so I will argue in the interpretive and constructive account that follows.

AUGUSTINE ON VIRTUE AND KILLING

I want to pursue this more expansive account of just-war morality by revisiting Augustine's ethics of desire and killing in self-defense and war. I do so because the just-war tradition traces its origins to Augustine and because he so clearly focuses on moral psychology, the affections, and human motivation in his discussion of killing.[15] Augustine frames his approach to homicide not in terms of applying moral norms to particular acts but in terms of assessing the effects of killing on the agent who performs it. He reminds us that the morality of actions must consider not only how one's action affects the well-being of others but also how one's action affects oneself. Augustinian morality in this sense is "agent-referring."

Summarizing his views about homicide in a letter written c. 397, Augustine states: "I do not approve of this, unless one happen[s] to be a soldier or public functionary acting, not for himself, but in defense of others or of the city in which he resides, if he act[s] according to the commission lawfully given him, and in the manner becoming his office."[16]

Here Augustine forbids private individuals from killing in self-defense but allows public officials to kill in defense of themselves and their community. He clarifies his views later in the *City of God*: "When a soldier kills a man in obedience to the legitimate authority under which he served, he is not chargeable with murder by the laws of his country; in fact he is chargeable with insubordination and mutiny if he refuses. But if he did it of his own accord, on his own authority, he would be liable for the charge of homicide. Thus he is punished if he did it without orders for the same reason that he will be punished if he refuses when ordered."[17] Note that Augustine's permission of public killing is not premised on the idea that love requires Christians to assume risks to help others, especially the weak, in need. That idea takes its origins from Augustine's teacher, Ambrose, and owes its influence today to Paul Ramsey, a follower of Augustine in several respects.[18] Love indeed informs Augustine's ethics of homicide, but not to justify coercive force as an expression of care or selfless protection of the innocent.

For Augustine, love is a virtuous desire when it disposes us to order our actions to their proper ends for their own sake.[19] We distort Augustinian thinking by confusing the virtue of love with acts of beneficence or by importing the deontic language of agape into a theological eudaimonism structured by the virtue of *caritas*. Augustine focuses not on principles instructing us to protect another from danger but on how our dispositions and attachments are organized in relation to various ends and how we affect ourselves through ordered or disordered activity. "Whatever you injure," Augustine remarks about acting in hatred, "you injure outwardly; notice what injury you do to yourself."[20] The evil posed by killing bears on one's character. That is to say, one key question for Augustine concerns the goods to which one assigns value and which provide the horizon for meaning and identity.

According to Augustine, those who kill in private self-defense act for "those things which can be lost against their will, and which they should therefore not love."[21] Self-defensive killing means, among other things, loving ourselves in excess and degrading ourselves in the process. Such killing implicates us in a disordered set of attachments according to which we rank the good of the mortal body above the value of the immortal soul and the value of the neighbor. About life in the body, Augustine writes, "perhaps one might doubt whether life is somehow taken from the soul when the body is slain. But if it can be taken away, it is of little value; and if it cannot, there is nothing to fear."[22] According to Augustine, killing in private self-defense necessarily implies excessive attachment to the transitory good of bodily life.

Killing in defense of the common good by public officers acting within the parameters of their official responsibilities is different. Augustine writes, "The natural order which seeks the peace of mankind, ordains that the monarch should have the power of undertaking war if he thinks it advisable, and that the soldiers should perform their military duties in behalf of peace and safety of the community."[23] He describes acts of justified homicide as "exceptions to the law against killing, made by the authority of God himself."[24] In Augustine's mind, especially during the latter part of his career, political life serves real, objective goods that can be defended in ways that allow for proportionate ordering of loves and commitments.[25] The public order embodies an image or replication of harmony—less perfect than the ideal, heavenly city, but providing a (relatively) good harmony nonetheless. The heavenly city—or "that part of it which is on pilgrimage in this condition of mortality, and which lives on the basis of faith—does not hesitate to obey the laws of the earthly city by which those things which are designed for the support of this mortal life are regulated; and the purpose of this obedience is that, since this mortal condition is shared by both cities, a harmony may be preserved between them in things that are relevant to this condition."[26] The earthly city serves a relative good, necessary for members of the heavenly city on their pilgrimage to their final destination. Accordingly, persons whose loves are properly ordered may attach relative value to the good that political life is meant to secure. Augustine writes, "[God] has given to mankind certain good things suitable to this life. These are: temporal peace, in proportion to the short span of mortal life—the peace that consists in bodily health and soundness, and in fellowship with one's kind; and everything necessary to safeguard or recover this peace."[27]

This account of the relative, instrumental good of political life leads Augustine to view its defense by public officials as justifiable. For Augustine the use of lethal force poses fewer dangers to the ordering of an individual's attachments when his actions are mediated by role responsibilities and organized toward the protection of the common good. Killing is less intimate for soldiers than for private persons insofar as it is carried out as a duty of public office. For that reason homicide can be more detached and disinterested—ordered by interests that go beyond a private person's immediate loves to include the commonweal. Augustine writes: "A soldier who kills the enemy is acting as an agent of the law, so he can easily perform his duty without inordinate desire."[28]

Augustine thus assigns fewer restrictions to public officials using violence in defense of the corporate body than to individuals who use force in defense of the private, individual body. The danger of disordered attachment appears greater to him in the latter case than in the former. That is to say, excessive attachment to bodily, mortal life is a greater temptation for private persons in relation to themselves than it is for public officials who act on behalf of the body politic.

This is not to suggest that one cannot commit wrongdoing as a public officer. For Augustine the real evil in war is not injury and death but "love of violence, revengeful cruelty, fierce and implacable enmity, wild resistance, and the lust for power."[29] Though justifiable in principle, war is also an occasion for concupiscence and the vice of *libido dominandi*. Soldiers and their commanders might act not in pursuit of justice but from a will-to-power. Their actions can become disordered by interests that swing wide from the virtues of fairness, prudence, temperance, and courage. These interests are real temptations, but in Augustine's view they can be resisted. And herein lies one key difference in his mind between private and public killing. For the private person excessive attachment to temporal goods is a *necessary* feature of private self-defensive violence. For the public official or soldier, in contrast, excessive attachment to temporal goods is only a *contingent* feature of violent action.

Understanding Augustine's ethics of homicide properly, then, means placing it within a wider framework of moral psychology and social roles, focusing on desire, the order of our attachments, and the temptations that such attachments pose in private and public life. We get nowhere reading Augustine's theological ethics until we understand that, for him, the good is prior to the right. In his ethics of killing it is crucial to grasp how homicide raises questions about one's internal psychic harmony, the ordering of one's loves. Homicide might derive from a lack of harmony and peace

from within. Peace within the soul is the sine qua non of peaceful relationships, relationships that are rightly ordered according to natural purposes
and patterns.[30]

Regarding the morality of soldiering, Augustine interprets the love
command to apply to the internal dispositions of public officers who are
commissioned to defend the common good. Augustinian love constrains:
public officers are not to act out of vengeance or a lust for cruelty, but they
are otherwise authorized to use force on behalf of the good of political
life. Attention to the duties of public office, individual interiority, and the
needs of the commonweal mediate Augustine's understanding of biblical
teaching. This is especially true regarding Jesus's command to "resist not
evil"—a command that would appear to prohibit all uses of violence.
That account of the love command, Augustine writes, pertains not to "a
bodily action, but an inward disposition. The sacred seat of virtue is the
heart."[31] The concepts of public responsibility, dispositional morality, and
the common good structure Augustine's account of social responsibility
and provide the framework for his interpretation of Jesus's command.
That structure provides rational concepts according to which Augustine
translates the teachings of Christian faith into the ethics of killing in
private and public life.[32]

Does Augustine authorize the use of force as an expression of neighbor love? This view is widely held among interpreters of Augustine and
the just-war tradition, but it courts confusion. The general idea is that
Augustine justifies killing when it aims to protect those who are otherwise helpless; such protection is an expression of Christian charity. Oliver
O'Donovan writes along these lines: "Augustine's famous letter to Boniface treats the obligation of military action as an obligation of love to
the neighbor."[33] Similarly, the U.S. Catholic bishops state that, according
to Augustine, "war arose from disordered ambitions, but it could also
be used . . . to restrain evil and protect the innocent. The classic case
which illustrated his view was the use of lethal force to prevent aggression
against innocent victims. Faced with the fact of attack on the innocent,
the presumption that we do no harm, even to our enemy, yielded to the
command to love understood as the need to restrain an enemy who would
injure the innocent."[34] The same idea finds its way into a letter signed by
sixty scholars and public figures, "What We're Fighting For." There we

read that "the primary moral justification for war is to protect innocent people from certain harm. Augustine . . . argues (echoing Socrates) that it is better for the Christian as an individual to suffer harm rather than to commit it." The authors then ask, "But is the morally responsible person also required, or even permitted, to make for *other* innocent persons a commitment to non-self-defense? For Augustine, and for the broader just war tradition, the answer is no. If one has compelling evidence that innocent people who are in no position to protect themselves will be grievously harmed unless coercive force is used to stop the aggressor, then the moral principle of love of neighbor calls us to the use of force."[35]

Augustine never articulates his justification of war in these terms. In the letter to Boniface to which O'Donovan refers, Augustine makes no connection between love and the duty to perform military service. He makes the more modest admonition that Boniface "not think that no one who serves as a soldier, using arms for warfare, can be acceptable to God."[36] The proper aim of soldiering is not to carry out a duty to the helpless neighbor but to secure peace through war, which must be waged only as a necessity. Indeed, Augustine speaks as if love as an exercise of will lies outside the bounds of war: "It ought to be necessity, and not your will, that destroys an enemy who is fighting you."[37] Claiming that proper recourse to military action arises as an expression of neighbor love goes beyond the plain meaning of Augustine's text.

Augustine's core position is that the use of force is justified in response to a grievance for the sake of civic peace and order when carried out lawfully by proper authorities. (In one letter, to the public official Macedonius, Augustine allows for forceful action by a private citizen to kill in self-defense, but in that case he is imagining a wayfarer outside the bounds of civic order and public authority—a traveler who kills a robber.)[38] Augustine nowhere justifies war as an expression of beneficent love in his various writings and discussions of war, such as *City of God*. Rather, as I indicated above, a just war operates in the service of peace, understood as including rightly ordered relationships between parts and wholes. The just warrior acts to defend or restore peace-as-order, not to protect the innocent neighbor selflessly, when carrying out violent acts.

Stated differently, Augustine justifies killing as a rightly ordered action toward defending the common good by public officials.[39] It bears repeating that the key to understanding Augustine's position is not a moral theory of duty, in which the right is prior to the good, but a broader, teleological ethical theory and moral psychology with a focal concern for psychic and social order. For Augustine, disordered attachments are illusory and dangerous. They are illusory because they mean putting oneself at the center of one's loyalties and, equally problematic for Augustine, allowing oneself to be the sole arbiter and center of value. Such are the dangers of the sin of pride: ignoring the ontological distinction between eternity and time, Creator and creation. Disordered attachments become dangerous because overstepping the boundary between Creator and creation leads us naturally to violate boundaries that structure our common life. Such internal disharmony leads to the problem the Greeks understood as *pleonexia*—grasping for power and advantage in order to overcome our fear about losing transitory objects of attachment. Confusing the distinction between temporal and eternal goods leads us to ignore the boundaries that properly separate persons from each other and that enable us to grasp our individuality and our differences. Hence the connection between theology, psychology, and morality in Augustine's discussion of homicide and the moral life more generally. When we privilege ourselves and our temporal needs, we are prone, anxiously and apprehensively, to overreach. For Augustine boundaries are both metaphysical and moral.[40]

Augustine's attention to the proper ordering of values and attachments directly informs his practical ethics of war. In that context one requirement is to avoid killing out of motives that mirror how unjust warriors behave. That is to say, the central danger from an Augustinian standpoint is imitating the wrong paradigm of action, falling prey to what might be called disordered *mimesis*. War for Augustine is a consequence of sin insofar as it is instigated by a lust for power and a partial remedy for sin when carried out justly.[41] Soldiers who kill out of "love of violence, revengeful cruelty, fierce and implacable enmity, wild resistance, and the lust for power" mimic the injustice that they are supposed to remedy and implicate themselves in the prideful evil they are commissioned to resist. Their character is diminished by the same disordered loyalties that motivate the actions of their (unjust) opponents. Soldiers who obey orders, in contrast, put aside their own judgments and attachments and act apart from their unmediated interests. Killing that is mediated by obedient submission to authority canalizes the aggressive passions of warriors in combat. Augustine writes: "For the good would even wage war with mercy, were it possible, with the aim of taming unrestrained passions and destroying vices that ought, under a just rule, to be uprooted or suppressed."[42] Indeed, Augustine believes that soldiers who obey orders are blameless if they commit wrongdoing at the behest of their superiors.[43]

For Augustine the soldier's ethic is a virtue ethic—one of psychic restraint, respect for boundaries, and orderly submission in the service of justice. Just war for Augustine operates in part within a penal and restorative paradigm—to punish wrongdoing, reset the balance upset by injustice, and restore a just and peaceable order.[44] But about the connections between virtue and other political offices, such as citizenship, Augustine offers us little guidance. As John M. Rist notes, "Augustine's attitude [toward political activity] is conditioned by the non-democratic principle that most people have no kind of official status as *de facto* public officials. He leaves little room for the authority and powers of the ordinary individual simply as a citizen, a member of society."[45] Perhaps because the empire was crumbling as he was writing the *City of God*, Augustine directed little attention to citizens' political responsibilities to the *res publica*. Augustine's political ethic is thus incomplete, for it ignores the vast space between the private morality of individuals and the public morality of soldiers, princes, and emperors. Attention to "orders of creation" that diversify public life would have to wait until Luther to gain a hearing, and even that hearing provides only a general sketch of the spheres and roles that naturally mediate human freedom and desire in civil society.

We must therefore expand Augustine's political morality to subsume a wider range of political responsibilities and practices. For that project his ideas provide a start. Indeed, as I hope to show, his ideas provide fruitful points of departure for considering the ethical dimensions of, and connections between, death, memory, and the desires that animate public culture. He reminds us that the morality of war is, in part, a morality of desire and love and that human attachments can be rightly ordered when they stand within a network of differentiated relationships and institutional responsibilities. That fact alone ought to alert us to the importance of the affections and how they are mediated by social processes and cultural norms.

For Augustine the commandment to love is not simple and straightforward; it is structured by our social affiliations and our natural interactions. However distant Augustine's views of citizen morality might seem, his ideas of moral formation have much to teach. So let us consider the synergism between culture and the affections as these ideas help shape an understanding of moral formation (and deformation) in the *res publica*.

WAR, THE AFFECTIONS, AND CIVIC VIRTUE

War typically arouses feelings of indignation and mourning—indignation at the injustices that surround one or both sides in war, mourning for the loss of life and goods associated with forming a common life. Doubtless for that reason Augustine described even a just war as marked by "heartfelt grief."[46] Indignation and mourning are more complicated than "unpleasant" or "uncomfortable" sentiments alone; they express esteem for what has been lost or what has been unjustly put at risk: security, friendship, peace, freedom, community, natural habitat. As I discussed in the previous chapter, Augustine makes a similar point about the emotions when he poignantly describes his feelings in response to his friend's death in book 4 of *Confessions* and, later in that same work, when he grieves the death of his mother.[47] Augustine's deep and anxious mourning tells him something about how he orders his loves—about whether they are virtuous or not.[48] Underlying that worry is the fact that, in Augustinian moral psychology, emotions are not merely raw feelings. They are moral responses, registering what we value through the passions. Our feelings thus presuppose norms that, properly recognized, prevent us from self-indulgence or inordinate attachment to worldly objects. Augustine writes: "In general, as a man's will is attracted to or repelled in accordance with the various character of different objects which are pursued or shunned, so it changes and turns into feelings of various kinds."[49] Emotions themselves are not a problem for Augustine; they express an interpretation of an event, the embrace or loss of an objective good. Ideally, indignation or mourning are forms of properly ordered appreciation, for we would not feel a loss were we not previously attached to something genuinely valuable that has now ceased to be.

Augustine would add that our affections are not merely individualistic; they are intersubjective and attach themselves to political and collective goods (among other shareable values). We "feel together" in ways that led Augustine to be keenly attentive to the moral quality of his friendships, as well as to matters that bear on a common life. "The life of a city is inevitably a social life," he writes.[50] He expressed these ideas most famously in his account of what constitutes a people. For Augustine, we understand a "people" to be an "association of rational beings united by a common agreement on the objects of their love" (*City of God* 19.24). Unity is experienced dialogically and intersubjectively, for which love and desire provide the social glue. Hence the fact that citizens in the *res publica* justifiably worry about injury to their attachments when injustice occurs— injury to their common goods, cherished traditions, and political values. For Augustine these goods are legitimate objects of attachment insofar as they furnish essential conditions of human freedom.

Grief about the loss of such goods is one way to express a sense of their importance. At the same time, grief's emotional and practical consequences can be morally precarious. They can produce a thirst for "revengeful cruelty, fierce and implacable enmity, wild resistance, and the lust for power" unless reformed by the virtues. For that reason alone the experience of collective indignation and mourning should require persons to assess their own society's conduct, hoping that what is done to others in response to a grievance is not an occasion for further misery. Actions that flow from the emotions should not be the cause of others' moral indignation. This is one reason to be concerned about justice— justice to ourselves and to others. For Augustine our sentiments should be constrained by fairness; we should not expect others to endure injustice any more than we do. Pride, "the perverted imitation of God[,] . . . hates a fellowship of equality under God, and seeks to impose its own dominion on fellow men" (*City of God* 19.12). Without properly ordered love the conditions necessary for such equality and fellowship are elusive. With that idea in mind Augustine rebukes the Romans in these terms: "As to the objects of that people's love—both in the earliest times and in subsequent periods—and the morality of that people as it proceeded to bloody strife of parties and then to the social and civil wars, and corrupted and disrupted that very unity which is, as it were, the health of a people—for all this we have the witness of history" (*City of God* 19.24).

Describing the affections in moral terms takes note of the fact that they are shaped by cultural influences. It is no stretch for Augustine to describe the emotions, as Paul Lauritzen does, as a "kind of cultural artifact."[51] Emotions cannot occur outside of a horizon of expectations, a moral world in which our conduct is indexed against a hierarchy of values. The quality of the emotions, says Augustine, lies in "the character of a man's will. If the will is wrongly directed, the emotions will be wrong; if the will is right, the emotions will not only be blameless, but praiseworthy" (*City of God* 14.6). In this way emotions are for Augustine rule-governed and depend on a wider system of shared meanings according to which the will directs itself. Emotions are expressions of agency shaped by standards of value, what Charles Taylor calls norms of "strong evaluation."[52] Such norms articulate goods toward which persons order their commitments and from which they derive their bases for self-interpretation.

This account also indicates that the emotions are learned. As culturally mediated, they are transmitted by those who powerfully articulate a society's standards of value. We gain a sense of how to interpret, respond to, and remember life's contingencies with the aid of culture's norms. Because our emotions are shaped by ethos and culture, it behooves us to consider how cultural images and political rhetoric bear on the imagination. That is to say, given the dynamic relationship between character and culture, moral assessment of the former cannot overlook the quality of the latter. It is therefore necessary to evaluate how cultures ask their members to imagine themselves and their opponents when they consider recourse to war. For these (broad) Augustinian reasons we can posit an ethics of heterology: cultural representations of the other should be subject to moral evaluation insofar as they condition, and perhaps corrupt, one's affective sense of what others are due.

The good of justice both issues from and helps to discipline the affections, enabling citizens to respond well to war's moral challenges to individual and collective character. Put differently, the collective experience of the emotions points to the importance of the virtues, especially civic virtue. Virtue refers to rightly ordered habits that incline us to act and feel in certain ways. Equally important, and often overlooked in moral theory, virtues have a political as well as a personal quality; they pertain to public and private life. They thus provide normative terms for informing and disciplining human feelings as we move from intimate into less personal settings.

Civic virtue consists of our dispositions toward and loyalty to the commonweal, typically requiring us to subordinate personal good to civic good when the two conflict.[53] The ideal of civic virtue holds great importance in the tradition of civic republicanism that traces its beginnings to Cicero. In that tradition true excellences are dispositions that incline an agent toward the common good. Augustine's own attitude toward civic virtue, to be sure, was ambivalent. He believed that civic virtue as practiced by the Romans was a counterfeit excellence. In his estimation Rome was founded and fueled by a love for glory. About Roman political history he writes, "It was this greed for praise, this passion for glory, that gave rise to those marvelous achievements, which were, no doubt, praiseworthy and glorious in men's estimation" (City of God 5.12).

Augustine's critique works less to discount civic virtue as a moral ideal than to dispute its goodness in the hands of the Romans. Indeed, his evaluation works on the assumption that civic virtue is a good that was honored in the breach. We should thus view the City of God in its entirety as a treatise on civic virtue given Augustine's relentless critique of Roman rule throughout that work.[54] He avows that Rome was founded on fratricide over envy and the pursuit of glory, recalling the story of Cain and Abel and the founding of the earthly city.[55] Roman deities "allowed the most terrible and abominable evils to have free play" (City of God 2.6), not only privately in the mind but publicly in games and the theater. Augustine cites Roman authorities themselves, including the historian Sallust, to support his view that the Roman republic changed "from the high of excellence to the depths of depravity," including the permission of such things as the rape of the Sabine women.[56] Roman gods were clear projections of human desires and the quest for flattery rather than sources of "right living" (City of God 2.15, 2.16). Recalling these and other facts of Roman history, Augustine writes: "I am sick of recalling the many acts of revolting injustice which have disturbed this city's history; the powerful classes did their best to subjugate the lower orders, and the lower orders resisted—the leader of each side motivated more by ambition than by any ideas of equity and morality" (*City of God* 2.17).

Augustine's polemics are well known but may lead us wrongly to conclude that civic virtue was only one of the many "splendid vices" of pagan thought and culture.[57] We should rather say that in Augustine's hands civic virtue can function as a critical principle or, more precisely, a disposition to practice social criticism. Political elites and cultural authorities who ask citizens to accept unjust practices corrode a "sense of justice," the virtue of equity and respect for others that should animate social institutions.[58] As a disposition that infuses a common life and inclines us to think about the moral quality of the commonweal, civic virtue describes a quality of mutual interaction that helps to constitute a collective way of being. Civic virtue thus coordinates and deepens an ensemble of collective desires—our "fellow feelings" toward ourselves as citizens linked by shared purposes for the common good.

Seen as a feature of civic virtue and the demands of justice, just-war morality can subsume more than a set of moral norms to assess political policy and military practice. The core claims of justice can also frame how ordinary citizens dispose themselves toward the common good as their leaders respond to political grievances. As a matter of moral and political psychology, we may query whether the popular desires that motivate support for war are desirable. We should thus examine how political authorities describe the stakes in war, how they represent our opponents, and how they attempt to appeal to our sense of fairness for popular support. Without such critical inquiry our responses to war can too easily curdle into expressions of what Augustine knew as *libido dominandi*, leaving the other vulnerable to one's self-deceiving and dangerous practices.

CONSENT AND DISSENT

We can view just-war morality, then, as emerging from an Augustinian attention to virtue and as mediating the desires of citizens toward (and beyond) the commonweal. Seen in these terms, just-war morality provides a framework that canalizes the affections and provides broad values for assessing how cultural processes structure the passions that underlie popular support for war. As a self-reflexive idiom for social criticism, just-war morality provides criteria for both evaluating the decisions of political elites and disciplining individual and corporate character. And in that way we can strengthen the otherwise tenuous connection between the ethics of war and the responsibilities of democratic social critics.

This is not to suggest that citizens who are alienated from political and social institutions should co-opt just-war morality or that those who protest against authority as their principal expression of political action should adopt just-war tenets as merely useful rhetoric for venting their views. Just-war morality provides substance for moral judgment and the expression of democratic consent or dissent.

When thinking about such judgments and practices of dissent, we do well to distinguish between *expressive* and *instrumental* forms. Expressive dissenters rebuke public officials as an end in itself, as an intrinsic good, and often find in such dissent a mode of self-articulation. They reject a priori the idea that government can enjoy the consent of the governed and perhaps find in political criticism an opportunity for ecstatic cathexis, anarchist aesthetics, or the manifestation of a sectarian ethic. But whatever the psychology of such dissent may be, such modes of disaffection undermine the prospect of genuine dialogue, deliberation, and consent as a matter of principle. Expressive dissent rejects the idea that the merits of one or another public policy are open for deliberation, evaluation, and popular approval. Such dissent might draw on nonmainstream political, religious, or cultural traditions, but it is antidemocratic in the context of modern, representative democracies insofar as it categorically rules out the prospect of consent, the very basis of democratic legitimacy.

Instrumental dissent, in contrast, is conditional. It is premised on the idea that, in principle, political institutions and policies can pass muster and may be worthy of popular support. Instrumental dissent aims at internal political reform, seeking to establish the proper basis for consent. It presumes that terms exist according to which respect should be assigned to public policy and its formation. Instrumental dissent is essential to, indeed constitutive of, the institution of consent, not a rejection of it. Informed by the idea that such dissent is part of civic virtue in modern, democratic polities, just-war morality enables citizens to evaluate political leaders' decisions in order to determine whether those decisions are worthy of approval and allegiance.

What virtues should be indexed to just-war morality and the habits it requires for instrumental dissent? I want briefly to identify three such dispositions: self-restraint, self-analysis, and the willingness to deliberate publicly. These virtues are implicit in modern democratic theory and augment the habits on which democratic practices rely. They presuppose moral goods that attach to democratic life, goods that redound to cultures in which equality and respect are fundamental principles that organize political roles and institutions. Moreover, they presume that self-reflection and dialogical deliberation help to constitute a good life. Equally important, they enable us to identify resources for an ethics of heterology that resists the temptations of xenophobia and self-justification to which Anscombe calls our attention in the comments with which we began this chapter.

Just-war morality calls forth the virtue of self-restraint in that it requires citizens, policy makers, and military personnel to situate the use of force within a wider set of moral (and global) goods. The practice of war is not an intrinsic good but should be ordered to the ends of peace and justice in the international arena. As ordained to such ends, war should have peace and justice as goods that are ingredients within its pursuits. For these reasons just-war tenets impose a kind of asceticism on public officials, combatants, and ordinary citizens. Self-restraint is explicitly required by the *ad bellum* criterion of last resort and the *in bello* limits on the conduct of war, and it is implied by the more general fact that war must be pursued in the light of moral ends. That latter idea requires citizens to situate their patriotic allegiances within a wider framework of moral purposes. Patriotic statements about the need to defend one's homeland, for example, must be chastened by reasonable appeals to moral purposes that should inform our conduct and character.[59] The habits of patriotism and allegiance—important to political motivation, civic identity, and public action—must be disciplined by the attention to a nation's wider aims, relationships, and responsibilities in the global common good. Just-war morality thus involves a spiritual exercise, demanding politicians, military planners, and citizens to organize their attitudes and practices according to the demands of fairness—including fairness to others whose interests may not be one's own.

Equally important, war requires a moral justification, an argument that appeals to the public reason of conscientious persons. War is not self-justifying, and it may not be sought in haste. For this reason just-war morality calls forth the civic virtue of critical self-analysis. As Plato understood in his design of the *Republic*, the institution of war must be framed by a broader set of parameters, in which self-reflection and contemplation of the Good mark the highest forms of human activity. Hence Plato's desire to subordinate the guardians to the philosopher-kings along with the need to rank warrior poetry below philosophy. The purposes that war might serve must stand within a framework that is self-reflexive and ordered to activities that do not glorify war as an end in itself. In just-war morality, reality is not organized in conflictual terms according to which martial virtues are goods in themselves.[60]

The need to produce a justification for war thus calls forth the disposition to deliberate, to place one's views within a larger dialogical context, when assessing the proper terms and course of military action. Deliberation in democratic contexts, Amy Gutmann and Dennis Thompson write, "asks citizens and officials to justify public policy by giving reasons that can be accepted by those who are bound by it."[61] Just-war morality serves such deliberative purposes by demanding a public accounting for war, enshrined in part in the *ad bellum* criterion of legitimate authority. That criterion requires those responsible for the common good to declare war and marshal a defense. In democratic contexts that fact puts the case of war in the public square, requiring policy makers, combatants, and ordinary citizens to weigh reasons for and against the case of war. The grievances to which a just war responds are not always obvious; a case must be made to those whose lives and welfare will be directly affected by its pursuit. Persons who are not disposed to deliberate about the morality of war join cause with those identified by Reinhold Niebuhr as "children of darkness," viewing war as incorrigible to morality.[62] They undermine grounds for assessing war as a duty of responsible citizenship.

Habits of self-restraint, critical self-analysis, and the willingness to partake in public moral deliberation echo dispositions valorized in classical Greek moral philosophy; they call to mind the virtues of temperance, wisdom, and courage. Such virtues require us to put political power to critical and moral scrutiny. In these respects attention to virtue requires us to develop the prophetic promise of just-war morality—its potential to generate social criticism and, when necessary, resistance to political power.

The virtues to which I have alluded thus possess radical implications for citizens considering the morality of war and, in particular, whether to join a standing army or to agree to conscription in military service. If I am correct about the role of the virtues for just-war morality, then individual citizens have a duty to settle matters of the *jus ad bellum* during times of conflict or impending conflict. Citizens cannot merely rely on a connection between patriotism and political obedience but should act on the notion that patriotism informed by a sense of justice requires moral reflection about the merits of a polity's demands on an individual's conscience. That notion implies higher expectations of moral assessment than has typically been the case in just-war theorizing and might require citizens to refuse participation or conscription in war.[63] Put differently, citizens who fail to engage in such reflection and who enter into an unjust war may be judged culpably negligent for choosing to be made into soldiers. To be sure, the social, political, economic, legal, and cultural forces that bear on an individual's decision are complex, making personal agency and moral deliberation in war an extremely complicated matter.[64] But just-war morality, properly understood, involves dispositions to resist sources of fear and to exercise courage and independence of mind regarding the merits of a polity's cause.

When just-war morality is expanded to connect with the habits of social criticism, it can contribute to the twin needs of legitimation and justification in democratic deliberations about the use of force. Obviously these points take us beyond Augustine and his vision of a just war. As a product of the premodern era just-war doctrine is typically viewed as enabling us to address a war's moral justification (or lack thereof). But legitimation is different. In modern democratic settings legitimation turns on the presence of consent (tacit or explicit) to acts authorized by public officials. Its value lies in the democratic commitment to hold authorities accountable to citizens and to provide a firm basis for political representation.[65] Concerns about legitimation are part of a broader theory of justified political coercion: reasons should be provided to persons whose liberties are restricted by a policy. Otherwise such restrictions are tyrannical, imposed heteronomously. Gutmann and Thompson remind us that legitimation is premised on the idea that "the moral authority of collective judgments about policy depends in part on the moral quality of the process by which citizens collectively reach those judgments."[66] Drawing on the habits of self-restraint, critical self-analysis, and willingness to deliberate publicly, the ethics of war can seek the best of both worlds. Just-war morality can provide moral resources for ensuring that we enter a war that reflects the popular will, one that does not seek to impose its will unjustly on others.

Earlier I stated that just-war morality involves a spiritual exercise—an ascesis—demanding political elites and ordinary citizens to discipline their attitudes, practices, and representations of the other.[67] I also said that such an idea suggests a controversial point that harks back to an idea from Augustine, namely, that virtue is grounded in the practice of confession. We are now in a position to see how that is so. Confession for Augustine was not solely or chiefly a matter of privately disclosing personal temptation and wrongdoing, as is often thought. Such personal reports are part of a more general practice of rendering oneself accountable to standards that one does not wishfully create (or project), objective norms by which to measure one's subjective leanings and desires. Confession, in short, is a matter of making oneself accountable to standards and purposes beyond one's immediate interests. For Augustine, and for those who follow in his path, self-knowledge quickly slides into excessive self-love and self-deception without objective reference points by which to measure oneself. Self-knowledge, including one's personal and social memories, must be tested by the principle of reality. Virtue for Augustine thus relies on the willingness to submit oneself to norms by which to evaluate one's loyalties and commitments. In our self-reflexive acts we must ask ourselves whether our self-interpretation is grounded in reality or fabricated with an eye toward self-justification.

MEANING, MEMORY, AND PUBLIC HISTORY

Seen in these terms, just-war morality can mediate civic virtue and, along with it, civic memory and the quest for meaning in the *res publica* by disposing citizens to evaluate public policy and public sentiment regarding war along with practices according to which war will be recalled in the future.[68] Such assessments are valuable for citizens across generations, bound as they are in political community. We do well to recall that as a political ethic, just-war morality presupposes the fact that political communities extend over time. They are, as Benedict Anderson famously argued, transgenerational imaginative structures in which past, present, and future members are conceived in solidarity.[69] Just-war morality thus includes virtues that dispose us to assess not only the sentiments of current citizens but also how public history will teach future generations to remember war in the formation of political identity and public culture.[70] Understood as providing a framework for social criticism, just-war morality provides a set of objective reference points that enable us to ask whether war is memorable for the right reasons and if the desires evoked by war are desirable and worthy of being transmitted to future citizens.

There is an intimate link, in other words, between collective memory, public history, and the life of a community over time. Collective memory provides what W. James Booth calls the "tectonic plates" on which communities sit—the deep structure according to which collective identities are forged (and conserved) across generations.[71] In that spirit we do well to recall the idea from George Orwell's *1984* that those who control the present control the past and that those who control the past also control the future.[72] Drawing on just-war doctrine, we (and they) can ask whether war was entered in a timely way, in pursuit of worthy ends, and carried out with restraint. Wars that fall short of those and other expectations leave citizens with less to be proud of, with less of a record to pass along to future generations as representative of a polity's history and character.

Augustine helps to shed light on these insights. Note that connections between the ethics of war and memory are strong indeed, joined at the outset in his discussion of Christianity and political morality in the *City of God*. That work is, among other things, an argument about how to remember the fall of Rome and whether Rome's decline should be understood as a consequence of embracing Christianity's putatively pacific virtues. According to Augustine, we must understand that Christianity is not a pacifist creed; it allows for the use of force to defend certain goods.

Equally important in Augustine's mind is the need to remember the true reasons for Rome's fall: its ongoing pagan sacrifices subsequent to its official conversion to Christian doctrine. This aspect of Augustine's thought has been universally ignored by theologians and philosophers who have worked in the just-war tradition. But we should not lose sight of what could be his most striking contribution to the ethics of war and peace. Often overlooked by readers of Augustine is the fact that he is defending the idea of a just war in response to criticisms about the political and cultural effects of accepting Christianity's moral norms. Thus, he queries at the outset of his magnum opus: "Why do our antagonists bring false accusations against the established Christian order, alleging that catastrophe has come upon the city just because it has left off the worship of its gods?" (*City of God* 1.15).[73] With that question in the background Augustine seeks to absolve Christianity for Rome's demise. In his account Rome's decline should not be remembered as a result of its conversion from Roman religion to Christian beliefs and practices. That argument is part of a larger agenda regarding the civic benefits of the Christian religion along with the core features of its political ethic.

Augustine's apology for Christianity and the idea of just war suggest a point that he and his interlocutors presumed as obvious, namely, that there is an ethics of memory—a duty to remember justly for the sake of history, self-understanding, and narrative recollection. He thus invites us to consider the obligations and virtues of what Ricoeur calls a "just memory."[74] Augustine's ethics is, as I noted above, "agent-referring": it attends to the moral effects of an action on the character of the person carrying out that action. He developed his agent-referring concerns, moreover, not by looking at the morality of individuals as isolated monads but as situated and affected by cultural forces that help shape character over time. The temporal quality of character and culture led him naturally to consider the virtues that surround memory, both individual and collective.[75] Given the intimate connection between memory and identity, there is an obvious obligation to remember for Augustine, a responsibility to remember truthfully. He thus worried about whether what people remember about themselves is prone to self-aggrandizement and, with that, self-deception. For these reasons we can say that an Augustinian ethics of war is, among other things, an ethics of memory. That Rome's morality "proceeded to bloody strife of all parties and then to the social and civil wars" is not his own personal judgment; it is, in his words, "the witness of history" (*City of God* 19.24).

Viewed in these Augustinian terms, just-war morality invites one to ask what a war means—how we interpret ourselves and others regarding matters of life and death. Death raises fundamental questions regarding horizons of meaning and desire, and war asks in the starkest terms whether its participants are willing to impose or take on the ultimate sacrifice. In this respect we continue to travel with Augustine, despite our chronological distance from him. For surely he would have us ask whether we possess a second-order framework for determining whether the desires aroused by killing, death, and sacrifice are themselves desirable. That is to say, Augustine would have us ask about the effects of killing on individual and corporate character and how death affects the practices of self-interpretation and the public history we wish to write about ourselves. War for Augustine was not only a matter of personal virtue and vice; it also raised questions of meaning and memory as these bear on the formation of civic identity and the construction of desire across generations.

In modern democracies the *ars memoriae* have been placed in the hands of the people, dispersed across various roles, ceremonies, institutions, and commemorative practices.[76] Understood self-reflexively, just-war morality can work in such contexts to ensure that war is remembered for the right reasons or, put more accurately, that what is remembered about war is right. In that way citizens can assess war and public history with habits and norms that enable us to resist the twin perils of self-aggrandizement and self-deception. That is no small need given how memories of past wars shape how subsequent wars are conceived, authorized, and fought. Viewed as an exercise of ascesis, just-war morality can discipline passions and actions that risk imposing on fellow-citizens and others the ultimate sacrifice. In the process it enables us to address Anscombe's anxious premonition: "The death of men, the curtailment of liberty, the destruction of property, the diminution of culture, the obscuring of judgment by passion and interest, the neglect of truth and charity, the decrease in belief and in the practice of religion—all these are the normal accompaniments of a war."[77]

9

THE MORAL AND POLITICAL
BURDENS OF MEMORY

FORGOTTEN MEMORY

In the previous chapter I said that Augustine's way of evaluating military conflict draws a compass that includes not only an ethics of war but also an ethics of memory. For Augustine, criteria for evaluating war enable us to evaluate public policy and military conduct along with the reasons and practices according to which war will be recalled now and in the future. In his mind, whether we are disposed to remember truthfully reveals something vitally important about our character and our capacities for virtue. Given that idea, Augustine would ask his readers whether their wars have been waged with a just cause, in pursuit of worthy ends, and with restraint. That evaluation would require readers to draw on virtues and norms for thinking soberly and unapologetically about the past. Wars that fall short of those expectations leave citizens with a morally questionable record to transmit to future members of their political community. One may infer in an Augustinian spirit that how friends remember their treatment of strangers during the heat and fog of war discloses something crucial about themselves.

In this chapter I step back from Augustine's ideas to take up more general philosophical matters regarding memory and justice along with the practices of memorialization and bearing witness. I want to ask, Do we have an obligation to remember people and events of the past? If so, what is the nature of this obligation, and who are the "we" who might be so obligated? Perhaps such an obligation should be viewed as a duty to the self given memory's therapeutic power and its importance to personal identity and communal solidarity. Yet it also seems true that personal well-being and collective coexistence may require us to forget or at least forgive—to "let go" of—some of our memories. Memory seems to be a source of stability and instability, resolution and anxiety, peace and conflict. How might we understand the ethics of memory and forgetting?

Strikingly, religious ethicists have expressed little interest in these questions.[1] I say "strikingly" in part owing to the importance of narrative and virtue theory in religious ethics. Narratives depend on memory to be recalled and transmitted in the formation of communities that bridge generations, and virtues rely on memory insofar as they exhibit habitual excellences, skills that we develop and perfect over time and that embody the effects of our past. As I noted in chapter 1, the concepts of narrative and virtue have provided grist for considerable work in religious and philosophical ethics in the wake of Alasdair MacIntyre's influential discussion of these matters in *After Virtue*.[2] Yet despite memory's clear link to these concepts, it has received little sustained attention in moral philosophy or religious ethics.

Apart from these connections among memory, narrative, and virtue, the subject of memory opens up fresh terrain for ethicists interested in the dynamics of psyche and culture. As I noted in my introduction, memory is one of our most intimate cognitive and affective activities and provides occasions for deep and intense experiences of our own intrasubjective alterities. It is central to moral psychology given its connection to personal identity and self-assessment, and it is informed and modified by cultural processes that embody tradition and heritage.[3] The topic of memory is thus of obvious interest to those seeking to navigate a cultural turn in religious ethics. Moreover, many religions regularly ask their adherents to recall foundational events, persons, and decrees. That memory has been generally neglected in the field of religious ethics is an odd fact indeed.

By *memory* I mean the recollection of the past so that it continues, in some degree or fashion, in the present. Memory is, as W. James Booth writes, "a kind of making present of the past, an (attempted) abolition of the distance created by the passage of time and the ensuring of the persistence of the past into the present."[4] Conservative and preservative, memory guards against the erosion of time. In that respect it has a single object: the past. But the concept of memory covers a wide range of experiences and phenomena. For the sake of introduction I will note three varieties.[5]

First is "procedural memory," or memory *how*. Procedural memory refers to abilities that are recalled in order to be performed in the present—for example, riding a bicycle, translating a foreign language, or tying a knot. Second is "propositional memory," or memory *that*. This form of memory, also called "declarative" or "semantic memory," consists of facts about the world—for example, that the Declaration of Independence was signed in 1776 or that Marx was buried in England. Third is "recollective memory," or memory *when*. This form of memory, also called "personal" or "episodic memory," consists of experiences in one's life—for example, a personal achievement, a natural catastrophe, or a national trauma.[6]

In what follows, I will examine five works that attend to these varieties of memory, focusing on critics who raise normative and political questions about memorial practices and events. I will proceed in the spirit of my argument in chapter 2, drawing together multiple, hybridizing discourses in religious studies: phenomenology, moral psychology, trauma studies, Holocaust studies, American religious history, theories of witness, hermeneutics, democratic theory, and cultural studies. Scholarship about memory today is keenly and creatively interdisciplinary. Yet even the range of discourses I have just listed provides a narrow picture. To offer something of a more general account of memory, I want first to place my discussion within a wider set of parameters. The experience of memory occurs in different embodied, vernacular, institutional, social, and political contexts, and that fact has important implications for any understanding of memory's ubiquity.

MEMORY: A TAXONOMY

To get a handle on memory from a normative standpoint, we should first distinguish between "deliberate" and "accidental" memory. Recollection is not only an experience that involuntarily "happens," like a dream or a hallucination. Memories also result from our effort to recall what we may have forgotten. Let us thus mark a distinction between "bidden" and "unbidden" memories, or memories as *praxis* and as *pathos*. The important point is that some memories are voluntary, that remembering is an activity we seek to do. Memory can thus implicate our agency and, with that, our moral responsibility.

Attention to moral agency should alert us to the fact that there are not only duties but also virtues of memory—habits or dispositions to remember that satisfy moral norms. We call such habits "excellences" on the premise that they meet a standard. That fact points to cultural and collective dimensions of deliberate memory. Remembering is a function of being a certain kind of people, of disposing ourselves toward certain ideals over time. Moreover, being a certain kind of people involves transmitting our ideals and dispositions to younger generations. Typically, societies want their children and younger citizens to share the commitments and values by which those societies develop and sustain their identity. We do well to note that political communities are not atemporal or static. As I noted in the previous chapter, political communities are transgenerational, imaginative structures in which past, present, and future members are conceived in solidarity.[7] We deliberately communicate our memories out of a desire to connect ourselves across generations. On this view we remember the past because of the future.

In other words, memories possess eros: they are energized by love, unity, and desire. We convey our memories in part owing to our attachments, our connections to other people. We look back on the past in light of goods and values, and we want to remember the past in the right way and for the right reasons as we transmit our heritage to our youth. On those terms I agree with Elie Wiesel: "To remember is to allow the past to move into the future and shape its course."[8]

The fact that memory can consist of praxes includes other distinctions as well. Here I have in mind the distinction between "habitual" and "active" memory. Habitual memory refers to the deep presence of the past in everyday life and practice. We might think of swimming as involving this kind of memory; similarly, in moral theory we understand the virtues as habitual excellences. The dense traces of memory can be literally embodied. Habitual memory differs from memories that I actively enlist for one or another purpose. Some memories I conjure up out of nostalgia, to reminisce. Or I bring them to mind in order to carry out one or another task—usually tasks that I do not regularly do. Translating a foreign language can involve this kind of active memory.

Earlier I made reference to certain cultural dimensions of memory, implying a distinction between individual and collective memory. Individual memories are those that come to the consciousness of a single person, remembrances that the individual can claim as a private possession. The memories of one person can hardly be transferred to the memories of another.[9] Collective memories are admittedly more difficult to pin down. I will presume, following Maurice Halbwachs, that the category of "collective memory" makes sense and that groups engage in memorialization processes that contribute to the formation of solidarity and corporate identity. Collective memories are not merely memories that groups have as a whole—as if there were something like a collective mind. Rather, such memories are those that individuals have as members of a group.[10]

Collective memories are not always and everywhere remembered by everyone in a group. Some collective memories are *common*, experienced by all members at once in an aggregate way, while other collective memories are *shared*, integrating "pieces" of memory into one version.[11] Common or shared memories occur routinely enough to define a group, allowing its members to assign a certain identity to themselves. Collective memories often occur "outside the mind" or "in the body politic," through the construction of monuments and memorial practices.[12] Memorial sites and rituals distill memories around aural and visual imagery that can be highly designative or suggestively symbolic.

Collective memories sort themselves out into different demographics, what John Bodnar calls "popular" and "institutional memory." Institutional memory, Bodnar writes, "originates in the concerns of cultural leaders or authorities at all levels of society. Whether in positions of prominence in small towns, ethnic communities, or in educational, governmental, or military bureaucracies, these leaders share a common interest in social unity, the continuity of existing institutions, and loyalty to the status quo." Popular memory, in contrast, develops in the vernacular. It originates from those "intent on protecting values and restating views of reality derived from first-hand experience in small-scale communities rather than the 'imagined' communities of a large nation."

Popular memory may (but need not) fall within the contours of official memory. Folk memory, countermemory, and memory that circulates outside the parameters of official accounts all help form popular memory. Such memories have a subversive potential. As Bodnar observes, popular memory's "very existence threatens the sacred and timeless nature of official expressions."[13]

Yet not all memories of a collective sort—be they institutional or popular—are confined to current members of a group. We must thus distinguish between collective memory of the sort Halbwachs considers, in which memories are transmitted by discrete social groups, and what Alison Landsberg calls "prosthetic memory." Distinct "from lived experience or from biological inheritance," prosthetic memory is mediated through film, television, and experiential museums. Such technologies of memory shape "'imagined communities' that are not necessarily geographically or nationally bounded and that do not presume any kind of affinity among community members."[14] Mass-mediated memories such as those provided by the television series *Roots*, Steven Spielberg's *Schindler's List*, or experiential museums such as the U.S. Holocaust Museum engage in a "visceral pedagogy" in which viewers or participants take on memories of events through which they did not live.[15] We become attached to such memories, like an artificial limb. The power of prosthetic memory lies in its capacity to diffuse the content and effects of memory across classes and groups. Landsberg writes, "Prosthetic memory has the ability to challenge the essentialist logic of many group identities. Mass culture makes particular memories more widely available, so that people who have no 'natural' claim to them might nevertheless incorporate them into their own archive of experience."[16]

There is also the distinction between different layers of memory, what also might be called "layers of forgetting." Here I am thinking about the distinction between "finite memory" and "repressed memory." These categories point to the limits of our powers of recollection, but they do so in different ways. There is information and emotion that I have forgotten simply owing to the feebleness of my mind. Some forgotten thoughts can be brought back to mind when I have my memory refreshed. Some memories are not entirely lost—but some are. Many of us likely do not retain a wide range of conscious childhood memories or regularly recall more basic data such as password codes, registration numbers, or previously learned scientific equations and mathematical formulas.

Distinct from information that we forget are repressed memories. Such memories are unavailable to consciousness, and in that way they resemble forgotten information. But repressed memories often seek expression. With repressed memories, as Freud argues, not only is repressed material (such as a traumatic memory) unavailable to consciousness, the very mechanism of repression is outside of conscious awareness.[17] Repressed memories are not those that I have forgotten but those that at some level I am afraid to remember. I have an interest in keeping a lid on them. And insofar as I do keep a lid on them, I may be deceiving myself about who I am, or about my personal history, or about why I am acting as I do. Freud's point is that memory and forgetfulness are not innocent; there is a kind of agency involved. We are reminded that both memory and forgetfulness can be driven by desire.

Closely related to repressed or forgotten memories is the distinction between "explicit" and "implicit" memory.[18] Explicit memory is that which I have in my consciousness, memories that I can recount and describe discursively. Implicit memories have more to do with mood, tone, feeling, and affect. These are the memories that resemble habit-memories, memories that are embodied. But implicit memories are unique insofar as they are brought about by sensual or aesthetic associations—by music, or taste, or smell. Marcel Proust's detailed descriptions of memories brought about by a sound, aroma, or color are of this implicit sort.

Memories of the kind I have mentioned—bidden and unbidden, habitual and active, individual and collective, and so on—fall into two general classes, what Sue Campbell has identified as "archival" and "reconstructive" memory. Archival memory stores a representation of our experiences in a way "that allows us to call them to mind on subsequent occasions." The key to archival memory is to represent a past experience "in ways unaffected by factors subsequent to it."[19] Archival memory thus consists of a kind of clear, untainted retention. Reconstructive memory, in contrast, is affected by subsequent factors, the conceptualization of which joins two theses. "The first," writes Campbell, "is that there are many different influences on the content and format that together yield the meaning of our rememberings." These influences "derive both from the continuous reprocessing of what we have learned, and from the specific circumstances in which we remember." Over time we conceive of our past in different ways, aided by new experiences, shifting emotional valences of memory, new occasions that prompt us to reframe our memories, changing media contexts, and objects that are keenly intertwined with the practices of memory. The second thesis is related: memories change over time, and such changes are normal features of our recollective processes.[20]

What I have said so far suggests that memory exists in layers rather than on one plane. But memory's layers are not necessarily arranged as distinct strata. It seems more accurate to describe memory as operating according to degrees of awareness and interpenetration, with some memories serving as foreground to other, more inchoate memories that operate in the background of one's mind. So, we might think of memory as *smooth and linear* in some respects and *jagged or interruptive* in other respects. As Booth remarks, "Some episodes stand out as identity-defining, as bathing all others in their light and investing them with a unifying meaning; some are not relevant."[21] In a similar vein Jenny Edkins speaks of "linear time" and "trauma time."[22] These distinctions indicate how some memories are shaped by other memories, the latter of which provide an organizing framework or horizon for self-interpretation and cultural self-description.

Last is the distinction between too little and too much memory. With repressed or finite memory we have information that at one level we may (eventually) want to recover but cannot. Yet there is also the fact of too much memory, of being haunted by the past. The past, we say, is too "present," perhaps because it is too recent, intimate, or violent to forget. We need time to get some distance on the past, which otherwise remains present. Here memory might suffer not from too much selective editing but from not enough.

A fable by Jorge Luis Borges, "Funes, His Memory," explores this facet of memory, the problem of memory's potential excess. Borges writes about a young man, Ireneo Funes, who never forgot anything, a man who was driven to madness by his condition. He could learn foreign languages effortlessly, and he invented a numbering system that preoccupied his mental imagining. But Funes's memory had a downside, Borges observes: "He was not very good at thinking." "To think," Borges writes, "is to ignore (or forget) differences, to generalize, to abstract. In the teeming world of Ireneo Funes there was nothing but particulars—and they were virtually *immediate* particulars."[23] Borges's story illustrates why anamnesis requires some measure of amnesia. We would not be able to organize our thoughts, to make decisions, to control our commerce with the world without some measure of forgetfulness that abstract thinking requires. And that forgetfulness must include some measure of freedom, some measure of control. I hardly need or want to remember the countless ways I have idled away my time or have lost myself in a flow of memories and related feelings. Such memories hardly help one shape the day, the week, or the year that lies ahead. This is a basic way of making a deeper point—namely, that we are more than our memories. We are not only shaped by our memories; we shape them: the relationship between identity and memory is circular. If we were *only* our memories, we would lack a framework for interpreting ourselves and for setting priorities for action-in-time. Everything would be "equally present" in our minds, and we would live out the philosophical perils of determinism. Borges's tale puts the point more starkly: if we remembered everything, we would go insane. Both Freud and Borges point to memory's potential for illness and the need for therapy—treatment that enables us either to recover from our past or place some distance between ourselves and our past. Memory exists in a complex dialectic with distanciation and forgetting.

Of course, memory is more fluid than all of these static categories and distinctions suggest. Following Campbell, we do well to note that memory is a dynamic process of remembering and forgetting that is constantly undergoing revision. And memory is multilayered: we remember that we can remember, and we even remember that we have forgotten certain ideas, feelings, or facts. Memory is thus keenly self-reflexive. Equally important, memory is coeval with our contingency and mortality—a struggle, however feeble, to overcome our finitude and the movement of the present into the shadows of the past. Why would we seek to remember if the past were forever present? Making matters more complicated is the fact that remembering is driven by voluntary and involuntary processes; our memories, and their selective editing, are not entirely under our control.

MEMORY THROUGH THICK AND THIN

Avishai Margalit's *The Ethics of Memory* focuses on deliberate, shared, explicit memory as well as jagged, interruptive, collective memories that surround political trauma and injustice. He addresses the question of whether we have an obligation to remember people and events from the past by saying that any answer depends on who is included in the "we." He begins his inquiry with an anecdote about an Israeli colonel who was met with public outrage after he admitted forgetting the name of a soldier who was killed under his command. The wrath heaped on the colonel led Margalit to reflect on the officer's obligation to remember and to consider whether, or on what terms, the officer should be considered at fault for forgetting.

Margalit pursues that question by invoking the Hegelian distinction between ethics and morality. Ethics, says Margalit, refers to thick relations and involves preferentiality. Morality, in contrast, refers to thin relations—relations between strangers and with humanity more generally. These two systems perform different kinds of work and involve different kinds of obligation. Over and against what he describes as the Christian project of transforming all relations into ethical ones, he defends the self-described Jewish project of keeping both sets of relations distinct. Moral relations, according to Margalit, are required of all persons: they are universal and nonpreferential. Ethical relations, in contrast, are optional. "There is no obligation," he writes, "to be engaged in ethical relations."[24] One may lead a solitary life. Caring, he adds, is what separates the two sets of relations. Care is an attitude at the heart of thick relations but not thin ones. Thin moral relations rely on reason instead. Indeed, Margalit argues, we need morality precisely because there are many about whom "we do *not* care" (32).

With these distinctions in view, what can we say about the ethics of memory? Margalit's main point is that we should understand the title of his book in light of the distinction between ethics and morality. Memory should generally be understood in ethical, not moral, terms. The caring of thick relations provides a connection between ethics and memory. To say that we care about a person is to say that we remember him or her.

Accordingly, a failure to remember would say something about our lack of care. The lack of care in thin relations indicates that there is no analogous connection between morality and memory. Our relations to strangers do not generally arise in contexts that call for or require memory: they are generally context-free, not context-bound.

Taking Margalit's distinctions together, we would say that memory does not play much of a role in the moral life. Memory should instead play a vital role ethically, in our thick relations. But for Margalit those relations and attendant obligations, as I noted, are optional. Memory, then, is important to that feature of our lives that is particular and preferential but not, strictly speaking, obligatory. On this account the colonel who forgot his fallen soldier's name violated an ethical duty, not a moral one. His failure to remember reflected a failure to care.

What about the relationship between memory, forgetting, and forgiveness? Margalit argues suggestively that forgiveness is not a blotting out of memory—a form of forgetting. Forgiveness rather consists in mastering motives of resentment in response to an injury. Forgiveness means "adopting . . . an exclusionary reason to counter reasons for action that are based on the injury done to us" (209). That is to say, to forgive is to adopt a second-order desire to overcome the first-order desire of "resentment and vengefulness" that stems from being a victim of injury (206).[25] Forgiveness, then, is part of the ethics of thick relations, in this case the relation to oneself. We owe it to ourselves not to dwell in a state of resentment with all of its psychological downsides. Successful forgiveness means that we no longer relive the feeling of resentment when the memory of an event comes to mind. So we may forgive the perpetrator while not having to forget his or her injurious deed.

One question that Margalit leaves unanswered is why anyone else should care about the colonel's failure to remember his fallen soldier's name. Margalit seems to assume that the colonel's ethical failure is one that others should be concerned about. But according to his own set of distinctions, that assumption makes little sense to those who exist outside of the thick relations in which the colonel found himself. If those who are outside those relations think that the colonel did something wrong by forgetting, then more concepts are necessary to make sense of that judgment. That is to say, Margalit needs a concept, in addition to care and reason, to indicate why others should be concerned about the colonel's failure. If that concern is based more broadly on our moral duties, then the distinction between moral and ethical obligations seems to do less work than Margalit presumes. An additional idea is needed to render intelligible why anyone outside a network of thick relations should care when others default on their ethical obligations.

The Ethics of Memory, as I noted, focuses attention on thick relations. Yet Margalit does not want to suggest that morality has nothing to do with memory (or vice versa). He argues that we do have a moral obligation to remember radical evil if, for no other reason, than to prevent future evil from occurring. Such evil seeks to undermine the very foundation of morality itself and aims to rewrite the past and control collective memory.[26] Failing to remember past crimes against humanity makes it easier for future crimes to occur. The cry, "never forget," in response to the Holocaust is, in Margalit's account, a moral plea to humanity in addition to being an ethical plea to (and from) the Jewish people. For Margalit we all have a moral obligation to remember massive injustice in order not to repeat it.

Crimes against humanity and other forms of radical evil require moral witnesses to preserve the memory of victims who have suffered injustice. Who should be charged with remembering for others? What kind of person is eligible to serve as a moral witness? Margalit's answer to these questions identifies several criteria: the witness must be an eyewitness of radical evil along with the actual suffering it caused, and the witness must have been at some risk herself either as sufferer or as observer (148). Moreover, the witness must express a sober hope "that in another place or another time there exists, or will exist, a moral community that will listen to their testimony" and that such testimony will play an active part in the unfolding of the story (155). In many respects a moral witness is reckoning with more than thin relations of morality. A moral witness speaks to an evil that is an assault on morality itself, but her testimony is most effective when it is based on thick relations with the victims (182).

Margalit's account of moral witnessing thus acknowledges that the distinction between morality and ethics (and their attendant obligations) is not always obvious. That fact raises a more basic question about his account, namely, where to draw the line between ethical and moral relations. One wonders, for example, whether coexistence in a liberal democracy would count as a thick or thin relation. At one level it would seem thick insofar as it presumes the partiality that attaches to being a citizen with a shared political history. But citizens in liberal democracies are often strangers to each other, connected less by common memories than by rights and political obligations. On first blush the distinction between thin and thick relations seems clear enough, but when we begin to think about the degrees of thickness and thinness in our social connections, difficult questions arise. Surely we care about others, even in thick relations, to different degrees.

Memory in democratic contexts seems to create especially interesting and thorny questions. Often we distinguish liberal democracies from traditionalist societies with ancient mythologies and social hierarchies that are shackled to the past. In Margalit's mind democracies rely little on memory: "A democratic regime, so it seems to me, anchors its legitimacy not in the remote past but in the current election. It would seem, therefore, that liberal democracies are exempt from an orientation to the past and rest their power on their vision of the future. Dwelling on the past in a democracy is as irrational as crying over spilt milk" (11–12).

Margalit acknowledges that "backward-looking emotions and attitudes" should play a role in democratic life (12), but he says little about how and why that ought to be the case. He neglects the extent to which democracies rely on foundational constitutional principles. Without the memory of constitutional arrangements and their historic origins, democracies would be reinventing themselves on a regular basis. Moreover, Margalit ignores the extent to which liberal democracies rehearse their legacies at both institutional and popular levels. That fact is a function of social groups' need to extend their institutional practices and ideals intergenerationally and to develop civic practices that cultivate political identity. Strikingly, Margalit's understanding of social relations devotes little attention to the temporal quality of communal life. By largely confining his understanding of the ethics of memory to thick relations, and by leaving our understanding of thickness vague, Margalit is unable to track how memory works in the ongoing life of modern liberal polities.

DUTIES AND DEBTS OF MEMORY

W. James Booth's *Communities of Memory* takes up matters of memory, political justice, and democracy by first advancing the idea that memory is essential to an individual's and community's need for temporal continuity. As a synthetic, "in-gathering" capability, memory is constitutive of individual and collective identity insofar as it connects us to our past and enables us to plot and plan our future. Against reductionist accounts of identity defended by Derek Parfit and David Hume, Booth (following Christine Korsgaard)[27] defends the notion of identity-across-time as a practical necessity arising from the idea of moral agency and its conditions. Insofar as we understand ourselves as responsible for actions in our past and as deliberators about our future, we presume the unity of agency and rely on the workings of memory. Memory is to be esteemed because it is central to identity, and identity is a necessary practical premise on which we base responsibility for the past and commitment to the future. Booth writes, "Memory-identity matters because, among other things, it is the ground of imputation, of the society (or person) as owner of its past and responsible for it, as well as identical to, and thus capable of, making commitments to a future, of binding its future by a present promise."[28] According to Booth's account, then, the obligation to remember is a kind of metaduty. We have that obligation as a condition of carrying out other duties such as acts of reparation or the fulfillment of promises. Without memory we would lack the practical identity on which we presume to hold ourselves accountable for the past or commit ourselves to future projects. For that reason, we can say that "identity, justice, and memory . . . emerge as tightly interwoven" (xiii).

Like Margalit, Booth focuses on what he calls "thick" memories. But Booth's designation adds to what we have seen from Margalit. Whereas Margalit understands "thickness" to refer only to close, familiar relations, Booth understands thickness also to refer to habit-memory and its density, what he refers to as the "non-explicit, nearly invisible values, behaviors, and beliefs that are the geological deposit of enduring relationships" (xi). Such memories, the "tectonic plates of our lives-in-common," have an agency of their own—what Booth also calls "autonomous" memory (x).[29]

But thick or autonomous memory is not to be taken for granted; it can be fragile. It must thus wage a defensive struggle against "the flow of time, and the erosion it brings to traces and to memory" (xi). The "low flame of remembrance," Booth writes, "is sometimes autonomous in the sense that it seems to return unsought, to impose itself on us, and at other (perhaps most) times it must be secured by the labors of memory and resistance" (71).

The idea of thick, autonomous (yet fragile) memory lies behind one key normative dimension of memory for Booth: the duty to remember is to honor a debt to community and to help secure its intergenerational connections. The obligation to remember is grounded in part on securing proper relations between present and past members of a community. Booth writes: "To neglect the memory of the community, not to preserve and transmit it, in short, not to bear witness to it, would be to damage the group's identity and violate a norm of reciprocity and co-responsibility: the debt, or quasi-contract, entailed by a life-in-common across time between the present in whose hands these memories (partially) rest and the absent past" (xii).

We have an obligation to remember, then, owing to our dependence on community for our particular character and tradition. Central to Booth's argument is the notion of intergenerational debt. Memory works in large measure as an expression of reciprocity to those on whom we have relied for our heritage and from whom we have benefited in broad and diffuse ways. What principally justifies the "pursuit of truth through the various private and public institutions of memory is the language of fidelity, of what is owed to the dead" (132).

This means, among other things, that memory is "radically particularistic." Memory is constitutive of identity, which means, Booth rightly notes, marking oneself off from others either as an individual or as a member of a group (171). On this premise Booth (following Halbwachs) understands memory to be confined to thick relations (as Margalit uses the term). Accordingly, claims about a supracollective or supranational memory can deploy the concept of memory only as a metaphor (174). Memory works to restore justice within discrete, bounded communities, not justice in some abstract or disembodied sense. It would be strange, then, for there to be a *moral* witness (using Margalit's language), a witness who speaks about crimes against humanity. For Booth, any such witness can only be an *ethical* witness. The work of memory-truth in witnessing "serves not so much to establish that such-and-such took place, that x was its perpetrator and y its victim, but rather to give voice to those rendered silent and absent, to reintegrate the lost into the unity of the community, and to reincorporate them into its justice." Witnessing is "in fulfillment of an obligation to the dead and for the sake of the continuity of the community across time" (138).

Booth, like Margalit, believes that liberal democratic norms exist in tension with the duties and debts of memory. For Booth this is because liberal democracy is premised on "past-less" principles, such as rights, whereas memory is dense, embedded in time, and particularistic (171). In his mind a certain kind of amnesia is necessary for democracy to exist. Booth writes that liberal theories require "a lessening of the weight of the past and of memory, and the refashioning of citizenship into a condition where the possession of the past is (mostly) irrelevant" (151). Liberal democracy is thus at odds with memory identity that invokes "autochthonous modes of belonging over the long duration. . . . A form of political life that rejects such a notion of identity and in its stead establishes a set of (roughly) universal-democratic norms must institute a type of forgetting (or a counter-memory), at least for its public space" (150).

Booth's equivocation—that liberal democracy involves forgetting *or* a countermemory—is revealing. It enables him to straddle the fence on matters regarding memory and democracy. Early in *Communities of Memory* he notes that democratic public culture involves its own form of civic rituals and memorial practices that unfold with an eye toward constructing civic identity. Recalling Alexis de Tocqueville, Booth observes, "Institutions transform the habits, the reflexes, in short the unreflective way of life of citizens, and in so doing fashion an unconscious and involuntary, almost habit-like memory of themselves and of the values and ways of living they embody. . . . As citizens, in the here and now, our instincts and habits have been educated by formal institutions and by informal practices that, inscribed in our habits and hearts, become our way of life, our mores, and thus a living presence of the past" (45).

Booth's view of democratic culture as relying on "past-less" principles seems to forget this Tocquevillian insight about habits of the heart. He ends up concluding his book by trying to lessen this tension between democracy and habit-memory and tradition. However, he does so not because he is mindful of formative influences of democratic mores but because liberalism presupposes a certain measure of freedom over our memories. Liberal democracy, Booth writes, "opens before us the prospect that we have some measure of choice in addressing the ties of memory-identity" (182). From this perspective democracy is not so much inimical to memory as reflective about it.[30]

It is not clear, however, that this claim about memory and reflection is coherent in Booth's account of autonomous memory. Who is the "we" who have a measure of choice over "our" memory-identity? Booth would do well to enlist some distinctions, such as first- and second-order desires, to indicate how layers of memory and reflective choice might be coherently coordinated. Any such distinction would do well to observe, as I noted above, that we are more than our memories. Our identity is not entirely beholden to memory; there is some space between memory and identity that allows the latter to exert some sovereignty and control over the former. Personal identity is such that it enables us to reckon critically with our memories, to sift and sort them out.

One way to think about memory and social criticism would be to say that we reside in multiple communities with different clusters of memory and that such communities provide multiple discourses for engaging in memory and critical reflection. Booth seems generally loath to acknowledge the fact of pluralism in his account of memory, but in places he notes that memories do exist along different strata. This insight emerges in Booth's discussion of institutional or official political memory. One problem with official political memories, he observes, is that they can flatten out more local and solidaristic memories. The forgetting required by liberal democracy "makes possible an accommodation between membership and diversity. The conflicting memories of various groups and the reflex of self-preference of the 'founding peoples' here give way . . . to a common political memory, that of the regime, its construction, constitution, and values" (152). We are not shackled to any one set of autonomous memories; rather, we depend on many memory streams insofar as we participate in different communities.

But that fact returns us to the problem of democracy as relying on "past-less" principles. The idea of distinct and conflicting memories might have been usefully deployed by Booth to lessen the putative tension between democracy and memory. If something like democratic institutional memory—what Booth describes as "political memory"—exists in tension with various local memories, then obviously the idea that democracies are memory-deficient makes no sense.

A more basic problem with Booth's reflections about memory and democracy is that the alleged tension between "past-less" democratic principles and memory-laden communities is, or can be, only heuristic. The tension can scarcely help us map social reality. Consider by way of example many Americans' visceral reaction to racial discrimination. It is no exaggeration to say that few American citizens think of the rights of racial equality without conjuring up memories (lived or prosthetic) of the civil rights movement. Appeals to liberal democratic rights often deploy modes of recollection, not forgetfulness.

Despite the perils of forgetting that Booth assigns to liberal democratic theory, he is not entirely against the notion. He recognizes that forgetting can serve a therapeutic purpose no less than remembering, that forgetting can unburden one from trauma. Forgetfulness "is the remedy for the bitter strife induced by too much memory." Hence a tension emerges: "Forgetting, memory, and justice . . . stand in an uncertain and perplexing relationship. To do justice is to remember, to preserve and guard in memory the injury, the victim, and the perpetrator. Yet peace and a life-in-common, the foundation of civic community, make their claims on us, one of which is that we allow the forgetting of past evils" (149). Forgetting and forgiveness overturn "the moral imperative of memory-justice . . . so that we may be oriented to the present and future, and not (or not solely) to the fulfillment of a debt to the victims or to the carrying out of the demands of justice for its own sake" (155).

Occasionally Booth recognizes that community is not a value always to be esteemed or, more accurately, that not all communities deserve to have their memories preserved. Unfortunately, he pays insufficient attention to this problem and its remedies. At most he talks about communities that transition from undesirable to desirable arrangements and the importance of amnesty for that process. But what do we say about communities and memorial practices that fail to undergo such transitions or forms of memory that celebrate injustice? Consider, for example, Confederate

Memorial Day in the American South.[31] In April and May (depending on the state) six southern states have a holiday to remember soldiers who fought for the Confederacy. State offices and schools are generally closed, the main library at the University of Georgia publicly displays the original Constitution of the Confederacy, and citizens across the South reenact Civil War battles in historical dress. Such practices meet the criteria to which Booth assigns the justice of memory: they bear witness to the past, repay a debt to the dead, and maintain identity and social boundaries across generations. However, in the process of performing "memory-justice," these events pay tribute to racial injustice insofar as they honor a way of life that could not exist without the institution of slavery. Sometimes the repayment of debts is a form of moral embarrassment. Booth seems too little aware of this fact.

Regarding problematic memories, Booth's main emphasis falls on transitional societies and their need to relinquish ties to the past for civic peace and progress. In that context he at times conflates forgiveness and forgetting in ways that Margalit would likely find incoherent. Booth describes amnesty, for example, as a form of "political-juridical forgetting" (155).[32] One might object that forgetting seems hardly to be a willful act. In any event forgetting, on Booth's description, is not unlike forgiveness in Margalit's account. In both instances the key point is that the act is justified as a duty to the self. In Margalit's case emphasis falls on the individual self, whereas in Booth's case emphasis falls on the community. The main point is the same: forgiveness and forgetting find their basis in the benefit in overcoming vengeful feelings. Booth writes that forgiveness "is the overcoming, on moral grounds, of resentment, and it is especially important in allowing human relations to continue that otherwise would be disrupted" (152).

To make sense of this idea, Booth would have done well (again) to think more about what, beyond memory, contributes to the construction of identity and the continuation of social relations. If the continuity of relationships depends on forgetting as opposed to remembering, it is not obvious that forgetting "erodes" identity or that such erosion is a problem. It would rather seem important to note how remembering can arrest individuals' or groups' growth, understood as existing in time and moving toward the future. Identity is not merely a backward-looking phenomenon. Imagination and its utopias, no less than memory and its ideologies, contribute to the formation of identity as a temporal phenomenon. Our second-order desires can modify our first-order desires by drawing on our moral imagination and hopeful expectations. Whatever willful forgetting (or forgiving) we perform is a function of our introspective powers and their several epistemic sources.

USES AND ABUSES OF MEMORY

Paul Ricoeur would restate my complaint above by saying that Booth emphasizes memory's "worldliness" (autonomous, habit-memory) at the expense of memory's "reflexivity" (the fact that *I* am remembering and am *mindful* of that fact).[33] That insight sits within a vast exploration of memory in Ricoeur's *Memory, History, Forgetting*, a work that weaves together many threads of his oeuvre into a crowning achievement: Ricoeur's lifelong dialogue with Husserl's phenomenology; Freud and psychoanalysis; Saussure on metaphor; Nietzsche, Heidegger, Foucault, and Derrida on modernity; Augustine and Aristotle on time and narrative; myths and symbols of evil; and Dilthey and Gadamer on history and hermeneutics. These topics and interlocutors, along with conversations with various theorists of memory—Halbwachs, Certeau, Ginzburg, Nora, White, Yerushalmi—all find their way into this expansive and ambitious work.

Ricoeur organizes his study according to three phases or investigations that correspond to the three parts of the work's title. What binds the three parts together is the "problematic of the representation of the past" (xvi). Memory and history both represent the past; these practices presuppose as the condition of their possibility the fact of human historicity and vulnerability, one key manifestation of which is forgetting. One of Ricoeur's aims is to sort out the goals and limits of memory and history, identify their reproductive and productive aspirations, and connect those insights to an account of the human condition. A related aim is a civic one: to help us address "an excess of memory here, and an excess of forgetting elsewhere," attending to what he calls "a policy of the just allotment of memory" (xv). Those efforts, he notes, are complicated by an aporia that lies at the heart of his investigation: memory is a presencing of that which is absent, a representation of that which is no longer but has not disappeared. This enigmatic gap between image and reality, recollection and experience, presence and absence frustrates any effort to provide a seamless analysis of memory, history, and their connections to our ontological condition as finite, historical subjects.

The first phase of the work, phenomenology, focuses on memory as *praxis* (a search) or as *pathos* (a reception). In either case memory must satisfy veridical criteria; it must be faithful to the past, but (like history) it cannot claim absolute certitude or infallible accuracy. That fact points to what Ricoeur calls memory's cognitive aspect, the idea that memory (unlike the imagination) must be true to something. Memory as praxis, moreover, involves the will and engages us more deeply. Ricoeur notes that various obstacles arise in ordinary experience, barriers to truthful memory that are erected either by the self or society. Memory's fidelity to the past can be impeded by psychological or ideological abuses of memory and forgetting. Here Ricoeur embarks on suggestive engagements with Freud on repression and Weber and Marx on ideology. Given these features of psyche and culture, memory's reliability is precarious indeed.

This fact all the more problematizes the very idea of a "duty of memory" understood either as an individual or collective obligation. Ricoeur endorses both of these modalities of memory, relying on Alfred Schutz's phenomenology of social relations and the notion that the experience of others is equiprimordial to the experience of self.[34] Following Schutz, Ricoeur writes, "The shared experience of the world rests upon a community of time as well as space" (130). To this insight he adds the idea, echoing Margalit and Booth, that some social relations are more proximate than others, that some relationships are with persons "who approve of my existence and whose existence I approve of in the reciprocity and equality of esteem" (132). We are left, then, with a threefold attribution of memory: to oneself, to one's close relations, and to others.[35]

The second phase of Ricoeur's analysis, epistemology, focuses on the work of history. Ricoeur conceives of history as moving along three interrelated phases: documentation, explanation/understanding, and representation. The documentation phase takes as its task the need to establish the historian's evidence; it ranges from statements of eyewitnesses to archival materials. This phase includes not only written and oral testimony but also places and spaces that evoke memory along with a set of assumptions about the historian's organization of time, scale of study, and attention to power and cultural norms. The explanation/understanding phase addresses the question, Why did things happen like this and not otherwise? Here the historian seeks to find root causes for events and to clarify accounts according to law-like generalizations.[36] Finally, the representative phase puts in written form the historian's construction of events and their causes. Both scientific and literary, it culminates in the historian's intention, which is to narrate the past and to assign to it human significance.[37]

Ricoeur correctly notes that these three phases are distinct in theory but not in practice.[38] "History is writing from one end to another," he states. "Explanation/understanding . . . finds itself encased, upstream and downstream, by two writings. It gathers energy from the former and anticipates the energy of the latter" (138). Indeed, the writing of history itself enters into history's flow: "The history book becomes a document, open to the sequence of reinscriptions that submit historical knowledge to an unending process of revisions" (234). Equally important is the fact that a historian's representations involve an implicit moral contract with the reader. When it comes to historical representation, "the author and reader . . . agree that it will deal with situations, events, connections, and characters who once really existed" (275). But this contract cannot proceed without due knowledge of what the historian produces: the presencing of an absence. The implications of this fact are considerable. Representation congeals around an absent thing that divides its absence into two domains—as a disappearance into the past and as an "existence" in the past. The aspect of existence "under the sign of the past" (280) is no mere logical paradox for Ricoeur; it brings us to a deeper truth, namely, the ontology of our historical being.

So we turn to the third phase in Ricoeur's account, hermeneutics, focusing at a second-order level on the *experience* of history and the burdens that accompany our historical condition. Ricoeur examines two dimensions of hermeneutical inquiry: attention to the limits of historical knowledge and attention to the existential conditions for such knowledge—our manner of being in the world. A critical hermeneutics of history, Ricoeur points out, has as its main claim that historical writing can produce no totalizing knowledge, no claim to "total reflection coming from the self-knowledge of history" (295). That awareness of our limits drives Ricoeur deeper into a Heideggerian analysis of our finitude—our being-toward-death and our fundamental contingency. At the same time, Ricoeur sees historians' work as not entirely ensnared by human finitude; it also functions as a power against death and a source of hope and creativity. The historian "appears as the one who, in a variety of ways, makes the dead speak" (368). Equally important, historiography can be productive. Against Heidegger's suspicions about the leveling effects of historical writing, Ricoeur rejoins that "historiography also understands the past as the 'return' of buried possibilities" (382). That is to say, we can recall the past with an eye to envisioning our present and future.

Ricoeur's allusion to a "return" offers a key for understanding his meditation on forgetting and its relationship to memory. Forgetting is both a threat to and a source of memory. One the one hand, it reminds us of our finitude: "forgetting is the emblem of the vulnerability of the historical condition taken as a whole" (284). But forgetting is not entirely to be lamented. In the active struggle to remember, we tacitly acknowledge an unconscious depth of traces and images of the past, both individually and collectively (429–30). Forgetting refers in part to memories that have been removed from the "vigilance of consciousness" (440), a reservoir of the past that lies outside our immediate powers yet nonetheless exists as their condition of possibility. The duty of memory is exercised against the backdrop of this wider horizon along with the intractable anteriority of our lives—the fact that "no one can make it be that [past things] should not have been" (280).

Memory, History, Forgetting takes up the concept of forgiveness outside the main body of the text, in the form of an epilogue. Forgiveness is the "eschatological horizon" (285) of the entire problematic of memory, history, and forgetting. That is because Ricoeur sees a distinction between the nonjudgmental nature of historical inquiry and the facticity of debt as a feature of our historical condition, on the one hand, and judgment regarding guilt (to which forgiveness is directed), on the other (285). So we move beyond the limits of reason when we approach this aspect of the phenomenon of forgetting. In that respect forgiveness for Ricoeur is a deeply theological concept.

In Ricoeur's estimation forgiving, as a form of forgetting, can be a kind of cheap grace, an effort to overcome the past for reasons of social utility. What is lost in that bargain is the capacity of a community to genuinely engage in its history, prevent future crimes, and partake in the benefits of democratic "*dissensus*" (455). In this respect Ricoeur shares Booth's worries about amnesty, what Ricoeur calls "commanded forgetting" (452). Forgiveness, however, can be different from forgetting. Like Margalit, Ricoeur sees forgiveness as a form of overcoming resentment and feelings of vengeance. Forgiveness is justified on the premise that we may distinguish between the agent and the act, thereby unbinding the agent from her past without forgetting her guilty act (490). For Ricoeur, then, forgiveness consists of more than a duty to the self. It is also a gift that frees an agent from her own past, offered in the hope of regenerating the guilty person to her better nature and rebinding her to social relations (468, 493). That is to say, forgiveness is not only a matter of self-care but an ethic of heterology understood as an act of grace offered to the other with an eye not to the past but to a new human future. On that optative, teleological note Ricoeur concludes his book with a meditation on happiness and its implications for thinking about memory, history, and forgetting.

* * *

As I noted earlier, *Memory, History, Forgetting* is arranged systematically along three phases, each with its own subsections. One challenge for the reader is grasping why Ricoeur locates his conversation with this or that author in one section rather than another. Despite his effort to guide the reader at the introduction of each section, some of his decisions remain counterintuitive, and some of what he includes or omits cries out for explanation. It is not obvious, for example, why history rather than memoir or autobiography should follow a discussion of memory. Ricoeur has little if anything to say about these other forms of memory work, and it seems facile to suppose that we should classify them under the rubric of history. To be sure, memoir and autobiography must heed certain historiographical conventions, but these forms of memory are written in the first person with an intimacy and mindfulness that history typically lacks.

At the very least, memoir and autobiography need not seek out law-like generalizations to validate their basic claims. It is odd that Ricoeur would omit an investigation into these expressions of memory.

Ricoeur's investigation of history likewise has curious omissions. He ignores deep methodological debates among historians about the relative merits of social history, intellectual history, oral versus written history, ethnographic history, and the like. Are we to assume that the "duty to remember" is equally well carried out by these different programs? Is it not the case, for example, that social historians claim that what intellectual historians "forget" as a condition for their work points to inexcusable lacunae? How would we adjudicate between these disputes over what is properly and improperly forgotten as conditions of these different historical programs? Ricoeur's discussion of history smooths over these deep fissures.

One of Ricoeur's aims, as I have noted, is to help us address "an excess of memory here, and an excess of forgetting elsewhere," attending to "a policy of the just allotment of memory." Those concerns enable us to articulate certain intuitions regarding the ethics and politics of memory, to ask why certain genocides and human rights abuses are memorialized while others are not. When, for example, will the Armenian genocide be appropriately remembered?[39] How and when will the massacres across the American West receive fitting modes of memorialization? What of the atrocities at Kampuchea, Nanking, Hiroshima, Rwanda, and Ground Zero?

Ricoeur's way of handling these questions is to pose matters of justice and responsibility as a *distributive* question regarding the "just allotment of memory." What he fails to help us with, however, is the justice or injustice of the memorial practices themselves, or what he calls the "abuses of memory—and of forgetting" (xv). That is to say, what we need from Ricoeur is a way to get a handle on substantive matters, not only distributive matters, regarding the ethics of memory. Consider, again, Confederate Memorial Day and assume, as I think we can, that Ricoeur would raise objections to it. Would those objections focus on the fact that "too much" attention is being paid to the Confederacy or that any attention at all is an "abuse" of memory or that memories of the Confederacy entail the "abuse of forgetting"—in this case the forgetting of slavery? On what criteria are these uses and abuses to be assessed in a second-order way?

Ricoeur might cite Confederate Memorial Day as an example of "manipulated memory"; it is faithful to a set of documented facts and testimonies, but it seems to be imposed coercively and draws on various practices that compound social pathologies. Yet that description belies the fact that Confederate Memorial Day has widespread approval in large segments of the South. More problematic is the fact that attending to the "manipulated" nature of the memory focuses on power dynamics and not, as I noted above, on the substance of the occasion. Drawing resources from Ricoeur for social criticism is gnarled by these facts.

Perhaps most puzzling is Ricoeur's invocation of Freudian concepts to explain forms of forgetting as unconscious reserves from which memory can draw. Ricoeur oddly leaves aside the idea that for Freud such repression is a function of agency and desire, outside the realm of self-awareness. Hence the obvious question arises: who, and on what terms, will provide the therapy according to which such repressive desires will be lifted? Ricoeur is hardly naive about the forces that distort memory, about what he calls "blocked memory" (69–80, 444–48).[40] But it remains unclear how desires that animate these repressive and oppressive forces can be identified and resolved for the common good. Nor is it obvious that all blocked memories deserve to have their obstacles removed or when it might be timely to do so. Put more generally, there is a critical ethics of desire that ought to mediate the work between memory and forgetting, recollection and repression. Forgetfulness understood as repression invites an account of remembering informed by a critical therapy of historical desire. Without those resources it remains unclear how Ricoeur's work can assist in the work of social criticism regarding matters of collective memory and injustice.

RESPONSIBILITY, IDENTITY, AND REMEMBRANCE

Echoing Ricoeur's desire to address "an excess of memory here, and an excess of forgetting elsewhere," Jeffrey Blustein's *The Moral Demands of Memory* takes up concerns about memory's excess and deficiency and situates those concerns within an overarching account of virtue. Like Margalit, Booth, and Ricoeur, Blustein asks how and on what terms we have a responsibility to remember people and events of the past, and he examines the "we" who might be so responsible. Distinctive in his account is the claim that there is no clear formula for striking a balance between memory's excess and deficiency—between what he calls the surfeit of memory and forgetfulness. We can be overly preoccupied and enslaved to our past no less than we can be willingly thoughtless about its moral and political importance. According to Blustein, we can chart a middle way between these extremes by adopting an "all things considered" perspective, looking at the value of remembrance in light of its impact on other social goods and obligations.[41] Virtues assist us in determining what other values to consider when determining "when, what, how, and how much to remember, and also in properly integrating this understanding into our lives" (15). Following Nietzsche, Blustein views virtue as having "a certain 'plastic power,' an ability to acknowledge and take up the past without becoming enslaved to it" (15). The task of determining a proper quotient of memory depends in no small part on the excellences of "prudence, restraint, and flexibility" (24).

Blustein thus views the moral demands of memory as requiring us to think about remembrance as a qualified good, the realization of which depends on a wider suite of excellences. His thesis is that "within limits and with respect to especially significant events, experiences, or people from the past, remembrance is an indispensable ingredient of a good life and a necessary condition of civic health" (2). Blustein develops this thesis by analyzing both individual memory and collective memory, the latter understood as forms of remembrance that are "communally shared and socially maintained" (138). Although distinct, these forms of memory are intertwined insofar as individual memories are informed by collective memories and vice versa. Blustein advances his analysis of both forms of memory within an overarching and capacious view of moral responsibility to identify memory's moral demands. In his account our mnemonic responsibilities should be understood in a fourfold way.

First, Blustein argues, we are responsible for remembering in order to keep past agreements, acknowledge previous blameworthy or praiseworthy actions, offer reparations, and the like. That is to say, in order to keep our promises or to account for prior injustice or heroism, we have the obligation to remember. Our moral responsibilities extend over time, and to meet them, we need to remember them (31). But the obligation to remember, Blustein goes on to argue, should not be limited to recalling events or facts that result from deeds that we freely and knowingly perform. Following the work of Bernard Williams and Margaret Urban Walker, Blustein argues that responsibility includes but goes beyond matters of moral agency to subsume aspects of the moral life that are not under our control. Responsibility is not only about deeds; it is also about character. It therefore requires us to take ownership of our past, including events to which we did not knowingly or willfully contribute in the formation of our character. When we take ownership of our past by managing how it influences the present, we can experience ourselves less as products than as persons with an augmented sense of self-command.

Second, and in a related vein, Blustein argues that taking ownership of our past—including its voluntary and nonvoluntary aspects—is constitutive of identity. As a duty to the self, Blustein argues, we have an obligation to remember. Our self-understanding is informed in no small part by the memories that inform a sense of who we are as particular persons. Having an identity is *itself* a source of value in a metapsychological way: an agent's identity makes it valuable for him or her to do certain things that might not be valuable to someone else. Understanding how memory encumbers duties to the self, it should be added, pertains to individuals as well as groups. Individuals and communities are diachronic in that they maintain a considerable measure of continuity over time. "Memory is critically important for personal identity," Blustein writes, because "it preserves and makes available for us the past experiences, actions, relationships and so forth that furnish our sense of self" (43). Thus understood, memory enjoys a reciprocal relationship with identity: it both forms and is informed by our efforts to answer the question of who we are. For that reason individuals and communities owe it to themselves to carry out memory work as expressive and constitutive features of their identities.

Issues surrounding communal memory raise specific questions that open up two additional reasons for justifying the responsibility to remember. Drawing on Margalit's distinctions between thin and thick relationships and between morality and ethics, Blustein argues that duties of remembrance obligate us in universal, as well as in particularistic, terms. Universal duties are heterological. They pertain, as they do for Margalit, to our obligations to strangers qua human. These are moral duties. More intimate or particularistic duties pertain to specific communal relationships, generating for Blustein (as for Margalit) an ethics of memory.

For Blustein, then, the moral demands of memory have far-reaching implications. They bear on (1) our understanding of responsibility, (2) the formation of individual and collective identity and (3) nonpreferential ties, as well as (4) preferential ties. Each of these four claims about memory's demands requires further unpacking.

The most fundamental reason to explain imperatives of memory is both backward-looking and forward-looking: we must take responsibility for what we have done and keep our promises about what we aim to do. The imperatives of memory thus require us to ensure that morally important aspects of our pasts are not lost or forgotten. But for Blustein understanding memory's obligations in such obvious terms is to overlook a wider range of morally relevant dimensions of our lives and agency. In addition to being responsible for our culpable acts and commitments, we are responsible for personalities and collective identities, including aspects of our identity to which we have not knowingly or volitionally contributed. This is not to theorize, as Booth does, about habit memory or the autonomy of memory, the idea that a silent, continuous flame of memory sustains the life of a community over time. Citing the example of how the 1921 Tulsa race riots were all but forgotten in the official memory of Oklahoma history, Blustein makes plain that memory *itself* is an object of obligation—that memory requires conscious and deliberate protection from the erosion of time. Hence one imperative for Blustein is to sustain memorial practices through civic and religious rituals.

Blustein's attention to the link between memory and nonvoluntary aspects of identity takes a different tack from Booth's. For Blustein the idea that nonvoluntary events and forces contribute to personality invites us to reckon with how they connect with personal self-knowledge and self-command. A healthy sense of agency derives, in part, from taking responsibility for one's fate. Accordingly, we are able to assume a measure of control over our past, to appropriate it and thematize its significance. Viewing memory as aiding that larger project of self-knowledge encourages us to learn from the past and understand its moral meaning, which may change as we acquire new insights, frameworks, and outlooks over time. Moral agency, in this view, is not merely a matter of having powers of self-knowledge and self-determination. Blustein instead endorses the idea of *judgmental* agency, whereby we determine not only whether we are culpable or praiseworthy for a deed but also whether some aspects of our past should be praised or criticized as we look back on them and seek to integrate their meanings into our individual or collective narratives. It is also the case, Blustein argues, that the experience of past injustice contributes to an individual's or group's identity. In some instances, in fact, the experience of injustice is essential to understanding the history and identity of a particular group or individual. For that reason as well, memory's link to identity and historical grievance helps us understand why memory is a proper object of obligation.

Taking responsibility for the past, as my previous comments make plain, includes but can go beyond events for which an individual or current members of a collectivity are directly responsible. Regarding individual moral responsibility, Blustein argues that being accountable for the past refers to prior actions, as well as "what one has *shown oneself to be like* by what one has done" (65). Echoing Aristotle's idea that we are responsible for the formation of our ends,[42] Blustein claims that there are patterns of conduct that point to relatively enduring personality traits that may well require one to change, insofar as one can, how one leads one's life. Responsibility thus consists of "taking control of how the past affects one's life now and going forward" (74). It is often within one's power to alter the significance of the past for one's life and relations to others, and responsibility encompasses duties to reckon with the past in that way.

Regarding collective responsibility, Blustein argues that successors can assume responsibilities for actions performed by a prior collectivity, moral aspects of which fall into consequentialist and nonconsequentialist modes of moral thinking. Collectivities can acknowledge past injustices in order to make amends, to reconcile with alienated groups, or to make sense of acts of reparation. When representatives of a community apologize for their predecessors' prior injustices, for example, they recontextualize the past and change its significance for the present. Understood in such terms, memory work seeks to produce favorable outcomes. But a consequentialist justification for memory work, Blustein repeatedly avows, captures only part of its moral dimensions. Drawing on the work of Elizabeth

Anderson, Blustein argues that memorial practices should also be understood in terms of *expressive* norms, norms that require us to express appropriate attitudes and feelings toward others.[43] How we remember "can be intrinsically valuable because it expresses valuable attitudes and emotions" (28). Respect, honor, admiration, and toleration exemplify acts that flow from expressive norms. Such norms offer a hybrid of deontic and areteic moral concepts in that they are principled and say something about the agent who expresses them, and they aim to realize intrinsically valuable goods. Symbolic acts of memory, acts that cannot be plausibly understood as aiming to change a state of affairs, arise from expressive norms insofar as they seek to acknowledge the moral standing of past victims and express a shared commitment to ethical principles that were breached in the past. The past is thus recontextualized: it no longer means that subverting the moral order represents the actual values of the community (143). Moreover, mainstream groups offer recognition to nonmainstream or marginalized groups when they recall the importance of past events that are integral to nonmainstream groups' ongoing self-understanding. Acts of remembrance that focus on the historical experiences of previously victimized groups thus help to secure their sense of distinctness and identity. Memorial practices, grounded in this way, support a sense of a group's "own worth and a dignified sense of its collective identity" (164).

The moral demands of memory, then, encumber our individual and collective lives on terms that are consequentialist and expressive and according to a capacious view of responsibility that has implications for understanding identity and agency. Having established these ideas as his platform, Blustein proceeds to discuss specific aspects of collective identity that refine our understanding of memory's moral demands. In this vein he notes that collective memory has a bipolarity that we do well to note. At one pole stand the demands of history, tied to the requirements of truth; at the other pole stand the demands of social cohesion, tied not only to the requirements of truth but also to forms of expression akin to myth. For Blustein truth is context-independent, while myth is context-relative, connected to particular identities and a common heritage. Collective memories seek to preserve true accounts of the past but also endeavor to promote social cohesion and integration. For that reason collective memory oscillates uneasily between the demands of history and those of myth.

With this distinction between history and myth in place Blustein engages Margalit on the difference between morality and ethics. Drawing on the distinction between thin and thick contexts of memory, Blustein places a higher premium on moral memory than does Margalit by claiming that such a morality responds to the impartial demands of truth as a regulative ideal. More precisely, the moral imperative of collective memory is "an obligation to remember accurately, to be conscientious in remembering and to strive to discover (and uncover) and, without distortion, obfuscation, and the like, convey the truth about the past" (213). That imperative is not merely to provide an accurate report of events and persons in the past but also to put "the facts together in a certain way in order to convey their import, moral, political, cultural, and so forth" (214). These demands are owed to others as fellow human beings, although they are properly "assigned to particular communities because they are best able or most qualified to discharge it" (216).

In contrast, the ethics of memory—drawing as it does from thick relations—pertains to our intimate relationships, to those near and dear. It thus includes context-relative, mythical aspects of remembrance that aim in part at social cohesion, communal identity, and transmitting a common heritage across generations. Collective memory in this respect is "more interested in symbolic meaning and resonance than in historical accuracy" (222). Communal remembrance "shapes a community's sense of its identity, draws the community's members together around a shared understanding of their past and its contribution to the present, and is capable of inspiring and motivating collective action" (222). The duties that attach to an ethics of memory, then, are internally related to the good of some particular form of collective life and the good of maintaining it.

The internal relationship between memory and social goods entails a moral standard, the effect of which is to disqualify some groups from making normative claims on behalf of their memorial practices. For Blustein, whether a certain communal relationship should be sustained through practices of collective memory "will at least partly depend on the moral character of the group in question and the relationships among its members" (225). That is to say, a group must satisfy some baseline moral criteria in order to lay claim to any ethics of memory. In this respect Blustein has an answer to the problem I put to Booth with my example of memorializing the Confederacy in the American South: groups that are bound together by ignoble traditions, however much their members may care about each other and seek to preserve a common heritage, have no justification for claiming the need for an ethics of memory. Making normative demands about the value of preserving the good of community through memorial practices presupposes that the community in question serves genuine moral goods. Groups that honor the memory of defending slavery fail to meet that standard.

Blustein then turns from that normative insight to broader metaethical questions regarding the ethics of memory. His aim is to make sense of why we ought to remember those who are near and dear, especially those who were close friends or intimates and are now deceased. What does it say about a relationship with someone if we forget about her during her lifetime or after her passing? Blustein replies that the duties that pertain to the ethics of memory can be explained by the idea that we owe it to remember others as an expression of love. Taking as his point of departure Søren Kierkegaard's idea that remembering the dead can be a work of love, Blustein embarks on a searching discussion of love, memory, and death.[44] Central to his discussion is the distinction between a conative, or desire-based, account of love, premised on the notion that a beloved satisfies a set of needs or wishes, and an evaluative account of love, premised on the notion that we love someone because we value him or her. For Blustein an account of love that properly explains the (ethical) duty to remember cannot be a desire-based account, for we would lose the motive to love once the object of love ceases to satisfy our desires by ceasing to exist. When, for example, we lose a close friend, our desire-based love loses its proper object or source of fulfillment, leaving us with motives to love only the memory of the deceased or the postmortem person. As an alternative Blustein advances an evaluative account of love, according to which love is a way of valuing a person. Following David Velleman, Blustein describes love as "an awareness of a value inhering in its object . . . an arresting awareness of that value" (256).[45] Memory-as-an-expression of love in this evaluative account would hold that we should not only love the memory of a person or the postmortem person but that we should remember "the person as I knew him; the person who possessed particular qualities that I came to love precisely because they were the qualities of someone I loved" (257). The work of love in remembering the dead is thus "a work of . . . continuing to value a loved one after his or her death, despite 'the multiplicity of life's demands' that press on us and make this valuing a challenge and an achievement" (260).

We remember loved ones on these evaluative terms, Blustein adds, for reasons that again sort themselves out along consequentialist and nonconsequentialist lines. There are desirable outcomes that attach to memorial practices in the ethics of memory, outcomes that include punishing those who deserve it, preventing future wrongdoing, enabling forgiveness when appropriate, and reconstructing social relationships. Our manner of valuing loved ones finds proper expression when we seek such ends. But these consequentialist reasons, however important, leave out something valuable in our experience of memory's ethical demands. We have obligations to remember in part because memorial practices enable us to express certain kinds of attitudes toward those who have died, and we express such attitudes in how we remember. On this expressivist account we "appeal to norms that tell us what attitudes to express toward the dead," attitudes of "appropriate evaluation" (268).

We can express appropriate feelings and values, Blustein observes, in three ways: by rescuing the dead from insignificance, by expressing enduring duties of love and honor to those who were special to us, and by carrying out memorial practices regarding others on the premise that we would want them carried out for ourselves. Taken together, these nonconsequentialist reasons point to complex motives in the ethics of memory. Blustein writes, "We ought to remember the dear departed because in doing so we declare that death has not eliminated what was distinctive and valuable about them; because we expect to be remembered after we die by those who are near and dear to us; and because we thereby give our predecessors the love and honor that we still owe, even after their deaths" (281).

Blustein concludes his study by turning to what he notes at the book's outset as one of the driving forces behind contemporary studies of memory—namely, the idea of bearing witness in the face of massive injustice. Bearing witness, he observes, intertwines individual and collective memorial practices. But bearing witness has non-mnemonic aspects that include getting at and telling the truth about another's suffering.

That is to say, like other forms of offering testimony, bearing witness as a form of remembrance includes the obligation to reveal a truth "that may be hidden or obscured or is one that others may, for various reasons, not want disclosed" (304).

More so than Margalit or Booth, Blustein examines the normative value of bearing witness. Consistent with his prior discussion of duties that are attached to the ethics of memory, he parses normative dimensions of bearing witness along consequentialist and expressivist lines. Bearing witness can have instrumental or consequentialist value insofar as it restores the mental health of survivors, catalyzes social reconstruction, prompts humanitarian assistance, and brings crimes to light (329). It may help to end oppression, restore lost possessions, and compensate victims when restitution is not possible (344). In addition, bearing witness has symbolic value that is normatively important on nonconsequentialist grounds. Such testimony expresses an allegiance to the good and a repudiation of the bad. It is a way of affirming the moral order itself over and against, say, values attached to efficiency or expedience. Bearing witness can thereby affirm the moral status of victims and their equal membership in the moral community—their status as free and equal persons. It allows victims to give voice to their justified grievances and rediscover their dignity in response to prior degradation. As such, bearing witness can empower victims by enabling them to recover their sense of moral agency or, when exercised by proxies, by affirming their agency. Furthermore, bearing witness can exemplify moral integrity, the capacity to abide steadfastly by one's convictions in the face of pressures to do otherwise. Put in terms I invoked in my introduction, bearing witness is a speech-act by the other, a petition that demands a hearing.

In these terms Blustein clarifies moral intuitions about the nonconsequentialist value of bearing witness, developing a line of argument about memory's intrinsic goodness about which he devotes considerable attention throughout *The Moral Demands of Memory*. His book is the most sustained and intelligent effort to bring normative theory to bear on memory. Blustein's work is important if for no other reason than that he clearly and persuasively defends his expressivist convictions and their distinctive implications for understanding normative aspects of memory. But regarding moral theory and memory, an ongoing tension courses through Blustein's argument. And there is the germ of an idea that is underdeveloped.

The tension is between consequentialist and expressivist reasons for remembering. These provide different grounds and compete in different ways with each other and with countervailing considerations. The core problem is this: it is unclear if we are to place these modes of moral theorizing on equal footing when thinking about the moral demands of memory. Thus it remains unclear how we are to adjudicate between them when they conflict with each other as moral foundations for performing memory work. The conflicts I have in mind are not only abstract or philosophical; they have concrete implications.

Put another way, Blustein's "all things considered" approach to the moral demands of memory is not helpful for social advocates or social critics of memorial practices. If we adopt a consequentialist line of reasoning, then ascertaining when and on what terms we are to carry out memory work would have us assess memory's instrumental value in relation to a cluster of other social goods. We would then ask if preserving or restoring the memory of this or that legacy is socially beneficial or if it should yield to other political or social priorities, thus allowing for political or other kinds of forgetting. But that analysis will not help us when thinking about memory's inherent value along expressivist lines. Preserving or restoring memory for the sake of redeeming the dignity of predecessors who have suffered injustice and degradation on expressivist grounds might have socially divisive or other deleterious consequences. If we are to adopt an "all things considered" approach to evaluating memory work, then we might justifiably decide to table or postpone the recovery of lost memories. But that decision would subject expressivist defenses of memory to consequentialist reasons. Blustein seems not to grasp how his two main moral theories for assessing memory's value create the need for moral or political adjudication at a higher level of theorizing.

Like Margalit, Blustein accepts the distinction between the morality of memory and the ethics of memory that relies on the distinction between thin and thick relationships. While Blustein is more mindful of memory's moral demands and the potential tension between them and the ethical demands of memory, he nonetheless fails to tell us why anyone outside of thick relations should care about memory's willful failures in those (thick) contexts. If the ethics of thick relations are so important, then one would think that its importance transcends the contexts of those thick relationships themselves. If I fail to remember an important friend or family member, does my failure have moral importance beyond the parameters of those relationships? May someone outside of those relationships fault me for failing to duly honor or remember a close family member of mine (but not hers)? Intuitively, an affirmative answer suggests itself. My forgetting would express something about me, and not only to other members of my family. But if that intuition is correct, then additional moral concepts are needed to make sense of how outsiders can judge the actions and dispositions of an individual in a thick relationship of which they are not a part. We often care about how (or whether) our close friends care about (and remember) others, and that fact requires more conceptualization than Blustein or Margalit provide.

One novel idea that we frequently encounter in Blustein's account is the connection between memory and a concept to which I refer in my introduction, namely, the concept of acknowledgment. Consider a few examples taken from Blustein's text. When speaking about the work done by truth commissions, he writes that "even after prosecutions and truth commissions have finished their work, these acknowledgments of the past can serve a useful social function" (24). When addressing what good comes from remembering, Blustein indicates as one reason that "we need to acknowledge what we have done in the past in order to make amends for it" (35). When speaking of a (fictional) individual who takes ownership of her unhappy past, he writes that "she takes up this part of her past and acknowledges it as her own, and her acknowledging it as her own uplifts her" (58; see also 73). When we expect a group to take responsibility for past wrongs, he observes, "we expect it to at least acknowledge the wrongs for which it is responsible, and . . . to remember what happened, why it happened, and to whom" (118). Similarly, Blustein describes apologizing for past wrongdoing as expressing the responsible party's "acknowledgment of the legitimacy of the victim's claim and the wrongness of the prior conduct" (143; see also 162, 165).

Blustein would have done well to unpack the various ways in which memory and acknowledgment are connected. It is clear from his account that memory-as-acknowledgment bears some resemblance to the Cavellian ideas I sketched at the outset of this book. In Cavell's view acknowledgment is a matter of my responding to something you are exhibiting—specifically, a matter of revealing a set of feelings or interests in response to a claim you place on me. When taken into the context of memory studies, the idea would be that the past places a claim on the present, thereby enjoying a certain entitlement. In that way we might say that the past, like the other, speaks in the imperative mood as a form of petition. On that view memory work operates according to an underlying set of normative commitments. To acknowledge the past is to respond to a claim by the past or from the past. And that claim is not about the value of remembering a prior moral accomplishment or wrongdoing. Blustein's capacious account of taking ownership of a past that bears on the present includes but goes beyond events or traits that have some moral valence. A person who takes ownership does so "for actions, episodes, or personal characteristics that somehow implicate his agency, and as one who takes responsibility for his past, he will acknowledge this fact" (64). Memory is a matter, in part at least, of reckoning with alterities that are one's own—intimate alterities—and responding to them. These ideas point to the fact that we do not come to memory in a neutral way; rather, memory is ethically charged from the ground up. Memory, in this reckoning, is not only a matter of duty or virtue. That is to say, memory is not only a matter about which, or toward which, we are related in terms of obligations or excellences. As that which invites acknowledgment, memory is a matter about which we are morally related in an inescapable way—as that toward which any stance we take exposes something fundamental about ourselves.

PLACE, CATASTROPHE, AND MEMORIALIZATION

As I noted earlier in my discussion of Ricoeur, there is a distinction between memory's "worldliness" and its "reflexivity," between "undergoing" a memory and "having" a memory. In political life these forms of memory coalesce in the effort to inculcate collective memory, that is, when we mindfully create occasions of memory with an eye toward habituating civic identity and communal solidarity. Such forms of memory might be classified as embodied or as habit-memory but not principally in the sense of being interiorized. Rather, some forms of memory are embodied and *exteriorized* in monuments and civic occasions—in "place memory" and commemorative events.[46]

Oren Baruch Stier and J. Shawn Landres's edited collection *Religion, Violence, Memory, and Place* takes up this feature of memory's exteriorization by examining contemporary ritualistic, spatial, and political features of memorial practice across a range of cultural contexts. Examining the "geography of memory," their book brings together theoretical chapters that explore aspects of place, mourning, and theology along with descriptive chapters that focus on memory and its contestation in specific locales: the Armenian diaspora, Auschwitz, Hiroshima, Rwanda, Herzegovina, South Africa, Haiti, South Dakota, New York City, and Washington, D.C. In contrast to Margalit's effort to "disentangle religion from the ethics of memory as far as it can safely and sensibly be defended,"[47] Stier and Landres propose an inextricable connection between the two.

To that end Stier and Landres advance two claims in the book's introduction: first, that memory is an essential dimension of religion and, second, that religion is an essential component of memory.[48] They document how a memorial dimension of religion has been almost entirely overlooked in religious studies and that any religious component of memory has received only piecemeal attention. Accordingly, their collection aims to show that memory is an essential ingredient of religion along the lines of Ninian Smart's sevenfold dimensionalization of religion as experiential, mythic, ethical, ritual, doctrinal, political, and social and that religion is "a multidimensional aspect that is part and parcel of human memorial activity."[49] The book organizes its subsequent thirteen chapters around philosophical issues in memory studies, followed by empirical/interpretive chapters on ritual and memory, space and politics, and challenges to the contemporary construction of memory. The book concludes with reflections on "haunted landscapes" by a leading scholar of American public history, Edward T. Linenthal.

Chapters that best coordinate reference to the book's four organizing rubrics of religion, memory, violence, and place are by Tania Oldenhage, Timothy Longman and Théoneste Rutagengwa, Terry Rey, and James Foard. But those four concepts do not find themselves integrated along

the same coordinates or to the same degree in each chapter. Two examples
help illustrate this fact. In her study of Holocaust remembrance in Germany, "Walking the Way of the Cross: German Places, Church Traditions,
and Holocaust Memories," Oldenhage describes the enactment of the
"Way of the Cross," a Christian procession patterned after the Stations
of the Cross that leads German Christians through the streets of their
hometowns so that they can learn the identities of Jewish families who
were once part of the community. She notes the highly ambiguous aspect
of remembering the Holocaust through the lens of the Christian passion
narrative, especially the German Christians' ritual use of an image that
places Jesus Christ at the center of a death camp. Her own view is that
this is an acceptable use of symbolism, not a form of Christian imperialism, given that each person needs an interpretive lens to make sense of
the past in a meaningful way. In contrast to this rendering of religion and
memory, Longman and Rutagengwa's chapter, "Religion, Memory, and
Violence in Rwanda," concentrates on religion not as an aid to memory
but as its target. They describe the Rwandan government's effort to discredit Christianity by associating Protestant and Catholic churches with
anti-Tutsi massacres. The Rwandan government's memorial efforts have
aimed to "de-sanctify" Christian churches in order to create a more cohesive postgenocidal social order on non-Christian terms. One might say in
the Rwandan case that remembering at one (institutional) level requires
forgetting at another (popular) level. In any event Oldenhage and Longman and Rutagengwa show that even where religion is a component along
with memory, violence, and locale, its role is hardly stable or necessarily
pertinent to all the presumed "rememberers."

Rey's chapter, "Vodou, Water, and Exile: Symbolizing Spirit and Pain
in Port-au-Prince," is one of the more successful efforts at coordinating
the four organizing concepts of the book. In 1995 the Haitian government commissioned the construction of the Monument to the Refugees to
commemorate the lives of those lost as "boat people" crossing the Carib-
bean. The monument, shaped as a sailboat, sits on the site of a natural
well that Vodou practitioners consider sacred ground. Rey describes how
Haitians saturate a public memorial with religious meanings that draw on
Christian and Vodou vocabularies, including the image of the dead being
"across the water" to honor those who have lost their lives at sea. Drawing

on ethnographic and historical analysis, Rey tacks back and forth between Africa and Haiti to identify dense layers of symbolic meaning attached to the Monument to the Refugees. The site recalls, among other things, enslaved ancestors as well as modern refugees. As a "vehicle of memory" the monument "represents death, rebirth, and the crossing of water (while also giving water to the people of Tabarre)"[50] and reflects "many important ideas, both pure and impure to Haitians: human origins and destiny; the structure of the universe; the spirits and the dead; the meaning of life and death; the pain of global economics; African rhythms and roots; and the desperate voyages of overcrowded, rickety sailboats."[51]

In "Vehicles of Memory: The *Enola Gay* and the Streetcars of Hiroshima," Foard focuses less on place as a determinate location than on how memory is "carried" by symbolic vehicles. Drawing on Margalit's notion of thick relationships, along with his recognition that radical evil challenges morality as a whole, Foard examines how Japan and the United States have handled the memory of the atomic bombing of Hiroshima.[52] In Japan, memorial practices have drawn from the tradition of ancestor worship and the need to establish a place for moral witnessing. With this tradition in the background, in 1985 the Hiroshima Electric Rail Company identified the location of every streetcar at the time of the bombing so that survivors could perform memorial rites to (and connect with) those who were killed. The 1994 exhibit of the *Enola Gay* at the U.S. Air and Space Museum, in contrast, drew from Judeo-Christian tropes of salvation and represented the aircraft as a vehicle of peace. For Foard the difference between the "ground level" symbolism of street cars and the "air level" symbolism of the airplane is telling. One set of symbols enabled solidarity and connection with the past, while the other symbol enabled distanciation and a fixation on the future. For the Japanese "the striking precision about place in the streetcar group serves both to authorize and make real their testimonies of the unique horrors of nuclear weapons and further to connect their moral witness to the repose of the particular dead for whom they feel a bond from the happenstance of sharing a streetcar ride" (122). For Americans Hiroshima became "only the prefiguration of a nuclear future approached with a biblically rooted combination of soteriological hope and existential dread"—a prefiguration that "allowed Americans to keep their distance from the particular dead and the particular place of Hiroshima" (119). The two vehicles of memory, moreover, represent "a dilemma posed by the jurisdiction over memory by less than universal communities even when the morality that binds universal humanity is threatened" (126–27). One conclusion that Foard might have drawn from the American example would put an ironic twist on Margalit's categories: sometimes ethical communities remember in ways that prevent them from expressing moral witness.

The remaining essays combine two or three of this book's organizing concepts. In "Indigenous Traditions, Alien Abductions: Creolized and Globalized Memory in South Africa," David Chidester describes the phenomenon of fabricated memory with the story of an influential charlatan, Credo Mutwa, and his efforts to market his brand of political memory (in person and in cyberspace) in postapartheid South Africa. The son of a convert to Christian Science, Mutwa worked for more than thirty years as an apologist for apartheid, a Zulu witchdoctor, an African tourist attraction, an employee of the South African Parks Board, a self-described liaison with extraterrestrial beings, and a self-appointed curator of indigenous memory. Of central importance for Chidester is that Mutwa effectively commercialized his authority and role as custodian of memory, thereby moving indigenous memory into the global marketplace, aided by the Internet. In Mutwa we see memory less as a matter of place than of displacement, less as a way to preserve identity than to manufacture it for self-interested ends. Flora A. Keshgegian's essay, "Finding a Place Past Night: Armenian Genocidal Memory in Diaspora," calls attention to Armenian-American nostalgia and utopian yearnings for what are essentially nonplaces in the homeland. Armenian diasporan memory, in her description, is keenly dislocated and imaginary, driven by traumatic memories of genocide and the need for restorative healing and a sense of place. Here memory elides into fixation on locale. As Keshgegian observes, for diasporan memories of this sort, "nation is . . . a remedy for trauma."[53] Michelene E. Pesantubbee's chapter, "Wounded Knee: Site of Resistance and Recovery," notes how memory of the massacre at Wounded Knee has functioned among the Lakota not only to organize commemorative pilgrimages but, more importantly, to mobilize contemporary activism among Native Americans on behalf of cultural rights. Lakota memorial practices have worked to restore a culturally dead tradition, materializing one hundred years after the historic atrocity and congealing around resistance to ongoing American colonization. Memory in this case has less to do with looking back than with looking ahead (as if to echo Ricoeur's point about the productive potential of memory).

In at least two instances the *absence* of explicit attention to religion in a site of violence and memory is noted. In "Memory, Religion, and Conflict at Auschwitz: A Manifesto" Jonathan Webber observes that religion is absent from the remembrance at Auschwitz and that traditional Jewish leaders do not believe that it requires its own specific religious or theological commemoration. Unlike other experiences of suffering and injustice in Jewish history, Auschwitz has not produced a fundamental change or development in Jewish ritual. Janet Liebman Jacobs's chapter, "Remembering Genocide: Gender Representation and the Objectification of Jewish Women at Majdanek," reinforces this point by noting that religion does little to frame the representation of female victims of the Holocaust in Eastern European Holocaust museums. In "The Stages of Memory at Ground Zero" James E. Young describes the World Trade Center Memorial Jury's deliberations and notes a concern for creating a 9/11 memorial that captures the twin motifs of "loss and renewal," but nothing more, as exemplified in the competitors' designs and the winning entry by Michael Arad and Peter Walker. These three chapters testify to religion's absence from sites that memorialize catastrophic violence. So the place of religion or religious themes in the sites under review is uneven at best.

All of this is to say that only some of the book's chapters actually carry out Stier and Landres's twofold proposal, and some defy it. One problem is that "religion" is understood too abstractly to serve as an effective organizing concept for the book. In some places *religion* refers to an ostensive tradition, for example, Christianity, Judaism, or Japanese ancestor worship; in other places it refers to the mobilization of traditional themes (for example, redemption); and in other places it is marked by general references to sacrality. In some chapters the memorialization under review is not religious in nature but rather the commemoration of violence carried out in the name of religion. For instance, in "In the Name of Mary: Sacred Space, Sacred Property, and Absolution of Past Sins" Juan A. Herrero Brasas describes the involvement of Franciscans in the mass killings and forced conversions in the former Yugoslavia during the Second World War. Noting religion's implication in the memorable violence at a specific locale (Brasas) is quite different from invoking religious idioms to frame the memory of violence at a locale (Oldenhage). These conceptual points and distinctions are lost in the generalities that shape Stier and Landres's desire to describe religion and memory as deeply intertwined.

That said, there is much to be gained from *Religion, Violence, Memory, and Place* if one steps away from Stier and Landres's strong theoretical proposals. The fact that memory is important to individual and collective identity across a variety of regions and cultures is documented in vivid detail. The experiential challenges of memorializing traumatic events and the tensions between the common good's need for justice and forgiveness are well documented. The fluid, contentious, enduring, and productive dimensions of memory likewise find ample expression. How memories of the same event play themselves out in different contexts invites comparative discussion and analysis. Most important, these essays demonstrate that memory is not merely a private or interior experience; it is willfully exteriorized in formal and informal ways. Memory has a public, material life.

* * *

These five works along with others I have cited open up a range of issues that can energize more sustained attention to the ethics and politics of memory in religious ethics and moral philosophy. They enable us to identify specific concepts and contexts in which attention to the interior and exterior features of memory invite normative analysis. Happy or unhappy, memories are a feature of everyday life in its private and public expressions. Memories both shape and arrest the development of individual identity and communities over time. Their link to religious traditions and practices, whether necessary or contingent, is impossible to ignore. That memory is contested in our personal and political lives is a tribute to its value, as well as to our sense of moral responsibility in the face of its fragility and potential for abuse.

As Ricoeur reminds us, the philosophy and ethics of memory enjoy an impressive pedigree, harking back to Plato, Aristotle, Augustine, and

Locke (among others). The five works under review here invite readers to pick up that legacy and to press it into new sociological, psychological, legal, theological, and ethnographic terrain. They capture memory's vital connections to matters of individual and intergenerational identity, justice, historiography, and human contingency. They also provide resources for exploring memory's complicated relationship with psychological aspects of forgiveness, as well as memory's potentially gnarled connections to liberal democratic public life and culture. More generally, they point to memory's dialectical relationship with social processes, civic formation, and material culture. Along the way they indicate how explorations of memory can broaden the agenda of a religious ethics that is attentive to the synergy of psyche and culture and the moral challenges that accompany the workings of conscience, political witness, and social criticism.

10

RELIGION, PUBLIC REASON, AND THE MORALITY OF DEMOCRATIC AUTHORITY

RELIGIOUS CONVICTIONS AND PUBLIC ARGUMENT

In the last chapter I said that public memory is often infused with matters that can be classified as religious. Public memory frequently has aspects that can be understood according to the heuristic account of religion that I offered in chapter 1. The objects of public memory often possess extraordinary qualities that entitle them to attitudes and related behaviors of reverence, fidelity, honor, devotion, and/or gratitude; have the capacity to bear importantly on human affairs independent of human volition; can resolve or appreciably lessen anxieties about our place, well-being, and experience in the world; can be a source of joy, wonder, awe, or kindred affections; and can be deep or far-reaching in effectuality and pertinence to human life. They can either lend an aura of sacrality to established political institutions, or they can work to weaken or destabilize efforts to legitimate the status quo. Moreover, public memory can identify individuals or groups with whom we connect by using ritual performances and other symbolic activities and can require discursive practices that are understood as having a transcendent quality. Whether by explicitly invoking traditional religious themes and images or by endowing institutions or social movements with timeless and sacred importance, public memory can lend an aura of legitimacy and enchantment to social practices and organizations.

Yet the manner in which religious beliefs, commitments, or ideas *should* inform public discourse and public life is a contested question in liberal, democratic societies. In this chapter I want to step back from issues of religion and public memory to take up more general matters regarding religion in democratic policy formation. In particular, I want to examine the moral appropriateness of using religiously authorized reasons in public policy and political deliberation in liberal democracies.

To focus this analysis, note the following: among the many things that religious adherents do, they argue. They stake claims over and against alternative beliefs and practices, and they do so in a number of ways—by drawing metaphysical distinctions, disputing sources and interpretations of authority, questioning matters of territorial rule, and defending hierarchies of value, for example. Religious believers understand their religious convictions as (among other things) cognitive matters that provide a vision of the good life that invites if not requires practical forms of implementation, including implementation in social and political institutions. Yet reasons that are intimate to religious adherents or that bind them to friends and communities may nonetheless fail to reckon with the other and the fact of difference in public culture and democratic life. Not surprisingly, how religious citizens ought to argue regarding public policy and public life—where their convictions can demonstrably affect the lives of other democratic citizens—is a matter of considerable dispute.

Let us approach the dispute this way: public policies have moral dimensions, and today we often talk, following John Rawls, of the ethical design of political and social institutions in a "well-ordered society."[1] When we think of policies regarding stem cell research, health-care reform, military conflict, or sexual orientation, for example, we are considering basic values regarding moral status, health and welfare, communal safety, or personal identity, among other things. And frequently those values find exponents who draw on religious convictions to justify their claims. Such exponents talk about persons born in the image of God, the virtue of neighbor love, the value of nonviolence, or the meaning of *shalom*, for example. It is difficult to imagine Western political and social history without hearing those voices. And those voices do not speak in general or abstract ways. Often, they are intentionally political. They aim at policy construction or institutional reform, and they speak in terms that they consider to be "reasons." They make claims about what they believe to be good and real for themselves as well as for others.[2]

In this chapter I want to think normatively about how religious adherents should address matters of public justice in pluralistic democracies. I do so out of an ongoing interest in the ethics of belief, attending as I think we should to religion's responsibilities to social order and public life. My basic question is whether religious citizens should be allowed to speak on matters of public policy in liberal democracies without any limits on how they express their deeply held convictions, or whether they should restrict their reason-giving to some political terms and values. Specifically, I want to discuss the extent to which religious ideas may operate within the canons of "public reason," an idea advanced by Rawls and a version of which I will describe to set the stage for determining whether or how religious reasons should inform the creation or revision of democratic public policy. Public reason is not simply about the notion that ideas should be publicly available in democratic discourse. It is certainly not about whether to accommodate religious practices in, say, courtrooms or in military service. Rather, public reason establishes a framework for assessing the *kinds of reasons* that may be introduced in democratic deliberations and decision making in the discourse of lawmakers, jurists, and ordinary citizens. It thereby constrains how religious convictions might influence decision making in issues such as democratic policy or reform.

Soon I will unpack these ideas in some detail. One aim of my analysis is to drastically reorient discussions of public reason *away* from self-regarding concerns about the personal importance of religious commitment and expressive freedom and *toward* an ethic of alterity. I want to change the subject regarding religion and public reason from mainstream concerns about the importance of religion to religious individuals or communities to concerns about forging a moral basis for grounding *authority* in pluralistic political regimes committed to the equal sharing of political power. Among other things, I want to make clear that matters regarding religion and public reason are not about "religion and public life" or "religion in the naked public square." Those frameworks are far too general and abstract for understanding the questions to which public reason addresses itself, and they often wrongly suggest that public reason stands or falls on empirical matters regarding religion's ubiquity or social value in the United States and perhaps other societies as well.

To advance my account of public reason as a heterological political ethic, I will introduce the idea of civic empathy, building on the account of empathy that I developed in chapter 4. Civic empathy is the disposition to see the political world—the world of democratic political institutions, roles, hierarchies, offices, policies, charter documents, and responsibilities—through the eyes of others, in a second-personal way. That fact should enable us to see more clearly one of public reason's core features, namely, that it is an other-regarding, egalitarian political ethic.

To sharpen and concretize these ideas, I will address four challenges to the idea of public reason, challenges that allege that it (1) alienates religious believers from their deeper convictions, (2) weakens morality's potential for robust social criticism, (3) fails to protect against wrong results, and (4) relies on an arbitrary distinction between faith-based and secular reasoning. To illustrate how public reason works, I will then turn to three policy cases—cases concerning the regulation of same-sex relationships, reproductive cloning, and racial desegregation. I will say more about why I selected these cases in due course. For one thing, they allow us to engage in some practical moral reasoning in religious ethics and to clarify what public reason, as I interpret it, permits and excludes in matters of public debate.

WHAT IS AND IS NOT PUBLIC REASON

Let us examine the basic idea of public reason. Rawls's defense of the doctrine has several elements that have been misunderstood or misrepresented in the vast commentary generated by his views. I want less to defend Rawls than to use his ideas as a touchstone to develop an account of public reason that clarifies and deepens its meaning for citizen-to-citizen relations in pluralistic democracies. Generally speaking, public reason is an ideal that includes features of all reason, such as inferential reasoning and relying on rules of evidence, as well as generally shared beliefs about the world, common sense, and noncontroversial methods of science. It is an ideal, moreover, that applies to "the basic moral and political values that are to determine a constitutional democratic government's relation to its citizens and their relation to one another."[3] "A citizen engages in public reason," Rawls writes, "when he or she deliberates within a framework of what he or she sincerely regards as the most reasonable political conception of justice, a conception that expresses political values that others, as free and equal citizens might also reasonably be expected reasonably to endorse" (581). The idea is to argue with "others . . . as free and equal citizens, and not as dominated or manipulated, or under the pressure of an inferior political or social position" (578).

The requirement to produce shareable reasons does not mean that public reason is, as might be assumed, secular reason. Secular reason is one example of what Rawls terms "comprehensive nonreligious doctrines" (583). Recalling his distinction between *political morality* and *comprehensive doctrines*, Rawls insists that public reason is a political matter, not one that presupposes a metaphysical vision for support (574). A doctrine is comprehensive, Rawls writes, "when it includes conceptions of what is of value in human life, and ideals of personal character, as well as ideals of friendship and of familial and associational relationships, and much else that is to inform our conduct, and in the limit to our life as a whole."[4] Comprehensive doctrines such as secularism aim to provide a worldview and supervise the way that reason directs individual or collective action. However much Mormonism differs from the secular humanism of Erich Fromm or the materialistic determinism of B. F. Skinner, all are comprehensive doctrines. The fact that secular reason is nonreligious does not make it less comprehensive than other totalizing worldviews or organizing practical beliefs. Public reason requires no totalizing vision, thereby providing a more capacious framework when considering views that are introduced in debates about constitutional issues and matters of basic justice.[5]

I want to isolate a concept from Rawlsian public reason to develop a central—but widely overlooked—concern, namely, the moral basis of democratic political authority. The main question to which the idea of public reason is addressed is this: on what basis may members of a pluralistic democratic society justifiably bind themselves on matters of constitutional essentials and basic justice? And what sorts of reasons, if any, may be used to restrict the liberties of other citizens? The main idea is that public policies may not justifiably lay claim to securing others' consent if the processes that led to such a policy made no effort to secure reasoned agreement. In a democracy the authority to rule others must be secured on terms that are shareable. In that way the policy expresses the "general will" or the "will of the people," and it aims to respect those who are addressed by the policy.[6] On the idea that political authority is shared, moreover, democracies ground themselves as politically autonomous in a literal sense: they are political entities that aim to be self-governing. Public reason thus aspires to find a common vantage point, a shareable language, according to which public policies may be evaluated. When thinking about the merits of a policy, citizens may draw from their self-defining beliefs for their personal moral guidance, but when deciding on that policy, they must restrict the appeals they make to reasons they reasonably believe can lay claim to being others' political reasons as well.[7]

Note that I am not saying that public reason puts restraints on religious language and beliefs that might be expressed in cultural debates about policy—say on television, at town hall meetings, in protest marches, and the like. Jeffrey Stout is among several critics with concerns about public reason's potential for placing a gag order on religious speech in those settings:

> I have heard that [Stanley] Hauerwas expressed the religious reasons for his criticism of U.S. militarism in public, before a religiously mixed gathering of citizens in the nation's capital, not long after September 11, 2001. . . . Hauerwas's audience on this occasion presumably included people who were concerned about such basic questions as whether states have a right to fight wars of self-defense and whether the constitutional provision requiring Congress to declare war continues to apply. These citizens were anxious to hear the arguments of a highly influential pacifist and also to hear those arguments subjected to public criticism from other points of view. Democracy would not have been better served, it seems to me, if these reasons had been circulated only behind the closed doors of churches and religiously affiliated schools, where they would have been somewhat less likely to face skeptical objections.[8]

But public reason is not about policing religious speech, or any speech, in inclusive, pluralistic cultural fora.[9] No restrictions are required when we discuss the merits of this or that policy in public culture.

Although Rawls is not always clear on this point, he labels this broad public realm the "background culture" or "the culture of civil society" as opposed to the more restricted realm in which we decide on a matter of policy.[10] On the view I am describing, debate that occurs in background culture can be freewheeling, and religious convictions can be expressed in whole cloth. Unbridled moral and religious discussion has the obvious benefit that through it we may come to change our minds, and democracy would be poorly served by limiting the moral resources on which citizens can and do rely. It may also be the case, as one of my examples will illustrate, that on some contested issues few if any nonreligious views enjoy widespread currency. Public reason is not about privatizing religion in the many fora of civil society.

To be clear: thus far I have been using the term *public* in a commonsensical way. Strictly speaking, however, debates in civil society are *private* insofar as they do not aim to provide a basis for legally coercing other citizens. Such debates might be loud and highly visible, and they might take place in open, inclusive settings—settings that pose no bar to anyone's participation—but they are nonetheless private. *Private* in the *precise sense* does not mean *secret*, *sequestered*, or *behind closed doors*. It should rather be understood on the model of private property: even when property is visible in public and has a public address, it is private insofar as an individual or group possesses authority over its alienation in market transfers absent state control. That which is *private* is in my possession, not the state's. Likewise, *public* in the *precise sense* refers to that over which popular sovereignty is exercised. It concerns matters about which democratic citizens as shareholders of power exert influence on each other in matters regarding policy formation or reform.[11] Recall that, for Rawls, public reason applies to "the basic moral and political values that are to determine a constitutional democratic government's relation to its citizens and their relation to one another."[12] As we proceed, I will be referring to public reason as pertaining to matters over which we share power as political sovereigns and subjects—as mutual stakeholders in our franchise as democratic citizens. I'll call this domain, following Rawls, the "public political forum."

Understanding "the public" in this way means that debates about public reason are not about "religion in the naked public square," or "religion in public life," as is often assumed.[13] The categories "public square" and "public life" are far too abstract, amorphous, and imprecise for understanding the problems and the forum to which the idea of public reason addresses itself. Moreover (and in a related vein), public reason takes no stand on the secularization thesis. It is in no way a threat to, or embarrassed by, the existence of religion in modern Western societies. The fact that religion exists in the "public square" or in "public life" is not a rebuttal—or some kind of answer—to those who defend public reason; that fact instead helps to launch the problems with which public reason is concerned. It is important to be precise about *the kind* of public square to which public reason applies. As I have noted, the kind of public square is a democratic one. The key term is *democratic*. The doctrine of public reason addresses itself to the proper terms according to which policies are evaluated and reformed within liberal democratic polities in which power is to be shared equally among citizens. Religious convictions or religious reasons are one set of the many possible kinds of reasons to which public reason applies itself.

This first clarification requires a second: public reason has as its target the ethics of political coercion and the underlying notion that democratic authority relies on popular consent. The core assumption is that limiting other citizens' legal freedoms shoulders a considerable burden of proof. Rawls conceives of the issue about "how, when constitutional essentials and matters of basic justice are at stake, citizens so related (as free and equal) can be bound to honor the structure of their constitutional democratic regime and abide by the statutes and laws enacted under it."[14] Without our grasping this issue regarding the ethics of political coercion, debates about public reason quickly default into arguments about freedom of religious expression or freedom of speech—*other* liberal democratic concerns. Criticisms of public reason often reduce matters to an intramural liberal squabble, even among antiliberals, about the meaning of political liberty. But public reason should be framed instead with an eye to matters of democratic legitimation—the requirement to secure authority based on popular consent. That concept—legitimation—requires us to ask, On what basis may a policy justifiably limit the freedom of democratic citizens in the domain for which the policy is designed?[15]

DEMOCRACY

To get a handle on the question of policy and individual freedom, and in keeping with my desire to frame public reason as a matter of democratic authority rather than as a matter of religion and public life, we should be clear about the idea of democracy. Democracy is, among other things, a form of collective self-governance in which political power is owned and shared by the people.[16] Equally important to my argument, democracy is value laden. As Corey Brettschneider argues in his study of democratic rights, democracy has a core set of values, producing what he calls a "value theory" of democratic institutional roles and cultural practices. Citing Abraham Lincoln, Brettschneider avows that the key elements of a democracy consist in a "government of the people, by the people, and for the people."[17] Following Brettschneider, we can say that democracy's principal values are equality of interests, political autonomy, and reciprocity. *Equality of interests* means that I count your interests as equal in importance to mine in political deliberations. *Political autonomy* refers to my freedom to deliberate about my current and future ends as a citizen. And *reciprocity* presupposes both of these values. In discussion of public policy, reciprocity requires citizens to view one other as "authors" and as "addressees"—as sharers of arguments in webs of political interlocution.[18]

These values of equality, freedom, and reciprocity are, to recall Rawls, "political, not metaphysical."[19] They need not proceed "all the way down" into an individual's personal identity. They do not stand within a single metaphysical doctrine or presuppose one comprehensive moral or religious vision. One important presupposition in public reason is that adherents of comprehensive doctrines should seek in their political life fair terms of social cooperation, recognizing that the free use of human reason can generate good faith disagreements about the ends of human life, as well as about the moral stakes and relevant facts regarding specific political controversies.[20] The sources of such disagreements, reflecting what Rawls terms the "burdens of judgment," include determining the relevance of concepts, assigning weight to such concepts, specifying them, and identifying facts that bear on the controversy at hand.

Understanding these burdens of judgment is crucial for grasping why toleration is a sound expectation in democratic life. They help us grasp what, in Rawlsian terms, makes any comprehensive doctrine, be it philosophical or religious, "reasonable." What makes a comprehensive doctrine reasonable is not that it might make good sense to others should they give it more thoughtful consideration or that it enjoys a historic legacy that implies some level of sanity or goodness when viewed from an outsider's ethical or political standpoint. Rather, a reasonable comprehensive doctrine knows that underlying the existence of moral differences are good-faith disagreements and that seeking to suppress such differences runs directly contrary to what it means to be a person endowed with the free use of reason.

Democratic authority thus understood amends the concept of authority that Bruce Lincoln develops in his work on the topic, about which I spoke in chapter 3. For Lincoln authority is "an effect characteristic of strongly asymmetric relations between speaker and audience, predisposing the latter to defer to the discourse of the former in ways that are often quite uncritical."[21] Note two things about this view: first, authority is an effect characteristic of asymmetric relations; second, the subordinate in the relation defers in ways that are often uncritical. But in *democratic* authority the adjective performs work that generates a different picture. Democratic authority that presupposes equal citizenship aims to create symmetrical, not asymmetrical, relations. Indeed, when authority is exercised in strongly asymmetrical ways in a liberal democracy, we typically raise questions about abuses of power. Vertical relations that are accepted are done so on the basis of prior, horizontally accepted procedures. Second, in democratic relations the discourse of one citizen or group might be accepted uncritically as a matter of fact. But ideally others' reasons are put to critical scrutiny. We hold lawmakers, jurists, and fellow citizens accountable to the sorts of reasons they invoke to support law or policy. Indeed, when others' ideas are uncritically accepted, as they often are in current politics, we bemoan that fact as corrosive of democracy itself. So democratic authority, normatively understood, is a horizontal not a vertical matter, one in which reasons are scrutinized rather than deferred to uncritically.

The values of political equality, freedom, and reciprocity ground democratic authority's normative dimensions insofar as they pertain to our *roles* as sovereigns and subjects. As citizens we have certain duties and rights in relation to each other as sharers of political power. We have certain entitlements that demand respect. That is to say, in the practices of collective self-governance, there are some things that we owe to each other. Abiding by public reason is one way of honoring our shared political obligations.

OBJECTIONS TO PUBLIC REASON

With these ideas in view let us turn to four concerns about the limits that public reason imposes on religious and moral discourse: the Self-Division Objection, the Attenuation Complaint, the Wrong Outcomes Challenge, and the Epistemic Critique. The Self-Division Objection claims that public reason alienates religious believers from their deeper convictions. The Attenuation Complaint claims that public reason weakens morality's potential for robust social criticism. The Wrong Outcomes Challenge claims that public reason fails to protect against wrong outcomes of a policy dispute. The Epistemic Critique claims that public reason relies on an arbitrary distinction between faith-based and secular reasoning. These ideas are commonly invoked to say that public reason violates certain duties to the self. Again, my view is that such self-regarding concerns eclipse attention to (among other things) the other-regarding aspects of coexistence in pluralistic democracies.

The first objection states that public reason is overly demanding, requiring religious believers to translate their values into terms that fail to capture the richness and integrity of their particular beliefs. Nicholas Wolterstorff puts the challenge this way: "It belongs to the *religious convictions* of a good many religious people . . . that *they ought to base* their decisions concerning fundamental issues of justice *on* their religious convictions. They do not view it as an option whether or not to do so. It is their conviction that they ought to strive for wholeness, integrity, integration, in their lives. . . . Their religion is not, for them, about *something* other than their social and political existence; it is *also* about their social and political existence."[22] Call this the Self-Division Objection. It complains that public reason's restraints appear to alienate an individual from her or his self-defining commitments. Accordingly, public reason is overly demanding, morally and psychologically speaking. It seems unrealistic, beyond ordinary human capacities.

More precisely: public reason imposes a double-consciousness on religious citizens. At one level a religious citizen is free to hold religiously authorized convictions not only about her own personal morality but about the morality or immorality of others. But when asked to articulate those convictions in the public political forum, she is required to speak in a different idiom, the language of political rights and duties. That fact suggests that something is lacking in her basic convictions— that there is something wrong with her moral resources. And that suggestion is offensive.

Yet this challenge leaves unanswered a more basic question: are the sorts of restraints imposed by public reason justified? Saying that such restraints pose an affront to religious practitioners, or that such restraints threaten to alienate them from themselves, begs a basic ethical question. That question is whether any such affront is a moral problem for democratic politics.

I claim that it is not. As I see it, we misstate the ethical stakes surrounding public reason insofar as we focus exclusively on first-personal questions regarding religious liberty, wholeness, and freedom of expression. The potential of the Self-Division Objection to calcify cultural and religious identity, encourage incuriosity, and fuel the culture wars in the name of religious freedom and integrity is difficult to overlook. But my chief response to this objection has less to do with its potential consequences than with the matter of political principle. The subject matter of public reason must first be understood as consisting of matters regarding justified coercion and the moral basis of democratic authority. Only when those matters are clear can we determine whether the Self-Division Objection has merit. In its most basic form public reason refers to a perspective and a language that citizens are to adopt when they defend or criticize coercive public policies. Our reason for endorsing a policy, in other words, turns not only on the fact that such reasons are good for me; it turns on the fact that my reason for accepting a policy relies on *others* having political reasons for endorsing it as well.[23] The basis that I have for endorsing a policy in democratic political regimes is that I can see that others have a reason—a shared political reason—to endorse it, too. Fellow sovereigns in a pluralistic democracy are entitled to reasons explaining to them why they are, or may be, coerced.[24]

On this description public reason is an ethic of alterity. Specifically, it is a kind of civic empathy, the disposition to place oneself in another's shoes and imagine how the political world looks and feels to that other person. As I indicated in chapter 4, empathy enables an outlook conditioned by our conception of another's feelings and frame of mind. In prototypical instances of empathy we feel as we take the other to feel, given our perception of his or her circumstances, and we are mindful of how our feelings have been so transformed. Indeed, when we show empathy, we can not only show others how they feel; we can show them that we agree with them about how to feel.[25] We show that we grasp their feelings and communicate our willingness to participate with them in a common life. This makes empathy central to the formation of like-minded groups. Far from being only a one-to-one dynamic, empathy can provide a basis for the formation of community.

Rawls was wary of invoking considerations of moral psychology when theorizing about justice, in part because he believed that utilitarian conceptions of justice required persons to sacrifice their individual interests for the good of the whole and that such conceptions presupposed, or relied on, a more general, shared sympathy that holds a collective together. Rawls avowed that such expectations were unrealistic and overly demanding. Overly demanding expectations, in turn, would weaken the appeal of justice and render any regime premised on a political psychology of self-sacrifice unstable. Rawls writes: "It is evident why the utilitarian stresses the capacity for sympathy. Those who do not benefit from the better situation of others must identify with the greater sum (or average) of satisfaction else they will not desire to follow the utility criterion."[26] Such dispositions, Rawls observes, are weaker than the requirements of reciprocity on which his account of justice-as-fairness hinges. Notable is the fact that "a marked capacity for sympathetic identification seems relatively rare" (500). Such feelings are thus less reliable as a basis for expecting persons to abide by the requirements of social justice when conceived in utilitarian terms, thus weakening utilitarianism's effort to generate a basis for its own support. Rawls adds: "Following the utilitarian conception [of justice] tends to be destructive of the self-esteem of those who lose out, particularly when they are already less fortunate." It is characteristic of a utilitarian doctrine "to demand self-sacrifice for the sake of a higher good and to deprecate the worth of the individual and lesser associations. The emptiness of the self is to be overcome in the service of larger ends. The doctrine is likely to encourage self-hatred with its destructive consequences" (500). For the purpose of establishing the stability of a theory of justice, something other than altruistic motivations, or motives of self-sacrifice, is needed.

But on this matter of political stability Rawls focuses on the demands of sympathy as providing the moral psychology that underlies utilitarian theory—the chief foil against which he develops his theory of justice-as-fairness. As we have seen, public reason as a form of *empathy* is different from *sympathy* and avoids its dangers. Empathy explains how citizens might establish democratic authority by aspiring to offer reasons not only *to* each other but also *for* each other. On this view I assess a policy by putting myself in others' shoes and imagine how the policy looks to them, along with how our political lives would be affected by the policy when it is enforced. The basis that I have for endorsing a policy lies in the fact that I can see, empathically, that others have a reason to endorse it, too. This is not to require that citizens lose themselves in the identities of another, only that they imagine themselves as if they were another.

Public reason can thereby rely on a realistic moral psychology—not one that is self-sacrificial but one that nonetheless draws us out of our particularist commitments to simulate others' vantage points.[27] Rawls is quite clear about the value of empathy for his theory of justice. Although he does not use the term explicitly, his argument clearly underscores the value of looking at the world from another's imagined point of view in his discussion of moral psychology and moral development in the third part of *A Theory of Justice*.[28] In that part Rawls seeks to establish the stability, or feasibility, of his theory of justice. Contrary to the more spare, antiempirical, and abstract forms of political and moral theorizing that characterize much of mainstream American philosophy, Rawls seeks to demonstrate that his theory aligns with facts about human motivations and psychological development. A concept of justice that accords with the processes of moral learning can commend itself as one that would generate sentiments and modes of cooperation that persons would find satisfactory in a regime organized according to Rawls's theory. They would thus have no motivations to create or reside in some other political regime or to defect from the norms of justice-as-fairness.

One argument in support of stability aims to show that general facts of moral psychology and moral learning, especially the development of a sense of reciprocity and a sense of justice, cohere with Rawls's theory of justice and make plausible his understanding of how principles of justice would be chosen from behind the "veil of ignorance" as he develops that idea earlier in his account.[29] Briefly stated, Rawls's view as put forth in *A Theory of Justice* is that the capacity to empathize begins to emerge in the second of three phases of moral development, namely, the phase in which children evolve beyond accepting morality as a matter of authority and begin to understand the importance of morality in their attachments and social relationships. Drawing from the ideas of William McDougall, Rawls sees moral development as occurring across three phases, namely, the morality of authority, the morality of association, and the morality of principles (461n8). During the second phase children experience morality in terms of goodwill and affection, which in turn increases their capacities for trust and fellow-feeling in their interactions with others. The foundational experiences of goodwill, trust, affection, and fellow-feeling continue into adulthood and enable us to understand and cooperate with others in various roles and relationships.

Key to the morality of association, Rawls writes, is the ability to know "that others have different things to do depending on their place in the cooperative scheme." Thus, one "eventually learns to take up their point of view and to see things from their perspective" (468). The skills necessary to adopt others' points of view are complex, requiring us to recognize that others may see the world differently than we do and that they have different wants, ends, plans, and motives. It also requires us to be able to identify what counts as especially important to others along with their beliefs and opinions. Lacking the ability to identify such matters, Rawls adds, "we cannot put ourselves into another's place and find out what we would do in his position" (469).

Rawls develops these ideas as a basis for believing that his view of justice does not ask too much of us from a psychological perspective. In our experience of the morality of association we learn about the benefits of give-and-take in social life and develop ties based on the experience of mutual advantage. Social stability arises from "the reciprocal effects of everyone's doing his share" (471). In this way Rawls suggests the importance of empathy as providing psychological resources for developing the capacities for reciprocity and a sense of justice on terms that respect the uniqueness and individuality of persons but that nonetheless help to strengthen social connections. My idea of civic empathy, or adopting the point of view of other citizens in the course of offering reasons to them in debates about public policy, echoes Rawls's more general ideas about how we acquire a sense of justice in moral development. Civic empathy is a species of reciprocity that maintains and strengthens social bonds. Equally important, the idea of civic empathy and its connections to public reason should allay worries about whether the doctrine is overly demanding.

A second concern about public reason attends to its putatively debilitating effects on moral conviction in public life. Michael Sandel regularly worries about separating philosophy from politics, about "bracketing moral and religious questions where politics is concerned."[30] Call this the Attenuation Complaint. It alleges that having to bracket religious discourse, or convert religious discourse into political language, requires religious adherents to weaken the full force of their views regarding a political controversy. On this account citizens feel muted by public reason's demands. Consider citizens who, on religious or moral grounds, wish to speak out against neo-Nazis who publicly display their anti-Semitism by marching in neighborhoods that are densely populated with Jewish families. Using public reason to express the offensiveness of anti-Semitism—saying, for example, that it is wrong because it fails to respect Jews' rights as citizens—requires critics to frame their judgments in an idiom that focuses on Jews' political liberties. Judgments and feelings of indignation about the grave moral evils of racism and religious bigotry find, at most, only qualified expression. And if a concerned citizen must cast judgment in that way, then it seems that public reason denudes public discourse of deeper moral convictions about the problems of injustice. Echoing Sandel's main complaint about Rawlsian liberalism, we might say that public reason fails to elicit the defining commitments of morally encumbered selves. Its arrival has, as its prerequisite, the absence of deeper and more demanding virtues of benevolence or respect for human dignity that can fuel robust social criticism.[31]

To this complaint I would reply that those who worry about the diminishing effects of using political language in moral and cultural controversies should think in comparative terms. By that I mean that such worries require contextualization, or attention to the circumstances of injustice, in order to be properly assessed. Consider again the case of neo-Nazis marching in Jewish neighborhoods. To be sure, having to refer to civic duties toward Jews does not invoke the strongest moral reasons for condemning the evils of racism and religious bigotry. The arrival of the language of political justice might indeed signal the prior absence of benevolence or respect for human dignity in public affairs. But the fact that anti-Semites exist indicates that something less than benevolence or respect for human dignity is *already* a feature of civic culture. In Rawls's language the case illustrates nonideal circumstances. That fact hardly allows us to say that reference to democratic values denudes political discourse of moral conviction. Political criticism of anti-Semitism aims to *improve* the morally and politically diminished conditions in which such bigotry is expressed. Public reason is sometimes necessary to address instances of injustice. If political justice and its ally, public reason, are in part remedial matters, aimed at correcting unjust states of affairs, that fact should hardly count against them. Drawing on the language of political values enables critics to express their indignation in ways that have conviction *and* exhibit democratic respect.

A third, related challenge regarding the effects of public reason observes that deliberations within its constraints might produce morally wrong results. Call this the Wrong Outcomes Challenge. It observes, correctly, that public reason is not right reason.[32] All that public reason asks is that participants discuss basic political issues in a common language that is provided by a family of reasonable conceptions of democratic justice. Because public reason is not right reason, a religious participant who abides by public reason might find herself on the losing side of a policy dispute. As a result she is alienated in two ways: first, by drawing on a different idiom and, second, by having to reside in a regime in which deliberations using that idiom have produced a morally unacceptable policy in her estimation.

In response to this complaint the proponent of public reason grants that it does not guarantee morally correct results. But the fact that a religious advocate might not succeed in public debate does not entail that public reason is to blame. Public reason does not impose more burdens on one set or kind of beliefs than it does on other comprehensive doctrines. All participants in public deliberation are subject to the same restraints, and no one religious doctrine can allege discrimination if it does not win in the give-and-take of public argument. Furthermore, losing in public debate hardly implies that religious voices were barred. The views of other religious adherents, duly translated into political values, might have prevailed. Equally important, public reason does not impose time constraints on those who find a public policy unacceptable. Although individuals or groups who lose in public argument might find that fact discouraging, they are not prevented from further participation and political activism.

None of this is to say that public reason requires one to accept a policy on the condition that other citizens, as a matter of fact, accept it, or will accept it, as well. It is only to say that public reason requires citizens to make good-faith efforts to articulate reasons that they think other citizens, similarly motivated by a desire to secure social cooperation, can accept. Abiding by public reason is a matter of being a conscientious citizen committed to mutuality, not a matter of ensuring consensus.[33]

A fourth challenge, the Epistemic Critique, poses an entirely different line of criticism. As developed by Christopher Eberle, this critique conceives of public reason as an "epistemic conception of public justification."[34] Eberle argues that public reason that excludes religious reasons is warranted only if we can establish the superiority of nonreligious reasons according to uncontroversial epistemic criteria. Those criteria include intelligibility, replicability, accessibility, and general reliability—norms that we use to judge a statement as rational. When we apply those criteria to nonreligious reasoning, Eberle argues, we find it to be no less arguable than religious reasoning.[35] When we think about knowledge based on ordinary sense perception, for example, we find that it hardly passes the tests of intelligibility, replicability, accessibility, and general reliability with flying colors. Nonreligious reasons should thus be viewed as another sectarian doctrine, no more neutral than faith-based political convictions.

If nonreligious reasons are no less controverted than religious reasons, then privileging nonreligious reasons as a basis for public policy relies on an arbitrary distinction.

Eberle also argues that the norm of respect and what he calls the "ideal of conscientious engagement" require everyone in pluralistic democracies to try to offer public justifications for their views as much as possible. His argument, in brief, is as follows: Our reasons are to take due account of the fact that everyone has higher order interests that they wish to pursue. All of us thus have a legitimate aversion to being coerced.[36] Accordingly, coercion must be justified on shareable terms as much as possible. That fact establishes a presumption in favor of seeking nonreligious reasons. By the same token, we must reckon with limit situations, namely, those in which citizens fail to find nonreligious reasons to support their views. In those instances—when citizens entirely lack nonreligious reasons—they may rest their arguments solely on religious convictions.

But here Eberle makes two errors. First, his description of the ideal of conscientious engagement presupposes the relative superiority of nonreligious to religious reasoning that his critique seeks to undermine. That Eberle allows citizens to invoke religious convictions only when they entirely lack nonreligious reasons presupposes the general desirability of the latter to the former. But Eberle can't have it both ways, endorsing the good of public justification while jettisoning the core distinction on which it relies. If, in Eberle's mind, the distinction between religious and nonreligious reasons is arbitrary, then it is not clear why he retains it. Second, Eberle fails to grasp the implications of his views for religious citizens in a pluralistic society. Suppose that you are a religiously devout citizen. Allowing for unrestrained reasoning in the formation of policy, even in the limit situation to which Eberle restricts his permission, means that you can be liable to coercion on others' religious grounds—grounds that violate your own account of religious truth. It is difficult to see how that outcome would be less alienating than relying on public reason alone.[37]

One way to think of public reason and the importance it attaches to shareable reasons is to consider matters of fairness. Restricting citizens' liberty with policies supported by reasons they cannot deliberate about and potentially accept is to deny them their due as shareholders of democratic power. Public reason seeks to ensure that we each have an equal share of power in the process of conceiving and authorizing a policy. Put another way: I treat others as second-class citizens by not offering them reasons that I sincerely think that they can count as good political reasons for themselves.[38]

Public reason, then, is tied to the notion of "citizen" as a public office. The idea of a "private citizen" for anyone in a democratic society is an oxymoron. Public reason is the effort to constrain our reasons so that the popular will authorizes a policy on terms according to which we communicate with each other as political equals. In this way we participate in a process by which we share ownership of a policy along with its fashioning. As Jeremy Waldron states, "We are all officials in a democracy."[39]

THE "PROVISO"

The idea that we are to aspire to offer reasons to each other as equal shareholders of political power—my organizing thesis—rules out one defense of public reason from which I want to distinguish my position. The argument I have in mind is proposed by Rawls in his effort to accommodate religious voices in the public political forum, and it finds a strong parallel in Brettschneider's understanding of public reason and democratic rights. According to Brettschneider and Rawls, when citizens debate and decide on matters of public policy, they need not bracket their deeper beliefs. The key requirement of public reason, they both avow, is that a policy proposal must find public justification at some (unspecified) point in time.

Rawls introduces this idea by first asking us to consider what he calls "the wide view of public political culture" in the effort to distinguish his account from more restrictive renditions of public reason. On the wide view, Rawls writes, religious or nonreligious comprehensive doctrines "may be introduced in public political discussion at any time, provided that in due course proper political reasons—and not reasons given solely by comprehensive doctrines—are presented that are sufficient to support whatever the comprehensive doctrines are said to support." Understood as "the proviso," this idea allows for "no restrictions or requirements on how religious or secular doctrines are themselves to be expressed."[40]

What is required is that, in due course, purely public reasons be introduced that are sufficient to justify the policy proposal in question.

Similarly, for Brettschneider, what is necessary for policy to pass the test of public reason is for that policy to be defensible on public terms. "The purpose of democracy's public reason," he writes, "is not to judge whether comprehensive conceptions are correct, but rather to evaluate whether laws, including those grounded in arguments derived from comprehensive conceptions, are consistent with citizens' shared status through the core values [of equality, autonomy, and reciprocity]."[41] So long as *someone* is able to justify a public policy on shareable political terms *at some point in time*, that policy passes Brettschneider's test of public reason.

In my view these permissions are too lax. While they are more inclusive than public reason is in my description, they have this problem: policy that fails to aspire to produce a public justification *now* fails to respect the political equality and autonomy of citizens who would be immediately bound by it. Rawls dodges this problem by asserting that determining when and by whom the proviso is to be satisfied are details that "must be worked out in practice and cannot feasibly be governed by a clear family of rules given in advance."[42] But the point at issue is not how to work out the details of the proviso but whether the proviso is warranted. As proposed by Rawls or restated by Brettschneider, the proviso's core problem is that it leaves policy to an after-the-fact public justification. It thereby subjects citizens in the interim to having their liberties restricted on terms that fail to count them as equal partners who share democratic authority. Any permission of post-facto justification leaves citizens vulnerable to being treated as political inferiors, contrary to the central aim of public reason itself.

To summarize: Public reason

1. is *political*, not *metaphysical*, requiring no totalizing vision for its support;
2. is about democratic authority rather than "religion in the public square";
3. says nothing to encourage (or require) the privatization of religion in *civil society*;

4. is a matter of *conscientious aspiration*, not a matter of ensuring actual consensus;
5. encumbers citizens in *real time*, not post facto;
6. draws its moral foundations from *democratic values* to ground how we are to establish *authority* in the formation of *coercive* public policy;
7. delivers an *understanding of authority* in which power is dispersed horizontally and subject to rational scrutiny; and
8. can be explained motivationally as an exercise of *civic empathy*, requiring citizens to imagine how a coercive policy matters politically to other citizens.

With these points in place I want now to turn to three cases with an eye to illuminating public reason as I have described it.

THREE CASES

LAWRENCE V. TEXAS

My first case is *Lawrence v. Texas*, the 2003 Supreme Court decision overturning a Texas statute that criminalized sodomy between consenting same-sex adults.[43] Let us imagine the case as having this background fact: one dissenting Supreme Court justice maintained the moral wrongness of sodomy as contrary to the natural law. In his view of the natural law, the justice adds, each sex act must be open to procreation, and sodomy lacks such openness.[44] Gerald Bradley and Robert George, scholars at the University of Notre Dame and Princeton University, respectively, submitted an *amicus curiae* to the Supreme Court in *Lawrence v. Texas* that took its inspiration from this natural law doctrine in the effort to express ideas on behalf of "a family-centered philosophy of public life" (1).[45] In their view same-sex sodomy should be criminalized in part because it lacks intrinsic openness to procreation, one of the purposes to which sexual activity and marriage are ordered by nature.

Moreover, Bradley and George argue, same-sex acts cannot occur in marriage, which is "a relationship between a man and a woman" (2).

Same-sex couples cannot marry, moreover, because "it is impossible for them to enter into bodily communion." Marriage is "a two-in-one flesh union of persons," and it is an institution that Texas law has a legitimate interest in promoting (17). In their view "Texas may constitutionally choose to protect marital intimacy by prohibiting same-sex 'deviate' acts, while tolerating similar behavior by unmarried opposite-sex persons." What explains the difference between sodomy in heterosexual and homosexual activity? Bradley and George write: "Deviate acts can never occur within marriage . . . or within any relationship that could ever lead to marriage" (3). Heterosexual sodomy, in contrast, can occur within or lead to marriage, and for that reason it can enjoy legal protection.

Our question is this: can this kind of natural-law argument pass the test of public reason in its effort to restrict the liberties of same-sex citizens?

On the face of things the Bradley-George brief makes natural law arguments that seem to abide by public reason. They focus on whether decriminalizing same-sex sodomy would weaken the state's promotion of the good of the traditional family. On their reckoning the family and its welfare are legitimate political values. They could easily point to laws that regulate sexual activity in the family, namely, laws against incest and polygamy. Policing the family might be seen as congruent with concerns about democratic equality and freedom: politically responsible and reflective citizens rely on strong educational and support structures, of which the family is (or can be) one. Indeed, any idea that the family is off-limits as a matter of policy fails to recognize the entire field of family law. Moreover, Bradley and George observe, the idea that nonmarital or same-sex activity enjoys fewer protections than sex in marriage stands squarely within the tradition of American legal reasoning. Discriminating against same-sex relations, as the Texas statute had done, is not arbitrary from the standpoint of legal precedent. Sodomy may be tolerated among heterosexual couples because marital relationships are of the sort that Texas may want to encourage. Indeed, for these authors heterosexual sodomy outside of marriage—in premarital or even in extramarital relationships—can be seen within an arc that they call "incipiently marital relationships" and on that basis can enjoy protection from the state (4, 23).

Regarding public reason it might seem that we could say, so far, so good. The core institutions—marriage and the family—are important for the development of democratic citizens. Among contemporary liberal theorists, Susan Moller Okin has argued on feminist grounds for applying norms of gender justice to the family, and Rawls himself includes the family in his understanding of what he calls the "basic structure"—those institutions to which a theory of justice applies.[46] The state has an interest in, among other things, its own continuation, and for that reason reproduction is an important political matter.

But public reason would place limits on the Bradley-George argument when they claim that the state may justifiably discourage same-sex acts insofar as the state is "authorized . . . by the common good . . . to *promote* marriage by respecting the privacy of the marital bedroom . . . and required by the common good . . . to discourage sexual acts outside of marriage" (9). Moreover, they argue, allowing same-sex intimacies appears to put law and policy on a slippery slope by easing cultural barriers to the legalization of same-sex marriage. This latter possibility, Bradley and George avow, undermines the idea that "marriage is characteristically procreative, or intrinsically ordered to having and raising children" (18).

Such appeals to a natural-law rationale for promoting heterosexual marriage seek to introduce a comprehensive account of human goodness into the Court's reasoning. And for that reason such appeals cannot qualify as public reasons until Bradley and George state them in terms of political rights and duties. For Bradley and George marriage has a certain intrinsic ordering, understood as a set of aims or activities toward which all marital relationships should be directed in order to count as morally legitimate. That understanding of marriage imposes on couples a metaphysical account of its purposes that public reason rules out.

Consider one concrete implication of this natural law argument as a basis for policy. The Bradley-George account of marital relations morally stigmatizes heterosexual couples who choose not to procreate given their commitments, values, and vision of a good marriage. Such couples are making decisions that do not abide by marriage's intrinsic ordering. Bradley and George need to identify the political rights and duties that are preserved by having citizens view childless couples of choice as having morally deficient marriages.

Moreover, Bradley and George's claims about heterosexuality and the common good make no sense on their own. In their minds the range of incipiently marital relations within which sodomy would be permissible includes couples having extramarital affairs or, as they put it, "men and women, sexually intimate and functioning as mother and father, but who cannot marry because one (or both) is estranged from a spouse." Bradley and George want us to believe that sexual activity that may threaten a family is nonetheless acceptable for the common good and for the good of marriage. They appear willing to destroy a family in order to save it.

What is clear in their account is not that sodomy should be criminalized as a matter of principle. Otherwise, heterosexual sodomy would be one target of their critique. Note the irony of their claims. For natural law theory heterosexual sodomy should be more problematic than homosexual sodomy given that a man and a woman have the choice to procreate through sexual relations. Obviously, two men or two women have no such choice. If Bradley and George want Texas law to encourage procreation, then it is not clear why it should restrict itself only to those who cannot procreate through sex.[47] What is plain from this discrepant application of procreative norms is that Bradley and George's brief aims to stigmatize homosexuality, not to protect family values.

The obvious objection to raise to these authors is that decriminalizing same-sex sodomy has no bearing on the legal or cultural status of heterosexual marriage and family for this simple reason: legalizing same-sex activity hardly prevents heterosexual couples from marrying and procreating. To permit same-sex relations is not to require such relations of everyone. In addition to the problems I just mentioned, that fact undermines efforts by these natural law theorists to invoke family values as a way of blocking the protection of same-sex liberties.

RELIGION, NBAC, AND REPRODUCTIVE CLONING

My second case stems from presentations invited by the National Bioethics Advisory Committee (NBAC) in the 1990s to explore how religious traditions might speak to the ethics of reproductive cloning. Commenting on that era and that topic for bioethics policy development, former NBAC member James F. Childress writes: "On the topic of human reproductive cloning, few philosophical discussions existed, and the major discussions in the literature were from scholars writing out of religious traditions. NBAC wanted to find illuminating contributions, whatever their origin or source, to the ethical analysis of human reproductive cloning and public policies toward it."[48] One speaker, Gilbert Meilaender, was asked to offer religious commentary in his capacity as a Protestant ethicist; Meilaender was one of several invitees who hailed from different religious traditions, and I want to concentrate on his arguments here.[49]

Meilaender's commentary on reproductive cloning draws on Christian theological claims to highlight its potential dangers. At the heart of his remarks is the biblically informed idea that there is a connection between sexual differentiation and procreation that reproductive cloning severs. "The creation story in the first chapter of Genesis," Meilaender writes, "depicts the creation of humankind as male and female, sexually differentiated and enjoined by God's grace to sustain human life through procreation." According to Meilaender, the connection between sexual differentiation and procreation enables parents to understand their offspring as gifts rather than as products—as begotten, not made. Here the focus is not on procreative norms but on the bearing of children as "unbidden." Among reproductive cloning's problems is that it could imperil the idea of the child as a mystery—"offspring of a man and a woman, but a replication of neither; their offspring, but not their product whose meaning and destiny they might determine." The point of the clone's existence "would be grounded in our will and desire." A begotten child, in contrast, "becomes the natural fruition of [parents'] shared love, something quite different from a chosen product." Viewing offspring as gifts rather than as products at our disposal affirms that "we are of 'equal dignity' with each other."

At the heart of Meilaender's argument, then, are these parallels: begotten:cloned::unbidden:bidden::gift:product. Reproductive cloning is thus wrong because (among other things) it is bad for the child as manufactured rather than as begotten. The idea that children should properly be viewed as unbidden has more than a few proponents. William F. May and Michael J. Sandel, members of President George W. Bush Jr.'s Committee on Bioethics, invoke that idea in their reflections on the ethics of genetic engineering,[50] and one observer of the NBAC meeting was reported to have been "especially moved" by Meilaender's testimony.[51]

But the critical question is whether this idea is admissible when deciding whether to ban, restrict, or permit reproductive cloning as a matter of bioethics policy. The doctrine of public reason would surely say that Meilaender, along with the other religious spokespersons invited by NBAC, is free to speak about sexual differentiation and procreation as he sees it theologically, "in whole cloth." There is no reason to think that he should translate his views into political values in order to make sense to the NBAC board. And, as I have indicated, we should have few qualms about that fact. All of NBAC's invitees expressed their views in civil society, not as persons commissioned to create or reform policy.

One way to summarize Meilaender's comments is to say that he called attention to the importance of human equality and the potential dangers of discrimination against persons who would be cloned. Cloned persons would be "at our disposal" in ways that "begotten" persons would not be. They would be too easily seen as things rather than as persons and subject to treatment as second-class citizens. In this way we can translate Meilaender's ideas into the language of public reason for those considering his testimony as providing material for policy formation.

Yet to some critics my translation fails to do justice to Meilaender's claims insofar as I abstract some political implications from his testimony, and such an abstraction does violence to his argument.[52] His understanding of equality is embedded within a holistic set of beliefs about God, gender difference, marriage, intercourse, biblical authority, and procreation—beliefs that hang together, without remainder. Extracting political values from this mix cuts into the interconnecting strands that constitute his web of beliefs. Holists question efforts to abstract something like a "thin" morality of equality and freedom from "thicker" beliefs and worldviews. Such abstractions are alleged to come at the cost of richness of the views on which the thin ideas rely.[53]

In response to this "richness" challenge we should ask, Richness to whom? Are we to infer that someone outside of the Protestant tradition cannot understand what a Protestant is saying? If that's the case, then why should he say it? It seems more plausible to say that whatever richness describes Meilaender's views might be lost *to the speaker* when we translate his ideas into a political idiom, but that hardly counts strongly against the desideratum of translation. In his remarks to NBAC Meilaender seems to urge the point that cloned persons would be at risk of exploitation and neglect, that they would be vulnerable to being treated as second-class citizens given the nature of their manufactured creation. That claim relies on the harm principle and the norm of nondiscrimination, and it depends on certain empirical predictions. Those concepts put his claims on solid grounds as candidates for public reason, and my rendition of them would doubtless satisfy Rawls's and Brettschneider's post-facto application of the doctrine.

Let us say that you side with Rawls and Brettschneider and conclude that Meilaender's views, duly translated, abide by public reason. There are still matters to consider regarding the coherence of his testimony. Meilaender's argument, focusing on the prospective harms of being a cloned person, leads to the odd conclusion that someone who is not created is better off than someone who is. This problem, known as the "nonidentity problem," makes it difficult to grasp how artificially producing someone is more harmful to that individual than not producing her at all. Typically (or intuitively), we understand "harm" as making a person or group worse off as a result of someone's actions. But because cloned persons would not have been conceived without the use of cloning, we cannot say that they have been made worse off by the procedure. Those who introduce the nonidentity problem thus argue that citing prospective harms as a basis for banning cloning relies on a category mistake.[54]

One way to get around this point is to proceed metaethically by revisiting what we mean when we cite the harm principle as a basis for restricting or banning a practice. Such a revisiting enables us to grasp that the harm principle applies to situations that include, but go beyond, circumstances in which a person or group is made worse off by another's conduct. What constitutes harm, Ronald M. Green writes, "is the outcome of a complex social and ethical decision aimed at discouraging conduct whose consequences we find undesirable."[55] The main purpose in using the concept of harm, Green argues, is to identify behavior that we want to discourage. The point can be illuminated by looking at other areas in the ethics of reproduction in which we might have good reasons to discourage practices that lead to the conception of children—for example, children who will have serious impairments. Bringing such children to a level where they can thrive, Green observes, "involves considerable social expense and effort" (121). Moreover, the fact that many seriously impaired children "must struggle through painful surgeries and other medical interventions is another reason for seeking to discourage practices leading to such births" (121). It is reasonable to conclude that if someone chooses to have a child, "they should try to see that the child is born within the existing parameters of good health. Failing to do this is conceptualized as committing a harm to the child" (121). On these terms it makes sense to consider the prospective downsides of a person's existence, including a cloned person, as a harm done to that person.

This is not to suggest that reference to such harms is sufficient to justify a ban on cloning, only that they cannot be discounted. The upshot is to leave open the question of whether prospective harms are *decisive* in banning or discouraging a practice. With that fact in mind consider this analogy: we would hardly ask racial minorities to cease procreating because their offspring would suffer discrimination, even though we are well aware of the pervasiveness of racism in American society. That fact shows that citing potential future social harms to offspring is insufficient as a basis for limiting reproductive liberties.

An additional problem with Meilaender's argument is that it is not obvious that a cloned child would be doomed to the status of manufactured product if we think about the narrative arc of a child's life. The idea that cloned persons would be construed as products rather than gifts presumes that a cloned child lacks the capacity for contributing to or overturning her parents' expectations and goals. Recall, again, the parallel: begotten:cloned::unbidden:bidden::gift:product. I see no reason for accepting this parallel when we think about the life of a child over a range of time. Cloned children no less than "begotten" children have the capacity to expand a parent's horizons—to challenge, grace, disturb, upset, and inspire—whatever mode of reproduction the parents have chosen. Put in the language of my argument in chapter 6, parents can be in debt to cloned offspring no less than to uncloned offspring. The idea that a cloned offspring would not be expected to defy expectations—as products that are at our disposal rather than as gifts that are begotten—could very well increase the offspring's chances of doing so. Put simply, there is no reason to think that a cloned child would behave any differently than an uncloned one would.

Perhaps most problematic is the fact that citing potential future harms to cloned persons is irrelevant to the core moral problem at hand, namely, whether cloned persons should fall within the scope of moral concern. Meilaender's position allows facts pertaining to the mode of reproduction to establish the basis of moral value. But, as Dan Brock observes, "it would be a mistake . . . to conclude that a human being created by cloning is of less value or is less worthy of respect than one created by sexual reproduction. It is the nature of a being, not how it is created, that is the source of its value and makes it worthy of respect."[56] Saying that manufactured individuals would be of lesser dignity in the eyes of their parents and of society only begs the question of moral status, leaving the determination of human dignity contingent on whether an individual will in fact be treated with respect.[57] Viewing moral status in those terms puts the cart before the horse. That is to say, when moral status is determined by the mode of reproduction, it loses its normative force when positioned vis-à-vis social sources of discrimination. If cloned persons would be subject to being discriminated against, as Meilaender suggests, that fact says less about them than about the family that produces them and the society that receives them.

"LETTER FROM BIRMINGHAM JAIL"

My third example draws from the arguments in Martin Luther King Jr.'s "Letter from Birmingham Jail."[58] King's letter mixes appeals to biblical theology, natural law, and democratic principles in the effort to reverse policies of racial discrimination and to critique moderate white churches' failures to support nonviolent direct action against segregationist policies in the South. The letter was addressed not to public policy makers but to clergymen in Alabama. At first glance King's letter would seem to be an easy case for public reason given that its forum is civil society rather than the public political forum. But advocates of public reason such as Rawls provide only qualified bases for affirming King's religiously based arguments within the "wide view" of public political culture. Rawls asserts that King fulfilled only the proviso, thereby implying that King failed to provide a straightforward example of public justification.[59] But King's public reason-giving is more clear-cut than Rawls suggests. For that reason I want to examine it here.

King's letter, like so many of his writings and oratory, routinely joins biblical imagery with liberal democratic ideals. He speaks of the "gospel of freedom,"[60] not in keeping with Martin Luther's understanding of *sola fides* or Christian liberty but in terms of racial freedom and equality. His imagery clearly joins religious and political idioms. When explaining the timing of direct action and nonviolent protest in Birmingham in 1963, King indicates that blacks in America "have waited for more than 340 years for our constitutional and God-given rights" (81). Segregation, King avowed, "is not only politically, economically, and sociologically unsound, it is morally wrong and sinful" (82). When justifying civil disobedience, he invokes the tradition of natural law reasoning, citing Augustine and Aquinas on the proper relationship (in their accounts) of human law and "the moral law or the law of God" (82). Given that laws of segregation are patently unjust, they fail to bind the conscience, and disobeying them violates no moral norm. King writes:

> A just law is a man-made code that squares with the moral law or the law of God. An unjust law is a code that is out of harmony with the moral law. To put it in the terms of St. Thomas Aquinas: An unjust law is a human law that is not rooted in eternal law and natural law. Any law that uplifts human personality is just. Any law that degrades human personality is unjust. All segregation statutes are unjust because segregation distorts the soul and damages the personality. . . . Segregation, to use the terminology of the Jewish philosopher Martin Buber, substitutes an "I-It" relationship for an "I-Thou" relationship and ends up relegating persons to the status of things. (82)

King consistently coordinates appeals to American democratic values, the natural law, and religious images and tropes. History is moving, he writes, "toward the promised land of racial justice" (87–88). He proclaims, "Now is the time to make real the promise of democracy and transform our pending national elegy into a creative psalm of brotherhood" (86).

King's letter is noteworthy in part because he is reckoning with a tension between claims of substantive justice, on the one hand, and democratic legislative procedures in the segregated South, on the other. King notes that the South's injustice stems both from its policy of segregation *and from the process by which that policy was authorized.* It is on this latter point that I want us to focus. King writes: "A law is unjust if it is inflicted on a minority that, as a result of being denied the right to vote, had no part in enacting or devising the law. Who can say that the legislature of Alabama which set up that state's segregation laws was democratically elected? Throughout Alabama all sorts of devious methods are used to prevent Negroes from becoming registered voters, and there are some counties in which, even though Negroes constitute a majority of the population, not a single Negro is registered. Can any law enacted under such circumstances be considered democratically structured?" (83).

Here King appeals to the moral wrongfulness of the *authority* of the Alabama legislature, not only to the moral wrongfulness of the policies that it produced. That is to say, King grasps a basic feature about the moral authority of public policy in democratic societies, namely, that authority must be secured on terms that aim to share power equitably. We do well to note the claims by political theorists Amy Gutmann and Dennis Thompson regarding the value of political legitimacy: "The moral authority of collective judgments about policy depends in part on the moral quality of the process by which citizens collectively reach those judgments."[61] On this matter King's effort to homologize Christian and political ideals never poses the danger of conceiving norms to evaluate policy formation solely on religious grounds. King spoke in terms of political values and the ethics of political coercion, however much he also spoke in the idiom and imagery of Christian theology.

Yet if political values suffice as a basis for arguing within the restraints of public reason, what merit is there in invoking religious ideals and images, of speaking in terms of the "gospel of freedom?" King's rhetoric makes plain that his use of political and theological idioms aims to address a specific audience. He criticizes his fellow clergymen for failing to energize their communities to agitate for civil rights and for questioning his use of nonviolent direct action as a form of political resistance. King's aim is not to speak in whole cloth about public policy as he sees it out of some concern for personal integrity or authenticity. It is rather to speak prophetically against religious practices and clerical leadership that leave the South's legal norms of racial inequality unchallenged. And King does so in a way that is mindful of the limits to which he should go in turning his own beliefs into a basis for a policy that would limit the political liberties of religiously motivated segregationists. His quest for equality was double-barreled, focusing both on matters of substantive justice and democratic procedure.

One conclusion we can draw from King's letter is that there is no obvious threat that religion poses to public policy formation or public discourse more generally. Equally important, King's invocation of democratic values and ideals poses no threat to his religious beliefs and values. Still, to some critics, expecting citizens to restrict their appeals to a fund of political values such as freedom and equality seems overly sanguine about the weight that these notions can bear as shareable reasons in the quest for producing morally acceptable authority in liberal, democratic societies.[62] But the fact that some democratic citizens cannot meet public reason's demands hardly counts against the doctrine. Public reason is a normative doctrine, not a descriptive one. King's example, however, supports optimism surrounding public reason's feasibility. His attention to the substance of public justice did not proceed at the expense of concerns about the proper basis of democratic authority. And on that latter point he spoke about the abuse of political authority in terms that everyone in a liberal democracy, regardless of religious or philosophical conviction, can grasp.

* * *

My three examples, admittedly brief and however different at first glance, share concerns regarding equality. They might swing wide of Rawls's understanding of the kinds of controversies to which public reason applies—he was never entirely clear on that subject. That said, these cases suggest a range of different policy arguments that address judicial, executive, and legislative branches of federal and state government in the United States. The Bradley-George example illustrates an argument that appears to abide by public reason yet fails to meet the doctrine's demands given its appeal to a comprehensive doctrine regarding family values and the purposes of marriage along with its contradictory articulation of the values central to that doctrine. The Meilaender example illustrates how a theological argument can be translated into terms that accord with public reason and then put to rational scrutiny on analogy with other ways in which we think about reproduction, harm, child rearing, and moral status. My civil rights example illustrates a case of successful public reason but on terms that are typically overlooked: King's argument targeted the injustice of antidemocratic procedure in the South, as well as the injustice of the policy outcomes of that procedure.

THE MORALITY OF DEMOCRACY AND VALUE-PLURALISM

To properly frame the question of public reason, we must begin by noting that it focuses our attention on matters of democratic authority, not about whether religion exists, or should exist, in public life. Public reason takes no position regarding the empirical merits of the secularization thesis. With that clarification in place, we should then note additional features about democracy—most notably that democracy is, among other things, a moral endeavor. When we enter into democratic debates about policies that will restrict citizens' liberty, we are not entering into a value-neutral sphere. To be sure, we are debating about various values and their implications, but our debates themselves are rule-governed activities.

Put another way: debates in pluralistic democracies are (or should be) reckoned with in a second-order way. Considerations of public reason begin by presupposing the fact or likelihood of good-faith moral and political disagreement. The challenge to which public reason assigns itself is how to handle such disagreement in the quest to generate public policy regulating citizens' conduct, in which some liberties will be restricted as a result. The values of equality, autonomy, and reciprocity constrain how we are to debate about *other* values and, more generally, how we are to comport ourselves in relation to fellow citizens who share a commitment to social cooperation and matters of public justice. Religious citizens who resist such values might be esteemed by their fellow religious adherents, and perhaps others as well, for the strength of their convictions. One thrust of public reason is to say that such persons, however sincere or committed, may nonetheless be antidemocratic. If, for example, a religious citizen sees all authority as deriving from God, then she must either count herself out as a democratic citizen or ascertain how divine authority is delegated equally to believers and nonbelievers in matters of democratic policy formation. The morality of democratic authority puts limits on any comprehensive doctrine that refuses to assign political authority on equal, horizontal terms.

To theorize about religion and public reason, then, is to theorize about *authority*—specifically whether and how appeals to *religious authority* align with the moral demands of *democratic authority* given democracy's understanding of how political power is properly to be shared.[63] Public reason thus provides terms that enable us to form a certain kind of association, a pluralistic democratic political one. It is not an association that aims to meet all our needs or to satisfy all our aspirations. But it is an association with norms that cut through, and perhaps against, the affiliations that bind people together in other groups and organizations. Our interactions in it are temporary and ad hoc, and they can vary in time and intensity from citizen to citizen. In those interactions we are to relate to one another as citizens who share power. Seen within this context, public reason is a feature of the role morality of citizenship. And in that role we are to argue in ways that acknowledge each other as citizens who are entitled to equal respect in the form of reciprocal reason-giving.

This heterological demand may draw citizens out of their deeper, more intimate convictions, and it may impose expectations that some citizens' firmly held beliefs might not endorse. But religions that teach their adherents to reckon with the fact of otherness have a framework in public reason for being true to some of their deepest commitments. According to public reason, when religious adherents argue, they encumber responsibilities that include norms that constrain all citizens in other-regarding ways. The fact that other-regarding norms restrict what a believer may do or say is scarcely an idea that is alien to many religious traditions in pluralistic democracies. Religious resistance to public reason is extremely odd. In any event democracy's norms constrain practices and dispositions that might otherwise seem uncontroversial to members of religious communities. For many individuals life in democracy requires contending with more than one source of authority and value.

EPILOGUE

SIGNPOSTS OF THE PAST AND FOR THE FUTURE

I BEGAN this book by proposing that a turn to culture opens up fresh territory for work in religious ethics by identifying ways to think about religion and ordinary life that are normally neglected by scholars in the guild. I set the stage for that proposal by charting current and potential future directions in the field, after which I embarked on a critical examination of the practice of cultural and social criticism and some special topics in religion, political affairs, and interpersonal matters of one sort or another. All of those discussions are relevant to scholars who draw on research traditions in religion, ethics, and culture. One goal is to identify a cluster of concepts that can catalyze experimental directions of inquiry; another is to revisit familiar ideas and discoveries and theorize about them from new angles. Coursing throughout each chapter is the dialectic of alterity and intimacy, the idea that our lives oscillate between knowing and acknowledging others, on the one hand, and remembering, reimagining, and reconfiguring our foundational onlooks toward self and world, on the other. The underlying idea is that cultures generate manifestations of and proclamations from the other that reveal something about our indigenous habits and attitudes given how we respond to them. More so that the symbols they help to express, more so than the practices that animate them, and more so than the habits they cultivate, cultures give rise to thought. They do so in light of the coeval, dialectical experience of alterity and intimacy. As features of our cultural lives, those twin ideas invite exploration that can avoid obscurantist and esoteric discourses that pervade academic discourses today. Future work in religious ethics might well benefit from noting these facts and following up on the opportunities that a cultural turn has to offer.

During the time I was drafting the chapters that found their way into this book, a number of monographs were published that reflect hybridizing work in religion, ethics, and culture. Below I will discuss six books that represent a cultural turn in the humanities—works by religious ethicists and cultural anthropologists that provide important signposts of the past and for the future. Not all of these works are equally successful; a few exemplify some of the problems regarding the turn to culture that I have addressed in the previous pages. But all of them coordinate an "ethics-distant" with an "ethics-near" approach to their materials, thereby working a hermeneutical dialectic between theoretical models and concepts, on the one hand, and ethnographic data from cultural immersion and field notes, on the other. As we will see, five of them address ethical and political matters in Islamic cultures, reflecting a genuine efflorescence in Muslim ethics. Together these works provide a chorus about how religion is keenly relevant to public and private life, often in ways that are overlooked by mainstream approaches to social and political thought, driven as those are by paradigms of research that embrace some version of the secularization thesis. Each book departs from—or challenges—reigning methodologies and research traditions in their respective areas of specialization and require us to reimagine some otherwise stable frames of inquiry that shape humanistic and social scientific scholarship. My aim here is to highlight their distinctive profiles and to identify important insights and blind spots that we do well to note.[1] Given how cultural differences and matters of identity can fossilize, foster incuriosity and anti-intellectualism, generate stereotypes, and impede human communication and amicable coexistence, careful studies of cultural and political non-elites and the ethical dimensions of everyday lives are a welcome feature of scholarship in the humanities and social sciences.

* * *

Saba Mahmood's *Politics of Piety: The Islamic Revival and the Feminist Subject* is an ethnographic study of the women's mosque movement in Egypt, focusing on the piety and practices of participants in three Cairene mosques that reflect a range of socioeconomic backgrounds. The women's mosque movement is part of a larger Islamic revival that has swept the Middle East, including Egypt, over the past four decades. Also known as the *da'wa* or piety movement, it has enlisted the energies of politically oriented groups but more generally seeks to imbue everyday life with a religious sensibility and ethos that has led to a dramatic increase in mosque participation by men and women, the proliferation of mosques and other institutions of Islamic learning, and marked displays of religious piety. As a reform effort, the *da'wa* movement aims to cultivate virtues and forms of reasoning that participants believe have become either marginalized or irrelevant in the context of secular state governance. Mosques have become the organizational center for many revivalist activities in Cairo, from disseminating religious knowledge and instruction to providing medical and welfare services to underserved Egyptians. The movement has become so popular that by the mid-1990s few neighborhoods existed in Cairo that did not offer religious instruction for women. Women who participated in the movement during Mahmood's years of research (1995–97) provided lessons that focused on Islamic scriptures, social practices, and forms of bodily comportment considered instrumental to cultivating the ideal virtuous self. Women's gatherings have altered the male-centered character of mosques and Islamic teaching, yet they have adhered to "a discursive tradition that regards subordination to a transcendent will (and thus, in many instances, to male authority) as its coveted goal."[2]

Mahmood grasps that rendering a patriarchal, nonliberal, authoritarian set of beliefs and practices intelligible to contemporary Western readers, especially Western feminists, is a difficult task. She is also aware of the challenges of studying a movement to which she is an outsider by virtue of her background and leftist commitments. In her mind the dangers of sounding ethnocentric, or clumsily applying Western categories that bear the weight of colonialist legacies, are real. Her effort to carry out her project with these concerns in mind is held together by three interlocking lines of analysis.

First is the effort "to analyze the conceptions of self, moral agency, and politics that undergird the practices of this nonliberal movement, in order to come to an understanding of the historical projects that animate it" (5). Mahmood thus examines a concept of agency that focuses on "embodied capacities" as a "means of subject formation" and the habituation of behavioral norms and ideals rather than on the assertion of autonomy (7). According to Mahmood, "what may appear to be a case of deplorable passivity and docility from a progressivist point of view, may actually be a form of agency—but one that can be understood only from within the discourses and structures of subordination that create the conditions of its enactment. In this sense, agentival capacity is entailed not only in those acts that resist norms but also in the multiple ways in which one *inhabits* norms" (15). Attending to matters of moral agency and the embodiment of virtue, Mahmood interrogates "how different forms of desire emerge, including desire for submission to recognized authority" (15).

Mahmood pursues this first line of analysis by drawing on the moral theories of Aristotle and Michel Foucault. Their work provides the basis for thinking about how external behaviors contribute to the formation of moral subjectivity, what Foucault calls "subjectivization." According to Mahmood, Foucault and Aristotle allow us to see ethics "as always local and particular, pertaining to a specific set of procedures, techniques, and discourses through which highly specific ethical-moral subjects come to be formed" (28). Of special importance is that Foucault and Aristotle enable us to grasp how repeated external behaviors, rituals, and practices are themselves causes rather than consequences of human subjectivity. Mahmood thus enlists the idea of *habitus* from her reading of Aristotle to attend to matters of moral cultivation and the formation of virtues that rely on an understanding of the self as embodied, contextual, and dependent on authorities and exemplars.[3] For Foucault and Aristotle, Mahmood writes, practices are important "in the *work they do* in constituting the individual" (29; Mahmood's emphasis).

Second is a metatheoretical argument. Mahmood wishes to examine "conceptual challenges that women's involvement in the Islamist movement pose to feminist theory in particular, and to secular-liberal thought in general" (2). Time and again Mahmood makes plain that she is trying to render the women's mosque movement intelligible in ways that operate outside the methodological canons of progressive feminism, either in its liberal or poststructuralist frameworks. Thus she does not ask how Muslim women in the mosque movement might be subverting or resignifying Islamic idioms with a liberative agenda in mind. Indeed, Mahmood states that her informants offer visions of human flourishing that have led her to parochialize her own political certitudes and assumptions (xi). For this reason Mahmood wishes to "make this material speak back to the normative liberal assumptions about human nature against which such a movement is held accountable—such as the belief that all human beings have an innate desire for freedom, that we all somehow seek to assert our autonomy when allowed to do so, that human agency primarily consists of acts that challenge social norms and not those that uphold them, and so on" (5). About having to deal with the women's mosque movement in light of her feminist commitments, Mahmood writes: "It has compelled me to leave open the possibility that my analysis may come to complicate the vision of human flourishing that I hold most dear, and which has provided the bedrock of my personal existence" (xii). That readers are not to assume that their political commitments will be vindicated by her work, Mahmood writes, "is the normative political position that underlies this book" (39).

Mahmood advances this second line of analysis by arguing that versions of human flourishing are quite evident in the women's mosque movement. She offers accounts of spirited discussions among women and female preachers about, for example, gender roles, the meaning of shyness, and how public weeping is practiced at mosque meetings in order to inculcate fear and awe among the practitioners. In addition, Mahmood seeks to illustrate how bodily practices such as ritual worship are the means of forming pious dispositions, how wearing the veil can instill humility, and how women justify their role as preachers in the mosque movement—a development that challenges the traditional role of men in that capacity. Mahmood also enters into a dialogue with one informant about how entering into a polygamous marriage may very well be the lesser of two evils facing single women in Muslim cultures. The overall result of these engagements, she proposes, is to "leave open the possibility that our political and analytical certainties might be transformed in the process of exploring nonliberal movements of the kind I studied" (39). Mahmood makes plain that her ethnography was regularly complicated by questions about moral authority and moral critique of the sort I discussed in chapter 3. She asks feminist readers: "Are we willing to countenance the sometimes violent task of remaking sensibilities, life worlds, and attachments so that women of the kind I worked with may be taught to value the principle of 'freedom'?" (38).

Mahmood's third line of argument ties into matters of religion and politics. She aims to have readers—especially secular progressives—overcome their discomfort about the prominent place of religion in public life. Although participants in the mosque movement do not seek to engage state institutions and political organizations directly, they have helped bring about discernible changes in public culture regarding styles of dress, comportment in work contexts, proper entertainment for adults and children, obligations to the poor, attitudes toward gender and marriage, and proper modes of public debate. The *da'wa* movement resists Western secularization in contingent and unforeseen ways, challenging the "nationalist-identitarian" movements in Egypt that look down on pietistic practices as forms of folk Arab tradition or see the revivalist movement as relying on sources of authority beyond that of the state (35, 75). The *da'wa* movement has been prompted in no small way in response to Western, secular influences and has increasingly become the target of state scrutiny and regulation in Egypt (73–75).

Mahmood proposes that the best political category for understanding the women's mosque movement is that of *community*. Although she distances herself from the liberal-communitarian debate in Anglo-American political philosophy, she sees potential in the concept of community for capturing what she calls the "unusual" (192) political space occupied by the mosque movement in Egypt. Rather than view the mosque movement in terms of identity politics or the politics of recognition, she encourages us to see the movement as a kind of community "that makes explicit those modalities of action through which embodied attachments to historically specific forms of belonging are forged." Virtues and practices that are cultivated by the women's mosque movement constitute an "extra-national" (194) form of belonging that holds great appeal in the postcolonial world.[4]

Readers drawn to Foucauldian theory would likely look to *Politics of Piety* as a showpiece of poststructuralist scholarship. Mahmood regularly and consistently intones against liberal humanist views of freedom, voluntarism, autonomy, and progressive politics as offering a reductive picture of agency, one that would prevent her from seeing the ethical and political dimensions of the women's mosque movement. But interpreting *Politics of Piety* as a signature example of poststructuralist theory might be to misread the book. Mahmood is not endorsing Foucauldian, poststructuralist thinking as *true*. She is rather drawing on Foucault's ideas as *useful*. She writes: "I find Foucault's analysis of ethical formation particularly helpful for conceptualizing agency beyond the confines of the binary model of enacting and subverting norms. Specifically, he draws our attention to the contribution of external forms to the development of human capacities, to specific modes of human agency" (29). Foucault enables Mahmood to get beyond Western feminist thinking that would have her see if Muslim women were engaged in one or another form of antipatriarchal liberative resistance in their meetings and discussions.

Using Foucault's ideas enables Mahmood to employ the phenomenological *epoche*—bracketing a set of commitments to allow the other to speak in her own terms. As I noted above, she is vexed throughout her work by questions of moral critique and moral authority, often expressing worries about seeming ethnocentric or colonialist in her treatment of a nonliberal religious movement. To avoid charges of sounding ethnocentric or of rehearsing ideas that are marked by colonialist associations, Mahmood silences her progressive, feminist commitments along with her dismay at the patriarchal, subordinationist practices and ideologies that she encounters in her fieldwork. Rather than read Mahmood as an advocate of poststructuralism as a philosophy of *truth*, it is more accurate to read her as deploying Foucault in order to carry out a rather familiar methodological procedure regularly used within the history of religions.

I hasten to add, however, that Mahmood's use of the *epoche* does not aim to make her study entirely value-neutral (the standard reason for invoking the *epoche* in the study of religion). Her effort to avoid sounding ethnocentric or colonialist should not obscure other normative dimensions of her argument. One instance emerges when she explains why she is not overly revulsed by the women's mosque movement. The Muslim women in her study, she states, are relatively harmless when compared to fascist or militant movements; nor do they seek to turn Egypt into a theocracy (37). The women in the revivalist mosque movement are safe subjects of study—they are not putting anyone in danger. That is to say, the women's mosque movement is deemed acceptable for academic study in part because they are not violating what is known in ethics as the harm principle.

If the women's mosque movement stirs up concerns among liberal feminists, Mahmood can dispel them by invoking Foucault and Aristotle to offer an alternative account of moral agency that has reflexive implications insofar as they might unsettle liberal and progressive assurances. Herein lies another normative feature of her work. Mahmood wants her account to parochialize Western feminist forms of scholarship. One cannot help but think back to chapter 2 and my discussion of how Marcus and Fischer describe anthropology as a form of cultural criticism that relativizes "our taken-for-granted concepts such as the family, power, and the beliefs that lend certainty to everyday life," thereby "disorienting the reader and altering perception," and locating "alternatives by unearthing . . . multiple possibilities as they exist in reality."[5] Mahmood speaks the same way. Describing the importance of suspending her feminist judgments, she writes: "'Intellectual inquiry' here entails pushing against our received assumptions and categories, through which a number of unwieldy problems have been domesticated to customary habits of thought and praxis" (196). Unsettling customary liberal habits of thought is one of the explicit normative aims of her work.

Another, less pronounced reason that *Politics of Piety* is not value-neutral has to do with Mahmood's underlying ideas about feminism as a whole. At the conclusion of her work she makes plain that her decision not to denounce the patriarchy and subordinationism of the women's mosque movement follows from a broader commitment to women's solidarity. Over the course of her research, she writes, "I came to reckon that if the old feminist practice of 'solidarity' had any valence whatsoever, it could not be grounded in the ur-languages of feminism, progressivism, liberalism, or Islamism, but could only ensue within the uncertain, sometimes opaque, conditions of intimate and uncomfortable encounters in all their eventuality" (198–99). In other words the other is given a pass owing to the process of the increased familiarization that comes with participant observation. The alterity of the women's mosque movement seems now to have vanished.

I devote considerable time unpacking Mahmood's study here—I'll be briefer in the other book discussions that follow—because it reflects several of the themes and anxieties I have examined over the course of this book. The questions with which *Politics of Piety* wrestles are textbook examples of issues that often arise in cultural anthropology that includes attention to religion and ethics. My problem with Mahmood has to do with the fact that she may not be entirely aware of what she is doing as she sets up the scaffolding to carry out her project. Specifically, she has failed to think about the terms and conditions according to which she may properly take the liberty to speak as a cross-cultural critic. The weaknesses of *Politics of Piety* become evident when we look at how Mahmood handles some of her categories and sources, especially when she (a) turns to moral theory and Aristotle's account of the virtues; (b) refers to "secular, liberal" ideas as the foil against which she argues; and (c) makes reference to feminist solidarity to explain her reluctance to criticize the women's mosque movement. The first problem pertains to her representation of Aristotelian moral theory and opens her to the charge of moral relativism in her treatment of pietistic virtues. It also leaves her open to the charge of overlooking the importance of intellectual virtue *and* its relevance to the practices of debate and reason-giving that she describes in her work. The second problem pertains to the fact that, despite her commitments to context, particularity, and history, she essentializes liberal thought and, in the process, eliminates a way to explain *the fact that* women join the mosque movement. The third problem exposes the question-begging nature of her feminist solidarity.

As to Mahmood's handling of Aristotle: in her eagerness to emphasize outward, bodily practices as inducing particular dispositions in the process of pietistic subjectivization, Mahmood conflates Aristotle's theory of virtue with Foucault's. As a result she fails to grasp the difference between Aristotle's view of virtue in relation to human flourishing and Foucault's view of virtue and aesthetic self-fashioning. Aristotle and those who follow in his tradition would question the attitudes and dispositions that the piety movement requires of its practitioners. Mahmood distinguishes Aristotle's views from Kant's by saying that the former focuses on "habituated virtue" rather than the "critical faculty of reason" (25). But that description overlooks how Aristotle's theory is organized by the idea that humans are rational animals and that virtue should be ordered to the active realization of basic potencies that are specific to human nature. Aristotle views virtues as instrumental and constitutive of a good human life, a form of practical moral activity that mobilizes one's reason in order to deliberate about how to live well. Moreover, and crucial to understanding Aristotle, is the fact that he understands human good and human flourishing in nonrelative ways. If the women in the mosque movement are indeed experiencing a form of human flourishing, as Mahmood maintains, then she needs to say what human potentialities are being realized in the practices she describes. She needs to identify by what criterion *flourishing* is to be understood so that we can distinguish between true and counterfeit forms. Without articulating and defending that criterion, her account defaults to a form of relativism that has us conclude that what the women in the mosque movement are doing is good, understanding the good to be relative to the values and traditions of the *da'wa* movement.

Mahmood misinterprets Aristotle in yet another way, one that prevents her from tracking the practices of reason-giving carried out by the women of the mosque movement. For Aristotle, intellectual and moral virtue, while distinguished, are intimately related: moral virtue requires excellence in deliberation just as good deliberation requires strong moral character.[6] Although she briefly acknowledges that "the question of motivation, deliberation, and choice in the Aristotelian tradition was important" (26), she says little about the cognitive dimension of virtue either in Aristotle or among her informants—despite evidence that she provides about the value of debate and overcoming interpretive questions about the meaning and weight of different scriptural and traditional sources. Mahmood shows how reasoning about moral concepts like humility, how to weigh and balance conflicting teachings from Islamic tradition, or how to conceptualize one or another authoritative account of the Prophet's life are all cognitive, interpretive activities that are important to the very people she describes. But none of that can be made sense of as a virtue given the picture of virtue on which she relies. Mahmood's understanding of virtue is palpably anti-intellectual insofar as it fails to grasp how deliberative activity is considered an excellence in the pietist movement. That is to say, her view of virtue as relying on repetitive, bodily, external practices blocks her from understanding and adequately representing *the value of reasoning to her informants themselves.*

As to Mahmood's reference to secular-liberal ideas as a foil: Mahmood tosses around references to the "secular-liberal" project (1, 75, passim) casually and carelessly. She fails to exercise due diligence about the variety of voices and theories that fall underneath that umbrella. When it comes to political theory, she is no particularist. Most problematic about her rejection of what falls under the "secular-liberal" banner is that it renders incoherent many of the things that Mahmood says about her informants, and it—along with her confused account of Aristotle—denies her a vocabulary for understanding the women in the mosque movement as acting for a purpose. Strangely, she states that the women in the mosque movement undergo "volitional training" on a path toward the goal of virtue and that they exhibit "self-willed obedience to religiously prescribed social conventions" (147–48). But she regularly rejects the idea of "an imaginary of freedom, one deeply indebted to liberal political theory, in which an individual is considered free on the condition that she act autonomously: that her actions are of her own choice and free will, rather than of custom, tradition, transcendental will, or social coercion" (148). Absent an understanding of the voluntary dimensions of human agency, however, we have no basis for explaining why Muslim women join the mosque movement in the first place. A liberal can easily say that the women in the mosque movement are exercising what is called second-order autonomy—choosing to submit themselves to traditional practices and ideals. Moreover, Mahmood confuses liberalism with secularism, entirely overlooking liberalism's important relationship with religious freedom and toleration. As I made plain in my discussion of Rawls in chapter 10, *political liberalism* is not a comprehensive secularizing doctrine. It helps to remember that what Mahmood calls the "secular, liberal project" (insofar as it is not a complete straw figure) differs from country to country—France and the United States being quite different instantiations of liberal ideas.

If, instead, Mahmood wants to turn to Aristotle to make sense of embodiment and virtue in order to put distance between that picture of the moral life and one that stresses liberal autonomy, he would remind her that virtue pertains to making a *choice*, one that lies at a mean between two extremes relative to the agent given her constitution and sensibilities and determined by a rational principle as understood by the person of practical wisdom.[7] Indeed, book 3 of the *Nicomachean Ethics* is devoted to sorting out the voluntary and involuntary dimensions of human action. Unfortunately, Mahmood reads Aristotle selectively and fails to grasp the importance of this voluntarist dimension of virtuous conduct in his moral theory.

Finally, regarding Mahmood and feminism: Mahmood's appeal to feminist solidarity to explain why she maintains studied moral silence about the women's mosque movement only begs the question about what feminist solidarity means. Surely it does not mean never criticizing other women. But Mahmood suggests that it does. As I noted in chapter 5, solidarity is a concept that enables members to draw lines to mark off an imagined community, and it does so by establishing criteria for determining who is in and who is out. Solidarity is an "in-group" idea that suggests a social psychology of collective resolve that draws its energy from members' real or vicarious shared experiences. Mahmood never makes plain how she understands the criteria that account for her view of feminist solidarity. How can feminist solidarity accommodate the desire for patriarchy?

Taken together, my complaints point to an underlying anxiety that runs throughout Mahmood's work, namely the worry about "sounding ethnocentric" by virtue of being an outsider to the lifeworld and practices she is studying. Mahmood's desire to avoid the charges of ethnocentrism or colonialism lead her to overreach and, in the process, overlook theoretical possibilities for her project and the suppressed normative claims within it. In my view Mahmood is certainly free to describe the women's mosque movement on their own terms, drawing on Foucault and other resources, but that shouldn't prevent her from expressing and defending her progressive, feminist concerns as well. Despite her efforts to be self-reflexive in her work, Mahmood fails to consider on what terms she can properly assume the stance of a social critic. As I made plain in chapter 3, norms and virtues exist to guide cross-cultural criticism, and they could directly inform the research and writing that resulted in *Politics of Piety*.

* * *

Farhat Moazam's *Bioethics and Organ Transplantation in a Muslim Society: A Study in Culture, Ethnography, and Religion* is a work in cross-cultural bioethics based on three months of immersion at a medical institution in Karachi that Moazam calls "the Institute," a public dialysis and renal transplantation unit renowned in Pakistan for providing the only free access to treatment and follow-up procedures and for its reputation of providing the highest level of medical care. A pediatric surgeon trained in Pakistan and the United States and a religious ethicist trained at the University of Virginia, Moazam returned to her home country in 2002 to study the distinctive social, cultural, economic, and religious factors that shape bioethical reasoning in Pakistan as part of her dissertation research. The chief aim of her book is to describe how bioethics is "particularized" in this Pakistani context and to show how its indigenous moral horizon differs from the framework provided by secular bioethics as developed in Anglo-American contexts. Her project is in part comparative, "juxtaposing a better-known landscape, that of live kidney transplantations in the United States, with the less familiar topography of how it is 'done' in an institution in Pakistan."[8] Citing the work of anthropologist Ruth Benedict as a model, Moazam went into her research assuming "that such attention to the 'other-ness' of a culture, its foreignness and 'oddities,' would also serve to test and clarify domestic assumptions and values" (9).

Moazam follows the work of five Institute staff members over the course of her study—three doctors and two social workers. She was openly welcomed to the Institute owing to her reputation as a physician, professor, and former university administrator in Pakistan prior to her research in biomedical ethics, and she made good use of her opportunity to enter into the lifeworld of the Institute as a participant observer. Her ability to quickly earn the trust of families, patients, and the Institute's staff enabled her to carry out more than one hundred interviews and to capture the complexities of treatment decisions and ethical trade-offs that were often required in an institution deluged by patients, many from poor backgrounds and in desperate straits. Because organ donations to nonfamily members were usually paid for in Pakistan, and because Pakistan banned the use of cadaverous organs, the Institute only accepted donations from living, related donors as a matter of moral principle. That fact, along with the complex kinship relations in a country that is 95 percent Muslim, made for difficult interactions and pressures among family members facing treatment decisions, especially when potential donors or recipients were women.

In her effort to contextualize and particularize the ethics of kidney transplantation in Pakistan, Moazam invokes a number of distinctions.

These distinctions sharpen the differences between Pakistani and Anglo-American moral horizons and highlight a particular set of ethical concerns surrounding gender and social injustice at the Institute. In contrast to the abstract nature of mainstream Anglo-American bioethics—a description often assigned to the work of Moazam's mentor, James Childress, and his collaborator Tom Beauchamp[9]—Moazam describes the moral world of the Institute as local and culturally specific, one that requires us to look at biomedicine's "micropractices." Furthermore, Moazam observes, Anglo-American bioethics focuses on the individual, isolated patient, whereas care providers at the Institute encountered their patients as nested in a dense web of family ties. Yet another contrast is between an Anglo-American ethic that accords primacy to autonomy and patients' rights and the ethic of care providers at the Institute who acted on a "ferocious benevolence" and commitment to social justice, often in ways that were not only directive but remonstrative and coercive of family members who declined to donate organs when they could (16). Whereas Anglo-American approaches to bioethics are premised on the idea of the equality of persons, moreover, Pakistani culture is hierarchical and androcentric in its understanding of role relationships. Physicians in Pakistan are viewed as agents of God in their curative powers and responsibilities, and they understand themselves as having strong duties to help those in need instead of delivering nondirective medical expertise to their "clients." Moreover, owing to the high value assigned to kinship relationships, staff members at the Institute were treated on the model of the family rather than as autonomous professionals (83–93). Finally, and most important, Anglo-American and Pakistani cultures look at the ethics of organ transplantation quite differently. The former regularly emphasizes organ donation as an altruistic gift from one individual to another, whereas at the Institute the donation was viewed as an obligation from one family member to another. In Western contexts the reward for donation is generally seen as an increase in self-esteem; in Pakistan the reward comes from securing God's favor (217–18).

Moazam thus found that within the moral horizon of transplant ethics in Pakistan, organ donation is a duty incumbent on family members; the medical profession enjoys a privileged moral status in Pakistani culture; family is a template for conceiving professional relationships; and medical care is shaped by benevolence in response to social suffering and social injustice. The language of individual rights, informed consent, autonomy, antipaternalism, and equality—standard fare in Anglo-American secular bioethics—is quite foreign to the world she studied. Summarizing these differences, Moazam writes: "Professional authority is used to bring about what is considered to be the best interest of the patient and, by extension, the entire family. In this process, the Western ideal of maintaining an objective, rational, therapeutic distance is replaced by emotional involvement in the lives of patients and their families" (219). The relationship is fiduciary, not contractual. And the circumstances are acute matters of social justice: fighting against poverty, limited medical resources, and the coercion of women to donate (220).

Yet it would be wrong to conclude from these contrasts that Moazam wants us to draw a sharp divide between "East and West" or between "Western" and "Muslim" societies. Her distinctions inform a context-sensitive examination of the moral problems that arose in the Institute and are thus modest in aim and scope. In fact, as she observes, the work of Beauchamp and Childress has become well known in Pakistan and in international bioethics more generally (222). In her view, however, to fully internationalize bioethics "the diversity of human voices and experiences must be brought into the fold"; moreover, American bioethicists should begin to reflect on their own particular and social assumptions about "what constitutes moral interactions between society and its healers" (225). She describes her work as taking one step in the direction toward comprehending "the many ways in which people experientially fashion and interpret concepts of dignity and respect for people, interpret caring for one another, and decide what constitutes ethical conduct between laypeople and those who assume responsibility for their health" (225).

Even as she argues on behalf of approaching ethics in a more particularized, context-sensitive way, however, Moazam does not lionize the values and practices of Pakistani culture. In particular, she argues that valorizing social relationships and family ties, so important to the context she studied, has a dark side. Moazam follows a number of families that put pressure on female family members to gift a kidney, even when a male member is better able to donate. She observes how male members avoided donating a kidney to a female sibling after agreeing to do so, often taking flight from their families and communities to avoid being shamed into donating. This fact of gender hierarchy regularly chafed against Moazam's feminist sensibilities. Summarizing her findings, she writes: "The double-edged sword of family dynamics that centers on a strong sense of mutual obligations among family members can result in the empowerment of donors or objectify and exploit the most vulnerable members of the unit" (170). Moazam is both even-handed in her description of cases and yet critical when assessing the beliefs and practices of her research subjects. About the temptations of reifying the ethics of one or another culture, she writes: "Just as it is reductive to conceive of individualistic cultures as always fragmented and uncaring, it is simplistic to consider interdependent, extended systems of kinship as absolute ideals of unity and selflessness" (170).

Moazam concludes her work by identifying problems she encountered in her role as a physician carrying out participant observation in a medical context. She is alone among those I am surveying in this epilogue for calling attention to ethical questions that attend to doing ethnographic work, questions that are classified under the rubric of "research ethics." Not unlike Mahmood, Moazam expresses self-awareness about her own training, background, and commitments, on the one hand, and her research subjects, on the other. And, like Mahmood, Moazam could not overlook matters of gender equity and the problems of women in an androcentric, hierarchical culture. But Moazam's questions had less to do with whether to bracket her own feminist commitments in her research and writing than whether to actively intervene and change the situations of subjects she was observing. In the course of her research, medical problems arose for patients whom she was following. "My own strong identity as a physician," she writes, "was never fully submerged during my fieldwork" (191). Questions about whether, when, and how to influence "natural" events she was observing left her ambivalent about the ethics of her dual role as physician and researcher. Despite emphasizing to house staff that she was carrying out ethnographic research, Moazam came to realize that when the faculty, residents, staff, families, and patients looked at her, they saw "a senior physician, a professor, and past chair of surgery" (186).

In more than a few instances Moazam decided to offer medical advice or to diagnose patients, and in several cases she decided to intervene.

Two cases concerning young female patients needing a transplant convinced her that it was time to leave the field. In both, she consciously assumed the role of a Pakistani surgeon taking steps to help achieve what she considered the best interests of a patient by actively seeking to persuade each patient's brother to donate his kidney (205). At that point in her research she realized that she had overstepped her role as a participant observer. She learned later that, despite her certainty surrounding the willingness of the brothers to donate, each fled the scene. "Ironically," she writes, "despite misgivings that I was overstepping my role as a participant observer, I had been unsuccessful after all in changing the course of events in the two cases in which I had interfered" (213).

In other words Moazam carries out a work that is both critical and self-critical. She is mindful of her background, relative affluence, feminist sensibilities, and training as a physician as affecting her perspective and actions as an ethnographer. But she has no hang-ups about possibly sounding "ethnocentric." That is because she is able to exercise the virtues I identified in chapter 3: She (1) gives reasons to explain and justify her judgments, (2) exhibits (general) moral and epistemic probity, (3) exercises due diligence in her work, (4) aspires to render a judgment that is informed by judicious perspective-taking, and (5) expresses herself with a style and a grasp of social location that is context-sensitive. Moazam is able to carry out fieldwork, identify important features of her background and perspective, and call herself out for intervening in the field of her research area. Owing to Moazam's ability to describe, evaluate, and self-evaluate, hers is a distinctive contribution to the interdisciplinary field of religion, ethics, and culture.

* * *

Charles Hirschkind's *The Ethical Soundscape: Cassette Sermons and Islamic Counterpublics* studies the circulation of Islamic cassette sermons and their role in subject-formation and the creation of an alternative public sphere for Muslims participating in the *da'wa* movement in Egypt. *The Ethical Soundscape* resulted from one kind of project made possible by the cultural turn that I described in chapter 2, namely, research that interrogates the role of media in public culture. Based on his ethnographic fieldwork in Cairo in the mid-1990s, Hirschkind provides a detailed picture of how the independent production of cassette tapes, starting in the 1970s, made it possible for popular Islamic preachers to transmit their fire-and-brimstone sermons without having to rely on established pathways for securing religious authority—typically in connection to a mosque tied to a specific community or as authorized through state regulated modes of certification in the effort to tie the religious sermon to the project of nation-building. Taped sermons are ubiquitous in Cairo—audible in cafés, family meals, public transportation, schools, informal gatherings, and the like—and are the source of spirited debates for those in the revivalist movement.

According to Hirschkind, popular cassette sermons have palpable visceral effects on their listeners and aim to open the hearts of Muslim listeners so that they can critically examine their dispositions and everyday activities in light of Muslim piety. That aim is driven by the revivalist desire to mitigate the effects of ubiquitous Western consumerist and sensual imagery, ideals, and values. By drawing on vivid poetic imagery from the Quran and hadith, affectively charged speech, shifting narratological perspectives, and the use of voice itself as sound instrument, revivalist preachers appeal as much to modes of rational deliberation as to subconscious modes of seeing and feeling, thereby addressing the "prerational ordering of the self upon which more rational practices depend."[10] Emphasis in popular Muslim revivalist oratory thus falls on moral psychology, ethical self-formation, and the cultivation of virtues, especially those of sincerity, humility, awe, regret, and fear, to guide moral action among listeners.

Axiomatic for Hirschkind is the idea, borrowed from the early twentieth-century anthropologist Marcel Jousse, of the listener as a "human compound," a term that aims to capture kinesthetic and empathic responses to the preached sound, image, or story. Based on his study of preliterate traditions, Jousse formulated an account of the stylistic features common to oral cultures, focusing especially on the rhythmic gesticulations of storytellers. Hirschkind points out that Jousse developed a picture of active, animated speaking and listening along with a theory that "language and consciousness are constructed upon a substrate of rhythmic motions, determined both by mnemonic faculties of the senses and the dynamics of bodily rhythms (respiration, pulse, heartbeat, and so on)" (77). Drawing on this idea of the indivisibility of body and mind, Hirschkind argues that the cassette sermon is a new medium not only for transmitting ideas or religious ideologies but, more importantly, for cultivating affective habits and sensibilities that are literally embodied among those who listen to them. "The soundscape produced through the circulation of this medium," Hirschkind writes, "animates and sustains the substrate of sensory knowledges and embodied aptitudes undergirding a broad revival movement within contemporary Islam" (2). In chapter 3, "The Ethics of Listening," Hirschkind states that listening to cassette tapes serves first to provide a form of relaxed attentiveness insofar as the sermon punctures the boredom and monotony of everyday life. "The relaxed attentiveness of this auditory practice," he writes, "invests the body with affective intensities . . . , latent tendencies of ethical response sedimented within the mnemonic regions of the flesh" (82–83). Hirschkind's informants "shared a common substrate of embodied dispositions . . . as instrumental to the task of [the] sermon audition. It is these sensory dispositions, . . . more than a commitment to normative rationality, that constitute the common ground upon which the discourses of a tradition come to be articulated, the 'reflexes' that make arguments about the status of Quranic references meaningful and worthy of engagement" (88).

Hirschkind develops his account of the ethical soundscape in Cairo to make a number of points about Islam in Egyptian society. He calls attention to two recurrent themes in the sermons themselves: the death of the individual, and communal pain. These two themes are taken up and amplified in the thanatological and eschatological idioms of Muslim pietist preaching. Death is emphasized not only as the individual's fate but also as a fact of life that should pervade the individual's everyday consciousness, values, and choices. Rather than marking an abrupt change in an individual's life, in Egypt consciousness of death pervades it in an ongoing way. According to Hirschkind, Muslim piety echoes Heidegger's concept of "being-toward-death" as an existential fact of ordinary existence. In a related vein Muslim preachers frequently speak of divine judgment and its implications for a person's choices, habits, and attitudes. That fact should instill pious fear in the individual and highlight the eternal stakes that attach to all temporal actions.

Political dimensions to the ethical soundscape exist as well. According to Hirschkind, the ethical soundscape sheds important light on the place of religion in postcolonial states that, at an official level, seek either to secularize the public square or, in the case of Egypt, to tightly control religious beliefs and practices. Drawing on the ideas of William Connolly, Talal Asad, and Michael Warner, Hirschkind argues that the revivalist movement in Egypt is a clear example of how religion—especially as embodied and felt—constitutes a "counterpublic" to the official aims of the Egyptian regime to regulate religious matters. Revivalism as a counterpublic also serves as a riposte to some versions of liberal political philosophy that picture religious belief as a private and politically irrelevant matter and view the public square as a site of open, transparent, and rational deliberation.[11] Indeed, the lively discussions prompted by cassette sermons cut across the divisions of private and public life that often shape liberal thinking. That fact makes plain that the revivalist movement is far from being a quietist and individualistic matter; it rather engages topics across a wide range of personal and political issues. Not unlike Mahmood, Hirschkind marks off the "unusual places" occupied by the da'wa movement.[12] Both scholars note that the public and political implications of revivalist Islam pertain less to electoral politics and ties to established institutions than to "the changes [the da'wa movement] effects in the social and moral landscape of Egyptian society" (209). By this Hirschkind means that the da'wa movement has focused not on political institutions but on relations between Muslims and Christian Copts, sometimes seeking to vilify or further marginalize Copts in ways that raise difficult issues about religious coexistence (209–12). Whether the da'wa movement can accommodate the desires and commitments of both religious communities, Hirschkind observes, "is hard to predict, but it would be premature to assume that such an outcome is impossible" (212).

Hirschkind concludes his work by arguing that the category of "fundamentalism" is entirely inadequate for describing the pieties, sensibilities, and practices of the Islamic revivalist movement. Here we see one palpable benefit of taking a cultural turn, namely, that it enables us to look not only at the moral life but also at how religion is practiced and theorized. In Hirschkind's mind the lifeworld of Egyptian piety is too variegated and contingent to be tagged with ideas associated with fundamentalist religions, namely, fundamentalism as "uninteresting" and contributing "very little to our understanding of human value and creativity, let alone our capacities of moral and political imagination" (205). Indeed, the challenge of dislodging the study of Islam from the cramped category of fundamentalism along with its polarized accounts of religion in the modern world is more than merely intellectual. The challenge, Hirschkind writes as he concludes his study, "is a moral one" (213).

For readers interested in culture, religion, and ethics Hirschkind's concluding sentence cries out for elaboration. Presumably the idea is that representing Islam as rich and variegated is "moral" in the sense that it is *just* to the individuals and movements being described in *The Ethical Soundscape*. Hirschkind suggests that it is now commonplace to view Islam as a fundamentalist religion and that focusing on the role of media and the unusual political place of the revivalist movement in Egyptian society helps to free the representation of Islam from simplistic and unfair clichés. His ethnography enables us to hear voices and encounter attitudes and feelings that a reductive, fundamentalist imaginary silences. In that respect *The Ethical Soundscape* is a project on behalf of fairness. Hirschkind's work thus stands within a tradition of social criticism launched by Edward Said, whom he favorably quotes as he concludes his book. Said and Hirschkind target orientalist attitudes and practices that judge Islam as culturally inferior to the West. Hirschkind's book may thus be read as an expression of social criticism seeking to reform Western readers of their biases and blindnesses. But Hirschkind sees a further danger, namely, the polarizing and dangerous effects that accompany closed-mindedness. Aiming to create a more complicated and variegated account of Islam, then, is "moral" because it aspires to contribute not only to the right but also to the good.

* * *

Jeffrey Stout's *Blessed Are the Organized: Grassroots Democracy in America* is not a full-scale ethnographic study but one that relies on a series of site visits and interviews with grassroots organizers and ordinary citizens in New Orleans and Houston after Hurricane Katrina, the borderlands of southern Texas, the neighborhoods of South Central Los Angeles, and an affluent community north of San Francisco to depict grassroots organizing and comment on the quality of democratic life and culture today. Focusing on groups affiliated with the Industrial Areas Foundation (IAF), a confederation of local or regional organizations that was founded by Saul Alinsky in Chicago in 1940, Stout introduces us to a wide range of ordinary citizens who meet in homes, synagogues, and churches; cultivate leaders; carry out power analyses; and take action to tackle problems of social justice in their locales. Bringing together his long-standing interests in Hegel, democratic theory, religion and public life, social criticism, and pragmatism, Stout takes us on a narrative journey in which we hear about the successes and failures of progressive grassroots organizing and, in the process, learn about the political, religious, institutional, psychological, ethical, social, economic, and intellectual dimensions of the people involved in the IAF. One aim of the project, Stout says, "is to bring the ideal of good citizenship down to earth. I want readers to experience something like what I experienced when talking, face-to-face, with citizens who believe that democracy's health depends on one-on-one conversations, small-group meetings, critical reflection, and organized action."[13] Moving back and forth between his conversations with various informants, on the one hand, and his critical reflections about citizenship, political organization, power, effective leadership, and American traditions of democracy and grassroots movements, on the other, Stout produces a reflexive study by adopting "a perspective that makes the dangers of our situation visible without simultaneously disabling the hope of reforming it" (259). The result is an exemplary piece of ethnographically informed social criticism and American public philosophy.

Stout begins his story in New Orleans sixteen months after Hurricane Katrina, meeting with members of a citizen's organization called Jeremiah, a network of churches, synagogues, parent-teacher associations, unions, and other nongovernmental groups that pay dues to fund the salaries of Jeremiah's organizers. Jeremiah is an affiliate of the Southwest IAF, which is supervised by Ernesto Cortés Jr., a legendary figure in grassroots organizing who mentored at Alinksy's Training Institute in Chicago, formed Communities Organized for Public Service in San Antonio, and now serves as a director of the IAF at the national and international levels (6). Stout recounts how members of Jeremiah sought to thwart the collusion of political and economic elites who saw in the devastation of Katrina an opportunity to "revitalize" New Orleans by making it a whiter and less-populated city. In the Houston Astrodome we learn how Renee Wizig-Barrios assembled local pastors to create "house-meetings for the homeless" aimed at organizing the evacuees and negotiating with Houston leaders to address some essential needs, such as extended cell phone coverage for those who could not pay and playground facilities for children. In the Rio Grande Valley we learn how grassroots leaders of Interfaith Valley successfully negotiated with Texan politicians to provide basic infrastructure after the press shamed business and political leaders with photographs of the miserable conditions of the *colonias*, a 150-mile stretch along the U.S.-Mexican border where the poorest of the poor reside in that state. There we meet Consuelo Maheshwari, a teacher in one of the borderland schools, who led an effort that persuaded local officials to provide greater police coverage and new streets around an elementary school that had been a safe haven for drug dealers. We also meet Father Pat Seitz, a local priest who secured concessions from the U.S. Postal Service to deliver mail where there were no street signs and who fought hard to win a grant to get sewage pipes installed in Las Palmas Colonia. We learn of Bishop Fitzgerald, who decided that his diocese would sponsor public radio and television stations so that residents in the valley could have better news and commentary. In Los Angeles County we meet Daniel May and Father David Velasquez of St. Rose Parish, IAF organizers who became part of a team of leaders tasked with tackling the problem of police checkpoints set up to catch unlicensed, undocumented workers, fine them, and impound their cars for thirty days in order to harass the local community and line the pockets of a local tow truck business and generate revenue for the city of Maywood. Stout concludes his journey with a visit to Kol Shofar, a synagogue in Marin County, north of San Francisco, where sixty delegates from a number of citizens' organizations in the Bay Area met for the first time to begin hammering out a regional plan on topics ranging from health-care coverage to the harassment of local workers in the wine country.

Stout develops these and other profiles and fills out their stories in rich, vivid detail. He describes not only their basic ideas about how and why they carry out grassroots organizing but also the passions and the virtues that motivate progressive grassroots action. Indeed, we learn more specifics about the lives, thoughts, and feelings of the informants in Stout's book than we do in Mahmood's and Hirschkind's ethnographic studies combined.

After taking us on his sojourn across the South and West, Stout steps back to comment on the health of democracy, contrasting his views with the practices and attitudes of "lifestyle liberals" who want political change but who shy away from grassroots organizing, the religious right, the pronouncements from the academic left, and the top-down presidential leadership of Barack Obama and the top-down organizing carried out by Organization for America, a group that Obama mobilizes to support policies he favors. If change is going to come, Stout insists, it must come from the bottom and must be carried out with methods that embody the democratic ideals that such methods aim to advance. His stories and examples aim to render the hope for change a realistic one.

Stout argues that democracy—specifically, a democratic republic—is organized around protecting against domination, providing "an inclusive, nonarbitrary criterion of citizenship" and "the modern democratic ideal of a nation dedicated to liberty and justice *for all*." This ideal, Stout adds, "is a core commitment in all of the citizens' organizations" that he examines in his study (57). But today, he observes, the ideal is in peril owing to widening patterns of disempowerment and disenfranchisement among those at the lower end of the economic ladder, increased economic stratification owing to the exponential increase in wealth of a small number of citizens over the last several decades, and the easy translation of economic power into political power. In Stout's view we live in a plutocracy, not a democratic republic. Grassroots organizing can be a form of counterpower against the increased hegemony of corporate and government elites whose decisions affect a vast swath of people in the United States and across the globe. Following the activities of those in the network of IAF organizations, Stout describes the slow, painstaking work of grassroots organizing that starts with face-to-face discussions and proceeds to house meetings, and then scales up to intentional and coordinated planning in this way:

> The meetings function as they do because hundreds of one-on-ones precede them and because they give rise to a power analysis, a research committee, and a core team of indigenous leaders charged with formulating

concrete proposals and a strategy for getting them enacted. When the proposals have been hammered out, the core team is in a position to identify allies and opponents in the upcoming fight. There will be public rites of commitment to clarify the difference and a phase of polarization in which allies are expected to stand forward. Opponents are held accountable for their opposition, and declared allies are held accountable if they fail to come through with their promises. Only when the fight concludes is it time for depolarization, at which point the process of taking a soundings at the one-on-one level can begin again. (265)

Stout adds that these grassroots experiences enable citizens to gain recognition and, in the process, discover something new and meaningful about themselves and their ties to others. The thread that unites the various grassroots organizers is the aim of holding political and business leaders publicly accountable and to do so in ways that are politically nonpartisan. Their efforts are being aided by new developments in the information age. Grassroots democrats now benefit from wider national and international networks, reflecting an expansion in the flow of information that holds great promise for organizing-from-below in our increasingly globalized world (106).

Blessed Are the Organized makes plain that democracy's problems do not end with the increased, arbitrary power of corporate elites and their allies in political office. Stout points out that our educational system fails to teach us how to organize or what democracy means in anything other than abstract and ahistorical terms. Equally unhelpful are members of the academic left who declare the end of democracy or the end of the nation-state. Stout uses his examples of grassroots activity to show that these political obituaries are premature. Toward the conclusion of the book he takes stock of what he's done:

The examples taken up in this book do not show that democracy is in good health overall. Disaster capitalism in New Orleans, the condition of resident aliens in Maywood, and the ethnic strife of South Central L.A. are evidence that momentous forces are at work, reshaping the landscape within which concerned citizens are struggling to get a foot-hold. It is indeed possible that the most powerful people in the world already have the means to exercise their power arbitrarily over us for the foreseeable future. It is also possible, however, that ordinary people have a fighting chance of winning some significant victories for liberty and justice. (285–86)

In Stout's mind grassroots organizing does not guarantee success, but it does provide evidence "that there are promising signs of democratic life all around us, if we care to look for them" (287). For readers interested in organizing, *Blessed Are the Organized* offers concrete models that justify giving it a shot (284).

One of Stout's points is not only that democratic grassroots organizing offers some hope to a democracy in peril but also that such activism is a tradition in its own right. He writes that in responding to "great scars of wrong," grassroots democrats "identify with a *tradition* of struggle against domination" (251; Stout's emphasis). His point in speaking favorably of such a tradition "is to call attention to the continuities, over time, in the ideals being hammered out in the practices of organizing and accountability in which those ideals have been embodied" (251). Other grassroots struggles against domination include abolitionism, the women's suffrage movement, and the civil rights movement. Writers such as Emerson, Whitman, and Thoreau give the tradition its voice.

Critics of Stout's work might point out that those other movements sought to protect against specific forms of domination—of slaves, women, and African American citizens—and that the IAF grassroots actions are far more wide-ranging and, as Stout observes, not restricted to single-issue activism. Nor do they aim at leveraging change in constitutional liberties and rights. Stout would likely reply that what holds all of them together as a tradition is a shared end—the protection against domination and the embrace of a nonarbitrary criterion of inclusive citizenship—along with the commitment to methods that reflect and embody those ends. That we now need a wider view about the dangers of domination, he could add, should not count against envisioning contemporary grassroots democrats as part of a tradition. Traditions change and respond to the demands of history, and today's problems are different from those of previous generations of grassroots organizers. For that reason the idea that grassroots democrats can be understood as belonging to a tradition seems plausible enough. But whether the grassroots organizers described in this work interpret themselves as part of such a tradition is not obvious. I will return to this point soon.

Another of Stout's main observations is that religion is a powerful force in the lives of grassroots activists and that anyone who believes in the secularization thesis is blind to the power and ubiquity of religion in American public life. Believers are going to want to exteriorize or objectify their deeply held commitments through concrete actions. Stout adds, however, that religious commitment is not a condition for membership in IAF affiliates, that they "neither exclude conceptions of sacred value from the discussion, nor require everyone to convert to a single conception of sacred value. Instead, they encourage citizens to speak openly about what matters most to them and to do so in the language most familiar to them, which is often the language of a religious tradition" (235). He observes one action that brought together Jewish, Christian, and Muslim clergy, and he points out that IAF groups are seeking to expand their constituencies beyond church congregants. Stout provides important details about the specific religious idioms and ideas on which his informants draw, and he organizes them under the rubric of the sacred, understood as designating intrinsically important matters that arouse reverence in response to them and horror at their violation.

Roman Catholics figure prominently in Stout's stories. As I considered their activism through the lens of their tradition and in light of what Stout says about the tradition of grassroots democracy, a question arose in my mind about how to conceive of the relationship between these two traditions. I'll focus on Catholics to sharpen my query.

Stout identifies biblical materials and the long tradition of Roman Catholic social teaching as important for some of those he met and interviewed. In one chapter he discusses Pope John Paul II's papal encyclical *The Gospel of Life*, and he observes that it is sometimes read by Catholics in ways that overemphasize the pope's teaching about prolife issues of abortion and euthanasia and play down the encyclical's stand on war, poverty, and capital punishment (186). Stout commends the fact that Catholic grassroots democrats venerate their tradition's affirmation of human dignity and the sanctity of life and render those notions concrete in their work on behalf of social justice.

Readers familiar with the tradition of Catholic social teaching know that it has not regularly encouraged democratic grassroots organization (although I see no reasons in Catholic social teaching that would oppose such activity). Both Stout and the tradition speak against viewing democracy solely in procedural terms (316n97). Catholic thinking about human dignity could be mobilized to justify democratic organizing but would likely relativize its value within a wider hierarchy of goods. For Catholics it would seem that grassroots organizing is a means to ends that they articulate in their terms, terms that have them think beyond what democratic justice is due to citizens. One Catholic priest in Stout's narrative, for example, organizes his ideas around the notion of a "preferential option for the poor" (190). I would imagine that others would act on some version of neighbor love or in light of the parable of the Good Samaritan.

If that is true, then it seems likely that Catholics (and others) view the relationship between their tradition and the tradition of grassroots democracy as political, not metaphysical. That is to say, democratic grassroots organizing by Catholics (and other religious organizers) suggests the existence of an overlapping consensus about the merits of grassroots democracy as a means to their ends—a consensus arrived at from a variety of starting points—rather than because they identify with a single, ongoing democratic tradition. I would have been helped by more discussion about how different accounts of sacred value (224) connect up with the values Stout identifies with the tradition of democratic grassroots organizing. One of Stout's informants says that "it's the issues that connect regardless of what our religious backgrounds are" (207). But how and why the issues are conceived as issues of justice by religious participants may draw on a wider or at least different cluster of ideas than those expressed in the tradition of grassroots democratic action.

* * *

Elizabeth M. Bucar's *Creative Conformity: The Feminist Politics of U.S. Catholic and Iranian Shi'i Women* is an ethnographic study in religious ethics that compares the rhetorical discourses of Catholic women in the United States and Shi'i women in Iran—women who hail from conservative and progressive camps in each tradition. Drawing on published materials and in-person interviews, Bucar shows how a number of American and Iranian women interpret and rearticulate authoritative pronouncements of male clerical leaders to revise ideas about moral agency, gender roles and relationships, reproductive ethics, women's dress, and moral leadership in terms that are congruent with the religious traditions they embrace. One of her main goals is akin to Mahmood's, namely, to break away from a paradigm of feminist research that would have her concentrate only on whether women are resisting or conforming to received religious teachings. Bucar's way of thinking about feminist politics has us look at how women interpret and rework the ideas of religious authorities, an approach to religion and feminism that relies on tools of rhetorical analysis and offers an alternative picture of women's agency.[14] The architecture of her study comprises several components.

One is Michel de Certeau's distinction between "strategies" and "tactics." *Strategies* are forms of thought and action that seek to rebel against and overthrow regimes of power; *tactics*, in contrast, are more modest. Bucar uses the latter concept to unpack the arguments she examines. Tactics take advantage of the opportunities within a field of power and turn them to one's advantage. Focusing on tactics thereby allows us to grasp what Bucar calls "creative conformity"—exploiting conceptual opportunities by using "clerical logics" and staying "within the game" while also generating creative "logical surprises" made possible by ruptures within the "clerical rulebook" (3–4).

In addition, Bucar proffers a theory of moral agency that she calls "dianomy." *Dianomy* is a neologism that aims to capture an account of agency that affirms human freedom as necessary for moral action while acknowledging that women's tactical terrain "is to some extent externally imposed" (4). Affirmations of women's autonomy emphasize feminist practices of dissent; notions of heteronomy situate women within a terrain of external forces and emphasize habituation and subject formation. Dianomy, in contrast, points to the unresolved tension between autonomous and heteronomous sources of the moral life and focuses our attention on the process by which individuals negotiate the dialectic according to which those sources interact. In Bucar's view the concept of dianomy opens up a neglected terrain for understanding sources that motivate and inform human agency. More important, however, is how the concept provides Bucar critical distance from her ethnographic subjects. Not infrequently ethnographic work takes the statements, self-understanding, or practices of its subjects at face value rather than as material that is ideological. Bucar seeks to distinguish her work from ethnographic studies that sentimentalize the religious lives and practices they describe. Focusing on "the process women use to construct their own visions of their moral lives using components of informal argumentation within a religious tradition," Bucar aims to show that when her subjects dissent from clerical logic, they nonetheless reproduce it and that when they reiterate clerical visions of women's proper roles, they in fact move those visions in new directions. The concept of dianomy enables Bucar to look at women's discourses in this bivalent way—and in terms that the women themselves might not endorse (8).

Another important concept for Bucar is the idea of charismatic authority. Referencing the work of Max Weber, Bucar reminds the reader of two ideal types of charismatic authority in Weberian sociology: pure and routinized charisma. The former denotes a leader's personal ability to generate excitement. The latter denotes what happens to a pure charismatic leader over time: his or her authority becomes routinized and institutionalized. The leadership of Pope John Paul II and the Ayatollah Khomeini—the two clerical leaders whose pronouncements provide the material for women's creative conformity in Bucar's study—show that Catholic and Muslim expressions of clerical authority draw from both pure and routinized versions. That fact suggests that we adopt a hybridized picture of their authority as well as a hybridized picture of how Catholic and Muslim leaders relate to their audiences. Bucar observes that charisma is a concept about a relationship, not only about a leader's qualities: an audience or group must ratify a leader's authority in order for it to be effective. From that observation Bucar proceeds to the book's main thesis: "I argue that a particular process of recognition of the audience (the women's discursive response to clerical rhetoric) contributes to the production of ethical knowledge within a community" (16).

The last important feature of Bucar's analysis is a box of tools from rhetorical theory she uses to sort through tactical modes of recognition that occur in response to clerical pronouncements. Several components shape her rhetorical analysis. From Stephen Toulmin she borrows resources for looking at the informal logical structure of justificatory arguments, and from Chaïm Perelman she borrows tools for examining the affective strategies and audience assumptions that contribute to an argument's persuasive potential. To these ideas she adds her own idea of "logics." As a middle term that mediates between the analysis of arguments and the contextual and communal assumptions regarding affective strategies, the "logics" of an argument enable innovations from within it. "Logics are the intellectual coherence behind transformations within a tradition," Bucar writes (23). When someone responds to an argument by selecting one small part of it to develop another argument, for example, she uses a "logic of concentration." When a person applies an idea from an argument to cases unanticipated by the speaker, she uses a "logic of expansion." The general aim of "logics" in an argument is to make possible new directions "without necessarily refuting the original argument" (23). Taken together, tools to analyze arguments, audience assumptions, and logics are what Bucar uses to "illuminate different aspects of persuasion and, ultimately, different opportunities for women to construct and articulate their own conceptions and practices of womanhood" (18).

With these components to shape her study—tactics, dianomy, authority, and rhetorical analysis—Bucar proceeds across five chapters to analyze a range of Catholic and Shi'i feminist responses to clerical teaching. Her principal focus is on how clerical leaders and religious women conceive of women's roles in the areas of moral exemplarity, motherhood, textual interpretation, embodied practices, and participation in public life. Bucar examines official teachings and how women respond to them in ways that rework clerical rhetoric for distinct purposes across both liberal and conservative lines (24). The topic of women as role models in clerical teachings has become an opportunity to discuss the injustice of women's actual social lives, for example. The idealization of women as good mothers in clerical rhetoric has provided an opportunity to think more expansively about the actual practices and experiences of mothering in feminist thought and, in the case of Iran, has led to a change in custody laws that now favor the mother in cases of divorce. Clerical teaching about the proper place of women as textual interpreters has become the occasion for feminist hermeneutics to illuminate the value of women's experience for interpreting texts in new ways. Authoritative pronouncements about women's ordination to the priesthood in Catholicism and veiling in Islam have become the occasion to theorize about the equality of Christian discipleship or to reimagine the meaning of freedom for Muslim women. Official teaching about religion in public life on matters of abortion and free speech have been taken up in ways that construct new parameters for public discourse in both traditions.

The overall result is to cast a spotlight on the productive power of creative conformity. The book makes plain that religions are not monolithic entities or communities whose members mindlessly defer to hierarchical authority. It also shows that feminist engagement with official teachings is not only about expressing dissent or ideological resistance. Bucar enables us to imagine feminist politics as a creative struggle *within* religious traditions. What we see is not that clerical authorities speak and religious adherents respond but that "both clerics and women engage in the rhetorical argumentation aimed at persuading the community about the moral life. Both interpret the tradition" (172). This way of focusing on interpretation enables readers to reimagine feminist rhetoric in Catholic and Muslim settings. Typically U.S Catholics appear to be dissenting, whereas Shi'ite Muslim women appear to be obedient (182). One merit of Bucar's study is to show how this dichotomy fails to capture the many ways in which discourse is put creatively to work. "Dissent" and "deference" don't map onto the Catholic and Muslim subjects of her study. More generally, Bucar shows that the religions of Catholicism and Shi'ite Islam do not only or chiefly rely on visceral, embodied affective registers, in contrast to Hirschkind's picture of Muslim revivalism in Egypt. While not gainsaying the affective dimensions of rhetoric, Bucar shows that the traditions she studies take reason and textual interpretation as crucial matters of interpretive rationality. In the picture she creates, both traditions are engaged in matters of justification and the adjudication of truth claims about gender roles, gender politics, and the place of religion in public life.

Bucar's study provides categories of analysis and classification that complicate how we might otherwise look at feminist rhetoric in Catholic and Muslim contexts. She thereby advances an understanding of what it means for feminists (and others) to engage their religious traditions with an eye to moving it in one direction or another. Her ethnographic experience made it clear to her that her categories and assumptions need to be deployed in a context-sensitive way as one feature of responsible ethnography. Context-sensitivity, as I argued in chapter 3, is indeed a virtue in any form of social analysis and social criticism. *Creative Conformity* nicely exhibits that fact.

Bucar's picture of women's creative conformity presumes that speakers and audiences are mutually interdependent in the production of ethical knowledge. An authority's recognition of the audience, she writes, "contributes to the production of ethical knowledge within a community" (18). What is unclear is whether Bucar's analysis adequately captures matters of moral authority as it shapes both the expression and the reception of such knowledge. Granted that ethical knowledge is creatively generated by religious women in Catholicism and Islam, what authority does that knowledge enjoy in the lives of lay audiences? How does that knowledge compare in authority with the authority of official clerical teachings? Each of the religious traditions in her study has a complicated understanding of moral authority and the credentials necessary to attain and exercise it. Even if the relationship between clerical speaker and audience is one of mutual interdependence, the actual relationship is nonetheless hierarchical. *Creative Conformity* would have been helped by exploring the relationship between the production of ethical knowledge and the credentials needed to express it authoritatively within the hierarchical institutional frameworks of Catholicism and Shi'i Islam.

* * *

Sherine Hamdy's *Our Bodies Belong to God: Organ Transplants, Islam, and the Struggle for Human Dignity in Egypt* is an ethnographic study of religious, legal, scientific, and moral debates about organ transplantation in late twentieth-century Egypt. Drawing on twenty-one months of fieldwork between 2001 and 2004 in Cairo, Mansoura, and Tanta, Hamdy organizes her study around whether the popular Muslim adage "our bodies belong to God" fully accounts for cultural reservations surrounding organ transplantation in Egypt from the late 1980s to the early 2010s. The adage makes plain that there are limits to what one may do with one's body given that it is created by God and is thus his property. Such limits would seem to suggest banning or severely limiting organ transplantation, however much a recipient might be suffering, since body parts are not an individual's property to reallocate. Indeed, until 2010, Egyptian law prohibited cadaverous organ transplantation.[15] A renowned mufti, Shaykh Sha'rawi, was outspoken against the practice, adding more authority to the ban. The ironic result of this arrangement was to drive the practice of organ transplantation underground, creating an international black market of organ sales and a relatively unregulated world of commercialized transplant medicine in Egypt, contrary to what a robust embrace of the Muslim adage might suggest.

Hamdy argues that a religious explanation for understanding Egypt's popular and official resistance to organ transplantation is a red herring. Nonreligious factors, especially class divisions, an underfunded social infrastructure, and an untrustworthy medical system, help to explain Egyptian reservations about the practice. Equally important, many who avow the idea that their bodies belong to God nonetheless endorse organ transplantation either as a matter of practical necessity or because they consider transplantation congruent with Muslim beliefs about duties to themselves and others. Indeed, other Muslim countries—Saudi Arabia and Kuwait—have national organ transplantation programs similar to those in Western countries. Many Islamic scholars in Egypt have publicly stated that organ transplantation is permissible. Moreover, Egyptian doctors helped to pioneer the field of transplant medicine. These facts indicate that seeking a simple "religious explanation" for Egyptian objections to organ transplantation is a nonstarter.

More important, such facts suggest that an entirely different way of thinking about the relationship between religious ethics, culture, and transplant medicine is needed to understand the role of religion in the lives of Muslim patients, families, and medical practitioners in Egypt. One of Hamdy's aims is to have readers get beyond stereotypical pictures of "religion" as a static, monolithic set of tenets that "map onto" biomedical controversies in an external, deductive, or absolutist manner. Instead, she argues for "rebinding" religious ethics and the social sciences to see how religion and ethical deliberation are embodied and contingent on a number of factors that do not easily admit of formulaic or apodictic conclusions about religion as, say, a "liberal" or "conservative" force in everyday life. With Hamdy, as with Hirschkind, we see one of the benefits of the cultural turn as a frame of reference for examining religious and ethical issues, namely, that it enables us to examine how *religion* is practiced and theorized in relation to ethics.

Hamdy develops her findings across seven chapters that address, for example, the crisis of political and religious authority in Egypt, authoritative Islamic teachings about the ethics of organ transplantation, patterns of ethical deliberation about whether to transplant an organ, and efforts to interpret or reinterpret Islamic religious and moral reasoning in light of various practical exigencies. In addition to her interview material and site visits she draws on films, newspapers and pamphlets, novels, archives of fatwas, policy statements, and historical data about the changing religious and political landscape of contemporary Egypt to provide a meticulously detailed picture of the lived experiences of Muslim patients, care providers, and family members who faced life-or-death decisions about the benefits and risks of donating or receiving bodily organs and tissues. She uncovers a complex field in which reasons for and against organ transplantation are debated in light of factors bearing on kinship relations, risk/benefit calculations, religious piety, concerns about poverty and exploitation, and cost.

Like Moazam, Hirschkind, and Mahmood, Hamdy portrays religion as deeply imbricated in a dense set of cultural, economic, political, and personal forces. That fact should prevent us from "hyperessentializing" religion to create an ahistorical, disembodied picture that is then deployed to explain how or why a particular policy is permitted or prohibited in a religious society. (Hamdy laments that policy makers in Egypt are now drifting precisely in that direction as they seek to articulate the "Islamic" position on organ transplantation [248–49].) But unlike Hirschkind, and more so than Mahmood and Moazam, Hamdy penetrates actual forms of practical reasoning and highlights the concepts, distinctions, values, range of considerations, and maxims that shape the practical reasoning of Egyptians about the ethics of organ transplantation. In Hamdy's view the tendency of medical anthropologists such as Arthur Kleinman, Renee Fox, and Judith Swazey to dismiss standard approaches to biomedical ethics because they often rely on abstract principles and focus on isolated or exotic cases goes too far. Hamdy is less worried about whether bioethics is "culturally specific" than whether it is "incomplete" (8). That is to say, Hamdy is less worried about "sounding ethnocentric" than with developing a justification for the criticisms and recommendations that emerge from her research. For Hamdy "ethics . . . remains a crucial site from which to expand the dialogue about social inequalities in health and to seek solutions" (8). More specifically, she recommends framing bioethics in a way that is "fully integrated in social analyses of the political, economic, and cultural terrains that are necessary for bioethicists to effectively promote social justice" (8). Referencing the work of Tom Beauchamp and James Childress, she adds: "The individual scale and the insistence on abstract principles, such as beneficence, justice, and autonomy, often miss what should be the targets of analysis by failing to capture the messiness of bioethical problems" (10, 258n10).[16]

Hamdy carries out her study with a sophisticated set of analytical tools to sort out moral arguments with an eye to their many layers and dimensions. Indeed, Hamdy's book is an exemplary study of Islamic biomedical casuistry. While affirming the embodied and agonistic nature of moral deliberation, she also grasps that Islam is a religion in which the use of reason is keenly important for everyday practitioners. She thus shows how people "came to bioethical decisions through the fluid and overlapping rubrics of Islam, biomedical efficacy, political-economic exigencies, and kinship" (12). Hamdy attends to how advice from religious authorities is attained and critically considered, how maxims are interpreted and reinterpreted, how judgments change depending on how the scale of a particular case or problem is conceived, and how cases are situated within the institutional matrices in which they ought properly to be resolved and in light of the political etiologies that help to explain them.

Of central importance is the meaning of *haram*—or wrongdoing—and how Islamic concerns about avoiding wrongdoing are informed by complex understandings of harm and multiple layers of risk analysis. Time and again Hamdy insists that alternative conceptions of the *scale* of a biomedical question affect moral deliberations. About the scale of risk, for example, she writes: "Different types of risk factor into the ethical decision making of patients and their family members. These include the *physical and environmental* risks predisposing patients and their families to disease, the *iatrogenic* risks of medical mistreatment, the *financial* risk of extraordinary debt and bankruptcy, the *spiritual* risk of doing something that can be potentially displeasing to God, and the significant *social* risks that come from the pressures that a transplant bears on kin relations" (174; Hamdy's emphasis).

In Hamdy's account, then, complex matters of practical reasoning, not a rigid or literalist understanding of Islamic tradition, shape how Egyptian Muslims deliberate about their religious and moral obligations in biomedical contexts. When her informants referenced the idea that their bodies belong to God, "they were not merely invoking the words attributed to Shaykh Sha'rawi as a memorized formula of Islamic 'orthodoxy'" (247). Instead, they reiterated that adage "in the context of their larger grievances against state mismanagement of resources, exploitation of the bodies of the poor, questionable outcomes of transplantation, and underground trafficking rings, as well as the context of cultural and social values that idealize dispositions of steadfastness and fortitude in the face of unavoidable suffering." Accordingly, religious beliefs about God in relation to human life "gain new meanings when they are uttered in social and political-economic contexts that constrain, define, and enable possibilities of how human life is lived" (247).

Reflecting her desire to connect bioethics with concerns of social justice, Hamdy calls attention to the crisis of political and religious authority in post-Nasser Egypt and the enormous economic disparities between the rich and poor that render irrelevant a single normative position about the ethics of transplant medicine. Political, social, and economic structures determine resource allocation and public health indicators, and as a result "patients are keenly aware that biomedical outcomes cannot be convincingly attributed to bad genetic luck or their own individual behavior" (13). They are sick because of water toxicity, lack of access to health care, and food-borne illnesses, all of which are a function of "Egypt's dismantling of public health care and the lack of oversight in public water and waste management, under both external and internal pressures of rapid privatization" (13). Owing to these facts, one cannot divorce concerns in biomedicine from the wider frameworks of political and social ethics.

These social factors play directly into the practical reasoning of Egyptian Muslims who must make treatment decisions in the face of organ failure. In many cases patients have nowhere to turn but to nonfamily members for an organ. They may decline an organ from a family member for reasons having to do with gender, age, or the family responsibilities of a potential donor. Even when family members can donate, they sometimes expect or receive payment for their organs, a fact that explodes the idea that family donations are altruistic whereas nonfamily donations are morally tarnished because they involve the exchange of money. Informants' casuistry created the permission for family members to receive a "gift" of gratitude after a donation while prohibiting the prior exchange of funds to incentivize organ giving. Moreover, the concern about exploiting the poor for organ purchases is not relevant to all cases. Donors in Egypt who seek payment are often middle-class individuals who need money because of a financial mistake. From the point of view of a procedure's risk/benefit analysis, moreover, it matters little whether an organ is purchased or given.

All of this is to say that numerous variables intrude on the plight of patients and families and factor into their decision making not only about whether to receive an organ but also about whether to buy one given the scarcity of available organs. Taking these various facts into account, Hamdy writes: "Too many terminally ill patients in organ failure had no kin to gift them kidneys. Many of them had families and young children to support. It made little sense to . . . doctors to police the boundaries between 'altruistic' and 'commercial' donations, especially when their experiences disproved the assumption that family donations are always altruistic and that commercial donations are necessarily more exploitative" (223). In her estimation, "allowing for paid organs is sometimes the most ethical course of action" (236). Going against a strain in medical anthropology that urges a ban on organ sales, Hamdy argues that a practical, interim solution would be "to make all organ donation transactions transparent rather than turning a blind eye to or criminalizing them. This way the donors can be given full information about the risks of surgery, the physicians can be held accountable for good surgical and medical outcomes, brokers can be eliminated, and donors might be more empowered, better treated medically, and decently compensated" (237).

Hamdy's practical conclusion may be controversial, but it is grounded in an extensive and detailed study that draws on insights from a wide range of individuals. To her credit she refuses to shy away from a normative proposal with strong arguments and information to support it. She refrains from throwing up her hands and concluding with the bromide that "everything is ambiguous," or that "things are complicated," or that "it all depends on one's perspective." Hamdy's work represents a new generation of anthropological scholarship that eschews bourgeois relativism.

In light of that fact we might ask how far her analysis departs from the framework of well-established work in Anglo-American bioethics. Recall her claim, referencing the work of Tom Beauchamp and James Childress, that "the individual scale and the insistence on abstract principles, such as beneficence, justice, and autonomy, often miss what should be the targets of analysis by failing to capture the messiness of bioethical problems." But determining the relevant scale of a problem is bread-and-butter work in biomedical ethics and elsewhere; messiness is the order of the day. No one in bioethics denies the reality of ambiguity, undesirable facts about the natural and social lottery, or the existence of moral conflict. (Hence Beauchamp and Childress cast their principles as *prima facie* rather than as absolute.) More to the point, all of Hamdy's analyses rely on considerations of justice, risk/benefit analyses of the sort that are central to judgments about beneficence and nonmaleficence, and questions about coercion that rely on respect for autonomy. Justice, beneficence, nonmaleficence, and autonomy are precisely the principles of bioethics articulated by Beauchamp and Childress. Indeed, the fundamental issue of organ transplantation in Egypt, as her interviews make plain, is whether it is permissible to harm one person to benefit another. One of her principal interviewees, Dr. Kotb, changed his mind about the ethics of transplant medicine when it became clear to him that "prevention of harm takes precedence over taking a benefit" (144). Moreover, Muslim deliberations about risk tolerance regarding organ transplantation mirror debates about "ordinary" and "extraordinary" means of treatment—concepts that have traditionally informed Catholic bioethics about how much burden a patient can reasonably be expected to bear. All of this is to say that debates about organ transplantation in Egypt seem to provide rich material for a comparative discussion of frameworks of practical reasoning in Anglo-American bioethics. Hamdy would seem open to such a project. At one point in her work—when discussing debates about brain death in Egypt—she expresses the desire to "expose the inadequacies of culturalist analyses that deepen the imagined divide between the Muslim world and the West" (48).

* * *

As the works of Mahmood, Moazam, Hirschkind, Stout, Bucar, and Hamdy make clear, carrying out an interdisciplinary research project with a sophisticated understanding of religion, culture, and ethics is no small challenge. It is time- and labor-intensive. Proficiency about different research protocols, concepts, distinctions, controversies, and traditions of scholarship is the sine qua non of any such work. So, too, are the requirements of practical reasoning both about the controversies one encounters in the field *and* about how to justify one's frame or frames of analysis when describing those controversies. Add to those facts that cultural immersion involves managing a long-term commitment to a project and negotiating contingencies, material and logistical frustrations, and interpretive barriers that are impossible to anticipate and that may redirect a researcher's plan of study. Expecting quick, efficient results that conform to the blueprint of an initial research prospectus in this aggressively interdisciplinary area of work is a fool's errand.

All of these scholars attend, in different ways and to different degrees, to matters of moral virtue and practical reasoning as these are shaped by the contexts in which they materialize. They all reflect the turn to "concrete particularity" of the sort I described in chapter 1. Naturally, each work bears the marks of its intellectual point of origin: The works of the religious and philosophical ethicists (Moazam, Stout, and Bucar) exhibit great fluency with concepts and categories that are the stuff of moral theory: virtue, feminist reasoning, principles of bioethics, democracy, and the like. Their work is constrained by limited opportunities and limited support for in-depth immersion and participant observation at the sites they visited. Given that grant funding to support the work of ethicists seeking research leave-time is rare, they must rely more on relatively brief visits and interviews to carry out their work. Their projects of necessity will lack the insights made possible by more longitudinal studies; they each make the very best of the opportunities available to them. Lengthy anthropological work (Mahmood, Hirschkind, and Hamdy), in contrast, reflects considerably more cultural immersion and fluency with tools to capture the wider aesthetics and ethos in which personal character is formed and moral and religious arguments are hashed out. Occasionally, however, fluency with basic concepts or sources of moral theory is less developed—as seen in Mahmood's inability to grasp basic features of Aristotle's moral theory or differences between Aristotelian and Foucauldian accounts of virtue.

More generally, all of these works develop normative considerations as central to their projects. This is to be expected in the work of Moazam, Stout, and Bucar, trained as they are in philosophical and religious ethics. But it is also true of Mahmood, Hirschkind, and Hamdy. They all depict human agency not on the model of calculating, rational action but as occurring within or in light of a broader horizon of value. And they understand their own scholarship as having ethical ramifications. Mahmood seeks to unsettle Western feminist pieties of scholarship. Hirschkind not only focuses on "the ethics of listening" but also states that detaching the *da'wa* movement from stereotypical pictures of fundamentalism is a moral act. Hamdy unpacks patterns of moral deliberation and concludes her work by taking a normative stand about procedures and practices of organ transplantation in Egypt. All of these scholars depart from older positivist, putatively value-neutral approaches to the study of religion, which either seek to bleach scholarship of normative ideas or quietly smuggle in normative judgments by lionizing, romanticizing, or exoticizing the practices and beliefs they describe.

Hamdy's work and Stout's work deserve special mention. My queries about some specifics in their projects should not detract from acknowledging their great success in coordinating insights in religion, ethics, and culture. Each work stands out as a standard-bearer for future scholarship that seeks to broaden the domains of religious ethics and cultural studies and bring them into dialogue with each other. If Hamdy's and Stout's works are evidence of how scholars working at the intersections of religion, ethics, and culture can proceed, that future looks very bright indeed.

NOTES

INTRODUCTION

1. Stanley Cavell, "Knowing and Acknowledging," in *Must We Mean What We Say? A Book of Essays*, updated ed. (Cambridge: Cambridge University Press, 2002 [1969]), 238–66.
2. Ibid., 263–64.
3. For a discussion of these ideas within Jewish philosophy see Robert Gibbs, *Why Ethics? Signs of Responsibilities* (Princeton, NJ: Princeton University Press, 2000). For a review of the concept of otherness in American literature see Giles Gunn, "American Literature and the Imagination of Otherness," *Journal of Religious Ethics* 3, no. 2 (1975): 193–215.
4. Cavell, "Knowing and Acknowledging," 264.
5. Thanks to Kevin Houser for helpful conversations about these ideas. See Kevin Houser, "Suffering, Acknowledgment, and the Ethical Space of Reasons" (PhD diss., Indiana University, 2015).
6. Clifford Geertz, *Local Knowledge: Further Essays in Interpretive Anthropology* (New York: Basic Books, 1983), 4.
7. Donald D. Evans, *The Logic of Self-Involvement* (London: SCM Press, 1963), 125.
8. Ibid., 128.
9. Thanks to Michael Rings for calling my attention to this feature of Kant's ideas.
10. Geertz, *Local Knowledge*, 3.
11. I am indebted to Matt Miller for this insight.
12. James Clifford, *The Predicament of Culture: Twentieth-Century Ethnography, Literature, and Art* (Cambridge, MA: Harvard University Press, 1988), 92.
13. See Bernard Williams, *Ethics and the Limits of Philosophy* (Cambridge, MA: Harvard University Press, 1986), 194–95.

1. WHAT IS RELIGIOUS ETHICS?

1. Michel Foucault, "Truth and Power," in *The Foucault Reader*, ed. Paul Rabinow (New York: Pantheon, 1984), 51–75, 74.

2. For exceptions see John P. Reeder Jr., "What Is a Religious Ethic?" *Journal of Religious Ethics* 25, no. 3 [25th Anniversary Supplement] (1997): 157–81; and David Little and Sumner B. Twiss, *Comparative Religious Ethics: A New Method* (San Francisco: Harper and Row, 1978), 24–52.

3. For an instructive discussion of objections to definitions in general, and definitions of religion in particular, see Thomas A. Tweed, *Crossing and Dwelling: A Theory of Religion* (Cambridge, MA: Harvard University Press, 2006), 33–42. I depart from Tweed by identifying a kind of definition, informed by Wittgenstein, that he fails to consider in his typology of lexical, empirical, and stipulative definitions, a typology that draws on the work of Robert Baird.

4. Bruce Lincoln, *Holy Terrors: Thinking About Religion After 9/11* (Chicago: University of Chicago Press, 2003), 2.

5. Ludwig Wittgenstein, *Philosophical Investigations*, 3rd ed., trans. G. E. M. Anscombe (New York: Macmillan, 1968), par. 66 (emphasis in original).

6. Ibid.

7. My heuristic definition borrows from Little and Twiss, *Comparative Religious Ethics*, 59–60. The reference to wonder or joy, (d), is informed by Tweed, *Crossing and Dwelling*, 69–73. The metadiscursive dimension, (h), follows Lincoln, *Holy Terrors*, 5–6.

8. See William James, *The Varieties of Religious Experience: A Study in Human Nature* (New York: Collier, 1961 [1902]), lectures 4–7.

9. See, e.g., Ernst Troeltsch, *The Social Teaching of the Christian Churches*, trans. Olive Wyon (Louisville: Westminster/John Knox Press, 1992 [1931]).

10. Stanley Cavell, "Knowing and Acknowledging," in *Must We Mean What We Say? A Book of Essays*, updated ed. (Cambridge: Cambridge University Press, 2002), 263–64.

11. Ibid., 264.

12. Wittgenstein, *Philosophical Investigations*, par. 66.

13. See James M. Gustafson, *Intersections: Science, Theology, and Ethics* (Cleveland, OH: Pilgrim, 1996), 35–55.

14. See, e.g., Lisa H. Sideris, *Environmental Ethics, Ecological Theology, and Natural Selection* (New York: Columbia University Press, 2003).

15. For exceptions see James M. Gustafson, *Protestant and Roman Catholic Ethics: Prospects for Rapprochement* (Chicago: University of Chicago Press, 1978); James M. Gustafson, "A Retrospective Interpretation of American Religious Ethics, 1948–1988" *Journal of Religious Ethics* 25, no. 3 [25th Anniversary Supplement] (1997): 3–22; Jeffrey Stout, *Democracy and Tradition* (Princeton, NJ: Princeton University Press, 2003), 270–86; and William Schweiker, "On Religious Ethics," in *The Blackwell Companion to Religious Ethics*, ed. William Schweiker (Malden, MA: Blackwell, 2005), 1–15.

16. Gustafson, "A Retrospective Interpretation," 3–22.

17. Ibid., 14.

18. See Albert R. Jonsen and Stephen Toulmin, *The Abuse of Casuistry: A History of Moral Reasoning* (Berkeley: University of California Press, 1988), 304.

19. Little and Twiss, *Comparative Religious Ethics*, 3.

20. Ibid., 18–19 (italics in original).

21. Ronald M. Green, *Religious Reason: The Rational and Moral Basis of Religious Belief* (New York: Oxford University Press, 1978); Roderick Hindery, *Comparative Ethics in Hindu and Buddhist Traditions* (Delhi: Motlial Banarsidass, 1978).

22. Gene Outka, *Agape: An Ethical Analysis* (New Haven, CT: Yale University Press, 1972).

23. Little and Twiss, *Comparative Religious Ethics*, ix.

24. See, e.g., Eric D'Arcy, *Human Acts: An Essay in Their Moral Evaluation* (Oxford: Clarendon, 1963).

25. See, e.g., the many editions of Tom L. Beauchamp and James F. Childress, *Principles of Biomedical Ethics* (New York: Oxford University Press, 2008); Richard A. McCormick, *Notes on Moral Theology, 1965–1980* (Washington, DC: University Press of America, 1981); Richard A. McCormick and Paul Ramsey, eds., *Doing Evil to Achieve Good: Moral Choice in Conflict Situations* (Lanham, MD: University Press of America, 1985); and John P. Reeder Jr., *Killing and Saving: Abortion, Hunger, and War* (University Park: Pennsylvania University Press, 1996).

26. See Sumner B. Twiss, "Comparison in Religious Ethics," in *The Blackwell Companion to Religious Ethics*, ed. William Schweiker (Malden, MA: Blackwell, 2005), 147–55.

27. See, e.g., Robert Gibbs, *Why Ethics? Signs of Responsibilities* (Princeton, NJ: Princeton University Press, 2000).

28. See, e.g., entries in William Schweiker, ed., *The Blackwell Companion to Religious Ethics* (Malden, MA: Blackwell, 2005).

29. See, e.g., Bernard Williams, *Ethics and the Limits of Philosophy* (Cambridge, MA: Harvard University Press, 1986); and Edmund L. Pincoffs, *Quandaries and Virtues: Against Reductivism in Ethics* (Lawrence: University Press of Kansas, 1986).

30. Alasdair MacIntyre, *After Virtue: A Study in Moral Theory* (Notre Dame, IN: University of Notre Dame Press, 1981).

31. See, e.g., Aaron Stalnaker, *Overcoming Our Evil: Human Nature and Spiritual Exercises in Xunzi and Augustine* (Washington, DC: Georgetown University Press, 2006); and David A. Clairmont, *Moral Struggle and Religious Ethics: On the Person as Classic in Comparative Theological Contexts* (Malden, MA: Wiley-Blackwell, 2011).

32. See Jeffrey Stout, "Traditions and Commitments in Religious Ethics," *Journal of Religious Ethics* 25, no. 3 [25th Anniversary Supplement] (1997): 23–56.

33. See, e.g., Jonsen and Toulmin, *The Abuse of Casuistry*; Richard Rorty, *Contingency, Irony, and Solidarity* (Cambridge: Cambridge University Press, 1989), 141–98; Martha C. Nussbaum, *Love's Knowledge: Essays on Philosophy and Literature* (New York: Oxford University Press, 1990); and Richard B. Miller, *Casuistry and Modern Ethics: A Poetics of Practical Reasoning* (Chicago: University of Chicago Press, 1996).

34. See, e.g., William R. LaFleur, *Liquid Life: Abortion and Buddhism in Japan* (Princeton, NJ: Princeton University Press, 1992); Charles Taylor, *Multiculturalism: Examining the Politics of Recognition*, ed. Amy Gutmann (Princeton, NJ: Princeton University Press, 1994); Saba Mahmood, *Politics of Piety: The Islamic Revival and the Feminist Subject* (Princeton, NJ: Princeton University Press, 2005); Stalnaker, *Overcoming Our Evil*; John Kelsay, *Arguing the Just War in Islam* (Cambridge, MA: Harvard University Press, 2007); and Elizabeth A. Bucar, *Creative Conformity: Feminist Politics of U.S. Catholic and Iranian Shi'i Women* (Washington, DC: Georgetown University Press, 2011).

35. I will examine exceptions to this generalization over the course of this book, especially in the epilogue.

36. See Kathryn Tanner, *Theories of Culture: A New Agenda for Theology* (Minneapolis, MN: Fortress, 1997), 27–28.

2. ON MAKING A CULTURAL TURN IN RELIGIOUS ETHICS

1. "Editorial," *Journal of Religious Ethics* 1, no. 1 (1973): 3.

2. Ronald M. Green, "The Journal of Religious Ethics, 1973–1994," *Journal of Religious Ethics* 25, no. 3 [25th Anniversary Supplement] (1997): 221–38, 232.

3. Ibid., 230.

4. Ibid.; Green is quoting from the 1973 "Editorial," 3 (see note 1 above).

5. The inaugural editorial of the *JRE* invites "'state of the discipline' essays . . . that will explore the critical issues of the moment and make suggestions for the future agenda of religious ethics." To those concerns this chapter is devoted. See "Editorial," 4.

6. See Alasdair MacIntyre, *After Virtue: A Study in Moral Theory* (Notre Dame, IN: University of Notre Dame Press, 1981), esp. 175–76, 188–89.

7. See Michael Walzer, *Spheres of Justice: A Defense of Pluralism and Equality* (New York: Basic Books, 1983); and Michael Walzer, *Interpretation and Social Criticism* (Cambridge, MA: Harvard University Press, 1987).

8. Onora O'Neill, *Towards Justice and Virtue: A Constructive Account of Practical Reasoning* (Cambridge: Cambridge University Press, 1996), 38–44.

9. See Michel Foucault, *Power/Knowledge: Selected Interviews and Other Writings, 1972–77*, ed. Colin Gordon (New York: Pantheon, 1980); and Michel Foucault, *The History of Sexuality*, vol. 1, *An Introduction* (New York: Vintage, 1980).

10. Ethicists' appeals to the authority of culturally unmediated experience suffer from pure subjectivism or naive realism.

11. See, e.g., Bernard Williams, *Moral Luck* (Cambridge: Cambridge University Press, 1981); MacIntyre, *After Virtue*; Charles Taylor, *Philosophical Papers I: Human Agency and Language* (Cambridge: Cambridge University Press, 1985); and Martha C. Nussbaum, *Love's Knowledge: Essays on Philosophy and Literature* (New York: Oxford University Press, 1990).

12. For instructive discussions see Lawrence Grossberg, Cary Nelson, and Paula Treichler, eds., *Cultural Studies* (New York: Routledge, 1992); Simon During, ed., *The Cultural Studies Reader* (New York: Routledge, 1993); and John Storey, *An Introduction to Cultural Theory and Popular Culture* (New York: Prentice-Hall, 1993). An introductory survey of cultural theory for Christian theologians is provided by Kathryn Tanner, *Theories of Culture: A New Agenda for Theology* (Minneapolis, MN: Fortress, 1997). For constructive engagements with many of the trends I examine in this chapter see Delwin Brown, Sheila Greeve Davaney, and Kathryn Tanner, eds., *Converging on Culture: Theologians in Dialogue with Cultural Analysis and Criticism* (New York: Oxford University Press, 2001). The essays in that volume connect the cultural turn in the humanities with historicist and postmodern accounts of the self and modes of knowledge. The present chapter aims to show why that account, and the distinction between classical and contemporary thought on which it rests, is simplistic.

13. Myles Burnyeat, "Culture and Society in Plato's *Republic*," Tanner Lectures on Human Values, Harvard University, Dec. 10–12, 1997, http://tannerlectures.utah .edu/_documents/a-to-z/b/Burnyeat99.pdf.

14. George E. Marcus and Michael M. J. Fischer, *Anthropology as Cultural Critique: An Experimental Moment in the Human Sciences* (Chicago: University of Chicago Press, 1986), 17.

15. Ibid., 165.

16. See William A. Barbieri Jr., "The Heterological Quest: Michel de Certeau's Travel Narratives and the 'Other' of Comparative Religious Ethics," *Journal of Religious Ethics* 30, no. 1 (2002): 23–48.

17. James Clifford, "Introduction: Partial Truths," in *Writing Culture: The Poetics and Politics of Ethnography*, ed. James Clifford and George Marcus (Berkeley: University of California Press, 1986), 1–26, 23.

18. Marcus and Fischer, *Anthropology as Cultural Critique*, x.

19. Ibid., 111, 116. In a similar vein Clifford observes that however much ethnographers must enter into power relations as part of their own research, their labors are "potentially counter-hegemonic" ("Introduction," 9).

20. See, e.g., David Little and Sumner B. Twiss, *Comparative Religious Ethics: A New Method* (New York: Harper and Row, 1978); Lee Yearley, *Mencius and Aquinas: Theories of Virtue and Conceptions of Courage* (Albany: State University of New York Press, 1990); Sumner B. Twiss and Bruce Grelle, eds., *Explorations in Global Ethics: Comparative Religious Ethics and Interreligious Dialogue* (Boulder, CO: Westview Press, 1998); Barbieri, "The Heterological Quest"; and Aaron Stalnaker, "Comparative Religious Ethics and the Problem of 'Human Nature,'" *Journal of Religious Ethics* 33, no. 2 (2005): 187–224. Twiss and Grelle seek to "bring the discipline of comparative religious ethics into constructive collaboration with the community of interreligious dialogue" (3). Twiss's introduction in that volume provides a helpful overview of comparative religious ethics as a background for developing this constructive collaboration.

21. Clifford Geertz, *Local Knowledge: Further Essays in Interpretive Anthropology* (New York: Basic Books, 1983), 57.

22. See, e.g., Nussbaum, *Love's Knowledge*; and Alex Kotlowitz, *There Are No Children Here: The Story of Two Boys Growing Up in the Other America* (New York: Doubleday, 1991).

23. See, e.g., Gene Outka, *Agape: An Ethical Analysis* (New Haven, CT: Yale University Press 1972); and John Rawls, *A Theory of Justice* (Cambridge, MA: Harvard/Belknap Press, 1971).

24. Geertz, *Local Knowledge*, 57.

25. Marcus and Fischer, *Anthropology as Cultural Critique*, 137–39.

26. Ibid., 165, 167.

27. See Charles Taylor, *Multiculturalism: Examining the Politics of Recognition*, ed. Amy Gutmann (Princeton, NJ: Princeton University Press, 1994), 25.

28. Ibid., 70, 67.

29. Marcus and Fischer, *Anthropology as Cultural Critique*, 138.

30. I discuss these problems as they relate to Taylor's views in *Terror, Religion, and Liberal Thought* (New York: Columbia University Press, 2010), 84–99.

31. Taylor, *Multiculturalism*, 72–73, 66–67.

32. See Susan Moller Okin, *Is Multiculturalism Bad for Women?* ed. Joshua Cohen, Matthew Howard, and Martha C. Nussbaum (Princeton, NJ: Princeton University Press, 1999).

33. Plato, *The Republic of Plato*, translated with introduction and notes by Francis Macdonald Cornford (London: Oxford University Press, 1941), 55.

34. Jonathan Lear, *Open Minded: Working Out the Logic of the Soul* (Cambridge, MA: Harvard University Press, 1998), 219–20.

35. Ibid., 221.

36. Ibid., 225.

37. Ibid., 226.

38. See Martha C. Nussbaum, *The Fragility of Goodness: Luck and Ethics in Greek Tragedy and Philosophy* (Cambridge: Cambridge University Press, 1986); and Nancy Sherman, *The Fabric of Character: Aristotle's Theory of Virtue* (Oxford: Clarendon, 1989).

39. Taylor, *Philosophical Papers I*, 53–55.

40. Charles Taylor, *Sources of the Self: The Making of the Modern Identity* (Cambridge, MA: Harvard University Press, 1989), 4.

41. Taylor, *Philosophical Papers I*, 48.

42. Paul Lauritzen, "Emotions and Religious Ethics," *Journal of Religious Ethics* 16, no. 2 (1988): 307–24, 308. Lauritzen elaborates on this cognitive or constructivist account of the emotions: "According to a constructivist view, emotions are culturally mediated or constructed experiences that are shaped by, and crucially dependent upon, cultural forms of discourse such as symbols, beliefs, and judgments. What a constructivist theory seeks to capture is the way in which emotions embody a sense of ourselves and our situations, the way in which they embody self-understanding and become intelligible when self-understanding is stripped away" (308).

Lauritzen proceeds on this account to raise questions about William James's moral psychology that seem sympathetic with, but go beyond, those developed by Charles Taylor, which I discuss below. See ibid., 309–13.

43. Plato, *The Republic of Plato*, 123.

44. One exception is the work of Stanley Hauerwas, who writes about the formation of distinctively Christian virtues within the Christian community. See, e.g., Stanley Hauerwas, *The Peaceable Kingdom: A Primer in Christian Ethics* (Notre Dame, IN: University of Notre Dame Press, 1983). Lauritzen engages Hauerwas on some substantive points regarding emotions in Lauritzen, "Emotions and Religious Ethics," 316–20.

45. Clifford Geertz, *The Interpretation of Cultures* (New York: Basic Books, 1973), 95.

46. For an exception see Charles Hirschkind, *The Ethical Soundscape: Cassette Sermons and Islamic Counterpublics* (New York: Columbia University Press, 2006).

47. Charles Taylor, *Varieties of Religion Today: William James Revisited* (Cambridge, MA: Harvard University Press, 2002), 88.

48. Wayne Meeks, *The Moral World of the First Christians* (Philadelphia: Westminster/John Knox, 1986), 11–13.

49. Geertz, *The Interpretation of Cultures*, 127.

50. Meeks, *The Moral World of the First Christians*, 97.

51. Ibid., 98.

52. Ibid., 100–103.

53. Ibid., 124–60.

54. In cross-cousin marriage, Trawick notes, "a man marries a woman in the category of his father's sister's daughter, his mother's brother's daughter, or in a few cases, his own sister's daughter." See Margaret Trawick, *Notes on Love in a Tamil Family* (Berkeley: University of California Press, 1990), 118. Subsequent citations of this source are referenced parenthetically in the text.

55. Ibid., 40.

56. Marcus and Fischer, *Anthropology as Cultural Critique*, 138.

57. Trawick, *Notes on Love in a Tamil Family*, 188.

58. See Robert Bellah, Richard Madsen, William M. Sullivan, Ann Swidler, and Steven M. Tipton, *Habits of the Heart: Individualism and Commitment in American Life* (Berkeley: University of California Press, 1985), 85–112.

59. See ibid., esp. 72–75.

60. William James, *The Varieties of Religious Experience: A Study in Human Nature* (New York: Collier, 1961 [1902]), 42 (James's emphasis).

61. Taylor, *Varieties of Religion Today*, 55.

62. Whether Taylor's reading of James is entirely accurate is another matter. James's descriptions of religious practitioners in *Varieties of Religious Experience*—saints, mystics, and ascetics; Christian Scientists, Roman Catholics, Unitarians, and Methodists, for example—include reference to their respective theological idioms, practices, and beliefs (e.g., faith, evil, grace, confession). James's descriptions would be unintelligible without these references to contextual and communal facts.

63. Taylor, *Varieties of Religion Today*, 75–107. Subsequent citations of this source are referenced parenthetically in the text.

64. See, e.g., Lee Yearley, "Conflicts Among Ideals of Human Flourishing," in *Prospects for a Common Morality*, ed. Gene Outka and John P. Reeder Jr. (Princeton, NJ: Princeton University Press, 1992), 233–53.

65. See, e.g., Robin W. Lovin and Frank Reynolds, *Cosmogony and Ethical Order: New Studies in Comparative Ethics* (Chicago: University of Chicago Press, 1985).

3. MORAL AUTHORITY AND MORAL CRITIQUE IN AN AGE OF ETHNOCENTRIC ANXIETY

1. Stephen Prothero, "My Take: Dalai Lama Should Condemn Tibetan Self-Immolations," http://religion.blogs.cnn.com/2012/07/12/my-take-dalai-lama-should-condemn-tibetan-self-immolations.

2. Bruce Lincoln, *Authority: Construction and Corrosion* (Chicago: University of Chicago Press, 1994), 4.

3. On locutionary, illocutionary, and perlocutionary acts see J. L. Austin, *How to Do Things with Words* (Oxford: Oxford University Press, 1962).

4. Cited in Choong Soon Kim, "The Role of the Non-Western Anthropologist Reconsidered: Illusion Versus Reality," *Current Anthropology* 31, no. 2 (1990): 196–201, 196.

5. Benson Saler, *Conceptualizing Religion: Immanent Anthropologists, Transcendent Natives, and Unbounded Categories* (Leiden: E. J. Brill, 1993), 9.

6. Of course *expressing disapproval*—in either impersonal or interpersonal terms— and *intervening* to change or eliminate the practice in question are different. Nothing about disapproval is sufficient for justifying interventions to change or eliminate a practice. Decisions to intervene involve moral and practical considerations about the potential effectiveness of an intervention, methods of intervening, the collateral effects of intervening, and the timing of an intervention, among other matters. But what I say about disapproval is necessary when considering whether to intervene to change or eliminate a practice. Otherwise the decision to intervene appears morally arbitrary. In those instances, to be sure, suspicions of chauvinism are warranted.

7. Here, and below, I follow a line of argument developed by G. A Cohen, "Casting the First Stone: Who Can, and Who Can't, Condemn the Terrorists?" *Royal Institute of Philosophy Supplement* 58 (May 2006): 113–36.

8. Theodor Adorno, *Negative Dialectics*, trans. E. B. Ashton (London: Routledge, 1990), 35–37. Adorno's idea is that relativism is a form of reason limiting itself, a self-imposed prohibition necessary to block awareness of the modes of production that underwrite bourgeois existence. In this way Adorno connects relativism with anti-intellectualism. On that premise he writes: "The perennial anti-intellectualism is more than an anthropological trait of bourgeois subjectivity. It is due to the fact that under the existing conditions of production the concept of reason, once emancipated, must fear that its consistent pursuit will explode those conditions.

This is why reason limits itself; throughout the bourgeois era, the spirit's accompanying reaction to the idea of its autonomy has been to despise itself. The spirit cannot forgive itself for being barred, by the constitution of its existence it guides, from unfolding the freedom inherent in its concept. The philosophical term for this prohibition is relativism" (37). My argument in this chapter, following Adorno's insight, is emancipatory. Worries about ethnocentrism can impose what he calls a prohibition on human reason and, with that, fuel anti-intellectualism and incuriosity. Providing therapy in response to anxieties about ethnocentrism can liberate the practice of nonchauvinistic cross-cultural critique.

9. Lee Yearley, "Bourgeois Relativism and the Comparative Study of the Self," in *Tracing Common Themes: Comparative Courses in the Study of Religion*, ed. John B. Carman and Steven P. Hopkins (Atlanta, GA: Scholars Press, 1991), 165–78, 166.

10. For a fuller account see my *Terror, Religion, and Liberal Thought* (New York: Columbia University Press, 2010), 84–99. See also Aaron Stalnaker, *Overcoming Our Evil: Human Nature and Spiritual Exercises in Xunzi and Augustine* (Washington, DC: Georgetown University Press, 2006), 299–301.

11. I borrow the locution *critical pluralism* from Michelle M. Moody-Adams, *Fieldwork in Familiar Places: Morality, Culture, and Philosophy* (Cambridge, MA: Harvard University Press, 1997), 203.

12. Here I follow, with some modification, Moody-Adams, *Fieldwork in Familiar Places*, 7. I prefer the language of descriptive cultural pluralism to descriptive cultural relativism in order to emphasize the facts of moral diversity on which some theories of moral relativism rely. See also Chris Gowans, "Moral Relativism," in *The Stanford Encyclopedia of Philosophy*, http://plato.stanford.edu/archives/sum2015/entries/moral-relativism/.

13. On abstinence and moral relativism see Steven Lukes, *Moral Relativism* (London: Profile Books, 2008), 37–38.

14. These distinctions are noted in ibid., 59–63.

15. Moody-Adams, *Fieldwork in Familiar Places*, 31–56.

16. For different perspectives on this topic see the essays in Gene Outka and John P. Reeder Jr., eds., *Prospects for a Common Morality* (Princeton, NJ: Princeton University Press, 1993); and Charles Taylor, "Conditions for an Unforced Consensus on Rights," in *Dilemmas and Connections: Selected Essays* (Cambridge, MA: Belknap, 2011), 105–23.

17. Lukes, *Moral Relativism*, 25.

18. Ibid.

19. Moody-Adams gets to this idea by arguing as an objectivist that practices that might seem to be either morally acceptable or beyond moral criticism because they occurred in the past (e.g., the slavery of Africans) can be explained as an example of what Aquinas calls "affected ignorance," understood as "choosing not to know what one can and should know," which is culpable. Moody-Adams invokes the idea of affected ignorance to rebut Bernard Williams's notion of the "relativism of distance." See Moody-Adams, *Fieldwork in Familiar Places*, 85–103.

20. Charles Taylor, *Multiculturalism: Examining the Politics of Recognition*, ed. Amy Gutmann (Princeton, NJ: Princeton University Press, 1994), 72–73.
21. Lukes, *Moral Relativism*, 141 (emphasis in the original).
22. Yearley, "Bourgeois Relativism and the Comparative Study of the Self," 166.
23. See notes 8 and 9 above.
24. Aaron Stalnaker, "Judging Others: History, Ethics, and the Purposes of Comparison," *Journal of Religious Ethics* 36, no. 3 (2008): 425–44, 434.
25. For one discussion see David Lyons, "Ethical Relativism and the Problem of Incoherence," *Ethics* 86, no. 2 (1976): 107–21.
26. For an example see Richard Rorty, *Objectivity, Relativism, and Truth: Philosophical Papers I* (Cambridge: Cambridge University Press, 1991), 1–17.
27. Lincoln, *Authority*, 4.
28. Abstaining from judging others is, of course, different from tolerating others— the latter being one kind of response to another who *is* judged. See my *Terror, Religion, and Liberal Thought*, 84–99; and Andrew Jason Cohen, "What Toleration Is," *Ethics* 115, no. 1 (2004): 68–95.
29. On confidence see Moody-Adams, *Fieldwork in Familiar Places*, 22–28.
30. I owe this idea of context-sensitivity to suggestions from Michael Ing, Dana Logan, and Danielle Murry-Knowles.
31. By "seeking the truth" here I mean, more colloquially, "getting to the bottom of things." I do not mean producing a comprehensive criteriological theory that enables us to distinguish between warranted and unwarranted beliefs.
32. Lincoln argues that authority is to be distinguished from coercion and persuasion by virtue of being accepted on trust. In his view the relationship of trust erodes (or has eroded) if an authority must threaten his audience coercively to ensure compliance or if he must proffer reasons to persuade his audience about his policies or pronouncements. One forfeits authority on Lincoln's account when he loses the trust necessary to abstain from offering reasons to legitimate his pronouncements. This claim seems counterintuitive, however, when we think about authority and persuasion. Lincoln provides no reason to believe that asking for persuasive reasons in an asymmetrical relationship is necessarily a sign of distrust. One could be asking for reasons to clear up an ambiguity or to deepen one's one understanding. In chapter 8 I will return to the topic of authority and asymmetries in relationships when thinking about public reason and democratic political authority. For Lincoln on authority, persuasion, and coercion see his *Authority*, 4–9.
33. Harry G. Frankfurt, *On Bullshit* (Princeton, NJ: Princeton University Press, 2005).
34. Thanks to Emma Young for pressing this point.
35. Cohen, "Casting the First Stone," 118, 122–23.
36. Cohen speaks in a more general way than I do here about this second form of discrediting critics in ibid., 124, 126.
37. Ibid., 126–33.
38. For a discussion see Cheshire Calhoun, "Standing for Something," *Journal of Philosophy* 92, no. 5 (1995): 235–60.

39. Thanks to Aaron Stalnaker for comments that clarified this idea.
40. See Mary Midgley, *Can't We Make Moral Judgements?* (New York: St. Martin's, 1991), 87–96.
41. Taylor, *Multiculturalism*, 72–73.
42. On acknowledgment see my introduction.
43. Will Kymlicka, *Multicultural Citizenship: A Liberal Theory of Minority Rights* (Oxford: Clarendon, 1995), 35.
44. I develop these ideas in *Terror, Religion, and Liberal Thought*, chaps. 1, 4, and 7.
45. Moody-Adams, *Fieldwork in Familiar Places*, 203.

4. THE ETHICS OF EMPATHY

1. Clifford Geertz, *Local Knowledge: Further Essays in Interpretive Anthropology* (New York: Basic Books, 1983), 59.
2. Ibid., 56.
3. Ibid.
4. Janet Hook and Christi Parsons, "Obama Calls Empathy 'Key' to Supreme Court Pick," http://articles.latimes.com/2009/may/02/nation/na-court-souter2.
5. Molly Hennessy-Fiske, Michael Memoli, and Scott Gold, "Obama Urges Americans to Debate 'In a Way That Heals,'" http://articles.latimes.com/2011/jan/13/nation/la-na-obama-memorial-20110113.
6. "Obama to Graduates: Cultivate Empathy," www.northwestern.edu/newscenter/stories/2006/06/barack.html; see also J. D. Trout, *The Empathy Gap: Building Bridges to the Good Life and the Good Society* (New York: Viking, 2009).
7. Kent A. Kiehl and Joshua W. Buckholtz, "Inside the Mind of a Psychopath," *Scientific American Mind*, Sept./Oct. 2010, 22–29.
8. Simon Baron-Cohen, *The Science of Evil: On Empathy and the Origins of Cruelty* (New York: Basic Books, 2011). The Hare Psychopathy Checklist is a widely used tool for diagnosing the lack of empathy; see www.hare.org.
9. Stephen Darwall, *The Second-Person Standpoint: Morality, Respect, and Accountability* (Cambridge, MA: Harvard University Press, 2006), 43–48. For an argument integrating empathy with care ethics see Michael Slote, *The Ethics of Care and Empathy* (New York: Routledge, 2007).
10. Marc Bekoff, *The Emotional Lives of Animals* (Novato: CA: New World Library, 2007); Frans de Waal, *The Age of Empathy: Nature's Lessons for a Kinder Society* (New York: Harmony Books, 2009).
11. Martin L. Hoffman, "Empathy and Human Nature," *Journal of Personality and Social Psychology* 40 (1981): 121–37. See also Robert Plutchik, "Evolutionary Bases of Empathy," in *Empathy and Its Development*, ed. Nancy Eisenberg and Janet Strayer (Cambridge: Cambridge University Press, 1987), 38–46; and Allan Young, "Empathy, Evolution, and Human Nature," in *Empathy: From Bench to Bedside*, ed. Jean Decety (Cambridge, MA: MIT Press, 2012), 21–37.
12. Robert L. Katz, *Empathy: Its Nature and Uses* (New York: Free Press of Glencoe/Collier-Macmillan, 1963).

13. Jeremy Rifkin, *The Empathic Civilization: The Race to Global Consciousness in a World Crisis* (New York: Penguin, 2009).

14. See cultureofempathy.com. The literature on empathy and childhood education is immense. See, e.g., David A. Levine, *Teaching Empathy: A Blueprint for Caring, Compassion, and Community* (Bloomington, IN: Solution Tree, 2005).

15. Dev Patnaik, *Wired to Care: How Companies Prosper When They Create Widespread Empathy* (Upper Saddle River, NJ: FT Press, 2009).

16. "Meryl Streep > Quotes," GoodReads, www.goodreads.com/author/quotes /700073; and "Meryl Streep Discusses the Role of Empathy in Her Life and Acting," YouTube, www.youtube.com/watch?v=c-wkAEoyTWE.

17. Suzanne Keen, *Empathy and the Novel* (New York: Oxford University Press, 2007), 11.

18. John Markoff, "Scientists Worry Machines May Outsmart Man," July 25, 2009, www.nytimes.com/2009/07/26/science/26robot.html.

19. Edward Titchener, *A Beginner's Psychology* (New York: Macmillan, 1915), 198, cited in Lauren Wispé, "History of the Concept of Empathy," in *Empathy and Its Development*, ed. Nancy Eisenberg and Janet Strayer (Cambridge: Cambridge University Press, 1987), 22.

20. Jean Decety and Kalina J. Michalska, "How Children Develop Empathy: The Contribution of Developmental Affective Neuroscience," in *Empathy: From Bench to Bedside*, ed. Jean Decety (Cambridge, MA: MIT Press, 2012), 167–90, 170.

21. See Nancy Sherman, "Empathy and Imagination," *Midwest Studies in Philosophy* 22, no. 1 (1998): 82–119; and Martin L. Hoffman, *Empathy and Moral Development: Implications for Caring and Justice* (Cambridge: Cambridge University Press, 2000). On the scientific literature see Alvin I. Goldman, "Ethics and Cognitive Science," *Ethics* 103, no. 2 (1993): 337–60; Stephen Darwall, "Empathy, Sympathy, Care," *Philosophical Studies* 89, no. 2/3 (1998): 261–82; Karsten R. Stueber, "Empathy," in *The Stanford Encyclopedia of Philosophy*, http://plato.stanford.edu /entries/empathy/; and Jean Decety and Meghan Meyer, "From Emotion Resonance to Empathic Understanding: A Social Developmental Neuroscience Account," *Development and Psychopathology* 20, no. 4 (2008): 1053–80.

22. Thanks to conversations with Bennett Bertenthal regarding these data. See also Stueber, "Empathy"; and Jean Decety, ed., *Empathy: From Bench to Bedside* (Cambridge, MA: MIT Press, 2012), esp. Sharee Light and Carolyn Zahn-Waxler, "Nature and Forms of Empathy in the First Years of Life," 109–30; Amrisha Vaish and Felix Warneken, "Social-Cognitive Contributors to Young Children's Empathic and Prosocial Behavior," 131–46; Nancy Eisenberg, Snjezana Huerta, and Alison Edwards, "Relations of Empathy-Related Responding to Children's and Adolescents' Social Competence," 147–63; and Decety and Michalska, "How Children Develop Empathy," 167–90.

23. By this I am not suggesting that the purported inclination *makes* empathy desirable.

24. Standard definitions include only the first two of my three conditions. For exceptions see Decety and Meyer, "From Emotion Resonance to Empathic

Understanding," 1055; and Daryl Cameron, Michael Inzlicht, and William A. Cunningham, "Empathy Is Actually a Choice," *New York Times*, July 10, 2015, www
.nytimes.com/2015/07/12/opinion/sunday/empathy-is-actually-a-choice.html.

25. See Nancy Snow, "Empathy," *American Philosophical Quarterly* 37, no. 1 (2000):
65–78, 66.

26. Katz, *Empathy*, 7; Darwall, "Empathy, Sympathy, Care," 270.

27. See the reference to the work of de Waal above. See, as well, the work of Mary
Gordon, www.rootsofempathy.org/en/mary-gordon.html.

28. Amy Coplan, "Will the Real Empathy Please Stand Up? A Case for a Narrow
Conceptualization," in "Spindel Supplement: Empathy and Ethics," ed. Remy
Debes, special issue, *Southern Journal of Philosophy* 49, s1 (2011): 40–65, 43.

29. Aristotle, *Nicomachean Ethics*, 1107a1–8, 1111b5–10.

30. Hoffman, *Empathy and Moral Development*, 197–220.

31. Ibid.; see also John P. Reeder Jr., "Extensive Benevolence," *Journal of Religious
Ethics* 26, no. 1 (1998): 47–70.

32. Dwayne G. Fuselier, "Placing Stockholm Syndrome in Perspective," *FBI Law
Enforcement Bulletin* (July 1999): 22–25.

33. See John Diegh, "Empathy and Universalizability," *Ethics* 104, no. 5 (1995): 743–63;
and Snow, "Empathy," 74. Similar issues are explored within the context of psychotherapy in Jodi Halpern, *From Detached Concern to Empathy: Humanizing
Medical Practice* (New York: Oxford University Press, 2001).

34. Hume and Smith focused on what they called *sympathy* and its liabilities.

35. David Brooks, "The Limits of Empathy," *New York Times*, Sept. 29, 2011, www
.nytimes.com/2011/09/30/opinion/brooks-the-limits-of-empathy.html.

36. Jesse Prinz, "Against Empathy," in "Spindel Supplement: Empathy and Ethics,"
ed. Remy Debes, special issue, *Southern Journal of Philosophy* 49, s1 (2011):
214–33, 228. See also Paul Bloom, "The Baby in the Well: The Case Against Empathy," *New Yorker*, May 20, 2013, www.newyorker.com/magazine/2013/05/20
/the-baby-in-the-well?.

37. Prinz, "Against Empathy," 229, 231.

38. John McDowell, "Virtue and Reason," *Monist* 62, no. 3 (1993): 331–50.

39. Snow, "Empathy," 74. See also Jeanette Kennett, "Autism, Empathy, and Moral
Agency," *Philosophical Quarterly* 52, no. 208 (2002): 34–57.

40. Snow, "Empathy," 74.

41. Linda Trinkaus Zagzebski, *Virtues of the Mind: An Inquiry into the Nature of Virtue and the Ethical Foundations of Knowledge* (Cambridge: Cambridge University
Press, 1996), 137.

42. See, e.g., Julia Annas, *Intelligent Virtue* (New York: Oxford University Press, 2011).
For an exception to a eudaimonistic theory see Zagzebski, *Virtues of the Mind*, which
develops a motivational view of virtue. See, as well, Kate Abramson and Adam Leite,
"Love as a Reactive Emotion," *Philosophical Quarterly* 61, no. 245 (2011): 1–27.

43. On harmony and concord see Augustine, *City of God* 19.13; on the lust for cruelty
see Augustine, *Confessions* 6.8; on conspiracy see ibid., 2.4–9; and on catharsis see
ibid., 3.2.

44. This point is driven home by William S. Babcock, "*Cupiditas* and *Caritas*: The Early Augustine on Love and Human Fulfillment," in *The Ethics of St. Augustine*, ed. William S. Babcock (Atlanta, GA: Scholars Press, 1991), 39–66, 46.

45. The distinction is deployed in J. David Velleman, "Love as a Moral Emotion," *Ethics* 109, no. 2 (1999): 338–74. Yet Augustine understands human desires as capable of undergoing transformation based on their objects of value, as I indicate below. For Augustine there is no sharp distinction between conative and evaluative bases for love.

46. Taricius J. van Bavel, "Love," in *Augustine Through the Ages: An Encyclopedia*, ed. Allan D. Fitzgerald (Grand Rapids, MI: Eerdmans, 1999), 509–16.

47. Augustine, *On Christian Doctrine*, trans. D. W. Robertson (Indianapolis, IN: Bobbs-Merrill, 1958), 3.10.16.

48. See, e.g., *The Confessions*, trans. Maria Boulding (Hyde Park, NY: New City Press, 1997), 4.6.11.

49. Augustine, *On Christian Doctrine* 1.22.20–21.

50. Anders Nygren, *Agape and Eros*, trans. Philip S. Watson (Chicago: University of Chicago Press, 1953 [1932, 1938, 1939]).

51. I discuss these matters in chapter 6.

52. Iris Murdoch, *The Sovereignty of Good* (London: Ark Paperbacks, 1970).

53. See Harry G. Frankfurt, *The Reasons of Love* (Princeton, NJ: Princeton University Press, 2006), 69–100.

54. As I will make plain in chapter 7, Augustine also understands disordered love as a vacancy, a privation.

55. John M. Rist, *Augustine: Ancient Thought Baptized* (Cambridge: Cambridge University Press, 1994), 165.

56. Augustine, *On the Morals of the Catholic Church*, chap. 15, par. 25, in *Christian Classics Ethereal Library*, www.ccel.org/ccel/schaff/npnf104.iv.iv.xvii.html.

57. For a discussion see John P. Langan, "Augustine on the Unity and Interconnection of the Virtues," *Harvard Theological Review* 72, no. 1 (1979): 81–95.

58. Snow, "Empathy," 69. See also Paul Lauritzen, *Religious Belief and Emotional Transformation: A Light in the Heart* (Lewisburg, PA: Bucknell University Press, 1992), 65.

59. Augustine, *On the Morals of the Catholic Church*, chap. 15, par. 25; chap. 24, par. 45, in *Christian Classics Ethereal Library*, www.ccel.org/ccel/schaff/npnf104.iv.iv .xvii.html; www.ccel.org/ccel/schaff/npnf104.iv.iv.xxvi.html.

60. In a similar vein Robert Merrihew Adams uses the language of "structural virtue" to describe how some virtues affect others by providing "personal psychic strength." See Robert Merrihew Adams, *A Theory of Virtue: Excellence in Being for the Good* (New York: Oxford University Press, 2006), 33–34. However, the discipline to which I am referring is as normatively substantive as it is psychological.

61. Thanks to many conversations with Kevin Houser for clarifying this point and its implications for thinking about good empathy.

62. In this respect empathy resembles romantic love as described and developed as a moral reaction by Abramson and Leite. In their account "love is an appropriate response to particular sorts of morally significant character traits such as generosity

and interpersonal warmth, forthrightness and sincerity, compassion, considerate-ness, steadfastness, and loyalty." Such qualities provide reasons for love. Yet, unlike their view of romantic love, good empathy need not rely on, or react to, "traits that are especially salient in the context of fairly intimate relationships." That is to say, virtuous empathy need not depend on attitudes or traits that the object of empathy expresses *toward* the empath. Rather, virtuous empathy can respond to attitudes or traits that the object of empathy expresses toward persons other than oneself. See Abramson and Leite, "Love as a Reactive Emotion," 2, 7.

63. For a discussion of empathy, human rights, and humanitarianism see Lynn Hunt, *Inventing Human Rights: A History* (New York: Norton, 2007).

64. On the idea of "building up" see Reeder, "Extensive Benevolence."

65. Augustine, *Morals of the Catholic Church*, chap. 26, par. 49, www.ccel.org/ccel /schaff/npnf104.iv.iv.xxviii.html.

66. These terms draw on Frankfurt, *The Reasons of Love*.

67. Velleman, "Love as a Moral Emotion," 343.

68. Reeder, "Extensive Benevolence," 58.

69. Nancy Sherman, "Empathy, Respect, and Humanitarian Intervention," *Ethics and International Affairs* 12, no. 1 (1998): 103–19; and Martha Nussbaum, *Love's Knowledge: Essays on Philosophy and Literature* (New York: Oxford University Press, 1990). For a cautionary note about the limits of narrative for cultivating empathy and for fostering prosocial behavior see Keen, *Empathy and the Novel*.

5. INDIGNATION, EMPATHY, AND SOLIDARITY

1. Karen Caffarini, "Union Official: 'Solidarity Is Key for Striking BP Refinery Workers," *Chicago Tribune*, Feb. 28, 2015, www.chicagotribune.com/suburbs/post -tribune/news/ct-ptb-bp-strike-rally-st-0301-20150228-story.html.

2. Michael Walzer, *Politics and Passion: Toward a More Egalitarian Liberalism* (New Haven, CT: Yale University Press, 2004), 110–30.

3. Walzer, "Deliberation . . . and What Else?" in ibid., 90–109.

4. Ibid., 91.

5. See Michael Walzer, "The Politics of Michel Foucault," in *Foucault: A Critical Reader*, ed. David Couzens Hoy (Cambridge, MA: Blackwell, 1986), 51–68.

6. Walzer, *Politics and Passion*, 122. See the historical study by Albert O. Hirschman, *The Passions and Interests: Political Arguments for Capitalism Before Its Triumph* (Princeton, NJ: Princeton University Press, 1977).

7. Walzer, *Politics and Passion*, 126.

8. Ibid., 130.

9. William Shakespeare, *The Tempest*, act 2, scene 2.

10. See Mark Kramer, "The Rise and Fall of Solidarity," *New York Times*, Dec. 12, 2011, www.nytimes.com/2011/12/13/opinion/the-rise-and-fall-of-solidarity.html.

11. Pope John Paul II, *Laborem exercens* (On Human Work), par. 8, w2.vatican.va /content/john-paul-ii/en/encyclicals/documents/hf_jp-ii_enc_14091981_laborem -exercens.html.

12. Pope John Paul II, *Sollicitudo rei socialis* (On Social Concern), pars. 38, 40, w2.vatican. va/content/john-paul-ii/en/encyclicals/documents/hf_jp-ii_enc_30121987 _sollicitudo-rei-socialis.html.

13. Ibid., par. 39.

14. See Richard Rorty, *Objectivity, Relativism, and Truth: Philosophical Papers I* (Cambridge: Cambridge University Press, 1991), 21–34, 35–45; and Richard Rorty, *Contingency, Irony, and Solidarity* (Cambridge: Cambridge University Press, 1989).

15. Rorty, *Objectivity, Relativism, and Truth*, 21.

16. Rorty, *Contingency, Irony, and Solidarity*, xv, 74 (following Judith N. Shklar's *Ordinary Vices* [Cambridge, MA: Harvard University Press, 1984], 44).

17. Rorty, *Contingency, Irony, and Solidarity*, 198.

18. Thanks to Barbara Klinger for ensuring that I make this point.

19. Peter Strawson, "Freedom and Resentment," in *Free Will*, ed. Gary Watson (Oxford: Oxford University Press, 1989), 59–80, 63.

20. Ibid., 70–72.

21. John Rawls, *A Theory of Justice*, rev. ed. (Cambridge, MA: Harvard/Belknap, 1999 [1971]), 421–29. Rawls appears to have Strawson in mind when he writes, "One who feels guilty, recognizing his action as a transgression of the legitimate claims of others, expects them to resent his conduct and to penalize him in various ways. He also assumes that third parties will be indignant with him" (423). But these feelings, Rawls adds, are "moral feelings" when they "presuppose an explanation by reference to an acceptance of the principles of right and justice" (427).

22. Ibid., 421.

23. Ibid., 416, 426.

24. Ibid., 426.

25. Rawls's point enables us to see another layer of solidarity that I cannot take up here. Insofar as the group in question is bound together by affiliative ties aimed at creating a better society, actions that aim to erode ties of solidarity—for example, by fomenting intrigue and generating misinformation—add to injustice. Such intrigue or misinformation violates more than an abstract principle; suspicion, rancor, rumor-mongering, and internal dissension weaken the ties of trust in an organization.

26. Nancy Snow, "Empathy," *American Philosophical Quarterly* 37, no. 1 (2000): 65–78.

27. Stephen Darwall, "Empathy, Sympathy, Care," *Philosophical Studies* 89, no. 2/3 (1998): 261–82.

28. See Jesse Prinz, "Against Empathy," in "Spindel Supplement: Empathy and Ethics," ed. Remy Debes, special issue, *Southern Journal of Philosophy* 49, s1 (2011): 214–33. My view of empathy, abbreviated for this chapter, takes stock of Prinz's critique by viewing it as a virtue in need of a suite of supplementary excellences. See chap. 4.

29. I draw the phrase "new traditionalism" from Jeffrey Stout, *Democracy and Tradition* (Princeton, NJ: Princeton University Press, 2004), 2.

30. See Jeffrey Stout's discussion of solidarity among grassroots organizers, and his description of religious belief and practice in their lives, in Jeffrey Stout, *Blessed Are the Organized: Grassroots Democracy in America* (Princeton, NJ: Princeton University Press, 2010).

31. See, e.g., Solidarity Sabbath of the Lantos Foundation of Human Rights and Justice, http://solidaritysabbath.org/about.

6. ON DUTIES AND DEBTS TO CHILDREN

1. James Clifford, "Introduction: Partial Truths," in *Writing Culture: The Poetics and Politics of Ethnography*, ed. James Clifford and George E. Marcus (Berkeley: University of California Press, 1986), 23.

2. G. Scott Davis, *Believing and Acting: The Pragmatic Turn in Religion and Ethics* (New York: Oxford University Press, 2012), 1–22.

3. Jeffrey Stout, *Blessed Are the Organized: Grassroots Democracy in America* (Princeton, NJ: Princeton University Press, 2010).

4. Todd David Whitmore, "Crossing the Road: The Case for Ethnographic Fieldwork in Christian Ethics," *Annual of the Society of Christian Ethics* 27, no. 2 (2007): 273–94; "Genocide or Just Another 'Casualty of War'? The Implications of the Memo Attributed to President Yoweri K. Museveni of Uganda," *Practical Matters* 3 (Fall 2010): 1–49; "Peacebuilding and Its Challenging Partners: Justice, Human Rights, Development and Solidarity," in *Peacebuilding: Catholic Theology, Ethics, and Praxis*, ed. Robert J. Schreiter et. al (Maryknoll, NY: Orbis, 2010), 155–89; "'My Tribe Is Humanity': An Interview with Archbishop John Baptist Odama," *Journal of Peace and Justice Studies* 20, no. 2 (2010): 61–75; "Religion, Ethics, and Armed Conflict: The Case of Uganda's 'War in the North,'" in *What Is War? Interdisciplinary Perspectives*, ed. Mary Ellen O'Connell (Leiden: Brill/Martinus Nijhoff, 2011), 227–39; "Whiteness Made Visible: A Theo-critical Ethnography in Acoliland," in *Ethnography as Christian Theology and Ethics*, ed. Christian Scharen and Aana Marie Vigen (New York: Continuum, 2011): 184–206; "Bridging Jesus' Missions to the Poor and the Wicked: Contributions from Attention to Culture," in *Violence, Transformation, and the Sacred: "They Shall Be Called Children of God,"* ed. Margaret R. Pfeil and Tobias L. Winright (Maryknoll, NY: Orbis, 2012), 193–209.

5. Elizabeth M. Bucar, *Creative Conformity: The Feminist Politics of U.S. Catholic and Iranian Shi'i Women* (Washington, DC: Georgetown University Press, 2011).

6. William F. May, *The Patient's Ordeal* (Bloomington: Indiana University Press, 1991).

7. I examine the monographs by Stout, Bucar, and several others working at the intersections of cultural ethnography, religion, and ethics in my epilogue.

8. See my *Children, Ethics, and Modern Medicine* (Bloomington: Indiana University Press, 2003). The name of the medical care center has been changed to protect confidentiality.

9. See James Clifford, "On Ethnographic Authority," in *The Predicament of Culture: Twentieth-Century Ethnography, Literature, and Art* (Cambridge, MA: Harvard University Press, 1988), 21–54.

10. Names of these persons are changed to protect confidentiality.

11. Interview by the author, March 1998.

12. Thanks to Melissa Seymour Fahmy for pressing this point.

13. The phrase is from Joel Feinberg, "The Nature and Value of Rights," *Journal of Value Inquiry* 4, no. 4 (1970): 255. For discussions of adult responsibilities toward children see William Aiken and Hugh LaFollette, eds., *Whose Child? Children's Rights, Parental Authority, and State Power* (Totowa, NJ: Littlefield, Adams, 1980); David Archard, *Children: Rights and Childhood*, 2nd ed. (New York: Routledge, 1994); David Archard, "Children," in *The Oxford Handbook of Practical Ethics*, ed. Hugh LaFollette (New York: Oxford University Press, 2003), 91–111; Michael W. Austin, *Conceptions of Parenthood: Ethics and the Family* (Burlington, VT: Ashgate, 2007); Jeffrey Blustein, *Parents and Children: The Ethics of the Family* (New York: Oxford University Press, 1982); Marcia J. Bunge, ed., *The Child in Christian Thought* (Grand Rapids, MI: Eerdmans, 2001); William Gaylin and Ruth Macklin, eds., *Who Speaks for the Child? The Problems of Proxy Consent* (New York: Plenum, 1983); Eva Feder Kittay, *Love's Labor: Essays on Women, Equality, and Dependency* (New York: Routledge, 1999); Rosiland Eckman Ladd, ed., *Children's Rights Re-visioned* (Belmont, CA: Wadsworth, 1996); Onora O'Neill and William Ruddick, eds., *Having Children: Philosophical and Legal Reflections* (New York: Oxford University Press, 1979); and Ferdinand Schoeman, "Rights of Children, Rights of Parents, and the Moral Basis of the Family," *Ethics* 91, no. 1 (1980): 6–19.

14. For autobiographical accounts of transformative relationships with children in family and professional settings, respectively, see Michael Bérubé, *Life as We Know It: A Father, a Family, and an Exceptional Child* (New York: Vintage, 1996); and Margaret Mohrmann, *Attending Children: A Doctor's Education* (Washington, DC: Georgetown University Press, 2005).

15. Michael J. Sandel, *Liberalism and the Limits of Justice*, 2nd ed. (Cambridge: Cambridge University Press, 1998 [1982]), 59.

16. See Tom L. Beauchamp and James F. Childress, *Principles of Biomedical Ethics*, 5th ed. (New York: Oxford University Press, 2001); and Miller, *Children, Ethics, and Modern Medicine*, 50–83.

17. Sandel, *Liberalism and the Limits of Justice*, 1.

18. John Rawls, *A Theory of Justice* (Cambridge, MA: Harvard University Press, 1971), 560.

19. Sandel, *Liberalism and the Limits of Justice*, 50–65, 55.

20. Rawls, *A Theory of Justice*, 572, 574.

21. Ibid., 574.

22. See John Rawls, *Political Liberalism*, exp. ed. (New York: Columbia University Press, 2005 [1993]), 133–72.

23. My argument draws on Sandel's commentary not to settle questions about Rawls's metaphysics in *A Theory of Justice* and later writings but to invoke Sandel's concepts and distinctions heuristically. In that capacity the terms that I borrow from Sandel aim to sharpen options and pathways for moral inquiry about obligation and indebtedness.

24. Tamara Schapiro, "What Is a Child?" *Ethics* 109, no. 4 (1999): 715–38, 730.

25. Ibid., 729.

26. See Immanuel Kant, *The Metaphysical Elements of Justice*, trans. John Ladd (Indianapolis, IN: Bobbs-Merrill, 1965), 79.

27. Schapiro, "What Is a Child?" 735.

28. Onora O'Neill, *Towards Justice and Virtue: A Constructive Account of Practical Reasoning* (Cambridge: Cambridge University Press, 1996), 194.

29. Miller, *Children, Ethics, and Modern Medicine*, 27–28.

30. Margaret Urban Walker, "Moral Luck and the Virtues of Impure Agency," in *Moral Luck*, ed. Daniel Statman (Albany: State University of New York Press, 1993), 235–50, 247, 241.

31. William F. May, "Comments to the President's Council on Bioethics," Oct. 17, 2002, http://bioethicsarchive.georgetown.edu/pcbe/transcripts/oct02/oct17full.html.

32. Michael J. Sandel, *The Case Against Perfection: Ethics in the Age of Genetic Engineering* (Cambridge, MA: Harvard University Press, 2007), 86.

33. Marcel draws the distinction between a problem and a mystery in this way: "A problem is something which I meet, which I find completely before me, but which I can therefore lay siege to and reduce. But a mystery is something in which I am myself involved, and it can therefore only be thought of as a sphere where the distinction between what is in me and what is before me loses its meaning and initial validity." Gabriel Marcel, *Being and Having: An Existentialist Diary* (1949; Gloucester: Peter Smith, 1976), 117 (emphasis in the original). By adverting to Marcel's distinction between problem and mystery to illumine different ontological orientations toward children, I do not mean to suggest that Marcel (or his ideas) romanticize children or should romanticize them. Marcel described fatherhood as a "hazardous conquest," in which feelings of tenderness can give way to "a growing irritation in the presence of a mewling, unclean creature who demands ceaseless attention and exercises a veritable tyranny over its relations." See Gabriel Marcel, *Homo Viator: Introduction to a Metaphysics of Hope* (1951; Gloucester: Peter Smith, 1978), 108, 121.

34. Throughout this chapter I am relying on the notion of gift in the commonsensical sense, as "a thing we do not get by our own efforts. We cannot buy it; we cannot acquire it through an act of will. It is bestowed upon us." See Lewis Hyde, *The Gift: Imagination and the Erotic Life of Property* (New York: Vintage, 1979), xi.

35. Søren Kierkegaard, *Works of Love: Some Christian Reflections in the Form of Discourses*, trans. Howard Hong and Edna Hong (New York: Harper Torchbooks, 1962), 172.

36. This account of debt recalls the Kantian resonances in Kierkegaard's idea that there exists a duty to remain in debt to love. Kierkegaard exclaims that such a duty

"is supposed to be the expression of the greatest contradiction to indifference, an expression of infinite love!" However, the distinct ontologies of duty and debt to which I am calling attention suggest either that Kierkegaard's attempt to conflate duty and debt is confused or that his account of debt trades on an ambiguity the effect of which is to mark out an obligation to cultivate a certain kind of moral character as one work of love. See Kierkegaard, *Works of Love*, 173.

37. I say "overlap" here instead of "merge" in order to allow room for debts to children in response to their intentionally beneficent actions. Caring adults' debts can emerge, then, owing to a child's beneficence and to a child's needs.

38. In the second edition of *Liberalism and the Limits of Justice*, Sandel disavows the communitarian label to describe his work, favoring the language of teleology instead. See his discussion of "where communitarianism goes wrong," in Sandel, *Liberalism and the Limits of Justice*, ix–xi.

39. Ibid., 58.

40. O'Neill, *Towards Justice and Virtue*, 194. In addition to O'Neill see, e.g., Martha C. Nussbaum, *The Fragility of Goodness: Luck and Ethics in Greek Tragedy and Philosophy* (Cambridge: Cambridge University Press, 1986); and Kittay, *Love's Labor*; and Walker, "Moral Luck and the Virtues of Impure Agency."

41. By "being available" I mean to recall Marcel's notion of *disponibilité*, the idea of being at another's disposal. See Gabriel Marcel, *Creative Fidelity*, trans. Robert Rosthal (New York: Farrar, Straus and Giroux, 1964), 38–57.

42. It also seems to ignore how this distinction marks a difference between absolutist and utilitarian theorizing, as Thomas Nagel observes. See Thomas Nagel, *Mortal Questions* (Cambridge: Cambridge University Press, 1979), 59–60.

43. I will draw on H. Richard Niebuhr in my comments below, although my previous analysis echoes ideas from Marcel. Niebuhr himself hybridized Mead's pragmatism and Marcel's existentialist phenomenology in *The Responsible Self: An Essay in Christian Moral Philosophy* (New York: Harper and Row, 1963).

44. Martin Heidegger, *Being and Time*, trans. John Macquarrie and Edward Robinson (New York: Harper and Row, 1962), 153–68.

45. Niebuhr, *The Responsible Self*, 65.

46. Ibid., 60.

47. Thanks to Mark Wilson for many hours of conversation about this and related points. See his formulation of "responsibility to" in Mark Wilson, "The Emotion of Regret in an Ethics of Response" (PhD diss., Indiana University, 2007).

48. Gerald P. McKenny, following Albert R. Jonsen, distinguishes three aspects of responsibility: imputability, focusing on the agent performing an act; accountability, focusing on the person or institution to whom (or which) the agent is responsible; and liability, focusing on the act for which the agent is accountable. Important for my discussion is the fact that, in McKenny's formulation, accountability expresses the idea of *responsibility to*. My account goes beyond McKenny's by probing a prejuridical account of responsibility as providing the background condition for considering these three specifications, including his second. In a prejuridical

account *responsibility to* points to the idea of responsiveness in a social context. See Gerald P. McKenny, "Responsibility," in *The Oxford Handbook of Theological Ethics*, ed. Gilbert Meilaender and William Werpehowski, 237–53 (New York: Oxford University Press, 2005); and Albert R. Jonsen, *Responsibility in Religious Ethics* (Washington, DC: Corpus, 1968).

49. Niebuhr, *The Responsible Self*, 71.

50. Jonsen reads the work of Robert Johann on responsibility in this way, as a normative principle to guide specific decisions. See Jonsen, *Responsibility in Religious Ethics*, 167–71.

7. EVIL, FRIENDSHIP, AND ICONIC REALISM IN AUGUSTINE'S *CONFESSIONS*

1. In what follows I depart from Charles Mathewes's discussion of Augustine's account of evil. For Mathewes, Augustine organizes his concepts of evil around the notions of *privation of being* and *perversion of human nature*. I concur with Mathewes regarding the first but not the second point, focusing as I do on Augustine's view of evil's origins. The notion that human nature is perverse describes Augustine's account of the effect and secondary cause rather than the primal origin of evil. See Charles T. Mathewes, *Evil and the Augustinian Tradition* (Cambridge: Cambridge University Press, 2001), 75–82. See also G. R. Evans, *Augustine on Evil* (Cambridge: Cambridge University Press, 1982); John Rist, *Augustine: Ancient Thought Baptized* (Cambridge: Cambridge University Press, 1994), 256–89; Aaron Stalnaker, *Overcoming Our Evil: Human Nature and Spiritual Exercises in Xunzi and Augustine* (Washington, DC: Georgetown University Press, 2006), 85–121; William E. Mann, "Augustine on Evil and Original Sin," in *The Cambridge Companion to Augustine*, ed. Eleonore Stump and Norman Kretzmann (Cambridge: Cambridge University Press, 2001), 40–48; William S. Babcock, "*Cupiditas* and *Caritas*: The Early Augustine on Love and Human Fulfillment," in *The Ethics of St. Augustine* (Atlanta, GA: Scholars Press, 1991), 39–66; William S. Babcock, "Augustine on Sin and Moral Agency," in ibid., 87–114; and J. Patout Burns "Augustine on the Origin and Progress of Evil," in ibid., 67–86.

2. Augustine, *The Confessions*, trans. Maria Boulding (Hyde Park, NY: New City Press, 1997), 4.6.11. All following quotations are from this translation and will be cited parenthetically in the text.

3. Augustine describes the act as "a craving to do harm for sport and fun" (2.9.17).

4. Ibid., 2.4.9. Augustine's theft would be classified by medieval thinkers as a "sin of malice." For Aquinas, no less than for Augustine, such a sin raises complex motivational questions. See Thomas Aquinas, *Summa Theologiae*, 1–2, Q. 78. For a discussion see John Langan, "Sins of Malice in the Moral Psychology of Thomas Aquinas," *Annual of the Society of Christian Ethics* 7 (1987): 179–98.

5. Augustine uses the language of "deficient" as opposed to "efficient" cause to describe Adam's movement of the will away from the Supreme Good. See *Concerning the*

City of God Against the Pagans, trans. Henry Bettenson (New York: Penguin Books, 1972), 12.7. All subsequent citations from *City of God* are taken from this edition.

6. The pear scene in *Confessions* recalls the garden scene in the book of Genesis. When trying to explain how the first sin occurred, Augustine concludes that Adam and Eve sinned "in secret." See *City of God* 14.13.

7. As Reinhold Niebuhr puts the matter: "Sin posits itself." See Niebuhr, *The Nature and Destiny of Man*, 2 vols. (New York: Charles Scribner's Sons, 1941), 1:252.

8. The point is put forcefully in Colin Starnes, *Augustine's Conversion: A Guide to the Argument of Confessions I–IX* (Waterloo, Ontario: Wilfrid Laurier University Press, 1990), xii.

9. The conundrum I am addressing differs from that which William S. Babcock explores. He focuses on Augustine's explanation of how evil can arise from a good will. See Babcock, "Augustine on Sin and Moral Agency," 107.

10. I use the word *imaginary* here, following Charles Taylor's locution of a "social imaginary," to focus on the way people imagine their surroundings, which is "often not expressed in theoretical terms, but is carried in images, stories, legends." See Charles Taylor, *Modern Social Imaginaries* (Durham, NC: Duke University Press, 2004), 23.

11. See Iris Murdoch, *The Sovereignty of Good* (London: Ark Paperbacks, 1970).

12. Donald D. Evans, *The Logic of Self-Involvement* (London: SCM Press, 1963), 125.

13. Ibid., 127.

14. Ibid., 128. In a similar vein Gene Outka invokes the idea of an onlook, focusing on its commissive and verdictive aspects, in his rendering of attitudinal and intentional features of Christian neighbor love; see Gene Outka, *Agape: An Ethical Analysis* (New Haven, CT: Yale University Press, 1972), 130–32.

15. James J. O'Donnell rightly identifies the parallel between this passage and Augustine's description of his friendship with his mother (more on this below). See James J. O'Donnell, "The *Confessions* of St. Augustine: Book 4," www.stoa.org/hippo/frames4.html. There is a difference, however, between Augustine's feeling "that my soul and his had been but one soul in two bodies" (describing his friendship with his unnamed friend, above) and experiencing friendship in terms of having "one life, woven out of mine and hers" (*Confessions* 9.12.30, describing his friendship with his mother, Monica). Augustine's first formulation, "unam fuisse animam in duobus corporibus" (had been but one soul in two bodies) comes from Ovid's description of the friendship between Orestes and Pylades (referenced in *Confessions* 4.6.11). The latter account defines Augustine's life and relationship with Monica following his conversion, described as "vita, quae una facta erat ex mean et illius" (one life, woven out of mine and hers).

16. Sigmund Freud, "Mourning and Melancholia," in *General Psychological Theory*, ed. Philip Rieff (New York: Touchstone, 1991), 164–79, 165. For Freud melancholics suffer from an excess of internalized self-reproach, the remedy for which is the lifting of the conscience, or superego, in order for the ego to adjust to the reality of loss. In that view we can properly mourn when the overbearing voice of conscience is silenced and the ego can adjust to the reality of another's passing. For Augustine

the remedy to melancholia is likewise a function of the reality principle. But that remedy is made possible not by the lifting of the conscience but by the transformation of the agent's onlook and priorities.

17. Peter Brown, *Augustine of Hippo: A Biography* (Berkeley: University of California Press, 1967), 52.

18. Augustine adds that he once considered evil to be a "substantial reality."

19. Jean-Luc Marion, *God Without Being*, trans. Thomas Carlson (Chicago: University of Chicago Press, 1991), 10.

20. Margaret R. Miles, "'Facie ad Faciem': Visuality, Desire, and the Discourse of the Other," *Journal of Religion* 87, no. 1 (2007): 43–58, 53.

21. Ibid.

22. Ibid., 52n42.

23. Ibid., citing Marion, *God Without Being*, 19.

24. On this distinction see Robert Sokolowski, *The God of Faith and Reason: Foundations of Christian Theology* (Washington, DC: Catholic University of America Press, 1982).

25. James Wetzel, "Book Four: The Trappings of Woe and Confession of Grief," in *A Reader's Companion to Augustine's Confessions*, ed. Kim Paffenroth and Robert P. Kennedy (Louisville, KY: Westminster/John Knox, 2003), 53–70, 69.

26. Eric Gregory, *Politics and the Order of Love: An Augustinian Ethic of Democratic Citizenship* (Chicago: University of Chicago Press, 2008), 286.

27. Wetzel, "The Trappings of Woe and Confession of Grief," 69.

28. Here I am following Boulding's edition, 236n151.

29. "Augustine will never be alone," observes Peter Brown while describing Augustine's early life. See Brown, *Augustine of Hippo*, 61.

30. This line of interpretation is put forward in Anders Nygren, *Agape and Eros*, trans. Philip S. Watson (Chicago: University of Chicago Press, 1953 [1932]). It was dispatched by John Burnaby, *Amor Dei: A Study of the Religion of St. Augustine* (London: Hodder and Stoughton, 1938), 92–100, 121–26.

31. Augustine, *Confessions* 9.13.36. Understanding how, for Augustine, grief can be hopeful is important for grasping how his response to Monica's death differs from his response to the death of his unnamed friend. O'Donnell notes this contrast as well: "The death of M. resembles and disresembles the death of A.'s friend in 4.4.7. His grief in both cases is great: accepting Christianity does not eradicate grief, but perhaps transforms it from hopeless to hopeful" (O'Donnell, "The *Confessions* of St. Augustine: Book 9," www.stoa.org/hippo/frames9.html).

32. Kim Paffenroth, "Book Nine: The Emotional Heart in the *Confessions*," in *A Reader's Companion*, 137–54, 147.

33. Murdoch, *The Sovereignty of Good*, 91 (emphasis in the original).

34. See Gabriel Marcel, *Being and Having: An Existentialist Diary* (Gloucester, MA: Peter Smith, 1976). For a discussion of Augustine, Marcel, and embodiment see Mark Wilson, "The Emotion of Regret in an Ethics of Response" (PhD diss., Indiana University, 2007).

35. Marcel, *Being and Having*, 169.
36. Ibid., 174.
37. Brown correctly understands the importance for Augustine of seeing the universe as consisting of differentiated goods, an insight made available to Augustine upon grasping Neoplatonic metaphysics. See Brown, *Augustine of Hippo*, 100.
38. I owe this thought to Margaret Mohrmann.
39. Book 9 of *Confessions* is followed by Augustine's searching discussion of memory in book 10.
40. Here Augustine seems close to John McDowell's notion of virtue as reason, understood as "an ability to recognize requirements which situations impose on one's behavior." See John McDowell, "Virtue and Reason," *Monist* 62, no. 3 (1979): 333.
41. On rules in relation to time in general, and the future in particular, see my "Rules," in *The Oxford Handbook of Theological Ethics*, ed. Gilbert Meilaender and William Werpehowski (New York: Oxford University Press, 2005), 220–36.
42. Aristotle, *Nicomachean Ethics*, in *The Basic Works of Aristotle*, ed. Richard McKeon (New York: Random House, 1941), 1106b20–24.
43. Augustine, "The Spirit and the Letter," in *Augustine: Later Works*, ed. and trans. John Burnaby (Philadelphia: Westminster Press, 1960), 215–16.
44. Reinhold Niebuhr, "Augustine's Political Realism," in *Christian Realism and Political Problems* (New York: Charles Scribner's Sons, 1953), 119–20.
45. Robin W. Lovin, *Reinhold Niebuhr and Christian Realism* (Cambridge: Cambridge University Press, 1995), 6 (emphasis mine).
46. Niebuhr gets at some of these ideas in his own way, drawing not from Platonic thought but from biblical and theological symbols in his essay "As Deceivers, Yet True," in *Beyond Tragedy: Essays in the Christian Interpretation of History* (New York: Charles Scribner's Sons, 1937), 3–24.
47. Stanley Hauerwas expresses this idea in his discussion of "freedom as the presence of the other," in *The Peaceable Kingdom: A Primer in Christian Ethics* (Notre Dame, IN: University of Notre Dame Press, 1983), 44–46. But rather than say, as Hauerwas does, that the other's "need is often the occasion of our freedom," Augustine's idea is that one cannot ascertain the alterity of the other without first being freed from self-preoccupation. On those terms he and Hauerwas would concur with the latter's claim that "the 'otherness' of another's character not only invites me to an always imperfect imitation, but challenges me to recognize the way my vision is restricted by my own preoccupation" (Hauerwas, *The Peaceable Kingdom*, 45).

8. JUST WAR, CIVIC VIRTUE, AND DEMOCRATIC SOCIAL CRITICISM

1. By "just-war doctrine" I refer to the body of reflection in Western theology and ethics regarding the ethics of going to war (*jus ad bellum*) and the conduct of participants in war (*jus in bello*). Contemporary works developing this general body of ideas include Paul Ramsey, *War and the Christian Conscience: How Shall*

Modern War Be Conducted Justly? (Durham, NC: Duke University Press, 1961); Paul Ramsey, *The Just War: Force and Moral Responsibility* (New York: Charles Scribner's Sons, 1968); Michael Walzer, *Just and Unjust Wars: A Moral Argument with Historical Illustrations* (New York: Basic Books, 1977); Michael Walzer, *Arguing About War* (New Haven, CT: Yale University Press, 2004); William V. O'Brien, *The Conduct of Just and Unjust War* (New York: Praeger, 1981); James Turner Johnson, *Just War Tradition and the Restraint of War: A Moral and Historical Inquiry* (Princeton, NJ: Princeton University Press, 1981); U.S. Catholic Bishops, *The Challenge of Peace: God's Promise and Our Response* (Washington, DC: National Conference of Catholic Bishops, 1983); James F. Childress, *Moral Responsibility in Conflicts: Essays on Nonviolence, War, and Conscience* (Baton Rouge: Louisiana State University Press, 1982); Jenny Teichman, *Pacifism and the Just War: A Study in Applied Philosophy* (Oxford: Blackwell, 1986); Ian Clark, *Waging War: A Philosophical Introduction* (Oxford: Clarendon, 1990); Richard B. Miller, *Interpretations of Conflict: Ethics, Pacifism, and the Just-War Tradition* (Chicago: University of Chicago Press, 1991); Lisa Sowle Cahill, *Love Your Enemies: Discipleship, Pacifism, and Just War Theory* (Minneapolis, MN: Fortress, 1994); Terry Nardin, ed., *The Ethics of War and Peace: Religious and Secular Perspectives* (Princeton, NJ: Princeton University Press, 1996); A. J. Coates, *The Ethics of War* (Manchester: Manchester University Press, 1997); Jean Bethke Elshtain, *Just War Against Terror: The Burden of American Power in a Violent World* (New York: Basic Books, 2003); Oliver O'Donovan, *The Just War Revisited* (Cambridge: Cambridge University Press, 2003); Brian Orend, *The Morality of War* (Orchard Park, NY: Broadview, 2006); Jeff McMahan, *Killing in War* (Oxford: Clarendon, 2009); and Nigel Biggar, *In Defence of War* (Oxford: Oxford University Press, 2013).

2. For a searching critique of this and related points see Reinhold Niebuhr's discussion of the morality of nations and political psychology in his *Moral Man and Immoral Society: A Study in Ethics and Politics* (New York: Charles Scribner's Sons, 1932), 83–112. Thanks to Matt Miller for calling my attention to this line of Niebuhr's thinking.

3. G. E. M. Anscombe, "The Justice of the Present War Examined," in *The Collected Philosophical Papers of G. E. M. Anscombe*, vol. 3, *Ethics, Religion and Politics* (Oxford: Basil Blackwell, 1981), 81.

4. Ibid., 72.

5. Ibid., 81.

6. The phrase is from Ramsey, *The Just War*, 367.

7. U.S. Catholic Bishops, *The Challenge of Peace*, pars. 279–329.

8. More general ideas connecting moral philosophy and sociology are found in Alasdair MacIntyre, *After Virtue: A Study in Moral Theory* (Notre Dame, IN: University of Notre Dame Press, 1981), 22.

9. The phrase is taken from Anscombe, "The Justice of the Present War Examined."

10. John Rawls, *A Theory of Justice* (Cambridge, MA: Harvard/Belknap, 1971), 454.

11. Alexis de Tocqueville, *Democracy in America*, trans. George Lawrence, ed. J. P. Mayer (New York: Doubleday/Anchor Books, 1969), 287.

12. See chap. 1.

13. See Paul Ricoeur, *Memory, History, Forgetting*, trans. Kathleen Blamey and David Pellauer (Chicago: University of Chicago Press, 2004), 68.

14. See Walzer, *Just and Unjust Wars*, 41. Walzer's approach avoids the charge of disembodiment that I raise in the next paragraph given his use of historical examples and connections to casuistry (ibid., xxx).

15. For discussions of Augustine and the just war see Herbert Deane, *The Political and Social Ideas of St. Augustine* (New York: Columbia University Press, 1963); Richard Shelly Hartigan, "Saint Augustine on War and Killing: The Problem of the Innocent," *Journal of the History of Ideas* 27 (April-June 1966): 195–204; Louis J. Swift, "Augustine on War and Killing: Another View," *Harvard Theological Review* 66 (July 1973): 369–83; Frederick H. Russell, *The Just War in the Middle Ages* (Cambridge: Cambridge University Press, 1975); Frederick H. Russell, "War," in *Augustine Through the Ages: An Encyclopedia*, ed. Allan D. Fitzgerald (Grand Rapids, MI: Eerdmans, 1999), 875–76; R. A. Markus, "Saint Augustine's Views on the 'Just War,'" in *The Church and War*, ed. W. J. Sheils (Oxford: Basil Blackwell, 1983), 1–13; John Langan, "The Elements of St. Augustine's Just War Theory," *Journal of Religious Ethics* 12, no. 1 (1984): 19–38; David A. Lenihan, "The Just War Theory in the Work of Saint Augustine," *Augustinian Studies* 19 (1988): 37–70; Robert L. Holmes, "St. Augustine and Just-War Theory," in *The Augustinian Tradition*, ed. Gareth B. Matthews (Berkeley: University of California Press, 1999), 323–44; Ramsey, *War and the Christian Conscience*, 15–33; Johnson, *Just War Tradition and the Restraint of War*, 150–65, 349–51; and Cahill, *Love Your Enemies*, 55–80.

16. Augustine, "Letter 47, to Publicola," in *A Select Library of Nicene and Post-Nicene Fathers*, vol. 1, ed. Philip Schaff and Henry Wace (Grand Rapids, MI: Eerdmans, 1956), 293.

17. Augustine, *Concerning the City of God Against the Pagans*, trans. Henry Bettenson (New York: Penguin, 1972), 1.26.

18. The key passage by Ambrose is notably brief: "He who does not keep harm off a friend, if he can, is as much in fault as he who causes it." See Ambrose, "On the Duties of the Clergy," in *A Select Library of Nicene and Post-Nicene Fathers*, vol. 10, ed. Philip Schaff and Henry Wace (New York: Christian Literature, 1896), 1.36.179. See also Ramsey, *War and the Christian Conscience*, 15–33; and Ramsey, *The Just War*, 141–47.

19. See William S. Babcock, "*Cupiditas* and *Caritas*: The Early Augustine on Love and Human Fulfillment," in *The Ethics of St. Augustine*, ed. William S. Babcock (Atlanta, GA: Scholars Press, 1991), 44; and John M. Rist, *Augustine: Ancient Thought Baptized* (Cambridge: Cambridge University Press, 1994), 174.

20. Letter 82.3 in *Works of Saint Augustine: A Translation for the Twenty-First Century*, part 3, vol. 3 (Sermons 51–94), trans. Edmund Hill, ed. John E. Rotelle

(Brooklyn, NY: New City Press, 1990), 370. Rist summarizes Augustine's position well: "'Private violence' demoralizes and brutalizes the agent." See Rist, *Augustine: Ancient Thought Baptized*, 194.

21. The comment is from Augustine's interlocutor, Evodius, but Augustine concurs with the premise in the dialogue. See Augustine, *On Free Choice of the Will*, trans. Thomas Williams (Indianapolis, IN: Hackett, 1993), 9.

22. Ibid.

23. Augustine, "Reply to Faustus the Manichean," in *A Select Library of Nicene and Post-Nicene Fathers*, vol. 4, ed. Philip Schaff (Grand Rapids, MI: Eerdmans, 1956), par. 75.

24. Augustine, *City of God* 1.21.

25. For a discussion of this and related points in the context of Augustine's developing views of killing and suffering see Kevin Carnahan, "Perturbations of the Soul and Pains of the Body: Augustine on Evil Suffered and Done in War," *Journal of Religious Ethics* 36, no. 2 (2008): 269–94.

26. Augustine, *City of God* 19.17.

27. Ibid., 19.13; see also 3.10. Carnahan instructively discusses these passages in "Perturbations of the Soul," 285. See also Augustine, *City of God* 19.14 and 19.17.

28. Augustine, *On Free Choice of the Will*, 8.

29. Augustine, "Reply to Faustus the Manichean," par. 74.

30. Augustine, *City of God* 19.12, 19.13, 19.17.

31. Augustine, "Reply to Faustus the Manichean," par. 76.

32. Miller, *Interpretations of Conflict*, 18–23.

33. O'Donovan, *The Just War Revisited*, 9. In the letter to Boniface (189) in question, Augustine writes that the obligation to extend mercy to the vanquished in war is an exercise of restorative justice, not that war's proper aim is to protect the innocent. For a discussion of Augustine and restorative justice see J. Warren Smith, "Augustine and the Limits of Preemptive and Preventive War," *Journal of Religious Ethics* 35, no. 1 (2007): 141–62.

34. U.S. Catholic Bishops, *The Challenge of Peace*, par. 81.

35. "What We're Fighting For," included as an appendix in Elshtain, *Just War Against Terror*, 189; see also Garry Wills, "What Is a Just War?" *New York Review of Books*, Nov. 18, 2004, 33.

36. Augustine, "Letter 189: Augustine to Boniface (417)," in *Augustine: Political Writings*, ed. E. M. Atkins and R. J. Dodaro (Cambridge: Cambridge University Press, 2001), 216.

37. Ibid., 217.

38. Augustine, "Letter 153: Augustine to Macedonius (413/414)," in Atkins and Dodaro, *Augustine: Political Writings*, 81.

39. In one context Augustine uses *benevolence* to describe the just warrior's proper ordering of dispositions toward certain ends. In a letter to Marcellinus, Augustine writes that Christians "should always have perfect benevolence in case we return evil for evil." Understood in that way, benevolence serves a negative, chastening

function. For those who claim that Augustine understands war as an expression of beneficent care for the innocent, it is interesting to note that in this letter he understands acting benevolently to mean that "people are often to be helped, against their will, by being punished with a sort of kind harshness." The beneficence involved, in other words, targets wrongdoers, not victims. See Augustine, "Letter 138: Augustine to Marcellinus (411/412)," in Atkins and Dodaro, *Augustine: Political Writings*, 38.

40. As William S. Babcock puts it: "It is *cupiditas*, the *amor* for things that can be lost against one's will (*De lib arb*. 1.4.10), that gives birth to this desperate sense that others constitute a threat to self. Fearing loss, it seeks to secure against loss by removing or dominating others so as to eliminate the threat they represent. . . . It sets one person against another; and the only answer to it is another love, or rather love for another object that is not vulnerable to loss." See Babcock, "*Cupiditas* and *Caritas*," 47.

41. I borrow this way of phrasing Augustine's view from Troeltsch's account of what he calls the relative natural law. See Ernst Troeltsch, *The Social Teachings of the Christian Churches*, trans. Olive Wyon, 2 vols. (Chicago: University of Chicago Press, 1981), 1:153.

42. Augustine, "Letter 138: Augustine to Marcellinus," in Atkins and Dodaro, *Augustine: Political Writings*, 38.

43. See Augustine, "Reply to Faustus the Manichean," par. 75. To the modern reader these comments and their attention to character say frustratingly little that echoes the idea that war is justified and limited in principled ways. While it is true that Augustine shows little interest in questions such as noncombatant immunity, the *jus in bello*, and the related idea of human rights, it requires little to draw out such ideas from his account. Intentionally killing innocent persons is symptomatic of a deeper set of disordered motives. Such killing is wrong on Augustinian terms because it flows from concupiscent affections. Others' claim to be left alone is violated by persons who seek to subject them to their avaricious desires. As Babcock suggests, attending to how virtues restrain human impulses enables us to see how Augustine could speak to such modern concerns. Langan's views on this matter are qualified, but he captures the general point when he observes that Augustine's warnings against being motivated by revenge "point the way to a limitation of the horrors of war by focusing on the virtues and attitudes of warriors. This does not eliminate the need for a rule of noncombatant immunity, but it is reasonable to think that care to develop a regard for certain moral virtues and values among soldiers would contribute in an important and perhaps decisive way to the preservation of many of the values which the rules of *jus in bello* are designed to protect." See Hartigan, "Saint Augustine on War and Killing"; Langan, "Elements of St. Augustine's Just-War Theory," 32; and Swift, "Augustine on War and Killing."

44. I say "in part" so as not to exclude the purpose of defending temporal goods, as I noted earlier.

45. Rist, *Augustine: Ancient Thought Baptized*, 195.

46. Augustine, *City of God* 19.7.

47. These two deaths are differently related to the virtue of hope, itself a fruit of Augustine's conversion. For instructive discussions of grief, time, hope, and the deaths of Augustine's friend and mother see Genevieve Lloyd, "Augustine and the 'Problem' of Time," in Matthews, *The Augustinian Tradition*, 41–45; Kim Paffenroth, "Book Nine: The Emotional Heart of the *Confessions*," in *A Reader's Guide to Augustine's Confessions*, ed. Kim Paffenroth and Robert P. Kennedy (Louisville, KY: Westminster/John Knox, 2003), 137–54.

48. See chap. 7 herein. Mourning is a response to death for Augustine and has deep connections to his awareness of human finitude and the power of time more generally. Mourning, then, has moral and ontological aspects. In that respect we must read Augustine's narrative account of his grief in relation to his theological account of humanity's being-in-time in book 11 of *Confessions*. As an act of memory, mourning for Augustine would be an act of what Ricoeur calls "being-in-the-face-of-death, against-death." See Ricoeur, *Memory, History, Forgetting*, 369; Lloyd, "Augustine and the 'Problem' of Time."

49. Augustine, *City of God* 14.6.

50. Ibid., 19.17. Subsequent citations of this source are referenced parenthetically in the text.

51. Paul Lauritzen, "Emotions and Religious Ethics," *Journal of Religious Ethics* 16, no. 2 (1988): 307–24, 308.

52. See Charles Taylor, *Sources of the Self: The Making of the Modern Identity* (Cambridge, MA: Harvard University Press, 1989), 3–24.

53. See Richard Dagger, *Civic Virtues: Rights, Citizenship, and Republican Liberalism* (New York: Oxford University Press, 1997), 13–14.

54. John Milbank's interpretation of the *City of God* seems to gesture in this direction, especially when he writes that Augustine achieves an immanent critique "or deconstruction of antique political society." See John Milbank, *Theology and Social Theory* (London: Basil Blackwell, 1990), 389.

55. Augustine, *City of God* 15.5. But Augustine adds a difference: the quarrel between Remus and Romulus "demonstrated the division of the earthly city against itself; while the conflict between Cain and Abel displayed the conflict between . . . the City of God and the city of men" (ibid.).

56. See ibid., 2.17–19.

57. For a discussion see Jennifer A. Herdt, *Putting on Virtue: The Legacy of the Splendid Vices* (Chicago: University of Chicago Press, 2008), 45–71.

58. Rawls, *A Theory of Justice*, 454.

59. On chastened civic virtue see Jean Bethke Elshtain, *Women and War* (New York: Basic Books, 1987), 252. For Elshtain's reflections on Augustine's theology, ethics, and politics see her *Augustine and the Limits of Politics* (Notre Dame, IN: University of Notre Dame Press, 1995).

60. See Aristotle, *Politics* 7.2. For a discussion of "militarism" see Coates, *The Ethics of War*, 40–76.

61. Amy Gutmann and Dennis Thompson, *Democracy and Disagreement* (Cambridge, MA: Harvard University Press, 1996), 52.

62. Reinhold Niebuhr, *The Children of Light and the Children of Darkness* (New York: Charles Scribner's Sons, 1944).

63. For an exception see McMahan, *Killing in War.*

64. See Walzer, *Just and Unjust Wars*, chaps. 3 and 19; and David R. Mapel, "Coerced Moral Agents? Individual Responsibility for Military Service," *Journal of Political Philosophy* 6, no. 2 (1998): 171–89.

65. See Hannah Fenichel Pitkin, *The Concept of Representation* (Berkeley: University of California Press, 1967).

66. Gutmann and Thompson, *Democracy and Disagreement*, 4.

67. On the idea of spiritual exercises see Pierre Hadot, *Philosophy as a Way of Life: Spiritual Exercises from Socrates to Foucault*, ed. Arnold I. Davidson (Oxford: Blackwell, 1995).

68. On memory see Maurice Halbwachs, *On Collective Memory*, ed. and trans. Lewis A. Coser (Chicago: University of Chicago Press, 1992); Mary Warnock, *Memory* (London: Faber, 1987); Elie Weisel, *Ethics and Memory* (Berlin: Walter de Gruyter, 1997); Edith Wyschogrod, *An Ethics of Remembering: History, Heterology, and the Nameless Others* (Chicago: University of Chicago Press, 1998); Edward S. Casey, *Remembering: A Phenomenological Study* (Bloomington: Indiana University Press, 2000); Avishai Margalit, *The Ethics of Memory* (Cambridge, MA: Harvard University Press, 2002); Ricoeur, *Memory, History, Forgetting*; and W. James Booth, *Communities of Memory: On Witness, Identity, and Justice* (Ithaca, NY: Cornell University Press, 2006). I will address issues of memory and ethics more extensively in the next chapter.

69. Benedict Anderson, *Imagined Communities: Reflections on the Origin and Spread of Nationalism*, 2nd ed. (London: Verso, 1991).

70. By "public history" I mean the recollection of a community's past in public documents, holidays, ceremonies, and commemorative practices.

71. Booth, *Communities of Memory*, 52.

72. George Orwell, *1984*, with an afterword by Erich Fromm (New York: New American Library, 1950), 35

73. See also Augustine's sermon "The Sacking of the City of Rome," in Atkins and Dodaro, *Augustine: Political Writings*, 205–14.

74. Ricoeur, *Memory, History, Forgetting*, 68. Memory for Augustine is subject to the power of time, also understood as the power of death. Book 11 of *Confessions*, exploring time as both a condition for and subject of memory, underscores finite humanity's being-toward-death, the fact that time is "the impending state of not being." See *Confessions* 11.14. Ricoeur engages Heidegger on memory, historicity, and death in *Memory, History, Forgetting*, 357–69. See also note 48 above.

75. Augustine's attention to collective memory is evident in *City of God*; to individual memory in *Confessions*, esp. books 10 and 11; and Augustine, *On the Trinity, Books 8–15*, ed. Gareth B. Matthews (Cambridge: Cambridge University Press, 2002), bks. 12–15. For a discussion of Augustine on individual memory see Roland Teske,

"Augustine's Philosophy of Memory," in *The Cambridge Companion to Augustine*, ed. Eleonore Stump and Norman Kretzmann (Cambridge: Cambridge University Press, 2001), 148–58.

76. On commemorative practices and public history see John Bodnar, *Remaking America: Public Memory, Commemoration, and Patriotism in the Twentieth Century* (Princeton, NJ: Princeton University Press, 1992); Dominick La Capra, *History and Meaning After Auschwitz* (Ithaca, NY: Cornell University Press, 1998); Jenny Edkins, *Trauma and the Memory of Politics* (Cambridge: Cambridge University Press, 2003); Edward T. Linenthal, *Sacred Ground: Americans and Their Battlefields* (Urbana: University of Illinois Press, 1991); Edward T. Linenthal, *The Unfinished Bombing: Oklahoma City in American Memory* (New York: Oxford University Press, 2001); Alison Landsberg, *Prosthetic Memory: The Transformation of American Remembrance in the Age of Mass Culture* (New York: Columbia University Press, 2004); David Simpson, *9/11: The Culture of Commemoration* (Chicago: University of Chicago Press, 2006); Oren Baruch Stier and J. Shawn Landres, eds., *Religion, Violence, Memory, and Place* (Bloomington: Indiana University Press, 2006); Marita Sturken, *Tangled Memories: The Vietnam War, the AIDS Epidemic, and the Politics of Remembering* (Berkeley: University of California Press, 1997); and James E. Young, *The Texture of Memory: Holocaust Memorials and Meaning* (New Haven, CT: Yale University Press, 1993).

77. Anscombe, "The Justice of the Present War Examined," 81.

9. THE MORAL AND POLITICAL BURDENS OF MEMORY

1. Two exceptions are Nigel Biggar, ed., *Burying the Past: Making Peace and Doing Justice after Civil Conflict* (Washington, DC: Georgetown University Press, 2001); and Bjorn Krondorfer, "Is Forgetting Reprehensible? Holocaust Remembrance and the Task of Oblivion," *Journal of Religious Ethics* 36, no. 2 (2008): 233–67.

2. Alasdair MacIntyre, *After Virtue: A Study in Moral Theory* (Notre Dame, IN: University of Notre Dame Press, 1981).

3. See Mary Warnock, *Memory* (London: Faber and Faber, 1987); and Edward S. Casey, *Remembering: A Phenomenological Study*, 2nd ed. (Bloomington: Indiana University Press, 2000).

4. W. James Booth, *Communities of Memory: On Witness, Identity, and Justice* (Ithaca, NY: Cornell University Press, 2006), x.

5. See John Sutton, "Memory," *Stanford Encyclopedia of Philosophy*, http://plato.stanford.edu/entries/memory.

6. As Sutton notes, the first form of memory is nondeclarative whereas the second and third are declarative. That is to say, the second and third forms of memory are representational: they claim to say something about the world. Propositional and recollective memory, then, must satisfy veridical criteria. When it comes to "memory that" or "memory when," we naturally distinguish between reliable and unreliable forms.

7. Benedict Anderson, *Imagined Communities: Reflections on the Origins and Spread of Nationalism*, 2nd ed. (London: Verso, 1991).

8. Elie Wiesel, *Ethics and Memory* (Berlin: Walter de Gruyter, 1997), 15.

9. See Paul Ricoeur, *Memory, History, Forgetting*, trans. Kathleen Blamey and David Pellauer (Chicago: University of Chicago Press, 2004), 96.

10. Halbwachs writes, "While the collective memory endures and draws strength from its base in a coherent body of people, it is individuals as group members who remember." Quoted in Lewis Coser, "Introduction: Maurice Halbwachs, 1877–1945," in *On Collective Memory*, trans. and ed. Lewis Coser (Chicago: University of Chicago Press, 1992), 22.

11. See Avishai Margalit, *The Ethics of Memory* (Cambridge, MA: Harvard University Press, 2002), 51.

12. Casey, *Remembering*, part 3.

13. John Bodnar, *Remaking America: Public Memory, Commemoration, and Patriotism in the Twentieth Century* (Princeton, NJ: Princeton University Press, 1992), 13–14.

14. Alison Landsberg, *Prosthetic Memory: The Transformation of American Remembrance in the Age of Mass Culture* (New York: Columbia University Press, 2004), 141–55, 8. Landsberg rejects the pejorative account of mass culture developed by members of the Frankfurt School and argues for mass culture's potential for inculcating empathy.

15. Ibid., 99–100.

16. Ibid., 8–9.

17. Sigmund Freud, *The Ego and the Id*, trans. Joan Riviere, ed. James Strachey (1923; New York: Norton, 1962).

18. Sutton, "Memory."

19. Sue Campbell, "Our Faithfulness to the Past: Reconstructing Memory Value," *Philosophical Psychology* 19, no. 3 (2006): 361–80, 362.

20. Ibid., 362–63. Campbell's distinction between archival and reconstructive memory echoes Husserl's distinction between "retention or primary memory and reproduction or secondary memory," as described in Ricoeur, *Memory, History, Forgetting*, 31–36. Ricoeur, echoing Campbell, assigns primacy to what Husserl calls secondary memory or what Campbell calls reconstructive memory.

21. Booth, *Communities of Memory*, 52.

22. Jenny Edkins, *Trauma and the Memory of Politics* (New York: Cambridge University Press, 2003), 15–16.

23. Jorge Luis Borges, *Collected Fictions*, trans. Andrew Hurley (New York: Penguin, 1998), 137.

24. Margalit, *The Ethics of Memory*, 105. Subsequent citations of this source are referenced parenthetically in the text.

25. For a related discussion see Jeffrie Murphy and Jean Hampton, *Forgiveness and Mercy* (New York: Cambridge University Press, 1998), 29.

26. Margalit, *The Ethics of Memory*, 79, 83.

27. See Christine Korsgaard, "Personal Identity and the Unity of Agency: A Kantian Response to Parfit," *Philosophy and Public Affairs* 18, no. 2 (1989): 101–32.

28. Booth, *Communities of Memory*, xiii. Subsequent citations of this source are referenced parenthetically in the text.

29. See also Casey, *Remembering*, 262–87.

30. See Barbara Misztal, "Memory and Democracy," *American Behavioral Scientist* 48, no. 10 (2005): 1320–38.

31. Thanks to John Lucaites for this example. See www.timeanddate.com/holidays/us/confederate-memorial-day.

32. Yet he also writes: "Pardon, mercy, and forgiveness . . . all calm vengeful memory without the need for forgetting" (152).

33. Ricoeur, *Memory, History, Forgetting*, 36–40. Subsequent citations of this source are referenced parenthetically in the text.

34. Despite setting the stage for considering the "duty of memory" at various points in this work, Ricoeur never systematically takes up the idea. See 69, 86–88, 90, 404, 413, 418, and 469.

35. Ricoeur, like Booth, understands memory to be linked to the imputation of responsibility. Following Locke, Ricoeur sees memory linked to identity in a forensic way, as the (practical) basis for holding individuals to account. See Ricoeur, *Memory, History, Forgetting*, 102–9.

36. Ricoeur would doubtless find much of what passes as the "use of history" in religious ethics as failing to count as scholarly history insofar as it fails to include this second phase. For Ricoeur, creating a narrative that draws on historical sources only invokes the first and the third phases of historical writing. History must also include the effort to address the "why" question with an explanation.

37. Readers familiar with Ricoeur's work should note that *Memory, History, Forgetting* is meant to form a trilogy with *Time and Narrative* (1984–88) and *Oneself as Other* (1992). Memory mediates between time and narrative, and it connects us to others in debt and shared responsibility.

38. Note that each main section, despite its focus on reproducing the past, gestures toward a productive present and future, typically in one or another form of sociality and self-awareness. The investigation into memory concludes with a discussion of its communal dimensions; the investigation into history concludes with a discussion of history's uncanniness in the face of history's various aporias; and the investigation into forgetting concludes with a discussion of amnesty not as commanded amnesia but as forgetfulness as "a wish in the optative mood" (*Memory, History, Forgetting*, 456). Together these three investigations converge at the horizon of forgiveness, about which I will say more below.

39. Peter Balakian, *The Burning Tigris: The Armenian Genocide and America's Response* (New York: HarperCollins, 2003).

40. See also Paul Ricoeur, *Freud and Philosophy: An Essay on Interpretation*, trans. Denis Savage (New Haven, CT: Yale University Press, 1970).

41. Jeffrey Blustein, *The Moral Demands of Memory* (Cambridge: Cambridge University Press, 2008), 21. Subsequent citations of this source are referenced parenthetically in the text.

42. See Aristotle, *Nicomachean Ethics*, 1114b1–8.

43. See Elizabeth Anderson, *Value in Ethics and Economics* (Cambridge, MA: Harvard University Press, 1993), 17–43.

44. See Søren Kierkegaard, *Works of Love*, ed. and trans. Howard V. Hong and Edna H. Hong (Princeton, NJ: Princeton University Press, 1995), 2nd series, IX, 345–58.

45. See also J. David Velleman, "Love as a Moral Emotion," *Ethics* 109, no. 2 (1999): 338–74.

46. Casey, *Remembering*, 181–215.

47. Margalit, *The Ethics of Memory*, 10.

48. Oren Baruch Stier and Shawn Landres, introduction to *Religion, Violence, Memory, and Place*, ed. Oren Baruch Stier and Shawn Landres (Bloomington: Indiana University Press, 2006), 1, 5.

49. Ibid., 7. Yet the editors seem to equivocate. Earlier in their introduction they back away from positing any essential connection between religion and memory when they state that memorial activity of a habitual sort "often is religious in nature" (5).

50. Tabarre is the neighborhood in which the monument is located.

51. Terry Rey, "Vodou, Water, and Exile: Symbolizing Spirit and Pain in Port-au-Prince," in Stier and Landres, eds., *Religion, Violence, Memory, and Place*, 204.

52. James Foard, "Vehicles of Memory: The *Enola Gay* and the Streetcars of Hiroshima," in Stier and Landres, eds., *Religion, Violence, Memory, and Place*, 118. Subsequent citations of this source are referenced parenthetically in the text.

53. Flora A. Keshgegian, "Finding a Place Past Night: Armenian Genocidal Memory in Diaspora," in Stier and Landres, eds., *Religion, Violence, Memory, and Place*, 105.

10. RELIGION, PUBLIC REASON, AND
THE MORALITY OF DEMOCRATIC AUTHORITY

1. John Rawls, *A Theory of Justice* (Cambridge, MA: Belknap, 1971), 453–62.

2. My terminology here follows John P. Reeder Jr., "What Is a Religious Ethic?" *Journal of Religious Ethics* 25, no. 3 [25th Anniversary Supplement] (1997): 157–81.

3. John Rawls, "The Idea of Public Reason Revisited," in *Collected Papers*, ed. Samuel Freeman (Cambridge, MA: Harvard University Press, 1999), 573–615, 574. Subsequent citations of this source are referenced parenthetically in the text.

4. John Rawls, *Political Liberalism*, exp. ed. (New York: Columbia University Press, 2005 [1993]), 13.

5. As will become plain below, public reason is "secular" insofar as it is nonreligious in its foundations. Public reason thereby enters into discussions of varieties of secularism. But again: the secularism from which public reason distinguishes itself is secularism as a comprehensive doctrine.

6. That is to say, authority is not secured on majoritarian grounds, as I will make plain below.

7. I say "reasonably" here to underscore the idealized understanding of public reason-giving, viewed in this way: the reasons offered are not those that appeal to the base interests of other citizens. They rather seek to appeal to values that citizens share as members of a democracy.

8. Jeffrey Stout, *Democracy and Tradition* (Princeton, NJ: Princeton University Press, 2004), 77.

9. See Stephen Macedo, "Liberal Civic Education and Religious Fundamentalism: The Case of God v. John Rawls?" *Ethics* 105, no. 3 (1995): 468–96, 492.

10. Rawls, "The Idea of Public Reason Revisited," 576.

11. Stout rightly grasps Rawls's understanding of "private" and "public" domains in his theory of public reason, but Stout's own view of *public* in an "ordinary sense" mars his discussion of religion and public reason in *Democracy and Tradition*. Aware that Hauerwas's presentation could well meet the test of public reason insofar as he was not speaking at a political campaign rally or before a congressional commit-tee, Stout offers another example: "Suppose another Christian pacifist did speak at a campaign rally for a political candidate representing the Green Party. Wouldn't it be good, all things considered, for her arguments to circulate publicly? How can we know in advance that they won't be persuasive?" As I will make plain, the ques-tion for democracy prescinds from having us ask whether such speech is good, "all things considered." The key is to determine whether such speech addresses others in ways that accord with basic democratic values. Stout further confuses matters, and considerably weakens the force of either of these examples, when he states that in his discussion of religion and public reason he is "not addressing the distinctive issues surrounding the roles of judge, juror, attorney, or public official." As I make plain below, public reason pertains to the role morality of those public offices. See Stout, *Democracy and Tradition*, 315n11, 315n14.

12. Rawls, "The Idea of Public Reason Revisited," 574.

13. See Robert Audi and Nicholas Wolterstorff, *Religion in the Public Square: The Place of Religious Convictions in Political Debate* (New York: Rowman and Little-field, 1997); and Richard Rorty, "Religion in the Public Square: A Reconsideration," *Journal of Religious Ethics* 31, no. 1 (2003): 141–49.

14. Rawls, "The Idea of Public Reason Revisited," 577.

15. Rawls, *Political Liberalism*, 217.

16. For an overview and typology see Amy Gutmann, "Democracy," in *A Compan-ion to Contemporary Political Philosophy*, ed. Robert E. Goodin and Philip Pettit (Oxford: Blackwell, 1993), 411–21.

17. Corey Brettschneider, *Democratic Rights: The Substance of Self-Government* (Princeton, NJ: Princeton University Press, 2007), 19–23, 19.

18. Ibid., 28–29.

19. John Rawls, "Justice-as-Fairness: Political Not Metaphysical," *Philosophy and Public Affairs* 14, no. 3 (1985): 223–51.

20. Rawls, *Political Liberalism*, 54–58; Rawls, "The Idea of Public Reason Revisited," 573–74.
21. Bruce Lincoln, *Authority: Construction and Corrosion* (Chicago: University of Chicago Press, 1994), 143.
22. Nicholas Wolterstorff, "The Role of Religion in Decision and Discussion of Political Issues," in Audi and Wolterstorff, *Religion in the Public Square*, 105 (emphasis in the original).
23. Charles Larmore, *The Autonomy of Morality* (Cambridge: Cambridge University Press, 2008), 199.
24. See Brettschneider, *Democratic Rights*, 75.
25. Robert L. Katz, *Empathy: Its Nature and Uses* (New York: Free Press of Glencoe, 1963), 7; and Stephen Darwall, "Empathy, Sympathy, Care," *Philosophical Studies* 89, no. 2/3 (1998): 261–82, 270. For an overview see Nancy E. Snow, "Empathy," *American Philosophical Quarterly* 37, no. 1 (2000): 65–78.
26. Rawls, *A Theory of Justice*, 500. Subsequent citations of this source are referenced parenthetically in the text.
27. On simulation and empathy see Nancy Sherman, "Empathy and Imagination," *Midwest Studies in Philosophy* 22, no. 1 (1998): 82–119.
28. Connecting Rawls's ideas to notions of empathy is not new; Susan Moller Okin argues that on a reconstructed interpretation of Rawls's idea of the veil of ignorance, empathy is a necessary requirement. See Susan Moller Okin, *Justice, Gender, and the Family* (New York: Basic Books, 1989), 101.
29. See Rawls, *A Theory of Justice*, 462.
30. Michael J. Sandel, *Democracy's Discontent: America in Search of a Public Philosophy* (Cambridge, MA: Harvard University Press, 1996), 19.
31. See, e.g., Sandel's criticism of justice-as-fairness as the first virtue of institutions in Rawls's *A Theory of Justice* in Michael J. Sandel, *Liberalism and the Limits of Justice*, 2nd ed. (Cambridge: Cambridge University Press, 1998 [1982]), 31–35, 168–69.
32. Thanks to Peter de Marneffe for raising this point.
33. See Christopher J. Eberle, *Religious Conviction in Liberal Politics* (Cambridge: Cambridge University Press, 2002), 104–8.
34. Ibid., 267. See also Wolterstorff, "The Role of Religion in Political Issues," 69, 82, 87.
35. By *religious* Eberle means "theistic."
36. Eberle, *Religious Conviction in Liberal Politics*, 84–102.
37. For a discussion see Vic McCracken, "In Defense of Restraint: Democratic Respect, Public Justification, and Religious Conviction in Liberal Politics," *Journal of the Society of Christian Ethics* 32, no. 1 (2012): 133–49.
38. Hence Rawls's description of public reason as connected to the "duty of civility" in "The Idea of Public Reason Revisited," 576.
39. Jeremy Waldron, "Religious Contributions in Public Deliberation," *San Diego Law Review* 30 (Fall 1993): 829.
40. Rawls, "The Idea of Public Reason Revisited," 591, 592.

41. Brettschneider, *Democratic Rights*, 62.
42. Rawls, "The Idea of Public Reason Revisited," 592.
43. See www.law.cornell.edu/supct/pdf/02-102P.ZS.
44. See Paul VI, *Humanae vitae*, www.vatican.va/holy_father/paul_vi/encyclicals /documents/hf_p-vi_enc_25071968_humanae-vitae_en.html.
45. Gerard V. Bradley and Robert P. George, "Brief Amicus Curiae of the Family Research Council and Focus on the Family in Support of the Respondent," http:// supreme.lp.findlaw.com/supreme_court/briefs/02-102/02-102.mer.ami.frc.pdf.
46. See Okin, *Justice, Gender, and the Family*; and Rawls, *A Theory of Justice*, 6.
47. See Andrew Sullivan, "Unnatural Law," *New Republic*, March 24, 2003, 22.
48. Email correspondence with James F. Childress, Jan. 16, 2011.
49. Gilbert Meilaender, "Begetting and Cloning," First Things, June/July 1997, www .firstthings.com/article/1997/06/005-begetting-and-cloning.
50. See William F. May, "Comments to the President's Council on Bioethics," Oct. 17, 2002, http://bioethicsarchive.georgetown.edu/pcbe/transcripts/oct02/oct17full .html.; and Michael J. Sandel, *The Case Against Perfection: Ethics in the Age of Genetic Engineering* (Cambridge, MA: Belknap, 2007), 45.
51. See Susan Cohen, "A House Divided," *Washington Post Magazine*, Oct. 12, 1997, 15.
52. Onora O'Neill addresses complaints about "abstraction," to be distinguished from "idealization," in Onora O'Neill, *Towards Justice and Virtue* (Cambridge: Cambridge University Press, 1996), 38–44.
53. For a discussion see Reeder, "What Is a Religious Ethic?" 157–81.
54. See John A. Robertson, *Children of Choice: Freedom and the New Reproductive Technologies* (Princeton, NJ: Princeton University Press, 1994).
55. Ronald M. Green, "Much Ado About Mutton: An Ethical Review of the Cloning Controversy," in *Cloning and the Future of Human Embryo Research*, ed. Paul Lauritzen (New York: Oxford University Press, 2001), 114–31, 120. Subsequent citations of this source are referenced parenthetically in the text.
56. Dan W. Brock, "Cloning Human Beings: An Assessment of the Ethical Issues Pro and Con," in *Cloning and the Future of Human Embryo Research*, ed. Paul Lauritzen (New York: Oxford University Press, 2001), 93–113, 110.
57. In his bioethical writings Meilaender makes plain that he does not abide by an understanding of moral status and human dignity as contingent on matters of social harm or social acceptance. He rather assigns moral status on the basis of biological development—specifically, when sperm and egg form a zygote, or soon thereafter. But Meilaender seems not to carry this line of thinking over into his considerations of cloning. See Gilbert Meilaender, *Bioethics: A Primer for Christians* (Grand Rapids, MI: Eerdmans, 1996), 30–31. For a sustained discussion of moral status see Bonnie Steinbock, *Life Before Birth: The Moral and Legal Status of Embryos and Fetuses* (New York: Oxford University Press, 1992).
58. Martin Luther King Jr., "Letter from Birmingham Jail," in *Why We Can't Wait* (New York: Penguin, 1964), 76–95.

59. Rawls, "The Idea of Public Reason Revisited," 593.

60. King, "Letter from Birmingham Jail," 77. Subsequent citations of this source are referenced parenthetically in the text.

61. Amy Gutmann and Dennis Thompson, *Democracy and Disagreement* (Cambridge, MA: Harvard University Press, 1996), 4.

62. See Stout, *Democracy and Tradition*, 67–68.

63. Put in terms of mainline Protestant theology, religious adherents who abide by public reason negotiate political life as a member of two kingdoms.

EPILOGUE

1. Other publications, about which I do not have space to comment here, are Anand Pandian, *Crooked Stalks: Cultivating Virtue in South India* (Durham, NC: Duke University Press, 2009); Leela Prasad, *Poetics of Conduct: Oral Narrative and Moral Being in a South Indian Town* (New York: Columbia University Press, 2007); and Christian Scharen and Anna Marie Vigen, *Ethnography as Christian Theology and Ethics* (New York: Continuum, 2011).

2. Saba Mahmood, *Politics of Piety: The Islamic Revival and the Feminist Subject* (Princeton, NJ: Princeton University Press, 2005), 2–3. Subsequent citations of this source are referenced parenthetically in the text.

3. Ibid., 136. Of course, Aristotle did not know the term *habitus*; he would instead use *hexis* to denote fixed features of character, both moral and intellectual.

4. Parallels with the interpretations of Christianity that emphasize forming "communities of character" or as relying on sources of authority outside the nation-state (by, e.g., Stanley Hauerwas and Stephen Carter, respectively) invite comparison here.

5. George E. Marcus and Michael M. J. Fischer, *Anthropology as Cultural Critique: An Experimental Moment in the Human Sciences* (Chicago: University of Chicago Press, 1986), 111, 116.

6. See Aristotle, *Nicomachean Ethics*, 1138a31–39b5. Mahmood misrepresents Aristotle and moral theory as well when, e.g., she writes that "the neo-Aristotelian tradition of 'virtue ethics' generally argues for the restatement of the priority of virtue as the central ethical concept over the concept of 'the good' or 'the right' in contemporary moral thought." This statement fails to grasp that virtue theory is one in which the good is conceived as prior to the right. Elsewhere in the book she states that Aristotle argues "that 'theoretical wisdom' is not the same as 'practical wisdom' since each are [*sic*] oriented toward different ends: the former pursues what Aristotle calls 'happiness' and the latter 'virtue.'" On the contrary: Aristotle understands forms of knowledge as virtues, as well as forms of happiness. See Mahmood, *Politics of Piety*, 28n48, 196n4.

7. Aristotle, *Nicomachean Ethics*, 1106b35–7a1.

8. Farhat Moazam, *Bioethics and Organ Transplantation in a Muslim Society: A Study in Culture, Ethnography, and Religion* (Bloomington: Indiana University

Press, 2005), 9. Subsequent citations of this source are referenced parenthetically in the text.

9. See the many editions of Tom L. Beauchamp and James F. Childress, *Principles of Biomedical Ethics*. Notably, this work is the first one Moazam cites. See Moazam, *Bioethics and Organ Transplantation*, 227n1.

10. Charles Hirschkind, *The Ethical Soundscape: Cassette Sermons and Islamic Counterpublics* (New York: Columbia University Press, 2006), 152. Subsequent citations of this source are referenced parenthetically in the text.

11. I say "some versions" to note that Hirschkind largely has Jürgen Habermas's views as his foil, not a robust and variegated understanding of liberal political philosophy. As with religion, so too with political philosophy: Hirschkind's warnings about reductionism apply.

12. See Mahmood, *Politics of Piety*, 192.

13. Jeffrey Stout, *Blessed Are the Organized: Grassroots Democracy in America* (Princeton, NJ: Princeton University Press, 2010), xvi. Subsequent citations of this source are referenced parenthetically in the text.

14. Elizabeth M. Bucar, *Creative Conformity: The Feminist Politics of U.S. Catholic and Iranian Shi'i Women* (Washington, DC: Georgetown University Press, 2011), 180. Subsequent citations of this source are referenced parenthetically in the text.

15. Sherine Hamdy, *Our Bodies Belong to God: Organ Transplants, Islam, and the Struggle for Human Dignity in Egypt* (Berkeley: University of California Press, 2012), 232. Subsequent citations of this source are referenced parenthetically in the text. Although Hamdy's research preceded the formation of a national policy in Egypt, at the time she published her book, she observed, that policy "has yet to go into effect" (232).

16. Hamdy omits reference to the fourth principle in Beauchamp and Childress's work, nonmaleficence. Yet concerns about avoiding harm directly inform the ethical deliberations of Hamdy's subjects, as I will make plain below.

INDEX